BORN TO REBEL

BENJAMIN E. MAYS

BORN TO REBEL

An Autobiography

With a Revised Foreword by

ORVILLE VERNON BURTON

The University of Georgia Press
Athens & London

University of Georgia Press paperback edition, 2003

Foreword by Orville Vernon Burton

Athens, Georgia 30602
www.ugapress.org

Printed digitally in the United States of America

Library of Congress Cataloging-in-Publication Data
Mays, Benjamin E. (Benjamin Elijah), 1894–1984.
Born to rebel : an autobiography / Benjamin E. Mays ;
with a revised foreword by Orville Vernon Burton.
lxvii, 380 p. : ill. ; 23 cm.
Originally published: New York : Scribner, 1971.
Includes index.
ISBN 0-8203-2523-6 (pbk. : alk. paper)
1. Mays, Benjamin E. (Benjamin Elijah), 1894–1984.
2. Morehouse College (Atlanta, Ga.)—Presidents.
3. African Americans—Civil rights. I. Title.
LC2851.M72 M38 2002
378'.112—dc21
[B] 2002043576

ISBN-13: 978-0-8203-2523-1

British Library Cataloging-in-Publication Data available

The original hardcover version of this text
was published by Scribner in 1971.

In memory of Sadie.

MY DEVOTED COMPANION

FROM AUGUST 9, 1926,

UNTIL HER DEATH,

OCTOBER 11, 1969.

CONTENTS

FOREWORD

The afterglow of Reconstruction had almost faded by 1894. In that year Benjamin Elijah Mays was born, about four miles from the crossroads settlement of Rambo (now Epworth) and ten miles from the town of Ninety Six, South Carolina. The rights of African Americans—especially the precious right to vote—had been seriously curtailed, although two African Americans sat in the General Assembly and one represented the state in Congress. Some thirty years after the Civil War, most African Americans in the South depended on white landowners for employment as sharecroppers, tenant farmers, and wage laborers. The chains of racial segregation were fastened more securely each year. From these difficult circumstances Mays, the youngest of eight children of former slaves, distinguished himself as a preacher, teacher, administrator, scholar, author, newspaper columnist, civil rights activist, and presidential adviser.

Mays had little interest in or curiosity about his own past. He knew only sparse details about his family, mostly about matters relating to the selling of his family to different states and the abuse and brutality his family suffered at the hands of whites. From an early age, Mays looked not to the past, but to the future, with its endless possibilities. In doing so, he distanced himself from traditional viewpoints and short-term goals. His support went to those causes that would best improve humanity.[1]

Mays was active in organizations and movements that embodied change in the South from the turn of the century until his death in 1984. He was coauthor of the influential 1942 Durham statement, which initiated a series of discussions resulting in the formation of the Southern Regional Council. He served as vice president and on the Board of Directors of the National Association for the Advancement of Colored People, as well as the Committee of 100, which supported the more activist NAACP Legal Defense and Education Fund. Mays served on the executive committees of the International Young Men's Christian Association and of the World Council of Churches, as president of the United Negro College Fund and of the Atlanta School Board, and as chairman of the National Sharecroppers and Rural Advancement Fund. He was a guiding force in the National Baptist Convention, the Urban League, and a host of other social justice and liberal organizations, such as the

Southern Conference for Human Welfare, the American Crusade to End Lynching, the Southern Conference Educational Fund, Civil Rights Congresses, and the Peace Corps Advisory Committee.

In his best-known role, as president of Morehouse College from 1940 to 1967, Dr. Mays transformed a struggling black college for men into perhaps the most prestigious African American institution of higher learning. In that office he trained and inspired a brilliant cadre of leaders, of whom Martin Luther King, Jr., was the shining star. Mays not only lived to see the "Second Reconstruction," the civil rights movement of the 1950s and 1960s, he also helped launch and sustain it. A 1971 article in the Harvard Theological Review pronounced Mays one of three "outstanding Black clergymen who have exerted a tremendous impact upon American life."[2]

The distinguished career of Benjamin Elijah Mays evolved from the black southern experience that he shared with so many African American youths who grew up the children of tenant farmers. Born during the heyday of racist demagogue Benjamin Ryan "Pitchfork Ben" Tillman, a U.S. Senator from South Carolina, Mays was one year old when South Carolina's 1895 constitution disfranchised African Americans. The following year, in *Plessy v. Ferguson,* the Supreme Court of the United States declared segregation legal. Mays's earliest memory was an encounter with whites in the Phoenix Riot of 1898. A group of armed vigilantes galloped up and cursed Mays's father, making him salute, remove his hat, and bow. In 1901, when Mays was seven years old, Booker T. Washington dined with President Theodore Roosevelt in the White House, and Tillman raged, "The action of President Roosevelt in entertaining that nigger will necessitate our killing a thousand niggers in the South before they will learn their place again." In 1909, when the NAACP was founded, Ben Mays was fifteen years old and, despite an insatiable desire for education, had never received more than three to four months of formal schooling in any one year. At the Epworth post office in 1915—the year of Booker T. Washington's death—a white doctor cursed and struck Mays because he was dressed in clean, neat clothes and stood tall with pride. That summer Mays became a Pullman porter and learned that racism infected Yankees also; he bought a drink in Detroit, and when he returned the glass from which he had drunk, the white waiter smashed it.

During World War I, while African Americans fought to make the world safe for democracy, they could not vote in the American South. Ben Mays registered for the draft, but he did not serve in the armed forces because he had decided to study for the ministry. During this time he gained an appreciation for the ideas of Eugene Victor Debs, president of the American Railway Union, organizer of the Social Democratic Party of America, and inmate in prison for his defense of those charged with sedition. Mays explained: "I'm deeply impressed with the words of Eugene Debs writing while a prisoner in a federal prison in Atlanta. These are the words: 'As long as there is a lower class, I'm in it. As long as there is a man in jail, I'm not free.' Eugene Debs inspired me greatly. To me, Eugene Debs has shaped my sensitivity for the poor, the diseased and those who have given their lives for the good of those sick and poor, the great and the small, the high and the low."[3]

Red scares and lynchings followed the wave of racial hatred that accompanied the beginnings of the great post–World War I black migration, when African Americans moved from the farms to the villages to the towns to the cities, especially to northern metropolises. While farm-reared Benjamin Mays was residing in Richmond, Chicago, Tampa, and Atlanta, Marcus Garvey's Universal Negro Improvement Association's Back to Africa movement caught the attention of many African Americans. Mays, however, shied away from Garvey's overt black nationalism and became more committed to Christianity and to expanding American democracy to include African Americans. By the time of the 1929 economic crash and the Harlem Renaissance's urban "New Negro," Mays had published "The New Negro Challenges the Old Order," an article about South Carolina's primarily rural race relations. Although Mays was not the urban Renaissance man, he was, as historian I. A. Newby wrote of Mays, "One of the New Negroes." In 1926, speaking at Benedict College, Mays announced: "I cannot and I would not apologize for being a Negro. We have a great history; we have a greater future. . . . we have a rendezvous with America." He continued, "I will live in vain, if I do not live and so act that you will be freer than I am—freer intellectually, freer politically, and freer economically." Mays implored the students: "Seek to serve your state, not as a Negro but as a man. Aspire to be great—not among Negroes, but among men! God knows I want to be a great teacher. I want no racial adjective modifying it. I want to preach the gospel of peace, good will, justice, and brotherhood—not to Negroes and for Negroes, but to men and for men." The editor who reported the speech added, "There was terrific applause following Mr. Mays's address but, outside, the Editor heard a representative of the 'Old Negro' saying: 'The young man has much to learn; he is quite radical.'"[4]

As the depression destroyed the tenant-farming economy of millions of African Americans, Mays grappled with the effects of poverty and discrimination in a southern city and researched the meaning of the African American experience through the black church. During World War II, when blacks were again asked to die for U.S. democracy, Mays, by that time president of Morehouse College, searched for a way to save his school, whose enrollments were depleted by the draft. Mays got philanthropic support for a program to allow gifted high school students to enter Morehouse as college freshmen; the first class to graduate under the new program was the celebrated class of 1948.

After World War II, when the United States became obsessed with communism and McCarthyism, Mays spoke out bravely and forthrightly about the injustices in American society: "For us in the South, the maintenance of segregation is more important than democracy; than the Christian religion; than, I was almost about to say, than keeping communism out of the country. I dare say a vast majority in the South would have preferred a Hitler victory to the elimination of segregation." In the 1940s and 1950s, when prejudice was ingrained in white churches throughout the country, Mays, the first African American to serve as vice president of the Federal (now the National) Council of Churches, cried out for integration and justice. Speaking at the World Council of Churches' Assembly in 1954, he warned, "It will be a sad commentary on our life and time if future historians can write that the last bulwark of segregation based on race and color was God's church."

After the Supreme Court ruled against segregated schooling in *Brown v. Board of Education,* the Southern Historical Association in 1955 asked Mays to present his views on the decision. Mays gave a speech titled "The Moral Aspects of Segregation": "No group is wise enough, good enough, strong enough to assume an omnipotent and omniscient role. . . . To do that is blasphemy. It is a usurpation of the role of God. . . . We are morally obligated to abolish legalized segregation in America, or reinterpret the Christian Gospel, the Old and New Testaments, and make the Gospel say the noble principles of Judaism and Christianity are not applicable to colored peoples and Negroes. Tell the world honestly and plainly that the Fatherhood of God and the Brotherhood of Man cannot work where the colored races are involved. Make no mistake—as this country could not exist half slave and half free, it cannot exist half segregated and half desegregated. If we lose this battle for freedom for 16 million Negroes, we will lose it for 145 million whites and eventually we will lose it for the world. This is indeed a time for greatness."[5]

In the 1960s, when African Americans protested their lack of civil rights in the American South, Mays was consulted as a longtime leader in the fight against segregation. By 1977 he was an adviser and confidant to President James Earl Carter, a fellow southerner and a born-again Baptist with whom Mays felt a spiritual kinship. Mays reflected, "How can you explain Jimmy Carter? God must have sent him." Mays believed Carter did more for civil rights than any other president, particularly in appointing forty-one African Americans to the federal courts. President Carter described Mays as "my personal friend, my constructive critic and my close advisor."[6]

Just as events influenced Mays, so did Mays influence events. Leading in the struggles against segregation, actively involving himself in the civil rights movement, writing a weekly newspaper column, pioneering in African American scholarship and education, and presiding over the desegregation of Atlanta's public schools, he helped inaugurate a new era of race relations. Lerone Bennett, Jr., in a tribute titled "The Last of the Great Schoolmasters," aptly labeled Mays part of the vanguard of the civil rights movement. He was one of the African Americans who were "bold enough, wise enough and selfless enough to assume the awesome responsibility" of bridging the gap between the first Reconstruction and the second. According to Bennett, "None tilled more ground or harvested a more bountiful crop than Benjamin Elijah Mays, a lean, beautifully-black preacher-prophet who served as Schoolmaster of the Movement."[7]

Though Mays's mother could not read, she instilled in her son the belief that he was inferior to no one. As Mays grew older he fortified that belief with the strength of his religious convictions and education. World travels introduced him to a more cosmopolitan view of race relations than that held by most Americans. So vehement was his conviction that whites and blacks were equal that he startled some African Americans who had been degraded by segregation. Mays understood issues and struggles on the grand moral plane, but the beauty of his life was that he immediately applied his principles to everyday problems. He lived in a segregated society, but he refused to support or be a part of segregation. He climbed stairs rather than ride a segregated elevator; he walked rather than support a segregated mass-transit system.

In writing his autobiography, Mays turned his attention to the past and provided a rich perspective on what it was like to grow up black in rural, segregated South Carolina a century ago. This autobiography describes an important and little studied period in American history: the nadir of race relations from the 1890s through the 1930s. During this time period, the Republican idealism of the Civil War and Reconstruction dissipated, and modern white America solidified its racist views of African Americans. Segregation and deteriorated race relations remained the order of the day until the changes brought about by the civil rights movement. Ben Mays lived through this nadir.

Born to Rebel, a classic work by a remarkable man, contains an abundance of historical material about the values and culture of the rural South. Chronicling Mays's life until 1970 and offering a commentary on race relations in the United States, this autobiography is an important story of the African American experience and a significant component of the American experience as well. The *Presbyterian Survey*'s assessment of Mays in 1954 applies to his autobiography also: "No one has more right to speak on race than Dr. Benjamin Mays. . . . because of his own integrity and understanding, . . . no one . . . says it with the simplicity and effectiveness with which Dr. Mays speaks." *Born to Rebel* provides a vivid glimpse of twentieth-century history from the African American perspective, which has too often been ignored or incorrectly interpreted in history books. Mays's life provides insight into the transitional years from Booker T. Washington's accommodationist philosophy to the Black Power radicalism of the late 1960s and early 1970s.[8]

With his special perspective and insight, Mays had some advice that is still relevant for today's young African Americans: "If I were you, I would count for something and no man would push me around because my skin is black or his eyes are blue. I would stand for something. I would count." On another occasion he said: "If I, and people like myself, can make it with every kind of stumbling block in our way, they ought to be able to make it when everything is open to them. They have plenty to gripe about, but not much in comparison. If they don't make it, may God have mercy on their souls. I'm not saying that everything is all right; we have much further to go. But we have come a long, long way, baby, from where we were."[9]

Dr. Mays, a careful student of history, asked before he died in 1984 that this foreword explain exactly "where we were," that it outline some of the discriminatory history of his native state. Mays grew up in a white-dominated world that kept black people "in their place." All his life he felt cheated by the lack of opportunities for schooling and the constant reminders of his second-class citizenship. To understand Mays, one must realize the different perspectives of African Americans and whites on the history of South Carolina. I. A. Newby, in *Black Carolinians*, explained: "To white Carolinians from Calhoun to Strom Thurmond 'states rights' and 'local self-government' were rallying cries against tyranny and synonyms for individual liberty and local democracy. To blacks they were code words for white authoritarianism, the very existence of which depended upon denying liberty and local democracy to blacks. . . . Tillmanism is the nearest thing to a genuine mass movement in the history of white Carolina, and whites in the state paid homage to it for over a generation. To students of black history and racial equality its most striking features are the extent to which it expressed the desire of white Carolinians to dominate blacks and the fact that much of its unity and force derived from its antiblack racial policies."[10]

Newby elaborated: "The central fact in the history of black Carolina has been the racism of white Carolina. Black Carolinians have been black folk in a society dominated by whites. Race was the criterion used to identify them, define their role, restrict their advancement, thwart their hope, limit their horizons. Their society isolated them as a racial group, educated (or failed to educate) them as a racial group, worked them as a racial group, exploited them as a racial group."[11]

From slavery to the more subtle institutional racism of the present day, scholars have found that South Carolina politics has chiefly revolved around the issue of the status of African American people, and ever present in antebellum South Carolina was the dread of a black revolt. Fearful that political conflict would somehow undermine slavery, South Carolina had a less democratic form of government than any state in the union. Candidates for the legislature were required to own property. White citizens could not vote directly for president, governor, or United States senator; and African Americans could not vote at all. South Carolina was the hotbed of nullification, "fire-eaters," and secession. Even after the Civil War ended and the national government molded South Carolina politics, the fear of black insurgency continued to dictate. Reconstruction, and in its wake white "Redemption," set the stage for Mays's life. The first South Carolina constitutional convention of Reconstruction, held in 1865, opposed extending the franchise to African Americans. "This is a white man's government," Governor Benjamin F. Perry asserted, "and intended for white men only." The South Carolina legislature also introduced a "Black Code," which imposed on African Americans a condition as close to slavery as was possible after emancipation.[12]

In response to the notorious black codes and to the terrorism accompanying the first year of emancipation, Congress enacted the Civil Rights Act of 1866. Under military supervision South Carolina convened its second constitutional convention of Reconstruction in November 1867. Well over half the people of the state were African American, and thus more than half the delegates, 76 out of 124, were African American. The new constitution gave the right to vote to every male resident of South Carolina twenty-one years of age or older "without distinction of race, color, or former condition."[13]

If Reconstruction could have succeeded anywhere, it was in South Carolina. African Americans formed a majority of the population, and Reconstruction lasted longer than in most southern states. The democratically elected legislature instituted public education from primary level to college for the first time in the state, and this education was open to former slaves. African Americans served in nearly every office at county and state levels except for the governorship; African Americans won half the seats of the lower house of the General Assembly and held a majority in the House for six years (longer than in any state at any time in American history), although never a majority in the Senate; and more land was distributed to former slaves than in any other state. During the years 1868–77, eight African Americans were elected to Congress and two became lieutenant governor. African Americans served on the South Carolina Supreme Court and as secretary of state, adjutant general, secretary of the treasury, Speaker of the House, and president protem of the state Senate. At the local level, African Americans were state representatives, sheriffs, probate judges, magistrates, postmasters, and school commissioners. All of this occurred, however, because federal troops were enforcing federal laws.

White Carolinians have created myths of the horrors of "black" Reconstruction, when barbaric, ignorant, inferior African Americans despoiled and prostrated a noble state. Until the 1960s white historians also severely criticized South Carolina's predominantly black Reconstruction governments for mismanagement and corruption, but most now view Reconstruction as a tragedy because, in spite of the tremendous pain and suffering of the Civil War and Reconstruction, African Americans still did not achieve equality, dignity, or the right to participate in the government under which they lived. Charges of graft among Reconstruction politicians are now considered in the perspective of the widespread tolerance of avarice and peculation that produced the Democratic Tweed Ring in New York City and the massive corruption of the white "Redeemers" during the "Gilded Age" that followed Reconstruction. Reconstruction South Carolina experimented briefly with idealism in the form of interracial democracy and responsive government, but most whites preferred racial discrimination, low taxes, and few government services.

Because white South Carolinians were never willing to share citizenship, let alone political power, with African Americans, violence accompanied Reconstruction. The Ku Klux Klan, active at least as early as the 1868 election, violently opposed black enfranchisement, and systematic terror reached a new intensity during the critical 1876 election. Even with federal troops in the state, Martin Witherspoon Gary coordinated a campaign of terror to return the state to the orthodox conservative white leadership that had governed South Carolina before the Civil War. Massacres throughout the state reflected the principles expressed in the twelfth and sixteenth points of Gary's "Edgefield Plan": "12. Every Democrat must feel honor bound to control the vote of at least one negro, by intimidation, purchase, keeping him away as each individual may determine, how he may best accomplish it. . . . 16. Never threaten a man individually—if he deserves to be threatened the necessities of the times require that he should die." Cold-blooded executions were common. As Benjamin Ryan Tillman later explained: "The struggle in which we were engaged meant more than life or death. It involved everything we held dear, Anglo-Saxon civilization included."[14]

"Redemption" put the moderate Democrat Wade Hampton in office. Moderation in this case meant that he preferred fraud and intimidation to meticulously planned multiple murders of African Americans. In 1878 Martin Witherspoon Gary explained: "We regard the issues between the white and colored people of the State, and of the entire South, as an antagonism of race, not a difference of political party. . . . White supremacy is essential to our survival as a people." Gary proposed that African Americans be excluded from the political process by barring them from the Democratic Party primary. Thus, the white primary was used informally after 1878 to resolve disagreements so that whites could present a united front in the general election. Because the Democratic primary was open only to whites from 1878 until 1944, it was the real election in most races. African Americans were effectively disfranchised for the next sixty-five years.[15]

In 1882 the South Carolina legislature passed the Registration and Eight-Box Law, developed by the moderate Hamptonite aristocratic historian Edward McCrady, Jr. By requiring that those who applied for voter registration take a literacy test, which included large loopholes for white Democrats, the law gave plentiful opportunities for administrative discrimination and provided an adequate "legal" substitute for intimidation and stuffed ballot boxes as a means of diluting the black vote. By 1884 African American registration in South Carolina had fallen to half the 1880 level because of the provision for separate ballot boxes for eight offices, the requirement that election officials move the boxes during elections without allowing African Americans to help one another find the correct boxes, and the requirement that registrants sign their names. To prevent whites from being disfranchised by these same rules, exceptions to the laws were made for those who were already on the registration rolls in 1857 and for those whom registrars recommended. The reapportionment that accompanied the Eight-Box Law of 1882 also created one of the most famous gerrymanders in the history of the United States: to pack African Americans into a single district so that other districts would be majority white, one congressional district ran half the length of the state, split six counties, and extended into the Atlantic Ocean. In a state that was 60 percent black, Republicans could seriously contest only one of seven seats. For some whites this was still too much.

In 1890 "Pitchfork Ben" Tillman won the governorship over an independent who courted the few remaining African American votes. Tillman declared, "The whites have absolute control of the government, and we intend at any hazard to retain it." Before Tillman's election, local governing bodies were elected by popular vote, and in counties with substantial black majorities, African Americans achieved control of government as long as federal officials supervised voter registration and elections. In his second term as governor, Tillman spearheaded the abolishment of elected local governments and provided for county officials to be appointed by the governor upon recommendation of the county's state senator and representatives. This law made it impossible to elect blacks as local officials even where African Americans were the overwhelming majority.[16]

In 1895 the state adopted Tillman's plan to disfranchise African American citizens permanently. First the legislature passed a re-registration act that was carefully administered in a racially discriminatory manner to prevent blacks from defeating a call for a constitutional convention. The distinguished historian David Duncan Wallace, who attended the 1895 disfranchisement convention, recorded that "elimination of the negro from politics as effectively as this could be accomplished by constitutional enactment was the one object for which the convention was called." The temporary chairman of the constitutional convention charged the delegates to write election laws to preserve "Anglo-Saxon supremacy." The 1895 constitution kept African Americans from having any real influence in the electoral process by establishing a literacy (or property) test, a poll tax, and an understanding clause.[17]

African Americans challenged both the literacy test and the poll tax that southern states enacted after Reconstruction, but the Supreme Court upheld both disfranchising tactics. In 1920 Congressman James F. Byrnes, who eventually became a U.S. senator, Supreme Court justice, and secretary of state, as well as governor of South Carolina, cautioned: "It is certain that if there was a fair registration they [African Americans] would have a slight majority in our state. We cannot idly brush the facts aside. Unfortunate though it may be, our consideration of every question must include the consideration of this race question." The effect of disfranchising legislation was profound: only three thousand blacks, or 0.8 percent of voting-age African Americans in South Carolina, were registered to vote in 1940.[18]

A major theme of political scientist V. O. Key, Jr., was that in the South the center of power as well as of extreme racism in the first half of the twentieth century lay in the "Black Belt"—counties with a black majority. During much of that period South Carolina as a whole had a larger percentage of African Americans than any state in the South. Although blacks were socioeconomically disadvantaged and effectively kept out of the political process, the number of African Americans in the state aroused concern among those who could vote, and blacks became scapegoats in a political environment that invited shallow demagoguery. From "Pitchfork Ben" Tillman and Cole Blease through Ellison D. "Cotton Ed" Smith, South Carolina demagogues rode the race issue to political prominence.[19]

After *Smith v. Allwright* overturned the white primary in 1944, Governor Olin Johnston, running for the United States Senate against the powerful incumbent, "Cotton Ed" Smith, called a special session of the legislature to draft measures to ensure the continuation of African American political suppression. In April 1944 Governor Johnston proclaimed: "history has taught us that we must keep our white Democratic primaries pure and unadulterated so that we might protect the welfare and homes of all the people of our State. . . . White supremacy will be maintained in our primaries. Let the chips fall where they may!" Although South Carolina's substitutes for the white primary were declared unconstitutional, Johnston won the Senate seat. Meanwhile the Democratic Party, which included practically all the white voters in South Carolina, organized itself into private clubs. African Americans could vote in primaries only if they swore to uphold separation of the races in education and society, if they took an oath that they believed in states' rights, and if they swore opposition to federal employment-discrimination laws. Judge J. Waites Waring, the aristocratic Charlestonian who had ruled against the white primary, declared the oath unconstitutional. (Waring was also the first federal judge to rule against segregated schools.) Representative Mendell Rivers vilified Waring in Congress, declaring: "He is as cold as a dead Eskimo in an abandoned igloo. Lemon juice flows in his frigid and calculating veins. . . . Unless he is removed there will be bloodshed." In 1950 the

South Carolina House of Representatives passed a resolution appropriating funds to purchase for Judge Waring and "his socialite wife" one-way tickets out of South Carolina and "to erect a suitable plaque" to the couple in the mule barn at Clemson College.[20] In 1952 Waring retired and left South Carolina for the more secure environs of New York City.

Despite this prosegregationist political atmosphere, Benjamin Mays chose to remain in the South, even though he received at least fourteen offers of prestigious and important jobs in the North, where "there was less segregation, where Negroes . . . thought they were free." He explained in 1957, "I stay in the South because I believe my best work can be done in the South." Neither did he stay within the comfortable and protective walls of Morehouse. Like Daniel staring down the lions, he confronted southern audiences: "Inherent in segregation is injustice; inherent in segregation is inequality. Segregation says to every white child in the South 'there's a man you can kick around.'" In 1949 Mays called upon southerners to "support the civil rights movement." He admonished: "We need to get rid of fears in the South. Fears of democracy and Christian religion. But we are a scared people. . . . We are scared to abolish segregation." The *Charleston News and Courier* complained that Mays was "inciting animosity of the rougher elements of the white population."[21]

Rougher elements made sure that racial violence did not cease. A gruesome measurement of racial terrorist activities is lynching. Twelve African Americans were lynched in South Carolina in 1889, eight in 1895, six in 1897, fourteen in 1898. In 1933 African American Bernie Thompson was lynched in Mays's hometown of Ninety Six. Writing about the lynching of a black man in Greenville, South Carolina, in 1947, Rebecca West explained that some white southerners believed lynching to be a "social prophylactic." Table 1 summarizes the reported lynchings of African Americans from 1882 to 1950 in states where Benjamin Mays had lived. Every black man knew that standing up to whites put life itself in jeopardy. Yet Mays, from the time he was a young man, proclaimed loudly and eloquently that African Americans should be, had to be, truly free and equal—that the pernicious institution of segregation, based on the implicit premise of black inferiority, must be destroyed.[22]

Mays's fearlessness freed him; he invariably spoke out against lynching and called for antilynching laws. He also attacked segregation. Legal segregation, he charged, was "worse than lynching. Segregation breeds lynching, injustice, and all kinds of discrimination . . . and advertises to the world that here is a group of people unfit to live as normal human beings." Moreover, he defiantly challenged southern politicians who claimed to oppose a federal antilynching law on the grounds that it interfered with states' rights: "If the South is earnest, is honest, if the Dixiecrats are honest, if the men who filibuster on the floor of the Senate against Civil Rights are honest, let them come back to Georgia, South Carolina, Mississippi, Alabama, Virginia

TABLE 1 Number of African Americans Lynched in States Where Mays Lived

Years	South Carolina	Georgia	Virginia	Florida	Illinois
1882–1903	109	241	70	115	10
1904–1908	14	52	4	13	2
1909–1913	18	75	2	44	4
1914–1918	10	79	4	23	2
1919–1923	10	58	3	34	0
1924–1927	4	5	2	18	1
1928–1932	3	8	0	6	0
1933–1937	3	13	0	8	0
1938–1942	1	6	0	7	0
1943–1946	lynchings not reported by state; total of 13				
1947–1950	1	2	0	0	0
Total	173	539	85	268	19

Source: Walter White, *Rope and Faggot: A Biography of Judge Lynch* (New York: Alfred A. Knopf, 1929), pp. 254–58; Jack Simpson Mullins, "Lynchings in South Carolina, 1900–1914" (M.A. thesis, University of South Carolina, 1961); Annual Report of the National Association for the Advancement of Colored People, each year has a different title (New York: NAACP, in named years).

Note: Years are not equally grouped. No African American was lynched in Maine from 1882 to 1950.

and let them stand up like men and say 'We don't want any federal anti-lynching bill. We'll have our own anti-lynching bill. We will abolish the poll tax. . . . We will do something about discrimination in employment, and I'll never believe they are honest until they do that."[23]

Governor J. Strom Thurmond declared in 1948 at his acceptance of the Dixiecrat presidential nomination, "There are not enough laws on the books of the nation, nor can there be enough laws, to break down segregation in the South." When South Carolina gave her native son 72 percent of the vote in the presidential election that year, Mays declared, "Today the South worships at the shrine of segregation"; he warned that before democracy could be realized, southern whites had "to get a new God to worship."[24]

As long as segregationist politicians controlled the political processes, educational opportunities for African Americans were extremely limited. Mays summarized the situation: "We can never have justice in education under a segregation law." Discrimination in schooling was blatant. In his 1911 inaugural address Governor Cole Blease declared: "I am in favor of building up the free school system so that every white child in South Carolina may be given a good common school education. . . . I am opposed to white people's taxes being used to educate Negroes. I am a friend of the Negro race. . . . The white people of the South are the best friends to the Negro race. In my opinion, when the people of this country began to try to educate the Negro they made a serious and grave mistake, and I fear the worst result is yet to come. So why continue?" In *Born to Rebel* Mays emphasizes the lack of educational opportunities for African Americans in the South, opportunities that black Americans have always seen as especially important. African Americans yearned to read the Bible. They also valued literacy because it was closely associated with freedom. As Mays poignantly recounts: "I really wanted to learn. . . . Vaguely, yet ardently, I longed to know, for I sensed that knowledge could set me free." While whites in America looked upon occupation as the chief indicator of status, African Americans (to whom many jobs were closed) saw educational achievement as the primary indicator of status. Understandably, education became the first and foremost target of the civil rights movement in the South.[25]

Education shows clearly and measurably how political discrimination affects people's lives. In Appendix A of *Born to Rebel*, in a section titled "Discrimination with a Vengeance," Mays reviews the discriminatory funding for black and white children in the South. Table 2 shows the expenditures of Mays's home county and of South Carolina in white-to-black ratios from 1896 to 1960, the last year for which figures for segregated expenditures were available. In 1900, for example, the state of South Carolina spent 4.21 times as much on each white child in school as on each African American child. If the ratios had been calculated according to the proportion of the total number of black and white children instead of by the number that attended school, the discrepancies would have been even greater. Ironically, in 1896, the year of *Plessy v. Ferguson*, the expenditures were less unequal than in later years. As the century progressed, the "separate but equal" system resulted in expenditures of more than eight times as much per white child as per African American child in the state. During Mays's first year in the Greenwood County schools, the county spent $6.29 for each white child attending school, but the expenditure for each African American child was only 23 cents. The white-to-black ratio of expenditures in that year was twenty-seven to one! In the last year before segregated statistics (but not segregated schools) fell into disuse, half a decade after *Brown* had replaced *Plessy* as the governing constitutional law in the United States, the state still spent 50 percent more on each white pupil than on each African American. A large portion of the discrepancy was due to differences in teacher-pupil ratios and teachers' salaries: African American teachers were paid less than white teachers to teach more children. The discrimination in the state's segregated institutions of higher education was even more flagrant.

TABLE 2 Racial Discrimination Ratios of Educational Expenditures in Greenwood County and in South Carolina, 1896–1960

Year	Greenwood County	South Carolina
1896	—	1.2
1900	3.9	4.2
1901	27.0	4.3
1902	5.8	4.2
1903	4.3	4.2
1904	7.5	4.8
1905	7.2	4.3
1906	6.4	5.3
1907	7.9	5.0
1908	9.8	5.7
1909	3.4	6.1
1910	6.3	5.4
1915	7.2	8.7
1920	10.4	8.5
1925	11.7	8.4
1930	9.3	7.4
1935	6.2	5.0
1940	4.2	4.4
1945	3.4	3.2
1950	1.7	2.4
1955	1.2	1.6
1960	1.3	1.5

Source: Annual Reports of South Carolina Department of Education in named years.

Note: During the italicized years Mays was enrolled in Greenwood County schools. Ratios were obtained by dividing (total educational expenditures on whites divided by white public school average attendance) by (total educational expenditures on African Americans divided by black public school average attendance). For a few years, enrollment figures had to be substituted for attendance. Every year was computed, but except for the years Mays was in Greenwood County public schools, I reported five year intervals. 1896 is the first year separate statistics for African Americans and whites are available. Greenwood County's expenditures are first recorded in 1899. 1960 is the last year for which segregated expenditures are available.

Mays's life as a student and as an educator reflected the difficulties inherent in a segregated society. In early-twentieth-century up-country South Carolina, cotton regulated the rhythms of life. As tenant farmers, Mays's family had to prioritize picking cotton over schooling. School for African Americans in the Ninety Six area ran from November to February. At the age of fifteen Mays left the neighborhood "Brickhouse" School (misnamed; it was clapboard) and traveled twenty-four miles from home to the better Baptist-association-sponsored McCormick School, yet he still received only four months of schooling each year. Two years later Mays entered the eighth grade at State College, which was also a high school. The decision to transfer was not easy. Mays's pastor and his teacher at McCormick wanted him to remain there to help instruct the younger children, and his father was vehemently opposed to his son's attending high school because he, like many farmers, believed that too much education made people foolish and dishonest. The fare from Ninety Six to State College at Orangeburg, 125 miles away, was three dollars and five cents. With his mother's prayers and blessings, and a ten-dollar bill his father had angrily thrown at him (ten dollars was a considerable sum for an African American tenant farmer in 1909), Mays attended his first "real" school. His brother sent what money he could spare, and Mays worked his way through school. He picked up paper on campus, worked as a janitor, painted houses, washed dishes, and after midnight, when other students slept, he cleaned outhouses. During his junior year, determined to continue his education, Mays rebelled against his father's authority and did not go home to help with the spring planting.

Mays was inspired by African American teachers at State College. When his math class had difficulty, Professor Nelson C. Nix challenged them: "You boys can't work these problems? The white boys at the University of South Carolina are eating these problems up!" Nix encouraged Mays and assured him that he knew as much as any white student, but Mays craved the best education he could get; he needed to prove to himself that he could compete with whites in education, an impossibility in the South.

Mays was twenty-one years old when he graduated from high school at State College. He tried to get into a northern college, but the best he could do was Virginia Union, another African American school in Richmond. The following year Bates College accepted him. Mays was determined to go even though his friends, especially the Yankee Pullman porters, warned that he would freeze in Maine. While working his way through college, Mays, an honor student, won the sophomore declamation contest and was on the debate and football teams. Bates College did not emancipate Mays, he professed, but "it did the far greater service of making it possible for [him] to emancipate [him]self, to accept with dignity [his] own worth as a free man." At Bates, Mays made his first white friends.

After Bates, Mays applied to Newton Theological Seminary but was rejected because he was African American. Instead, following up on an idea that Professor Nix had earlier planted in his mind, Mays decided to go to graduate school at the University of Chicago. The contrast between Chicago and Bates College was enormous. At Bates teachers had never refused to acknowledge their African American students, and all local restaurants served blacks; in Chicago most cafes near campus would not serve African Americans, white students did not eat at the same tables with blacks, and some white teachers did not speak in public to their African American students.

After only three semesters, John Hope, president of Morehouse, lured Mays away from Chicago to teach math and algebra at his college in Atlanta. After graduation from Bates, Mays had married Ellen Harvin, a schoolmate at State College, and Morehouse gave Mays the opportunity to be near his wife, who was teaching in South Carolina. Their time together was short, however; Ellen Mays died in an Atlanta hospital less than two years later.

Mays began teaching math, psychology, and religion at Morehouse in 1921 and earned a reputation as a fair but demanding teacher. He accepted nothing less than a student's best effort, whether the student was an athlete or a member of the debating team (which he coached), light- or dark-skinned, from a deprived background, as he had been, or from the bourgeoisie.

While teaching, Mays also fought segregation from the pulpit. As pastor of Shiloh Baptist Church, Mays found that working with people in his congregation kept him in touch with the lives of those African Americans who were not sheltered in the elite world of the college-educated. As a preacher, Mays had to speak their language. He was proud to be from the rural proletariat and never insulted their intelligence or underestimated them. His people were always part of his heart, and he drew strength from them. Mays entitled his last book, written in 1981, *Lord, the People Have Driven Me On.*[26]

After three years at Morehouse, Mays decided to resume his studies for an advanced degree from the University of Chicago. In 1924 Chicago was still rife with racial prejudice, but here, at the age of thirty, Benjamin E. Mays made his first southern white friend, W. O. Brown.

In 1925 Mays finished his M.A. He considered remaining at Chicago as a candidate for the Ph.D., but once again he was lured away—this time to his high school alma mater, South Carolina State, to teach English. Here he met his second wife, Sadie Gray. The two were married during the summer of 1926, while they both did graduate work at the University of Chicago.

Because married couples were prohibited from working together at South Carolina State, the newlyweds took jobs with the National Urban League, which in 1926 sent Mays farther south, to Tampa, Florida. Working with separate black and white communities was difficult for a man of integrity who opposed segregation. While the Mayses struggled with problems of poor housing, low pay, poor recreational facilities, and second-class citizenship in Tampa, they continually reached out and cared for others. When an African American appeared in juvenile court, either Sadie or Benjamin Mays was there too, and soon delinquent black youths were sent to the Urban League instead of the home for juvenile offenders. In a newspaper article titled "It Costs Too Much," Mays challenged the segregation laws that confined African Americans to balconies and rear seats, carefully laying out the important distinction between "obeying unjust laws through sheer necessity and the voluntary acceptance of a law which one did not have to accept." Mays kept this distinction clear in his life and encouraged his students to do so. As he wrote later in *Seeking to Be Christian in Race Relations:* "Segregation crushes manhood, creates fear in the segregated and makes him cowardly. It develops in the person segregated a feeling of inferiority to the extent he never knows what his capabilities are. His mind is never free to develop unrestricted. The ceiling and not the sky becomes the limit of his striving."[27]

In Tampa, Mays and his wife went beyond the job description of improving the "lot of Negroes in employment, recreation, housing, health, education, and juvenile delinquency." This Mays did and did well, but what challenged the Tampa community was his earnest belief that his job was also to help African Americans "build respect for and pride in themselves despite the strangling chains of segregation." Believing they would eventually be dismissed because of their refusal to accept the status quo, the Mayses resigned from the Urban League in 1928 and moved to Atlanta, where they lived for the next six years. Mays became the student secretary for the National YMCA, a job that involved working with African American students in South Carolina, Georgia, Florida, Alabama, and Tennessee, while Sadie found employment first with the Georgia Negro Child Welfare Department and later with the Atlanta University School of Social Work. The YMCA, segregated in the North and the South, became partially integrated under Mays's secretariat.

In 1930 Mays left the YMCA to study the African American church in the United States. Under the auspices of the Rockefeller Institute of Social and Religious Research, Mays and a fellow minister, Joseph W. Nicholson, began their pioneering study of 609 urban congregations and 185 rural churches. They spent fourteen months researching and another ten months writing *The Negro's Church* (1933).

Studying and writing stirred again Mays's dream of a doctorate, and he re-entered the University of Chicago in 1931. After returning to Chicago at thirty-seven years of age, Mays protested campus discrimination and demanded equal seating at public affairs and equal housing in the dormitories. His wife received an A.M. degree from the School of Social Science Service, and Mays finished his class work in 1934 and received his Ph.D. from the University of Chicago School of Religion in March 1935.

In the summer of 1934, while working on his dissertation, Mays became dean of Howard University's School of Religion in Washington, D.C. Although Howard admits students of any race, color, and national origin, it has always been a historically black university whose special role has been the education of African American students. It is jointly supported by congressional appropriations and private funds. Because the United States Constitution requires the separation of church and state, the School of Religion was in a particularly vulnerable situation. In *Born to Rebel* Mays recounts both his successes and his failures as dean. One of his successes was his guidance toward accreditation by the American Association of Theological Schools; Howard was the second black seminary to qualify. While Mays is modest about his career at Howard, the distinguished faculty he gathered and the number of African American leaders who graduated from Howard prove that his accomplishments were nothing less than extraordinary.

Mays's success as dean of the School of Religion at Howard brought recognition to the former South Carolina farm boy. During his six years there, Mays was able to travel abroad for the first time, attending world conferences in Europe and India. On his travels Mays broadened his understanding of race, discrimination, and segregation, and he discovered that prejudice against African Americans was not confined to the United States. On ships he had a double cabin to himself and was seated alone at dinner. When a letter mistakenly informed a London hotel he was the distinguished president of Howard University, he was treated well; but when he returned to the same hotel without a letter, he discovered that for an African American man there was no room in the inn.[28]

On his travels Mays also learned that the plight of blacks was even worse in South Africa than in the United States. Mays also studied the plight of the Indian "untouchables" and concluded that their situation paralleled that of African Americans. Mays learned that Moslems and Hindus in India had a strong sense of unity within each group, however, and that they could not understand why Christians would segregate or lynch other Christians in the United States.

In India, Mays met with Mahatma Gandhi. In *Born to Rebel* he recounts this conference with the man who made Indians proud of their culture and history, who equated himself with the "untouchables," and who used the techniques of nonviolence to start a movement for India's independence that eventually led to the dissolution of the British Empire. Mays urged Gandhi to oppose the entire caste system and not just "untouchability." Although Mays had practiced nonviolent protest for most of his life, Gandhi introduced him to a broader perspective. Gandhi articulated implications for change beyond Mays's individual challenges to segregation and advocated mass campaigns of passive resistance to bring about change. When Mays later gave his famous Tuesday morning Morehouse talks, he drew upon his discussion with Gandhi to encourage young African American men who had to live in a prejudiced society.

On 31 May 1940 Benjamin Elijah Mays became the sixth president of Morehouse College. Morehouse, established in 1867 and named in honor of Dr. Henry Lyman Morehouse, secretary of the American Baptist Home Mission Society, was "dedicated to the task of building men: first by enlightening their minds, then by freeing them from the shackles of a psychological conditioning brought about by nearly two hundred and fifty years of slavery." Mays believed in the need for African American colleges only because of the discriminatory effects of segregation. Mays asserted, "If white historians had cared enough, had been knowledgeable enough, had been sensitive enough, good enough—and if the Founding Fathers had had the black man in mind when they wrestled the thirteen colonies from England and founded this country [—]there would have been no need . . . of Negro colleges." If it were not for black colleges, Mays argued in 1976, the education of minority students would have been "blotted out." Schools such as Morehouse provided "images, the things that tell people they are somebody, that they count."[29]

At Morehouse, Mays found morale low and the endowment on the point of losing a million dollars. The school was in the least favorable position among the colleges that formed the Atlanta Affiliation. Morehouse, "the stepchild in the Affiliation," was "fast becoming a junior college." Atlanta University controlled Morehouse's budget and finances; Morehouse students ate meals on the Atlanta University campus; and Spelman provided medical care for them.[30]

When soliciting the cooperation of students, faculty, trustees, alumni, and friends of the school, Mays promised to "give to Morehouse College all that I have . . . the best of my mind, heart, and soul. . . . I will give . . . my money until it reaches the sacrificial point. . . . I will serve this institution as if God Almighty sent me into the world for the express purpose of being the Sixth President of Morehouse College." After accepting the presidency, Mays immediately planned for the expansion and growth of Morehouse. His program included raising four hundred thousand dollars to match an endowment offer; securing annual contributors; constructing a new dormitory, dining hall, chapel, gymnasium, and classroom building; encouraging alumni to recruit new students; providing faculty housing; collecting past-due debts from students; increasing faculty salaries; and improving the credentials of the faculty. Not only did Mays accomplish his initial goals, but during his twenty-seven-year tenure he raised over fifteen million dollars for Morehouse College. In addition to the five buildings included in the original plan, Morehouse constructed thirteen others, including seven dormitories, a music building, and a science laboratory.

Mays was not, however, a president who focused on building. These accomplishments were minor compared to the special spirit he helped create at Morehouse College. Former student Samuel DuBois Cook, later president of Dillard University, believed that "Mays's genius was as an inspirer and motivator as well as a transformer of young men. . . . the Mays legacy is one of the great possessions of Black people and America." Under Mays's leadership, the faculty and teaching improved, student participation in extracurricular activities increased, the curriculum was constantly strengthened, available resources were used wisely and additional resources were steadily acquired, and full accreditation was obtained. Mays used honorary degrees to instill pride in young African American men; in 1943, Morehouse became the first black college to award an honorary degree to Paul Robeson. At the ceremony, Mays introduced Robeson as "a man who embodies all the hopes and aspirations of the Negro race and who, despite crippling restrictions, breathes the pure air of freedom. . . . You represent in your person, in your integrity, and in your ideals the things for which this college stands and for which it shall continue to stand." In 1968 the most prestigious of academic honor societies, Phi Beta Kappa, established a chapter at Morehouse, a school that had begun in a church basement with thirty-eight former slaves as students. When Mays accepted the presidency of Morehouse, he declared, "If Morehouse is not good enough for anybody, it's not good enough for Negroes." By the time of his retirement, Morehouse was an excellent college by any standard.[31]

Mays never lost sight of his goal: to create the best possible environment for the coming of age of young African American men. According to the historian David Lewis, "The personality of the statuesque and white-maned Dr. Mays permeated the milieu of the college with firm but unobtrusive moral guidance." The July 1965 *Morehouse College Bulletin* devoted a twenty-page supplement to Mays's administration. Included in the appraisal of his service was the following: "Under the far-reaching leadership of Benjamin E. Mays, Morehouse College has gone beyond mere academic respectability. Morehouse's bigness is not in student populations nor financial resources, but in the quality of an educational program that has led to earned recognition as a front-rank liberal arts college."[32]

At a Founders' Day address in 1963, the alumnus speaker gave Mays credit for nurturing Morehouse "from young adulthood to maturity." Predecessors laid the foundation, but Mays molded and gave to the great institution the form it is today. The celebrated "Morehouse man" is very much the Benjamin E. Mays man. Mays fulfilled his initial promise; he served as if heaven sent, gave as if his very existence depended upon it, and led Morehouse toward success.[33]

Every Tuesday morning for nearly thirty years, President Mays addressed Morehouse students on the state of the college and answered their questions. Again and again in his Tuesday talks, Mays encouraged Morehouse students to be men, not "black" men who had to play second fiddle to white men, but rather African American men who were not afraid to walk side by side with whites. Mays's most famous disciple, Martin Luther King, Jr., realized when he entered Morehouse that "nobody there was afraid." Mays encouraged students to fight fear and racism. "If you are ignorant," Mays told students, "the world is going to cheat you. If you are weak, the world is going to kick you. If you are a coward, the world is going to keep you running."[34]

Admired by many, Mays also had critics. When he was a youngster, others found him too studious and serious. As a preacher, the young Mays was sometimes perceived as a hopeless modernist who strayed from the conservative doctrines that African American Baptists accepted as orthodox. Some faulted what they believed to be inconsistencies in Mays's fusing of civil rights, social gospel, democracy, and Christianity in theology. As a college teacher and administrator, he was criticized as too demanding—he graded too strictly; he was against athletics.

Both African Americans and whites found many of his actions as a civil rights leader threatening. When President John F. Kennedy named Mays to the Civil Rights Commission, the Senate refused to confirm the appointment because Mays was a desegregationist and therefore unable to make "impartial" decisions. Georgia's two senators, Richard B. Russell and Herman E. Talmadge, protested that Mays's strong stance on integration was too narrow minded! Moreover, like many who fought for civil rights and challenged the social hierarchy of a segregated society during the 1930s and 1940s, Mays was wrongly accused of being a communist. Because of Mays's association with groups interested in social justice, groups that may have had communist members, the Georgia senators claimed that Mays had communist leanings. They cited *Communism and the NAACP*, published by the Georgia Committee on Education in 1958, where the Mays entry included thirty-one "communist" actions, such as his sponsorship of a dinner honoring W. E. B. Du Bois, his support of the American Crusade to End Lynching, his chairing a conference on discrimination in higher education for the Southern Conference Educational Fund, his membership on the nominating committee of the Southern Conference for Human Welfare in 1947–48, and, of course, his leadership in the NAACP. Mays, who perceived communism as anti-Christian, was outraged to be labeled a communist. Although Mays denied the allegations, Kennedy withdrew the nomination and tried to compensate by appointing Mays as one of the initial members of the Peace Corps Advisory Committee.[35]

Some African Americans thought that Mays should have confined his critique of American society to black-white issues. Mays's opposition to the Vietnam War and his broad views on social justice sometimes upset more conservative civil rights leaders who believed that African Americans should be supportive of President Lyndon Johnson's foreign policy because Johnson was supportive of civil rights legislation. Mays, however, as at his 1968 commencement address at Michigan State University, argued that Americans had to battle three major enemies of man: war, poverty, and racism. He warned, "Make no mistake: We will abolish war or war will abolish mankind."[36]

Mays was principled but practical. As chairman of the Atlanta School Board, he made decisions that angered people, African Americans and whites, on both sides of the political spectrum. In order to make integration work and to keep Atlanta from becoming an all-black city surrounded by white suburbs, Mays accepted what has become known as the Atlanta Plan as a compromise. Although the Atlanta Plan is generally hailed as one of the most successful school desegregations in the United States, some civil rights leaders believe Mays could have demanded more according to the law of the land.

Mays did not give blind support to all African American causes. The civil rights movement was divided, and Mays's unwavering support of Martin Luther King, Jr., angered some of the African American leadership. The old-line integrationist disappointed some young African American separatists when in 1967 he criticized the Student Nonviolent Coordinating Committee for an absence of "constructive ends. . . . Anything that tends to set white against black, I think does harm." He later said, "I don't think the Black Panthers are going to emancipate the black people from the problems of hunger, housing and more economic stability."[37]

Many younger activists advocated violence or—reared in an increasingly secular urban culture far removed from Mays's origins—rejected Christianity, which they considered the opiate of the black masses in America. To this later generation the aging warrior Mays appeared dated. But even some of the most vociferous of these African American activists still acknowledged the greatness of Mays and pointed to him as a positive role model, a mentor, and even as a "cultural hero."[38]

Mays's abolitionist-temperance tradition at times offended those from sophisticated backgrounds. He spoke his mind, often giving unsolicited advice. For example, he advised his faculty to observe three don'ts—don't drink, don't smoke, don't borrow money. Mays's only indulgence was the five or six teaspoons of sugar he heaped in each of the several cups of coffee he drank every morning. Dr. Richard Barksdale, an African American professor of English who had worked with Mays, once suggested that the coffee and sugar may have provided Mays's legendary energy. And, indeed, his energy was legendary. In 1981 Mays talked about "the spirit of urgency" and how he "worked all [his] life as if eternity was in every minute." Many people attribute Mays's nickname "Buck Benny" to his quick pace; he seemed to bounce as he sped from one place to another. Others ascribe it to his determination to "buck" the system. Mays, however, said that he acquired the sobriquet during his early days at Morehouse, when he initiated austerity programs to save the college and insisted that students repay outstanding debts.[39]

Although *Born to Rebel* demonstrates clearly why people honored and respected Mays, the autobiography, with perhaps too much reserve, omits many of the incidents that inspired devotion. Stories about the "puritan" Mays could mislead one into thinking he was ascetic in personality as well, but this kind and gentle man gave his acquaintances many reasons to love him. As president of Morehouse, he made it his business to meet and get to know each and every student, and he invited them into his home for visits. He was intelligent and witty, a wonderful conversationalist and a great raconteur. A classmate from the University of Chicago described Mays as "one of the greatest personalities in the world." Yet he was a very modest man. In 1980 as he received numerous honors, Mays explained: "I have never done anything for the purpose of being honored, to have my name on the front pages of the newspapers. I have done what I believe I was sent into the world to do: worship my God and serve my Fellowman." Even after all the recognition and awards he could say: "we all travel the same road from our mother's womb to the grave. So there's no need of anybody getting chesty. We travel the same highway."[40]

Mays does not relate that he offered to pay fines incurred by Martin Luther King, Jr., and others involved in civil rights work. He discusses how he firmly required Morehouse students to pay defaulted debts, but he neglects to mention his generosity in paying for students' educations. Although they had no children of their own, he and his wife supported the education of relatives and needy students. A former Harvard Divinity School student who was a Danforth Seminary intern at Morehouse remembered: "After receiving personal financial favor from Dr. Mays during a crucial and critical phase of my academic career, I tried to repay him. He refused my attempt by simply saying, 'If I have helped in any way, pass it on.' And for the rest of my life, I will try to pass it on."[41]

Mays was devoted and loyal to family, friends, and institutions. He often returned to Ninety Six for family reunions, celebrations, and funerals. He served loyally as president of the alumni association of South Carolina State, and a speaker at the eighty-fourth Founders Day said that Mays was "remembered in the Orangeburg community for his outstanding speeches at the annual Easter service held in the old White Hall campus for twenty-five years. This event drew a capacity audience each year."

Another example of people's devotion to Mays and Mays's reciprocal loyalty is in the small African American country school in Pacolet, South Carolina. In 1953 this school adopted the name Ben E. Mays High School. The students voted to have a Ben E. Mays day each year in honor of the school's namesake, and Mays never missed the day. The superintendent of the school said: "We think it noteworthy when an internationally known figure takes time out from a busy schedule to spend a day with boys and girls in a small rural school. Dr. Mays' presence annually should serve as an inspiration to the students of this institution." Teachers felt "that the presence of Dr. Mays [served] as an aid to the holding power of the high school," and more and more students stayed in high school and graduated. Mays also established ranking male (who, of course, went to Morehouse) and female scholarships for the senior class.[42]

Mays was democratic in his personal life just as he was in his political beliefs. Everyone—students, faculty, administrators, politicians, and endowment donors—wanted some of his time, and he was open to all, on a first-come, first-served basis. If he had agreed to speak to a small rural congregation on a particular day, he would not break his commitment to make room for a more prestigious engagement. In 1980, when an African American congregation in Ninety Six renamed their church Mays's United Methodist, he said that he was more touched by that honor than by any other he had ever received.

For Mays, religious faith lay at the very center of his life. "The first Christian light . . . to shine upon human relationships," he wrote in *Disturbed about Man,* "is the conviction that God is the author of all life, the source of human life is not blind mechanistic force, not blind chance, not natural laws; the source of human life is God." In his younger years, Mays, greatly inspired by the faith of his father and the piety of his mother, plowed a row, hitched his mule to a tree, and prayed, asking "the Lord to make it possible for [him] to get an education." And in his later years, no less religious, Mays the theologian wrote, "Man cannot leave God alone, and God cannot leave man alone; so someday, man will yet learn that the ways of the Lord are just and righteous altogether and that in obedience to God's command man will make the earth a place of love, brotherhood, justice, and peace."[43]

With a strong background in the liberal Protestant tradition, Mays drew heavily upon its theology to critique the social and economic conditions that African Americans experienced every day. For Mays, the world was filled with sin that manifested itself in terrible injustice and suffering, and it was the mission of the Christian to work to correct the injustice and to strive to better humanity. As a result, human experiences, instead of divine revelation and heavenly salvation, became central to Mays. Religious beliefs, according to Mays, needed to permeate every aspect of a Christian's life, every decision, and every thought. Mays found great comfort and purpose in his faith and the meaning it brought to his life.[44]

Being at peace with the omnipresent, omniscient, and omnipotent God enabled Mays to walk fearlessly in a land of prejudice and segregation. In "The Obligations of the Individual Christian" Mays argued: "The Christian cannot excuse himself by saying, 'I cannot go against tradition; I cannot buck the mores; I cannot jeopardize my political, social, or economic future.' The true Christian is a citizen of two worlds. Not only must he answer to the mores, but he must give an account to God. And with God's help he can be loyal to the highest and to the best he knows." Expounding on freedom in a speech, he again turned to the individual's relationship with God: "The free man, walking the high road moves on faith in the rightness of his position, takes the next step, trusting where he cannot prove, leaving the consequences to God." With God as his friend Mays feared no white man and no white man's unjust law.[45]

Giving religious support to Mays's rejection of segregation and racial injustice was his belief that God created each human being with intrinsic worth and dignity. Moreover, Mays believed, God created humanity in unity; therefore, segregation or any other attempt to destroy or divide humanity was to defy God's will. At the same time, Benjamin E. Mays understood the humanity of his oppressors, whom he was always ready to forgive. He argued that the "chief sin of segregation is the distortion of human personality. It damages the soul of both the segregator and the segregated. . . . It is difficult to know who is damaged more—the segregated or segregator." He believed that people had the power to change for the better. He once said that he was always happy to award an honorary degree from Morehouse to someone who had once been an oppressor of African American rights but had become a champion of civil rights because he understood how difficult and courageous such changes were. Such actions illustrate why Julian Bond said of his college president: "I am kneeling at the feet of a giant. Making friends of enemies has been the lifelong mission of Benjamin Mays."[46]

An extremely proud man, Mays was also meek, meek in the biblical sense, as Jesus and Moses were meek. Like Jesus, who drove the money changers out of the temple and challenged the Pharisees, and like Moses, who confronted Pharaoh and led his people out of Egypt, Mays followed his God and his conscience to fight injustice and segregation throughout the world and to free his people in the American South from the oppression of racism. Mays asserted during a commencement address at Bucknell University: "The test of good religion is not how we treat our peers and those above us, but how we treat those beneath us, not how we treat the man highest up, but how we treat the man farthest down. . . . the real test of my religion would be how I treat the man who has nothing to give me—no money, no social prestige, no honors. Not how I treat the educated, but how I treat the man who can't write his name." Mays took the text on Lazarus and Dives as a call for social conscience. Speaking on poverty and disease in the world, he told Bucknell graduates: "we must be concerned about the plight of other people. Whether we like it or not, our destiny is tied up with their destiny, and their welfare is ours. Jesus, in the twenty-fifth chapter of Matthew, makes it clear that our relationship to God is dependent upon our relationship to man. 'Inasmuch as ye did it unto the least of these, ye did it unto me.' Dives goes to hell not because he was rich and not because he was bad. Dives was a good man, a decent respectable, law-abiding citizen. He went to Hell because he had no social conscience. He did not care."[47]

Mays never hid his deep and abiding faith in God. Whether giving a sermon or delivering a speech before a secular audience, Mays never failed to use "a series of related biblical references." He stated about his public speaking, "I drew upon my theological training." Mays never criticized without providing constructive suggestions, no matter whether his audience was a graduating class at a huge midwestern state university, the congregation of a tiny rural black church, or a president of the United States. "We should begin in the kindergarten to develop people who believe in our Christian principles and democratic ideals," he asserted. "Goodness is as important as literacy. An honest heart is as important as a brilliant mind."[48]

Although he had been tutored in speech and became one of the most celebrated educators and orators of the twentieth century, he never rejected his roots. Professor Charles V. Willie of Harvard University, a former student of Mays's, maintains that Mays took his inspiration from the Bible and incorporated the "wisdom of the folk in his speeches and sermons." He integrated "folk wisdom and formal knowledge" so that each informed the other. When asked about his speaking, Mays explained that he used literary sources, psychology, philosophy, "everything I have learned," and "the experiences of the people sitting out in front of me, experiences I know they have had. We are all bothered by the same things—birth, courtship, marriage, sickness, death, anxiety." According to Mays, a successful speaker "must first have a message to give with the ultimate purpose to teach, not teaching so much to learn, but teaching to make people think. The speaker must first believe in what he is saying. . . . The truth is essential." Mays aimed "to not only make them feel, but to think deeply as well."[49]

Whatever the occasion, Benjamin Mays prepared meticulously for each speech, but he never used written notes before he was forty-five, and he was sixty before he relied on a manuscript. For Mays, speaking was a creative act, and he prepared for each and every audience accordingly. In an analysis of his speaking style, scholar Doris Levy Gavins observed that Mays always talked with people, rather than reading speeches. Encouraged at the age of nine by a standing ovation from the congregation for his recitation of the Beatitudes, Mays captivated and inspired audiences until his death. He relied on reason over emotion. He retained the grace of simplicity and the charm of the farm boy but was as much at ease addressing heads of state as delivering a sermon to the members of a small African American congregation. Partly because Mays treated all audiences with respect, his speaking impressed his listeners with its "sheer power." Robert Brisbane, founder of Morehouse's political science department, once described Mays's appearance as "regal," and Daniel Thompson, vice president of academic affairs at Dillard University, stated, "His presence was so great that anything he said would have gone over well." Bell Irvin Wiley, president of the Southern Historical Association, described Mays's 1956 talk on segregation as an "impassioned commentary on these moral inequities; the eloquence and the force with which the speaker stated his views was evidenced by the fact that he was twice interrupted by vigorous applause—a phenomenon without precedence in the Association's history—and by the tremendous ovation that he received at the conclusion of his remarks."[50]

Mays demanded perfection of himself in his scholarship just as in his speeches and his educational work. His account of the Phoenix Riot in Appendix A of *Born to Rebel* is first-rate historical investigation combining techniques of oral history with more time-tested traditional sources. Although he lived through the Phoenix Riot in 1898, Mays did not depend on memory for his account; he did extensive research. His work pointed to the economic underpinnings of the riot and made important distinctions between renting and sharecropping that most historians miss today. Mays understood rural society, and his writings and research reflect a unique perspective on the agrarian South.

Mays's greatest contribution as a scholar lies in his combination of the study of race relations and religion. Scholars of African American religion today still start with *The Negro's Church,* by Mays and Joseph W. Nicholson, and Mays's book *The Negro's God as Reflected in His Literature.* According to Mays and Nicholson, the origin of the African American church clearly distinguished black from white religion in the United States. Five themes underlay the origins of the African American church: various periods of growing racial consciousness, group and individual initiative, splits and withdrawals from established churches, African American migration, and the mission of other churches. Both these books pioneered the analysis of the liberating aspects of the African American church; members in control of their church, for example, were not "Uncle" and "Auntie" but "Mr." and "Mrs." Drawing upon his own experience as a youth in rural South Carolina, when he "was motivated by people in the church who made [him] believe that [he] could become something worthwhile in the world," Mays argued that the black church provided a safe haven and an escape from the segregation and discrimination that marked every day in the lives of African Americans. To "be recognized and to be 'somebody,' has stimulated the pride and preserved the self-respect of many Negroes who would have been entirely beaten by life, and possibly completely submerged. Everyone wants to receive recognition and feel that he is appreciated. The Negro church has supplied that need."[51]

The Negro's Church also criticized the poorly trained ministers who often encouraged socially irrelevant patterns of escape by preaching compensatory, your-reward-is-in-heaven, pie-in-the-sky Christianity. Again reflecting his own upbringing in rural South Carolina in his understanding of African American religion, Mays wrote in *The Negro's God* that he had "heard the Pastor of the church of [his] youth plead with the members of his congregation not to try to avenge the wrongs they suffered, but to take their burdens to the Lord in prayer. . . . invariably after assuring them that God would fix things up, he ended his sermon by assuring them further that God would reward them in Heaven. . . . Being socially proscribed, economically impotent, and politically browbeaten, they sang, prayed, and shouted their troubles away. This idea of God had telling effects upon the Negroes in [Mays's] home community. It kept them submissive, humble, and obedient. It enabled them to keep on keeping on." While Mays opposed the concept that religion should keep people "submissive, humble, and obedient," he thoroughly approved of a religion that helped a downtrodden people endure—"to keep on keeping on." His analysis was not one-sided.[52]

Mays was more than a scholar of African American religion, and his view of religion was more than a vague anthropological explanation for the world. For Benjamin E. Mays, religion and Christianity were vital forces. At the time of the study (during the depression), Mays was able to capture the pulse of the African American church. As a result of his research, Mays identified problems that the church needed to solve. In retrospect, it is clear that much of what Mays discussed was an accurate prediction of the later needs and feelings of the African American community. Mays suggested consolidation to relieve economic problems of the black church and to encourage more cohesiveness in congregations and better leadership from the African American community. He criticized the static, nonprogressive nature of the church and noted that it had failed to retain the loyalty of many of the most critically minded African Americans. His list of the shortcomings of the black church is long: pastors were poorly educated; too many sermons betrayed a magical conception of religion; teachers in church schools too often lacked college educations; there were too many African American churches for the number of black churchgoers; the churches struggled under a heavy load of indebtedness; they were too little concerned with social problems such as juvenile delinquency.

In spite of the problems, Mays asserted that the good outweighed the bad in the African American church. The church was the first area of life outside the family where African Americans, particularly men, enjoyed freedom. "And it was to the advantage of the Negro that he proved his worth as a preacher," Mays and Nicholson noted, "because as a result, in spite of continued restraints, prohibitions, and anti-Negro legislation, a few liberal-minded whites encouraged the Negro minister and actually helped to make it possible for him to fulfill his mission as a preacher." *The Negro's Church* also discussed the preacher's importance in African American society. Black preachers were leaders, politicians, orators, bosses, and idealists. The ministry was one of the few professions open to talented African American men in the nineteenth and early twentieth centuries. In 1930, blacks accounted for less than a tenth of the population of the United States, while African Americans accounted for nearly a fifth of the total number of preachers. The black church was, and still is, a foundation of pride and self-respect for African Americans, and they could, and still can, become leaders and hold responsible positions within its administration.[53]

Mays intrigued students by pointing out how the African American church could foster social change. The pulpit of a black church provided a forum for discussing world problems, including racial difficulties, and for dispensing practical advice. Through adult education, the church could reach poor and uneducated African Americans. For generations of African Americans, the church had been the center of intellectual life as well as religious and moral teaching. Benjamin Mays remarked that whites practiced politics in government while African Americans practiced politics in the church.

For the rest of his life, Mays continued to research and write about African American religion. In *Seeking to Be Christian in Race Relations,* written three decades after *The Negro's Church* and *The Negro's God as Reflected in His Literature,* Mays discussed the value of nonviolent protest and noted that Martin Luther King, Jr., drew upon his Christian and African American heritage in preaching his gospel of nonviolent change. Mays maintained that nonviolent protest took root in African American culture the first time a slave sang a spiritual. As songs of protest about slaves' suffering and pain, spirituals refuted the white myth that African Americans were satisfied with life in white America and helped African Americans bear the burden of racism. Mays argued that songs and praise of Jesus, the founder of nonviolent protest, helped to prevent the hatred and bitterness that otherwise would have developed into violence and race war. Mays pointed to Frederick Douglass and Harriet Tubman as practitioners of nonviolence in their efforts to free the enslaved. Mays discovered nonviolence in the quiet persuasiveness of Booker T. Washington and the eloquent bitterness of W. E. B. Du Bois. Mays pointed out that, since 1935, when Donald Murray won a court case enabling African Americans to attend the University of Maryland Law School, the NAACP had been peacefully using the courts to gain larger citizenship rights for African Americans. The courts were also used to lessen the disparity between blacks and whites in salaries and educational facilities. Change was coming slowly through legal channels, but the people were persevering, gaining strength of spirit from their relationship with God and their nonviolent efforts for change.

"Among all things," as Julian Bond insisted, "Dr. Mays is a teacher. It is his reason for being. His teachings are based on his faith and his faith is based on the feeling that man is a rational being able to build a better world." Mays once described his motivation in his weekly newspaper column: "I behave as I do because I know that as long as I am treated as a Negro, a caste man, this thing isn't right, and until my dying day I shall insist first on being a human being and incidentally, a Negro. In my protest, I am not fighting to be *with* anybody. I just want to be human and allowed to walk the earth with dignity." Mays's unrelenting opposition to racism was a logical consequence of his belief in the unity of the human family, a family with kinship to God. He strongly believed that segregated schools denied the God-given unity of mankind. The purpose of education was to strengthen human dignity and kindness. "I think the great need is an education with a social conscience," he said; "science has made the world a neighborhood. It is left for all of us—leaders in education and religion—to make it a brotherhood."[54]

In a commencement address delivered at the University of Liberia in 1960, Mays said: "Generally speaking, education is designed to train the mind to think clearly, logically and constructively; to train the heart to feel understandingly and sympathetically the aspirations, the sufferings, and the injustices of mankind; and to strengthen the will to act in the interest of the common good. To state the purpose in Christian perspective, the aim of education should be [to] glorify God and to serve mankind." For Mays, the responsibilities of the teacher extended far beyond the classroom.[55]

Mays's influence reached far and wide. Local African American leaders in many southern towns and urban centers, working for civil rights in their own communities, testify to the crucial impact Mays had on their lives. In 1980, on "Benjamin Elijah Mays Day" in Washington, D.C., Alex Haley told the audience how his father had driven over a hundred miles so that young Haley and his brother could see the great educator. In my own research on the era from Reconstruction to the modern civil rights movement, I personally was told by African American descendants of Reconstruction political leaders that many black activists learned from Mays "behind the veil," to use W. E. B. Du Bois's phrase. In 1982 Andrew Young, mayor of Atlanta and former ambassador to the United Nations, said essentially the same thing; in every city in the United States, the leading African American doctor, the most important African American attorney, "most certainly one of the key preachers and probably most of the black elected officials owe where they are to Dr. Mays." Coretta Scott King said to Mays: "Most of the black male leadership in our country during the last forty years has in some way been inspired by you. . . . Martin Luther King, Jr., called you his spiritual mentor and was greatly influenced by your life and example. . . . you've been a great inspiration to me."[56]

Mays's relationship with Martin Luther King, Jr., is the most famous example of how he encouraged others. Historian Stephen B. Oates wrote in *Let the Trumpet Sound* that at Morehouse, King "found his calling under the guidance and inspiration of Benjamin Mays," who "as a preacher and theologian was out to renew the mission of the black church. . . . At Morehouse chapel, this tall and erudite man, with his iron-gray hair and hypnotic voice, mesmerized his young disciples by preaching stewardship, responsibility, and engagement. 'Do whatever you do so well,' he counseled, 'that no man living and no man yet unborn could do it better.' Here at Morehouse, he was not turning out doctors or lawyers or preachers, Mays said. He was turning out *men*." Accordingly, King "saw in Mays what he wanted 'a real minister to be'—a rational man whose sermons were both spiritually and intellectually stimulating, a moral man who was socially involved. Thanks largely to Mays, King realized that the ministry could be a respectable force for ideas, even for social protest."[57]

It would be human nature for a teacher to claim credit for a former student who achieved greatness. But Mays was extremely modest about his relationship with King, saying that he did not realize his influence until King wrote about it in *Stride toward Freedom*. Martin Luther King, Jr., symbolized hope and courage for African Americans, but Mays was that symbol to King. King turned to Mays for advice, and Mays often helped King in the struggle for civil rights. The influence of Benjamin E. Mays on his most distinguished disciple could be a book unto itself. Their friendship lasted from King's collegiate days to his death in 1968.

In 1944, when Mays was fifty years old and in the fourth year of his presidency at Morehouse, King entered the college at the age of fourteen in Mays's special program for gifted high school students. Mays, a powerful pulpiteer with impeccable academic and scholarly credentials, stirred his college students with addresses based on commonplace observations but spurred by intensity and intimacy. King often stayed behind to discuss the sermon, and by the time he was in his junior year at Morehouse, the two men talked regularly in Mays's office. Whether they agreed or disagreed, these discussions, which Mays encouraged with all Morehouse students, inspired King. King's fame overshadows Mays's, but I believe there could not have been a Martin Luther King, Jr., if there had been no Benjamin Elijah Mays. From their days together at Morehouse, through the years of the civil rights struggle, and until King's death, the pair shared the same philosophy and goals.

Martin Luther King, Sr., described the effect of Mays's oratorical skills upon his son: "Dr. Mays, an elegant speaker, offered the tempering of drama with calm assurance and unassailable reason. . . . Martin Luther was clearly impressed by those first three years and told his mother one evening he would enter the ministry." Describing the "insistent call to the ministry" that her husband felt, Coretta Scott King explained that "the decision that finally led to that path was largely due to the example of Dr. Benjamin Mays, president of Morehouse College. . . . From first to last Dr. Mays took a great interest in Martin. It was not that he deliberately guided him towards the ministry as that he influenced Martin by his example. For although Dr. Mays was brilliant, he was not removed from the heart of the people. In the pulpit he talked a great deal about social justice; you might say he preached a social gospel. This conformed exactly with Martin's views, and it helped to form them. . . . At Morehouse listening to Dr. Mays preach . . . Martin came to see that the ministry could be intellectually respectable as well as emotionally satisfying. When he accepted this fact, it opened the way for him to go into the church."[58]

King's enemies also recognized Mays's influence. One pamphlet, *America's Betrayal: Martin King, Red Tool,* quoted a Louisiana legislative committee report that King's "un-Americanism" began at Morehouse, "where he was noticed by President Benjamin E. Mays, a notorious negro radical with a public record of affiliation with some twenty-five fronts of which . . . several were Communist Party fronts operating amongst the negroes." According to the pamphlet, Mays "saw that King had possibilities as a rabble-rouser and . . . played a major part . . . in putting King's feet on the road which eventually led to Montgomery" and the bus boycott.[59]

Mays's support of King and the Montgomery bus boycott was crucial in 1956. King had been visiting with his parents in Atlanta. Word reached him there that a Montgomery grand jury had resurrected an antiquated antiboycott law (once used to hinder unionization) to indict King and eighty-eight others and that he would be arrested if he returned to Alabama. Distressed because his son would be part of mass arrests, because he might be harmed, and because as an African American civil rights leader he would not receive due process in the Alabama courts, the elder King invited his most trusted friends to counsel against his son's returning to Montgomery. Attorneys, educators, and newspapermen, fearing that Montgomery was ready to explode, advised Martin Luther King, Jr., against returning to the city. King, however, announced that he had decided to go back. He later wrote: "In the moment of silence that followed I heard my father break into tears. I looked at Dr. Mays, one of the great influences in my life. Perhaps he had heard my unspoken plea. At any rate, he was soon defending my position strongly. Then others joined in supporting me."[60]

King was arrested, but the boycott became a major cornerstone of the civil rights movement. In June 1956, a United States district court ruled that racial segregation on city bus lines was unconstitutional, and in November, the Supreme Court affirmed the district court's ruling. By December, the buses in Montgomery were integrated and the second Reconstruction was underway.

The next year, Mays honored King at the Morehouse commencement. "You did not betray that trust of leadership," the college president began. "You led the people with quiet dignity, Christian grace and determined purpose. While you were away, your colleagues in the battle for freedom were being hounded and arrested like criminals. When it was suggested by legal counsel that you might stay away and escape arrest, I heard you say with my own ears, 'I would rather spend 10 years in jail than desert people in this crisis.' At the moment my heart, mind and soul stood up erect and saluted. I knew then that you were called to leadership for such a time as this. You are a symbol of hope and courage for oppressed people everywhere."[61]

In 1964, when King won the Nobel Peace Prize, Mays initiated a plan to have the entire city of Atlanta celebrate their distinguished native son. Mays recounts how he was able to overcome jealousy and division within the African American community and the objections of white racists to organize a committee for the gala. Pressure from the *New York Times* and encouragement from Mayor Ivan Allen turned the tide; the dinner was a great success for both King and publicity-conscious Atlanta. Four years later, after King's assassination, Mays delivered his eulogy. It has been said that when Mays preached King's funeral, he "extracted the essence not only of Martin but also of Benjamin. Either man could have been speaking of the other."[62]

Mays, an exceptionally dedicated and principled man, struggled against great adversity to gain an education and to maintain a sense of self-worth while living in a society that, at every turn, expressed its belief that he was worthless. He spoke out firmly but peacefully against the injustices of race relations in America. Mays could have contended, as many others did, that things have improved vastly since the 1890s, that we should count our blessings, that we should not rock the boat, but he steadfastly refused to do so. Having lived through some of the worst times that racism spawned in America, he looked back through seven decades of social progress and concluded that we must not be satisfied with that progress. He continued to be active in educating, advising, and encouraging others to democratize America.

At the age most people retire, the indefatigable Mays began a whole new career as chairman of the Atlanta School Board for twelve years. Mays also remained active in support of reform. Typical is the letter that he and Martin Luther King, Sr., wrote in support of the boycott of J. P. Stevens and Company in 1977: "Racial justice today is dependent on economic and social justice" and an "issue of conscience has arisen which demands our involvement." Workers, black and white, male and female, young and old, "need our help urgently if justice is to be served." When African American children were being murdered in Atlanta, the *Christian Century* interviewed the "long-time national black leader and highly respected president of Atlanta's school board." Mays informed the reporter: "the situation should be a challenge to the churches. Take our black churches—almost every one, however beautiful it may be, is only a stone's throw from youngsters not going to Sunday school, maybe selling dope, maybe becoming thieves. . . . Housing projects are very near my church; we ought to bring the children into our church and let them know we care. The church could give them incentive." The writer commented, "When the 86-year-old educator sees a youth out of school during school hours, he marches right up to inquire why." In 1983, he was the cochairman of South Carolina Senator Ernest Hollings's presidential steering committee. When at eighty-seven, he retired as "the oldest board president in the United States . . . Mays said, 'I have several things to do before I die.'" He started working on three books, a collection of his articles, a recounting of his twenty-seven years at Morehouse, and a history of *Brown v. Board of Education*. "I plan to die in the harness," said Mays.[63]

Mays's unceasing efforts have made a difference in the United States, and he recorded those struggles in *Born to Rebel*. Mays believed strongly in the power of the voting booth and asserted that "the right to vote is the most sacred thing a man can have." Because the right to vote had been taken away from African Americans in 1895, he would tell audiences: "My father voted, so what's all the argument about? It's nothing new. And 25 years from today your children will be amazed at all this hullabaloo about nothing." A major accomplishment of the civil rights movement was the passage of the Voting Rights Act of 1965, which abolished most of the overt legal impediments to African American voting, such as the literacy test and the poll tax. The civil rights movement impelled African Americans to register and vote in greater numbers than one would expect in light of their lower than average income and level of education; lower income and education levels usually inhibit political participation. Interest in voting is acquired as a consequence of what scholars call "political socialization." The children and grandchildren of African American citizens who were discouraged from voting in the years before the Voting Rights Act are less likely to register and vote than whites of similar ages whose parents and grandparents did vote. Mays wrote his autobiography partly to help offset these lingering effects of past discrimination. The Current Population Survey (November 2000) puts the non-Hispanic white/African American voting disparity at 5 percent (61.8 versus 56.8). That is a modest disparity when we consider the difference in the socioeconomic status of African Americans and the apathy produced by a lack of candidates representing their interests. Moreover, close to a quarter of young African American males are disfranchised because of felonies, even though many have already paid their debt to society. Yet, a surprising number of African Americans continue to vote. The spirit of Mays lives on because he and other civil rights leaders so inspired a generation that their sons and daughters, grandsons and granddaughters, have inherited their fervor.[64]

The South of 2002 is not the South in which Mays grew up; legal barriers have largely been broken down, and the psychological restraints that minimized African American participation during the Jim Crow segregation period are now dissipating. Today, African Americans register in much of South Carolina about as freely as whites. Mays advised African American youths that they were "standing on the shoulders of others who have endured and fought through the ballot and the courts." About those who did not break the obstacles to voting, Mays charged, "Any man who is ashamed of his background is a slave."[65]

Today many younger African Americans and whites do not remember the old blatant segregation. Today's racism—and racism it is—is more subtle. White bloc voting persists, as does antiblack racial gerrymandering, but many of the devices of the 1970s and 1980s have been overthrown in legal procedures; African American plaintiffs have filed and won many (but not all) cases against at-large elections and reapportionment plans designed to keep white incumbents in office and exclude minorities. Today's battles involve the new states' rights focus by the 5-4 majority on the Supreme Court, which encourages resegregation of schools, the end of antidiscriminatory regulations (on the ironic view that they are not color blind), and discrimination in redistricting. Just as Mays had to fight different battles than his father had, so Mays's legatees have to recognize and fight against the more subtle forms of discrimination. Mays understood the differences between the past and the present, and he exuded hope for the future.[66]

The life of Dr. Benjamin Elijah Mays illustrates the ironies of southern history. Born in an area known as the "dark corner" of a county notorious for its violent extremism, Mays emerged as the great advocate of nonviolence. This area of the South Carolina up-country has produced many national, regional, and state leaders of distinction. One can tell much about what a people value by what they select to preserve as historical and by the sites they deem significant enough to mark with plaques and monuments. A marker in Ninety Six commemorates Congressman Preston S. Brooks, the congressman who assaulted the senator from Massachusetts because Senator Charles Sumner gave an antislavery speech insulting to a kinsman of Brooks and to the state of South Carolina. In the words of Brooks: "I struck him with my cane and gave him about 30 first rate stripes with a gutta percha cane.... Every lick went where I intended.... I wore my cane out completely." In 1856, a grand assembly at Ninety Six honored Brooks; the *New York Times* reported it to be the largest gathering ever in the up-country. At that celebration, thousands of canes were presented to Brooks to replace the one he had destroyed while beating Sumner. The Edgefield Chapter of the United Daughters of the Confederacy maintains the home of Martin Witherspoon Gary, the "Bald Eagle of the Confederacy." The Gary home is a shrine that houses memorabilia for the Red Shirts, the paramilitary group that violently repudiated South Carolina's experiment in interracial democracy. This area is also the home of Senator J. Strom Thurmond, who used his presidential nomination by the "white supremacist" Dixiecrat party in 1948 as a starting point from which to maneuver his way into a political dominance unmatched in the state since the days of political theorist and defender of slavery John C. Calhoun. A life-size statue of Thurmond faces the Edgefield courthouse.[67]

As a young boy, like many others in that community, I took note of the two local historical markers decorating downtown Ninety Six. One commemorated a Revolutionary War battle at the nearby Star Fort, and the other celebrated Preston Brooks. Although Ninety Six is also the home of Benjamin E. Mays, the long-time president of Morehouse College, the spiritual mentor of Martin Luther King, Jr., and the godfather of the modern civil rights movement, I did not learn of Mays in any memorial in the town of Ninety Six nor in the local schools. No statue or plaque commemorated this native son, this apostle of peace whose very life represented a heroic struggle for dignity and for civil rights. The world in which I grew up had not changed much from the segregated world into which Mays was born, and I remained unacquainted with the African American oral tradition regarding Mays. It was only in my senior year at Furman University when I heard Dr. Mays speak during a Religious Emphasis week that I learned that this great educator had come from my hometown. The small town white fathers, as well as white women's auxiliaries, did not value Mays for a memorial. The greatest South Carolinian in the twentieth century was from Ninety Six, and I had not even known who he was!

Readers sense in *Born to Rebel* a deep hurt. As a young man, Mays believed: "I could never do what I hoped to do or be what I aspired to be if I remained in the state of my birth. I had to seek a new world." In his preface, Mays wrote of the "indignities" and the "injustices and brutalities heaped upon Negroes during [his] lifetime." One purpose of his writing *Born to Rebel* was "to expose the snaillike progress which we have made in Negro-white relations in the South and in the nation." Mays was constantly aware of the racial inequities in the American South. Yet this is not a bitter book, fraught with pent-up rage at the circumstances of life in the segregated South. It is instead a quiet, rational insistence that all is not well in America.

Mays completed his autobiography in 1970 (most of the writing was done years before). At that time, he wrote that he never felt "at home in [his] native county."

His experiences—watching the Phoenix Riot, "observing the way [his] people were treated, noting the way in which they responded to this treatment, never having had a white friend from Greenwood County, and having always lived in a rented home"—left him with "a feeling of alienation from the county of [his] birth. The chasm was so wide between black and white in [his] day that [he] never felt that any white person in Greenwood County or in South Carolina would be interested in anything [he] did."

Mays, however, lived to see the South's acceptance of him and of the kind of life he preached. In 1977, Richard Raymer, a white member of the Atlanta School Board, said of Mays: "He is the most widely respected citizen in Atlanta today. If you took a poll he would come out on top. He is the kind of man we would like our kids to grow up to be." In 1974, Lander College in Greenwood, South Carolina, awarded Mays the thirty-fourth of his forty-nine honorary degrees, and Representative W. J. Bryan Dorn entered the tributes and Mays's acceptance speech into the *Congressional Record.* Furthermore, Dorn added: "Greenwood County has produced no more illustrious son than Dr. Mays, who was, I am proud to say, born only a short distance from where I now live. . . . [He is] one of the world's most renowned and distinguished educators. Dr. Mays, a superb orator and gentleman, has been an ambassador of culture, good will, brotherhood and understanding throughout the world." Dorn attributed to his friend Mays the credit for much of his transformation from a defiant segregationist to a supporter of African American rights, including busing. On a later occasion, Dorn listed some of the world's leaders he had known, including presidents and generals; he went on to say, "The greatest man I have ever known is my friend and neighbor, Dr. Benjamin E. Mays." In 1979, when South Carolina named a new veterans' administration hospital in honor of this thirteen-term congressman, Mays was asked to address the assembly. This African American man, who had believed no white from Greenwood County could be interested in anything to do with him, who had thought he would never have a white friend from his home county, told the gathering, "With all due respect to you great people who have assembled here today, I'm here for one purpose, because I'm a friend of William Jennings Bryan Dorn."[68]

Times were changing for this modern-day reformer. Like the prophets of old, called to chastise and preach repentance and justice in the country, Mays had met with fierce resistance, but finally Mays the prophet was honored in his own country. As Mays put it: "Yes, Lord, South Carolina has changed. I, myself, have changed." In July 1980, his portrait was hung in the South Carolina State House in Columbia; he was the second African American (after Mary Bethune McCloud) to be so honored. On that occasion Mays exulted, "I am no longer an alien in my native state, I feel as free as the wind that blows, free as the birds that fly." He was also inducted into the

South Carolina Hall of Fame. And on a crisp Friday in early November 1981, dignitaries including Coretta Scott King, together with white and black home folk, gathered at a ceremony to name the intersection of Scott Ferry Road with U.S. Highway 178, six hundred feet from his birthplace, "Mays Crossroads." A tall granite marker pays tribute to Mays as "one of the state's most distinguished native sons / one of the great forces for civil rights not only in this country but around the world."

Lamenting that Greenwood County had been "too slow in honoring Dr. Mays for his accomplishments," Larry A. Jackson, president of Lander College, went on to describe one of the reasons for the tribute to Mays: "to remind us, the citizens of this place who will pass on this road from time to time, of the message and the quality of his life. . . . You have given us a vision of what human life is supposed to be like and we will remain always in your debt."[69]

Although *Born to Rebel* ends with an indictment of the South, Mays, in the decade after its publication, found a special peace with the homeland that had treated him and other African Americans so badly for so long: "I am happy, I am glad, in fact I am extremely proud that my native state has done so much to honor Benjamin Mays, son of the soil, son of the farm, son of slaves."[70]

He continued, "My father was born into slavery nine years before Lincoln issued the Emancipation Proclamation and my mother was born into slavery before Congress made slaves citizens." Mays reminded the crowd gathered to honor him that he was fifty-two years old when he was first allowed to vote, that African Americans in South Carolina could not vote until 1946. "Yes, Lord," he said, "the people have changed for the better in my native state of South Carolina." Mays recounted the Phoenix Riot, his first childhood memory, and told the crowd that the mob of white vigilantes murdered his cousin. "There was a time," he said, "when I hated my native state, not the people but for what the politicians did—segregating me so that I could never rise to be what God intended all men to be—free." Most of his life he had not sung "Dixie," but now he could because, he noted, "'Dixie' [was] no longer to [him] the world of the segregated society." He concluded by telling the integrated crowd that "the South is destined to play a great role in democratizing the United States. . . . Yes, I can sing 'Dixie' but I can also sing, 'My country 'tis of Thee, sweet land of liberty.' . . . I love my friends, I love my South Carolinians. . . . I shall not, and I can not and I would not even if I could, let my native state down."[71]

Less than three years later, at a memorial service for Mays on 1 April 1984 at Mays Crossroads, the state senator for Greenwood and McCormick counties, John Drummond, said: "We are glad that history will always link his name to this church, to my home town of Ninety Six, and to the little community of Epworth where he entered this world. We will say with pride that we were his home folks. And we will be the beneficiaries of the works of a man who found this world a troubled place, and made it better."[72]

The obituary for Mays in the *New York Times* extolled him as "a noble and powerful combination" of "teacher and preacher." Charles G. Adams, pastor of the Hartford Memorial Baptist Church in Detroit and president of the Detroit Central Branch of the NAACP, wrote of Mays: "The epitome of manhood, Benjamin Elijah Mays was tall, stalwart and wise. Having perfected the art and diplomacy, refinement, taste, style, common sense, faith, thrift, diligence, discipline, patriotism and total dedication to human betterment, Dr. Mays was the Benjamin Franklin of Black America. His indomitable faith, personal integrity, capacity for hard work and concern for others fueled and fired his meteoric rise from abject poverty and mean obscurity to the highest-ranking scholar, author, activist and educator that one could know. Without a doubt, he was the most distinguished pulpiteer and educator that America has ever produced. . . . [He instilled] faith and character. . . . Never before has America seen a more perfect blend of faith, intelligence and courage. . . . At 89, he died, still dreaming, still writing, still fighting for justice, still striving for excellence. May his memory and his character live long in the hearts and minds of those whose lives he touched."[73]

Charles V. Willie has written that Mays had found satisfaction in a life where he responded effectively to constant challenges; for Mays, to live was to struggle. Writing about the endemic racism in white society in 1977, Willie drew upon the theory of the social philosopher René DuBos and the example of Benjamin E. Mays. According to DuBos's theory, society needs rebels who become the "standard bearer of the visionaries who gradually increase man's ethical stature"; rebels provide "hope that our societies can be saved." Willie argues that this is why the redoubtable fighter Mays entitled his life story *Born to Rebel*. In this age of the antihero, it is perhaps difficult to grasp fully the heroism of Mays's rebellion; it was a rebellion of poetic elegance, both pertinent and passionate. According to Samuel DuBois Cook, Mays understood that "the heart of the ethical consciousness is the cry of the human heart and soul for something better, nobler, higher, and richer." Dr. Mays was "a philosopher of the heroic life. The heroic life is defined in moral, religious, intellectual, humanistic and institutional terms." Heroism demands tough choices, and Mays once said, "I would rather go to hell by choice than to stumble into heaven by following the crowd."[74]

When my friend Dr. Mays asked me to edit this wonderful and inspiring autobiography, he pointed out that many whites were unaware of his story and that having a white scholar of race relations introduce his book would be a good thing. Actually, since the time Mays wrote, even some African American scholars, no longer confined to historically black colleges, also fail to recognize the name of Dr. Benjamin E. Mays.

Yet this story of Benjamin Mays is important to all people because it proclaims a truly heroic example of striving for a better world. Mays's life was one of sacrifice and accomplishment. His Christian philosophy drove him to speak truth to power and call the United States to its ideals of justice and brotherhood. Generations born since the Vietnam War have found it difficult to believe in heroes, but as we study the life of Benjamin Mays, we can see how individuals make a difference in history and why we can still believe in heroes.

ORVILLE VERNON BURTON

Notes

I would like to acknowledge the assistance of Matthew Cheney, Bill Hines, Chris Vilas, and Georganne Burton; their suggestions and editorial comments helped clarify and focus this foreword. I shall always be thankful for former University of Georgia Press Director Malcolm Call for his belief in this project and our shared admiration for Benjamin E. Mays. Everyone at the University of Georgia Press has been outstanding in support, and I especially appreciate the efforts of my editor, Derek Krissoff, and the astute suggestions of Project Editor Jon Davies. Thank you also to the Research Board of the University of Illinois at Urbana-Champaign.

1. Charles V. Willie, "Educational Leaders Past and Present—the Education of Benjamin Elijah Mays: An Experience in Effective Teaching," in *Walking Integrity: Benjamin Elijah Mays: Mentor to Generations*, ed. Lawrence E. Carter, Sr. (Atlanta: Scholars Press of Emory University, 1996), p. 391.

2. Richard I. McKinney, "The Black Church: Its Development and Present Impact," *Harvard Theological Review* 64, no. 4 (1971): 477; Doris Levy Gavins, "The Ceremonial Speaking of Benjamin Elijah Mays: Spokesman for Social Change, 1954–1975" (Ph.D. diss., Louisiana State University, 1978), p. 185. Quotations and information derived from *Born to Rebel* are not cited.

3. Editorial, *The Colored American*, Nov. 1901, p. 78; Donald Norton Brown, "Southern Attitudes toward Negro Voting in the Bourbon Period, 1877–1890" (Ph.D. diss., University of Oklahoma, 1960), p.151; "Address of Dr. Benjamin Elijah Mays at the Ceremony Dedicating the Historic Marker at Mays Crossroads near the Birthplace of Dr. Mays at Epworth, S.C., Nov. 7, 1981," tape transcription, p. 5.

4. Orville Vernon Burton, "The Rise and Fall of Afro-American Town Life: Town and Country in Reconstruction Edgefield County, South Carolina," in *Toward a New South? Studies in Post–Civil War Southern Communities*, ed. Orville Vernon Burton and Robert C. McMath, Jr. (Westport, Conn.: Greenwood Press, 1982), pp. 152–92; I. A. Newby, *Black Carolinians: A History of Blacks in South Carolina from 1895 to 1968*, Tricentennial Studies, no. 6 (Columbia: University of South Carolina Press, 1973), pp. 232–34; Mays, "The New Negro Challenges the Old Order" and "Address Delivered at Older Boys' Conference, Benedict College, Feb. 26, 1926," both in Asa H. Gordon, *Sketches of Negro Life and History in South Carolina* (1929; reprint, Columbia: University of South Carolina Press, 1971), pp. 192–212.

5. *Columbia Record*, 3 May 1949, pp. 1, 4; *Editorial Reprints from the Petal Papers* and personal comments by P. D. East, editor (Petal, Miss.); James W. Silver, "The Twenty-first Annual Meeting," *Journal of Southern History* 22 (Feb. 1956): 61.

6. Mays, address at Epworth, 7 Nov. 1981, p. 5; "Remarks by Sen. John Drummond, Senator, Greenwood, McCormick Counties, Mt. Zion Baptist Church, Greenwood, S.C., April 1, 1984," pp. 2–3.

7. Lerone Bennett, Jr., "The Last of the Great Schoolmasters," *Ebony* 32 (Dec. 1977): 74–79.

8. Rachael Hende, *Presbyterian Survey,* June 1957, photocopy in Benjamin E. Mays file, South Caroliniana Library (hereinafter cited as SCL).

9. Grace Jordan McFadden, "Quest for Human Rights: The Oral Recollections of Black South Carolinians," interview with Mays, Instructional Services Center, Film Library, University of South Carolina.

10. Newby, *Black Carolinians,* p. 12.

11. Ibid., pp. 15–16.

12. "Speech of B. F. Perry," *Journal of the People of South Carolina, Held in Columbia, South Carolina, September 1865* (Columbia: Julian A. Selby, 1865), p. 14; South Carolina, *Constitution of 1865,* art. 1, sec. 14, and art. 4; South Carolina, *Laws,* 1865, pp. 271, 276, 293, 295–96, 299, 303–4; Laughlin McDonald, "An Aristocracy of Voters: The Disfranchisement of Blacks in South Carolina," *South Carolina Law Review* 37, no. 4 (1986): 557–82. My discussion of discrimination and the history of vote dilution draws heavily on Orville Vernon Burton et al., "South Carolina," in *The Quiet Revolution in the South: The Impact of the Voting Rights, 1965–1990,* ed. Chandler Davidson and Bernard Grofman (Princeton: Princeton University Press, 1994), pp. 191–232, 420–32, and on Orville Vernon Burton, "'The Black Squint of the Law': Racism in South Carolina," in *The Meaning of South Carolina History: Essays in Honor of George C. Rogers, Jr.,* ed. David R. Chesnutt and Clyde N. Wilson (Columbia: University of South Carolina Press, 1991), pp. 161–85.

13. United States, 14 *Stat.,* 27, 428, 15 *Stat.* 2, 14, 41; *The Constitution of South Carolina, Adopted April 16, 1868* (Columbia: John W. Denny, 1868).

14. Orville Vernon Burton, "Race and Reconstruction: Edgefield County, South Carolina," *Journal of Social History* 12 (fall 1978): 31–56; "Plan of the Campaign of 1876," in the papers of Martin Witherspoon Gary (SCL); Benjamin R. Tillman, "The Struggle of 1876: How South Carolina Was Delivered from Carpet-Bag and Negro Rule," speech at the Red-Shirt Reunion at Anderson, S.C., 1909.

15. *Charleston News and Courier,* 4 June 1878.

16. Tillman Inaugural in South Carolina *House Journal,* 1890, pp. 130–54.

17. David Duncan Wallace, *The South Carolina Constitution of 1895* (Columbia: Bureau of Publications, University of South Carolina, no. 197, 15 Feb. 1927), p. 35; George Brown Tindall, "The Question of Race in the South Carolina Constitutional Convention of 1895," *Negro History Bulletin* 15 (Jan. 1952); *Journal of the Constitutional Convention of the State of South Carolina* (Columbia: Charles A. Calvo, Jr., 1895), 10 Sept. 1895, pp. 1–2; *Constitution of the State of South Carolina, Ratified in Convention, December 4, 1895* (Columbia: R. L. Bryan, 1909), especially art. 2, sec. 4; Susan Bowler and Frank T. Petrusak, "The Constitution of South Carolina: Historical and Political Perspectives," in *Government in the Palmetto State,* ed. Luther F. Carter and Davis S. Mann (Columbia: Bureau of Governmental Research and Service, University of South Carolina, 1983), pp. 27–44.

18. James F. Byrnes to William Watts Ball, 18 Jan. 1920, in the papers of William Watts Ball, Perkins Library, Duke University; Winfred B. Moore, Jr., "The 'Unrewarding Stone': James F. Byrnes and the Burden of Race, 1908–1944," in *The South Is Another Land: Essays on the Twentieth Century South,* ed. Bruce Clayton and John Salmond (Westport, Conn.: Greenwood

Press, 1987), pp. 3–27, quotation p. 9; Arnold Derfner, "Racial Discrimination and the Right to Vote," *Vanderbilt Law Review* 26, no. 1 (1973): 523–84; Newby, *Black Carolinians*, p. 291.

19. V. O. Key, with the assistance of Alexander Herd, *Southern Politics in State and Nation* (New York: Knopf, 1949), pp. 130–55; Jack Bass and Walter De Vries, *The Transformation of Southern Politics: Social Change and Political Consequence since 1945* (New York: Basic Books, 1976). Key entitled chapter 7 "South Carolina: The Politics of Color," and when Bass and De Vries deliberately updated Key, they called their South Carolina chapter "The Changing Politics of Color."

20. Burton, "Black Squint," pp. 171–72; McDonald, "An Aristocracy of Voters," pp. 573–76; U.S. *Congressional Record*, 80th Cong., 2d sess., 1948, 94, pt. 8:9752; *Charleston News and Courier*, 22 July 1948, p. 1; Robert Lewis Terry, "J. Waites Waring, Spokesman for Racial Justice in the New South" (Ph.D. diss., University of Utah, 1970); Tinsley E. Yarbrough, *A Passion for Justice: J. Waties Waring and Civil Rights* (New York: Oxford University Press, 1987); South Carolina, *Journal of the House of Representatives*, 88th General Assembly of the State of South Carolina, 2d sess., H.B. 2177, 15 Feb. 1950, p. 440.

21. Mays, address at Epworth, 7 Nov. 1981, p. 6; Mays, "Full Implementation of Democracy," *New South* 12, no. 3 (1957): 10–12; *Columbia Record*, 3 May 1949, pp. 1, 4; *Charleston News and Courier*, 8 May 1949, p. 4.

22. *New York Herald-Tribune*, 10 Oct. 1933; Rebecca West, *A Train of Powder* (New York: Viking Press, 1955), p. 77; Stewart E. Tolnay and E. M. Beck, *A Festival of Violence: An Analysis of Southern Lynchings, 1882–1930* (Urbana: University of Illinois Press, 1995); W. Fitzhugh Brundage, *Lynching in the New South: Georgia and Virginia, 1880–1930* (Urbana: University of Illinois Press, 1993); Terrence R. Finnegan, "'At the Hands of Parties Unknown': Lynching in Mississippi and South Carolina, 1881–1940." (Ph.D diss., University of Illinois, Urbana-Champaign, 1993) and "Lynching and Political Power in Mississippi and South Carolina," in *Under Sentence of Death: Lynching in the South*, ed. W. Fitzhugh Brundage (Chapel Hill: University of North Carolina Press, 1997), especially p. 193.

23. Bass and De Vries, *Transformation of Southern Politics*, p. 253; *Columbia Record*, 3 May 1949, pp. 1, 4.

24. *Columbia Record*, 3 May 1949, pp. 1, 4.

25. Ibid.; "Governor Blease's Inaugural Address," *House Journal of South Carolina*, 1911, p. 92ff., reprinted in Lewis K. McMillan, *Negro Higher Education in the State of South Carolina* (Orangeburg, S.C.: privately printed by the author, 1952), pp. 257–59.

26. Mays, *Lord, the People Have Driven Me On* (New York: Vantage, 1981).

27. *Tampa Bulletin*, 7 Apr. 1928; Mays, *Seeking to Be Christian in Race Relations* (New York: Friendship Press, 1957), p. 46.

28. Miles Mark Fisher IV, "Dr. Benjamin Elijah Mays: The Howard Years," in *Walking Integrity*, ed. Lawrence E. Carter, p. 130.

29. Benjamin Brawley, *History of Morehouse College* (Atlanta: Morehouse College, 1917); Edward A. Jones, *A Candle in the Dark: A History of Morehouse College* (Valley Forge, Pa.: Judson Press, 1967); Dereck J. Rovaris, Sr., *Mays and Morehouse: How Benjamin E. Mays Developed Morehouse*

College, 1940–1967 (Silver Spring, Md.: Beckham House Publishers, [1994?]); *Presbyterian Outlook* 158, no. 17 (1976).

30. Jones, *Candle in the Dark,* pp. 137–38.

31. Bennett, "Last of Great Schoolmasters," p. 73; Dorothy Butler Gilliam, *Paul Robeson: All-American* (Washington: New Republic, 1976), pp. 113, 159; Marie Seton, *Paul Robeson* (London: Dennis Dobson, 1958), pp. 141–43.

32. David Levering Lewis, *King: A Biography,* 2d ed. (Urbana: University of Illinois Press, 1978), p. 19; *Morehouse Alumnus,* July 1965 (special supplement), p. 1; Jones, *Candle in the Dark,* p. 267.

33. *Morehouse Alumnus,* Apr. 1963, p. 5; Jones, *Candle in the Dark,* p. 265.

34. Lewis, *King,* p. 21.

35. Ted Poston, "Mays and King," *New York Post,* 10 Apr. 1957; *Atlanta Constitution,* 2 Mar. 1961; *America's Betrayal: Martin King, Red Tool; Report of Hearings by the Louisiana Joint Legislative Committee,* 6–9 Mar. 1957, p. 57, and the U.S. *Congressional Record,* 23 Feb. 1956, p. 2831, photocopies of above both in Mays Folder (SCL); U.S. *Congressional Record,* 88th Cong., 1st sess., 1963, 109, pt. 10:13611.

36. Mays, "The Universities' Unfinished Work," commencement address, Michigan State University, East Lansing, 9 June 1968; Gavins, "Ceremonial Speaking of Mays," p. 229.

37. "A Black Thorn in the White Conscience," *Atlanta Journal and Constitution,* 18 Jan. 1970, sec. M, p. 9.

38. Willie, "Educational Leaders Past and Present," p. 391; Nathan Wright, Jr., "Education of Black Youth," *Newark Star Ledger,* 9 May 1971, p. 27.

39. Mays, address at Epworth, 7 Nov. 1981, p. 4.

40. Ibid., p. 5; Mays, typescript of speech at Mays portrait unveiling, State Capitol, Columbia, S.C., 12 July 1980, p. 7; George A. Singleton, *The Autobiography of George A. Singleton* (Boston: Forum Publishing, 1964), p. 142.

41. Charles G. Adams, "Benjamin Mays: An Amazing Man," *Michigan Chronicle,* 7 Apr. 1984, sec. A, p. 6.

42. Letter from Mays, Class of '16 alumni president, 1925, Mays file (SCL); "Mays Honored," *Black News,* 16 Feb. 1980; "Ben E. Mays School, Pacolet, S.C.," *Journal of PEA* 10, no. 6 (1958): 12.

43. Mays, *Disturbed about Man* (Richmond, Va.: John Knox, 1969), pp. 17, 19; Barbara Lewinson, "Three Conceptions of Black Education: A Study of the Educational Ideas of Benjamin Elijah Mays, Booker T. Washington, and Nathan Wright, Jr." (Ph.D. diss., Rutgers University, 1973), pp. 18–30, 128–32.

44. Randal M. Jelks, "The Academic Formation of Benjamin E. Mays, 1917–1936", in *Walking Integrity,* ed. Carter, pp. 106–7

45. Mays, "The Obligations of the Individual Christian," in *The Christian Way in Race Relations,* ed. William Stuart Nelson (New York: Harper, 1943), p. 225; Mays, "Each in His Time," eulogy of Emory O. Jackson, Sixth Avenue Baptist Church, Birmingham, Ala., 16 Sept. 1975; Gavins, "Ceremonial Speaking of Mays," pp. 281–87.

46. *Editorial Reprints from Petal Papers; Greenwood Index-Journal,* 6 Jan. 1984.

47. Mays, "His Goodness Was Not Enough," commencement address at Bucknell University, Lewisburg, Pa., 13 Sept. 1954; Gavins, "Ceremonial Speaking of Mays," pp. 205–11.

48. Mays, "The Universities' Unfinished Work"; Gavins, "Ceremonial Speaking of Mays," pp. 24, 235.

49. Charles V. Willie, foreword to *Quotable Quotes of Benjamin E. Mays,* by Benjamin E. Mays (New York: Vantage, 1983), p. ix; Gavins, "Ceremonial Speaking of Mays," pp. 24–27.

50. Gavins, "Ceremonial Speaking of Mays," pp. 30–31; *Editorial Reprints from Petal Papers;* Silver, "Twenty-first Annual Meeting," p. 61.

51. Mays and Joseph W. Nicholson, *The Negro's Church* (1933; reprint, New York: Russell and Russell, 1969), p. 281; Mays, *The Negro's God as Reflected in His Literature* (1938; reprint, New York: Russell and Russell, 1968), p. 15.

52. Mays, *The Negro's God,* p. 26.

53. Mays and Nicholson, *The Negro's Church,* p. 3.

54. *Greenwood Index-Journal,* 6 Jan. 1984; Mays, "My Views," *Pittsburgh Courier,* 7 May 1966, p. 13, and Apr. 1955, reprinted in *New South,* Jan. 1964, p. 45, copy of second article in Mays file (SCL); Lewinson, "Three Conceptions of Black Education," p. 31.

55. Mays, "Education—to What End?" University of Liberia commencement address, 8 Jan. 1960; Gavins, "Ceremonial Speaking of Mays," p. 214.

56. Leonard Ray Teel, "Benjamin Mays: Teaching by Example, Leading through Will," *Change* 14, no. 7 (1982): 15; *The Ninety Six Star and County Review,* 11 Nov. 1981; *Greenwood Index-Journal,* 3 and 11 Nov. 1981.

57. Stephen B. Oates, *Let the Trumpet Sound: The Life of Martin Luther King, Jr.* (New York: Harper and Row, 1982), p. 19.

58. Martin Luther King, Sr., with Clayton Riley, *Daddy King: An Autobiography* (New York: William Morrow, 1980), pp. 140–41, 171; Coretta Scott King, *My Life with Martin Luther King, Jr.* (New York: Holt, Rinehart and Winston, 1969), pp. 85–86.

59. *America's Betrayal.*

60. King and Riley, *Daddy King,* pp. 170–71; Howell Raines, *My Soul Is Rested: Movement Days in the Deep South Remembered* (New York: G. P. Putnam's Sons, 1977), pp. 64–65; Lewis, *King,* pp. 73–74; Oates, *Let the Trumpet Sound,* pp. 92–93.

61. Coretta Scott King, *My Life with Martin Luther King, Jr.,* pp. 158–59.

62. Teel, "Benjamin Mays," p. 22.

63. *Christian Century,* 26 Oct. 1977, p. 975; Linda Marie Delloff, "It Is Clear," *Christian Century,* 1–8 July 1981, pp. 692–93; "Atlanta Educator to Retire," Associated Press article [1981?] in Benjamin Mays file, Greenwood County Regional Library.

64. Bureau of the Census, "Voting and Registration in the Election of November 2000," prepared by Amie Jamieson, Hyon V. Shin, and Jennifer Day (Washington, D.C., Feb. 2002), table B, p. 6.

65. *Greenwood Index-Journal,* 15 July 1980; *Columbia Record,* 3 May 1949, pp. 1, 4; Mays, "The Road to Blessed Immortality," *The Pulpit: A Journal of Contemporary Preaching* 28, no. 1 (1957): 30–31.

66. Burton, "'Black Squint'"; J. Morgan Kousser, *Colorblind Injustice: Minority Voting Rights and the Undoing of the Second Reconstruction* (Chapel Hill: University of North Carolina Press, 1999); Frank R. Parker, *Black Votes Count: Political Empowerment in Mississippi after 1965* (Chapel Hill: University of North Carolina Press, 1990); Chandler Davidson and Bernard Grofman, eds., *Quiet Revolution in the South: The Impact of the Voting Rights Act, 1965–1990* (Princeton: Princeton University Press, 1994).

67. Preston Brooks to James Hampden Brooks, 23 May 1856, in P. S. Brooks Papers, South Caroliniana Library, University of South Carolina, Columbia, S.C.; Orville Vernon Burton, *In My Father's House Are Many Mansions: Family and Community in Edgefield, South Carolina* (Chapel Hill: University of North Carolina Press, 1985), pp. 93–95, and "In My Father's House Are Many Leaders: Can the Extreme Be Typical?" in *The Proceedings of the South Carolina Historical Association, 1987* (Aiken: The South Carolina Historical Association, 1988): 23–32; Richard Maxwell Brown, "South Carolina Extremism and Its Violent Origins: From the Regulator Movement to the Edgefield Tradition, 1760–1960," in *Strain of Violence: Historical Studies of American Violence and Vigilantism* (New York: Oxford, 1975), pp. 67–90.

68. *Greenwood Index-Journal,* 15 July 1980 and 18 June 1974, p. 4; Bennett, "Last of the Great Schoolmasters," p. 79; "Speech Made by Dr. Benjamin E. Mays, at the Dedication of the Dorn VA Hospital, June 14, 1979."

69. *Ninety Six Star and County Review,* 11 Nov. 1981; *Greenwood Index-Journal,* 3 and 11 Nov. 1981.

70. Mays, speech at portrait unveiling, p. 6, and address at Epworth, 7 Nov. 1981; *The Ninety Six Star and County Review,* 11 Nov. 1981; *Greenwood Index-Journal,* 3 and 11 Nov. 1981.

71. Mays, address at Epworth, 7 Nov. 1981, pp. 6–7; *Ninety Six Star and County Review,* 11 Nov. 1981; *Greenwood Index-Journal,* 3 and 11 Nov. 1981.

72. Drummond, "Remarks at Mt. Zion Baptist Church," p. 3.

73. *New York Times,* 1 Apr. 1984; Adams, "Benjamin Mays."

74. Samuel DuBois Cook, introduction to *Quotable Quotes of Benjamin E. Mays,* p. xviii; Charles V. Willie, *Black/Brown/White Relations* (New Brunswick, N.J.: Transaction Books, 1977), p. 214.

PREFACE

Few men in my time have observed and experienced more indignities in Negro-white relations than I, who by choice have elected to live in the South, though hating, as early as I can remember, the injustices and brutalities heaped upon Negroes during my lifetime. No one has agonized more over the race problem than I have. It has weighed heavily on my mind ever since I saw my first mob when I was only four or five years old. That mob I still see. I hope this book will help to expose the snaillike progress which we have made in Negro-white relations in the South and in the nation since Emancipation and since the turn of the century.

This volume may also help to bridge the wide gap in thinking and experience between my generation and the present generation and thus give our youth a sense of history. Young people born just before and since World War II, and certainly since 1954, do not have the faintest idea what Negro-white relations were like in the South and in my native South Carolina in the days of my youth. Young black Americans have made great contributions to improve human relations through sit-ins, boycotts, and demonstrations which those of us who are older could hardly have made in our time; and yet the present generation of young people have built on foundations laid by their elders through "blood, sweat and tears," and through the innocent deaths of millions of Negroes who lived a long time ago.

Even white contemporaries of mine can never know the humiliating conditions under which Negroes had to live because of enforced segregation in my day. The segregated system was so cruel, so inhuman, and so destructive to the development of manhood and character that white America can never really know the damage it did to the mind and spirit of millions of Negroes who lived and died under that system. It may be that this book will fill the vacuum in the thinking of young Negroes and whites as well. If certain conditions are unbearable now, they were a hundred times worse at the turn of the century and during the first fifty years of the twentieth century. This is not to say that we can afford to be complacent and satisfied with the progress recently made in Negro-white relations. No such inference must be drawn from this book.

The United States is a rich country, the most prosperous nation in history. Despite this fact, there are millions who live in despair and poverty or on the brink of poverty. Millions live in slums and hundreds of thousands are unemployed. Many young people drop out of school and become delinquents; they see no hope, and some take to rioting. All of these things take place in one of the most literate and enlightened countries in the world. It is conceivable, therefore, that some American youth, confused and frustrated, as I surely was, may get a glimmer of hope from reading these pages and go forth to accomplish something worthwhile in life in spite of the system.

I would be glad indeed if this book would in some way make a modest contribution toward enabling us to see more clearly what the United States must still do to make the American dream a reality for every American and thus motivate us to fulfill that dream, not in the next century but now.

If any of these things should be accomplished, I will feel richly rewarded.

In brief, this book is the story of the lifelong quest of a man who desired to be looked upon first as a human being and incidentally as a Negro, to be accepted first as an American and secondarily as a black man—but without complete success. This is the age-old quest of man: to be judged on the basis of what he is, of what his potentials are, and on what he aspires to be.

Benjamin E. Mays
Atlanta, Georgia, 1970

Acknowledgments

I am indebted to many people who assisted me in various ways during the three years I was collecting data and writing this autobiography.

The following persons were helpful in appraising the proposed project: Walter R. Chivers, James E. Conyers, Tilman Cothran, Leslie Dunbar, Butler Henderson, George Kelsey, Charles R. Lawrence, Charles Merrill, John Monro, Eugene Patterson, Benjamin Quarles, James Silver, Charles H. Thompson, L. M. Tobin, Bell I. Wiley, E. B. Williams, Samuel W. Williams, and Charles Willie.

In order to give more validity and depth to my own experiences as a black man in a white-dominated world, the following persons interviewed 118 contemporaries of mine for the purpose of comparing my experiences with theirs: Bernita Bennette, Helen Caruthers, Mildred Coats, Rodney Dobbins, C. B. Fagan, Eddie Gaffney, William Howard, Anna Mary McCall, Albert Thompson, Jr., Isabel Tobin, and Flotilla Watkins. In addition to the 118 persons interviewed, certain persons were requested to respond direct to questionnaires seeking the same information sought by the interviewers. Twenty-one responded: S. S. Abrams, Genie Chaires, Mattie Dean, Tom Dean, Sam Glenn, Susie Glenn, Emory Gray, Sr.,Gordon Hancock, H. C. Hamilton, Carrie B. Harper, Thomas J. Henry, Blair T. Hunt, W. M. Jackson, Susie Massey, Eloise Milton, Josephine Murphy, S. A. Owens, Lewis Robinson, Albert Robinson, L. M. Tobin, and Arthur H. Yancey.

I am indebted to research assistants who researched magazines, newspapers, and legal and official documents to ascertain the degree of racial discrimination that existed throughout South Carolina and the South. They were: Robert Allen, New York; James Bell, Arkansas; Hope Blackwell, Virginia; James A. Boyer, North Carolina; C. W. Florence, Virginia; Minnie L. Fountain, Louisiana; Jack L. Gant, Florida; C. G. Gomillion, Alabama; J. L. Hardy, Mississippi; Charles Meadows, Georgia; Richard McKinney, Maryland; Bernard Parks, Georgia; Marie Robinson, Atlanta; Allen Stokes, South Carolina; S. E. Warren, Mississippi; and Glenda Diane Alexander, Karen Gail Alexander, Gloria Wise, William Dendy, Lloyd Sanders, Jewel Wise, Parris Stanley—all of Atlanta.

I am indebted to the following persons for their visitations to churches and night clubs to ascertain the racial situation in churches and night clubs in Atlanta in 1969: Richard Allen, Frazier B. Bradley, James Brown, Martin Bryant, Calvin Butts, James Colly, Edward Fye, John S. Harris, Robert Jackson, William McFarland, Randolph Scott, Harry Slay, Maceo Sloan, Osker L. Spicer, Jr., Julius Stephens, Ed Stewart, Glenn Taylor, Wayne G. Thompson, Calvin Thornton, Robert West, Mr.

and Mrs. Adrian Abercrombie, Mr. and Mrs. James Edmondson, and Mr. and Mrs. Roy Thompson.

As for the future of the private Negro colleges, in connection with my chapter on Morehouse, I received helpful statements from F. D. Patterson, Luther Foster, James M. Nabrit, James E. Cheek, Vivian Henderson, Hugh M. Gloster, and J. H. Holland.

In addition to my own Atlanta experiences and observations as to why Atlanta is different now than it was in the 1920s, I received letters from Grace Hamilton, Police Chief Herbert Jenkins, Richard H. Rich, Mayor-Emeritus William B. Hartsfield, Mayor Ivan Allen, Jr., Jesse O. Thomas, Sinclair Jacobs, James P. Brawley, Eliza Paschall, W. A. Robinson, Josephine Murphy, and Ludie Andrews.

Special information was furnished me by Samuel Gandy of Howard University; Blake Clark of *Reader's Digest*; Ruth Wilson, Bates College; and Charles Hadley and Roland A. Wakefield, graduates of Bates College.

The editors of several newspapers made available to me, through microfilm, copies of their newspapers published around the turn of the century, authentic data of the black-white conditions at the time of my birth and during my early years in the 20th century. They are *The Index-Journal*, Greenwood, South Carolina; *The Columbia State*, Columbia, South Carolina; *The Charleston News & Courier*, Charleston, South Carolina; *The Birmingham News*, Birmingham, Alabama; *The Nashville Tennessean*, Nashville, Tennessee; *The Richmond News Leader*, Richmond, Virginia; *The Raleigh News and Observer*, Raleigh, North Carolina; *The New Orleans Times-Picayune*, New Orleans, Louisiana; *The Atlanta Constitution* and *The Atlanta Journal*, Atlanta, Georgia.

The Atlanta University librarians were most cooperative in gathering microfilms from newspapers and making it possible for me to do research in the Atlanta University Library: M. M. Jackson, Gaynelle Barksdale, and Julio Hernandez.

Special acknowledgements must be given to Samuel DuBois Cook, Professor of Political Science at Duke University, presently on leave with the Ford Foundation; and to John Hope Franklin, Chairman of the Department of History at the University of Chicago, for reading critically the entire manuscript and offering invaluable comments that gave strength to the book; also to Jeannette Hume, Professor of English at Morehouse College, and Professor Eloise Thetford of Chicago who read each of the twenty-two chapters, giving the author the benefit of their skill in the use of the English language to make the book more readable; to Cordelia Blount of Georgia State University for reading the galley and page proofs; and to Sylvia Cook, wife of Samuel DuBois Cook, who read the manuscript along with her husband and made independent, encouraging comments helpful to the author. Too much credit cannot be given to Evarie Stuart Thompson, creative, intelligent, and competent, who for three years served as my secretary and assistant. Without her concern and skill, the completion of this work would have been much more difficult and less well done.

Before her serious illness which began on August 27, 1969, and ended in her death on October 11, 1969, Mrs. Benjamin Mays served as my reading audience and listened critically to what I read and gave valuable comments that added strength to the book.

Finally, without a three-year grant from the Rockefeller Foundation, through Dr. Leland DeVinney, this book could not have been written. The Rockefeller grant ended June 30, 1970 after three years. I am indebted to the Ford Foundation, through Doctors James W. Armsey and Samuel DuBois Cook, for a grant to continue the work on the book from July 1, 1970 to the date of publication, February, 1971, and to begin a new project.

Introduction

Reflections on a Rebel's Journey

Samuel DuBois Cook
The Ford Foundation *

My chief problem in this introductory essay—which I am terribly honored to write—is to try at once to do justice to the man and his book and to remain a half-step this side of idolatry. Success in the endeavor is not easy. I unabashedly revere Bennie Mays for his genuine contributions, strength of character, gifts of mind, vision, ability to grow and courage to change, creative restlessness and zest for life, stubborn moral courage, prophetic imagination, deep commitment to social justice, boundless energy and eagerness to tackle new tasks, devotion to academic excellence, capacity for independence of thought and critical judgment, single-minded commitment to the most precious and enduring values of the human enterprise, and life-long romance with the world of higher possibilities. He is a wise man. His spirit is indomitable, his will inexhaustible.

He is a powerful disturber of the human conscience and an implacable foe of every form of complacency, mediocrity, self-righteousness, moral conceit, and hypocrisy—individual and collective. His prophetic concerns are not limited to technical moral and religious dimensions but extend to the whole institutional life and process of culture and history. He is a hard taskmaster. He is mighty difficult to please because of his vision of, and commitment to, the higher possibilities of human life—the deep longing for something better. Mays is a modern prophet.

His life, echoing and expressing the tragedy and the glory of the black encounter, has been that of desperately walking the tightrope in several dimensions of "being" and "becoming," believing and doubting, Spartan immersion in activity and stoic resignation to the inevitable, continuity and change, rebellion and adjustment, the saying of "yes" and "no" to history and culture. It has been rough going, but what a magnificent and inspiring odyssey and product! The story tells us something profound about the human spirit at its best—richness, vitality, creativity, resourcefulness, resilience, and wonder.

The achievements of the man would be astonishing for anybody; they are almost incredible in light of the environment of his childhood and formative years. Dr. Mays has earned an international reputation in religion,

*On leave from Duke University.

higher education, public speaking, public life, and the struggle for social justice. He has been honored by Presidents of the United States.

A tireless worker, he has authored more than half a dozen books, contributed chapters to some twenty more, penned about one hundred articles, and produced hundreds of reports, pamphlets, and other materials aimed at specialized audiences. Since the mid-1940's, he has written a weekly newspaper column. A silver-tongued orator and eloquent preacher, he has delivered thousands of public speeches and sermons. His list of honors and awards is legendary.

Dr. Mays has, for example, received more than twenty-five honorary degrees from a variety of institutions of higher learning. He graciously refused the first honorary degree offered him. He did so on the ground that his achievements then did not make him deserving of the honor. His standards of excellence are high both for himself and for others.

The man is inexhaustible. He is, as Jacques Maritain said of the Angelic Doctor, always about his Father's business. He lives in the world not of memory but of anticipation, not of the land conquered but of new challenges and new worlds to conquer. He is driven by higher possibilities. It has been well said that "to dwell in the past is to stop work and what is life without any new tasks which drive us."[1]

So, at the age of seventy-five, Bennie Mays, always eager to serve his fellows, responded to popular pressure to run for his first elective public office—a seat on the Atlanta Board of Education. Although he did only a small amount of campaigning, the election returns gave him a landslide victory. A few weeks later, Atlanta confronted one of the worst crises in its history, involving a court-ordered comprehensive plan for the desegregation of the public schools. Both racial communities were up in arms. Tensions mounted. Fears increased. Doubts grew. White opposition was organized, articulate, and emotion-laden. Hundreds of teachers allegedly threatened to resign. Parents were upset, and many said they would withdraw their children from the schools. Mass rallies were held. Large numbers of students, encouraged by high public officials, marched on the State Capitol. Because of the commanding role of leadership in the resolution of social conflict, the election of the new president of the School Board took on crucial significance. Citizens waited.

Since Dr. Mays commanded near-universal respect and faith in the Atlanta community, his fellow members elected him the first black man to serve as president of the Atlanta Board of Education. Accordingly, Dr. Mays today is devoting massive time and energy to the improvement of public education in Atlanta. That is a mark of the character, concerns, and commitment of the man. The only thing "retirement" means to him is a shifting of the chief residence and focus of responsibility. In a variety of capacities, he is as involved, busy, and energetic as ever. His life, therefore, continues to be full of excitement, meaning, zest and productivity. It has not been dulled by the passage of time.

Dr. Mays' autobiography is a remarkable document. It is a moving account, laced with wonder, grace, and dignity, of the spiritual, intellectual, and social journey of a great human being. The book is not self-serving. It is a portrait of the human heart, mind, and spirit embarked on a magnificent adventure—sensitively and creatively encountering self, men, events, circumstances, and perceptions of ultimate reality. It is the saga of a dreamer in a land of ambiguity, ambivalence, and "impossible possibility."

But the book is more, much more, than the odyssey of one man. It is a collective autobiography, disclosing the inner and outer experiences of Negroes—their lonely and tragic search for incorporation into the promise and performance of American life, their long night of struggle for equality of citizenship and humanity. In a gentle and luminous way, it captures the essence of the black experience in the New World—the agonies, wounds, fears, tears, humiliations, hopes, anguish, triumphs, inching progressive movements, inner terrors of mind and spirit, exilement at home, burdens, setbacks, breakthroughs, affirmations, and boundless faith in the ideals and promises of the land. Mays goes to the heart of the spiritual adventure of black people.

"The first thing I can remember," Dr. Mays observes, "is a white mob looking for a Negro to lynch." The statement is fraught with symbolic meaning as well as historical significance. Every reflective and sensitive black man, in the deeper levels of being, is haunted by the symbolic mob of racism perpetually flashing on the screen of consciousness and sensibility; the picture is inescapable—just as Dr. Mays cannot escape the memory of that physical mob during his childhood.

The book is also a social and historical document about America—particularly the legacy, depth, and persistence of white racism with all its tragic consequences not only for black people but for the whole country as well. It probes and illuminates the tangled roots and many-dimensional character of the current racial crisis. This country "is tramping out the vintage where the grapes of wrath are stored." It is experiencing the feedback of three and a half centuries of racial injustice and tyranny. The anger, bitterness, resentment, and hatred in large sectors of the black population are the fruit of a long period of oppression, insensitivity, neglect, and moral hypocrisy. The chickens of the years are coming home to roost. Mays tells the story in beautiful and eloquent language.

A chief virtue of the book is that it provides perspective. Historical perspective is crucial. It liberates us from the tyranny and narrow throes of the moment. This book reminds us both of the progress that has been made in race relations over the past few decades and of the distance the country has to go before equality of opportunity and dignity cleanses, enriches, and fulfills the land. And Dr. Mays points the way out of the racial tragedy.

What is the meaning of this man's life? The mind cries out for an answer, even as it perceives the perils lurking in the search. Since the life of every human being is filled with mystery and wonder, attempts to deal with questions of the meaning thereof are risky and hazardous business. But I would hardly show fidelity to the teachings of Bennie Mays if I failed to try.

The chief meaning of Dr. Mays' life is the significance of personal responsibility in the human encounter and adventure. It is an affirmation of ethical individualism. The ideals we cherish at the core of our selfhood, the dreams that drive us by day and haunt us by night, the industry and discipline we muster, our will and intelligence, the choices we make, our vision of possibilities, and the faith we live by make a difference in the quality of our lives and the level of our achievements. No shallow determinism can do justice to the radical freedom (within, of course, limits) of the individual persons. And to the extent that men possess freedom, to that extent they have responsibility. The human spirit is not ordained by the nature of things to be enslaved to the structures of culture. Reinhold Niebuhr has observed that, paradoxically, men are both creators and creatures of the historical process.

Another structure of meaning in the life of Bennie Mays is another ancient, though often neglected, truth. Individuals, particularly those in strategic positions of organizational leadership, have enormous influence on the lives of others—especially the young. Imitation of systems of thought and belief and patterns of behavior is a fundamental fact of life. We imitate, appropriate, and incorporate into our own structure of meaning the values and visions of others, particularly those we respect and esteem. What we are and believe—or appear to be and to affirm—spill over into the lives of others and flow into the rivers and currents of their being. Individuals' lives, therefore, have significant bearing on, and consequences for, others who appropriate their meanings and values. Bennie Mays has touched, enriched, and inspired, in various ways and degrees, the lives of a staggering ,indeterminate number of people. Martin Luther King, Jr. is simply the most famous one. Imitation and citation, consciously and unconsciously, of Dr. Mays is a common occurrence. He has a rather special gift of memorable epigrammatic utterance and powers of persuasion and motivation.

A third meaning of the life of Dr. Mays is the tragedy of racism. Racism is a search for meaning that is, in a variety of ways, self-defeating. It diminishes life. It impoverishes funded experiences, knowledge, and shared values. It militates against the whole of community. Long ago, Myrdal noted that the "Negro genius is imprisoned in the Negro problem."[2] Because racism is a demonic evil—Reinhold Niebuhr calls it a form of original sin[3]—Dr. Mays has spent endless time, energy, and talent trying to combat it. The investment has been more than justified. For racism is a problem of the human spirit.

But if racism were not such a cancerous reality and social force, Dr. Mays could have spent his time, industry, and gifts of mind on the ultimate issues of religious and philosophical thought. His union of seminal intellect and inexhaustible energy perhaps marked him as a potential Paul Tillich, Reinhold Niebuhr, Karl Barth, Rudolph Bultmann, Nicolas Berdyaev, Josiah Royce, Martin Buber, Jacques Maritain, Emil Brunner, or Walter Rauschenbusch. He could have added significant original propositions to the corpus of religious and philosophical thought. Consequently, the intellectual enterprise is the loser.

Finally, the life of Benjamin Elijah Mays suggests that while the life of reason may be out of style, it is not out of clout and muscle; it is not devoid of creative power and productivity. It is filled with constructive possibilities. The old ship of reason, while not without handicaps in negotiating the turbulent waters of the contemporary world, is not completely disabled. It is a good and secure ship—built especially for the troubled waters of the human journey. It is the most reliable ship in the whole harbor of civilization. It is old but ever young. There is no substitute for rational and experimental exploration and evaluation of alternative conditions, possibilities, and consequences, the cool calculation of the probable consequences of each option, the counting of the cost, and the bringing of what is out of sight into view.

To a degree, the message of this remarkable rebel and dreamer has had a transformative impact—not enough but some—and the final harvest is not yet in. Seeds planted in the garden of the continuum of human experience have a way of sprouting, multiplying, and bearing fruit in their own good time. Showing fidelity to the life of reason, Dr. Mays has been a catalyst and instrument of social change for the better—in race relations, education, and religious meaning and relevance. He is, of course, quite dissatisfied with his impact, but his contributions have improved, in a significant measure, the quality of life and promise in the land.

For decades now, Dr. Mays has been in the habit of quoting the prophet Micah: "He has showed you, O man, what is good; and what does the Lord require of you but to do justice, and to love kindness, and to walk humbly with your God?" The feeling is inescapable that the words have a peculiar meaning for Dr. Mays, sum up his total philosophy of life, and express the ultimate depths of his being. "The ideals cherished in the souls of men," said Whitehead, "enter into the character of their actions."[4]

To the limits of human possibility, Bennie Mays has done justice, loved kindness, and walked humbly with his God. Neither the heights of achievements and the bright lights of triumph, nor the depths of disappointment and sorrow have been able to separate him from these ideals. Perhaps it is true, after all, that, in this tragic world, a good conscience is our only sure reward. Bennie Mays is deserving of a good conscience.

But—and this is symbolic of the paradox at the heart of the ethical life—he will never enjoy a good conscience. Only men of genuine ethical sensitivities and deep and abiding humane sympathies are truly and constantly troubled by the miseries, woes, tragedies, and follies—individual and collective—of the human condition. Their own heroic efforts are insufficient to eradicate their moral tension and agony. Their sense of guilt is incurable. For it is born of their moral view of the universe and their anguish over the predicament of men and society. The pangs of conscience are always there—nudging, twinging, pressing, demanding more, reminding of the ethics of duty. They cannot have an easy conscience when they know that a better life is a cosmic imperative and within existential reach. Ethically insensitive men are free to wallow in the trough of indifference, moral complacency, and self-righteousness, but the sensitive and creative is ever demanding more of itself, something better, nobler, purer. It is dynamic, not static.

Because of a divine moral restlessness implanted in his Puritan conscience and cultivated and cherished in the depths of his being, Bennie Mays will always be morally restless, anxious, and demanding. While understanding the foibles and moral afflictions of human nature, he is a moral perfectionist. He will not achieve moral peace; his ethical consciousness is too deep, intense, and demanding for that. The world contains too many evils and therefore challenges for the man to take a moral vacation. He is too self-demanding to have a complacent conscience. Too much remains to be done for him to become a spectator of the events, struggles, and encounters of the contemporary scene. His vision of the higher possibilities of human life is too grand; his zest for life too immense; and his concern for the lot of his fellows too vast and deep for him to have a satisfied conscience. He is moved by a vision of nobler things that will not let him go; neither will he let it go. He grips the vision and the vision him.

It is a precious, humbling, and unforgettable experience to know Bennie Mays. It is also, at times, somewhat embarrassing to us ordinary mortals whose vision of life is less majestic and imperative or who find habitation of the mountaintop—beyond periods of brief duration—too dazzling.

1. *A Dreamer's Journey* (Glencoe, 1949), p. 280.

2. Gunnar Myrdal, *An American Dilemma* (New York, 1944), p. 28.

3. *Reinhold Niebuhr on Politics*, Harry R. Davis and Robert C. Goods, eds. (New York, 1960), p. 232.

4. Alfred North Whitehead, *Adventures of Ideas*, Mentor ed. (New York, 1955), p. 49.

Chapter I
In the Days of My Youth

I remember a crowd of white men who rode up on horseback with rifles on their shoulders. I was with my father when they rode up, and I remember starting to cry. They cursed my father, drew their guns and made him salute, made him take off his hat and bow down to them several times. Then they rode away. I was not yet five years old, but I have never forgotten them.

I know now that they were one of the mobs associated with the infamous Phoenix Riot which began in Greenwood County, South Carolina, on November 8, 1898, and spread terror throughout the countryside for many days thereafter. My oldest sister, Susie, tells me, and newspaper reports of that period reveal, that several Negroes were lynched on the ninth and others on subsequent days.

That mob is my earliest memory.

Susie says I was born on August 1, 1895. The 1900 United States Census gives my birth date as August 1, 1894, and this date I accept. My birthplace is ten miles from the town of Ninety Six, South Carolina,[1] and fourteen miles from Greenwood, the county seat. The first post office I recall was named Rambo; later it was renamed "Epworth." Epworth is four miles from my birthplace, six miles from Ninety Six, and ten miles from Greenwood. The train ran through Ninety Six, which is seventy-five miles from Columbia. My birthplace is about midway between Greenwood and Saluda, not far from Edgefield.

Both my parents were born in slavery, my father, Hezekiah Mays, in 1856 and my mother, Louvenia Carter Mays, in 1862. My mother was too young to remember anything about slavery, but Father could, for he was nine years old when the Civil War came to an end in 1865.

I know virtually nothing about my ancestors. I have been told that my grandmother, Julia Mays, and her two children were sold as slaves by someone in Virginia to a buyer in South Carolina. Her daughter died early, and her son was shot to death in the field by a white man. After coming to South Carolina, she married my grandfather, James Mays. Six children were born to them, four girls and two boys: Frances, Roenia, Janette, Polly, Hezekiah (my father), and Isaiah.

I never knew my grandfather, James Mays, but I remember my grandmother, Julia, quite distinctly. She lived to be ninety or more years old. As I remember her features, I think she might have had a strain of Indian or white blood. However, I do not recall ever hearing her or my parents make any reference to white ancestry. I never knew my maternal grandparents. My mother had three brothers and two sisters: Abner, Harper, John, Sarah, and Susie.

My mother and father were very dark-skinned, and the color of their children ranged from black to dark brown. Color was never a problem in my family, nor did we ever feel any discrimination based on color among Negroes in my community, whose colors ranged from black to white. To protect the "purity" of the white race, South Carolina had decreed that any person with one-eighth of Negro blood in his veins belonged to the Negro race.[2] So there were a good many mulattoes and white Negroes in my area. We never felt sorry for ourselves because we were dark, and we accepted Africa as the home of our ancestors. Although I can appreciate the current emphasis on blackness, I am mighty glad I didn't have to wait seventy years for someone in the late 1960's to teach me to appreciate what I am—black! Many times my mother, unlettered and untutored though she was, said to us children, "You are as good as anybody!" This assurance was helpful to me even though the white world did not accept my mother's philosophy!

My heroes were black. Every once in a while, some Negro came along selling pictures of, or pamphlets about, a few Negro leaders. Pictures of Frederick Douglass, Booker T. Washington, and Paul Laurence Dunbar hung on our walls. In my high school days, Booker T. Washington meant more to me than George Washington; Frederick Douglass was more of a hero than William Lloyd Garrison; Dunbar inspired me more than Longfellow. I heard about Crispus Attucks and was thrilled. The Negro preachers and teachers in my county, I worshiped. I didn't know any of the white preachers and teachers. (I doubt that I would have worshiped them if I had!) The Negroes in the South Carolina Legislature during the Reconstruction and post-Reconstruction years were the men held up to us in high school history classes as being great men, and not the Negro-hating Benjamin Ryan Tillman and his kind, who strove so long and hard to deprive the black man of his vote. I had identity.

My mother could neither read nor write. She enjoyed having me read to her, especially sections of the Bible. Until this day, I regret that I didn't teach my mother to read, write, and figure. Father could read printing fairly well but not script. I often wondered how my father—a slave for the first nine years of his life—had learned to read as well as he did. My sister Susie, ninety years old now, told me much about our parents when I visited her in the summer of 1967 as I was beginning this book. She remembers well two of my father's stories. He frequently told how the slave children on his master's plantation were fed. While the slaves were working in the fields, the master's wife would feed the slave children. She would pour milk into a trough and then call the slave children—my father among them. The children would rush to the trough, scoop up the milk in their hands and slurp it into their mouths. The other story is delightful. The slave master's son liked my father very much. Though it was unlawful to teach a slave to read, this white boy would take my father down in the woods to a secluded spot and there teach him to read.

I am the youngest of eight—three girls and five boys: Susie, Sarah, Mary, James, Isaiah, John, Hezekiah, and Benjamin—me. I never knew Isaiah, who died early. Hezekiah was the only one of my siblings to finish high school. The others went hardly beyond the fifth grade in our ungraded one-room school. The maximum school term of the Negro school was four months—November through February. The white school usually ran six months. Discrimination and farm work accounted for the shorter term for Negroes. Most of the cotton was picked in September and October; and early in March work on the farm began. It would never have occurred to the white people in charge of the schools that they should allow school to interfere with the work on the farms. I was nineteen years old before I was able to remain in school for the full term.

Education was not considered essential in those days, not even by or for whites. By law, slaves were kept illiterate. Consequently, when four million Negroes were freed in 1865 most of them were unable to read or write. It is not surprising, therefore, that, according to the Census of 1900, 57 percent of the Negro males of voting age in my county were illiterate.[3] Even the 43 percent who could read and write could not vote. In the state as a whole 52.8 percent of Negroes ten years old and above were illiterate in 1900 as against 64.1 percent in 1890. I suppose that the literacy in my family was slightly above the average of Negroes in my county.

Two of my brothers, James and John, tried farming. James stuck with it until he was killed at the age of forty-eight or fifty by a brother-in-law.

Earlier, however, John had left for the city. Another brother, Hezekiah, after an altercation with Father, pulled off his sack and left the cotton field and his home, never to return except on visits to the family. My three sisters all married farmers in the community.

It could hardly have been otherwise than that most of the Negroes in my county at the turn of the century were wage hands, sharecroppers, and renters. Only a very small minority owned farms or were buying them. How could it be different? Thirty-five years earlier, Negroes had been freed without being given a dime or a foot of land by the federal government. Emancipated from Southern slavery in 1865, the Negro was promptly deserted by the North. Had forty acres and a mule been given to each emancipated slave family, as had been proposed, the economic plight of the Negro would have been greatly ameliorated. Today the harvest might well have been of wheat and not tares.

In 1900, Greenwood County, in which I lived, had a population of 28,343, of which 18,906, or 66.7 percent, were Negroes. The fact that Negroes so far outnumbered the whites contributed to the whites' determination to exclude them from politics. The evil result of this determination was the infamous Phoenix Riot. Negroes in my county were heavily dependent upon the white people for land to till; the whites were equally dependent upon the Negroes to get their farms worked. In 1900, close to 20 percent of the Negro farmers in South Carolina owned their homes. However, in Greenwood County in 1910 only 112 Negroes owned their farms free of debt; ninety-five had farms but they were mortgaged; sixty-eight were part owners; 1,230 were cash tenants; 1,296 were share tenants; forty-three share-cash tenants; and eighty-nine were not specifically designated.[4] These figures add up to 2,933 farms run by Negroes. The free-of-debt owners, plus the owners with the mortgages, and the part-owners totaled 275, or 9.4 percent who had some ownership in their farms. Roughly speaking, only one Negro farmer in ten owned his land, and only one in twenty-six owned a farm absolutely free of debt. Ninety percent of the Negro farmers in Greenwood County were renters, sharecroppers, and wage hands. Despite poverty, however, Negro life was very stable. As a rule, men did not desert their families. There were not many illegitimate children in my community. A girl who had an illegitimate child was usually looked down on as having brought disgrace to her family.

My father was a renter. As far back as I can remember, I think we owned our mules. Any man who owned his mules or horses, buggy, wagon, or other farm equipment occupied a little higher status than the one who worked for wages or was a sharecropper. The wage hand was one who worked by the month for ten, twelve, or fifteen dollars a month. The sharecropper, or the one who worked on "halves," had his house, mules, and other farm implements provided for him. The owner of the land received half of all the sharecropper made.

As I recall, Father usually rented forty acres of land for a two-mule farm, or sixty acres if we had three mules. The rent was two bales of cotton, weighing 500 pounds each, for every twenty acres rented. So the owner of the land got his two, four, or six bales out of the first cotton picked and ginned. Many Negroes rented as many as sixty acres of land, paying as rent six bales of cotton weighing 500 pounds each. From the first bales ginned, Father got only the money that came from selling the cottonseeds. I was elated when that time came, for my father always celebrated by buying a big wheel of sharp yellow cheese out of the first cottonseed money. I still enjoy the taste of cheese. I have eaten the finest varieties in many parts of the world, but nothing has ever tasted as good to me as the cheese my father used to bring home from the sale of cottonseeds.

Although I do not recall that we were ever hungry and unable to get food, we did have very little to go on. To make sixteen bales of cotton on a two-mule farm was considered excellent farming. After four bales were used to pay rent, we would have twelve bales left. The price of cotton fluctuated. If we received ten cents a pound, we would have somewhere between five and six hundred dollars, depending upon whether the bales of cotton weighed an average of 450, 475, or 500 pounds. When all of us children were at home we, with our father and mother, were ten. We lived in a four-room house, with no indoor plumbing—no toilet facilities, no running water. When my oldest brother got his own farm, and after the death of Isaiah, there were eight of us; and things changed as my sisters got married and the oldest brothers, James and John, began to fend for themselves. If we were lucky enough to get twelve or fifteen cents a pound for cotton, things were a little better. But six or seven hundred dollars a year was not much when Father had to pay back, with interest, money borrowed to carry us from March to September, and when shoes, clothing, and food for all of us had to be bought out of this money. Then there were the mules, the buggies, wagons, and farm tools to be bought and paid for.

We were never able to clear enough from the crop to carry us from one September to the next. We could usually go on our own from September through February; but every March a lien had to be placed on the crop so that we could get money to buy food and other necessities from March through August, when we would get some relief by selling cotton. Strange as it may seem, neither we nor our neighbors ever raised enough hogs to have meat the year round, enough corn and wheat to insure having our daily bread, or cows in sufficient numbers to have enough milk. The curse was cotton. It was difficult to make farmers see that more corn, grain, hogs, and cows meant less cash but more profit in the end. Cotton sold instantly, and that was *cash* money. Negro farmers wanted to *feel* the cash—at least for that brief moment as it passed through their hands into the white man's hands!

Though never hungry, we were indeed poor. We supplemented our earnings by working at times as day hands, hoeing, chopping, and picking cotton for white farmers in the neighborhood. The price paid for this work usually was forty cents a day, sometimes only thirty-five, though when a man was desperate for help on his farm he would pay fifty cents a day. One made more money picking cotton, especially if he were a good cotton picker. The pay was forty or fifty cents per hundred pounds. All of us worked on the farm, including my sisters. Except in cases of dire necessity, Negro fathers preferred to have their daughters work on the farm rather than cook in the white man's kitchen. My sisters did not plow or cut wood, but they hoed and chopped and picked cotton. We usually got to the field about sunup and worked until sundown.

It was and still is a belief among Negroes that most white people who had Negro tenants cheated them. This belief had no lack of confirming evidence! Many Negroes did not know how to keep their own accounts, and even when they could, all too many of them were afraid to question a white man's figures. His word was not to be disputed, and if he said a Negro owed him so much, questions were not in order and no explanations were forthcoming. If he told John, "We broke even this year; neither of us owes the other," even if John knew he had cleared a hundred dollars, he would ask no questions, register no protest.

To support my own recollections about a great deal of my past, I have either personally interviewed or had someone else interview 118 Negroes who were born about the same time I was.[5] The majority believed that Negroes who worked for white people in the South were grossly cheated by their white "bosses." Of the 118 interviewed for this study, 101 (85.6 percent) expressed the belief, from their own experiences and observations, that Negroes were cheated by white people. One was emphatic: "Whites didn't cheat Negroes—they robbed them!" Seven disagreed. Ninety-one (77.1 percent) were convinced that Negroes were also cheated in the courts.

I share these majority opinions. In my county, whenever a white man was involved, the Negro was automatically guilty. As these interviews showed, it is difficult even now to get Negroes to believe otherwise. They know that Negroes were cheated in slavery, were worked and treated like animals. They know that Negroes are still cheated by whites on such things as rentals or contract buying, so they are certain that Negroes were taken advantage of on the plantations of the South after emancipation.

Despite the fact that I share this widespread belief, I feel that William Mays (no relative of mine), on whose land we lived, was fair in his transactions with my father. I did not know Dr. Childs, on whose place we lived until we moved to the "Bill" Mays place; but according to what I heard my parents say about him, he was a kindly white man. I never knew Bill Mays well. In my entire youth, for that matter, I did not know any white person well. I never had a white playmate. I saw Bill Mays when he made fairly frequent visits to the farm to see how Father was getting along, and occasionally we saw him in Greenwood. I suppose I never talked with him ten minutes at one time during our whole tenure on his place. I got the impression that he took some interest in Father's welfare. I do not believe William Mays ever cheated my father; but I was really hurt one day when I heard him tell Father, when I was trying to get away to school, that he should keep me home to work on the farm. From that moment on, I put him down as being against me. In fact, I considered anyone my enemy who was not in sympathy with my aspiration to get an education. I never forgot what Mr. Mays said to my father. A few years later when I was home from school and he visited the farm, my mother asked me to go out and speak to him and I refused. I felt that he was still against my going away to school. If Bill Mays did not cheat my father, I am sure that there must have been other white men in the South—however few—who did not cheat Negroes who worked for them.

I believe my mother had a kind of affection for the wives of Dr. Childs and Bill Mays, and for their children, who sometimes paid brief visits to our house. I recall that on more than one occasion the sons of Betty Childs came to see Mother after their family had moved to Greenville, and Mother always appeared glad to see them. As I recall, one of them gave Mother a half dollar. The way Mother spoke of Betty Childs and Nona Mays indicated affection for them—an affection which my father, I am sure, did not share. My own contact with them and their children was so slight that I never had a chance to develop any real friendship or affection. In Greenwood County, for the most part, black was black and white was white, and never the twain did meet except in an *inferior-superior* relationship; this relationship I never sought, cherished, or endured.

I did not know the meaning of it at the time, but I recall going to Greenwood with my mother when she went to see "Miss Nona," as she was called by the Negroes. Mother and I went to the back door. I do not know whether "Miss Nona" required this, or whether Mother was following the custom for Negroes to go to the back door when they went to a white man's house. I remember seeing Negroes go to the back door of a white man's house even when the white people were sitting on the front porch. Most of the 118 persons interviewed for my study reported that Negroes went to white people's back doors in their communities. When asked "Why?" forty of them, or 33 percent, said it was custom or tradition. Eighteen said white people demanded it. One person said, "It would have been accepting Negroes as equals if whites had allowed them to enter the front door." Another said that Negroes were sent to the back door because they were not considered persons. As for me, I learned the hard way, later on when I was in Orangeburg, South Carolina, that a Negro was not to go see a white man by way of the front door. But as a child, even when we had "worked out" by the day, the back-door custom had not struck me as odd, for we had no need to go to the front door, the noon meal being served on the back porch, as a rule, and not in the dining room.

I did not leave the farm because it was repulsive to me. I enjoyed work on the farm and am proud to proclaim that I was a *good* farmhand—much better than the average. At the age of twelve, I was able to take the lead row in hoeing and chopping cotton. I was an excellent "fodder puller" at the same age. I "knocked cotton stalks" in preparation for the next crop. Whenever we had three mules, I could, with sack and horn, keep ahead of three plow hands, pouring the guano in the furrows. I was not much at cutting cordwood. We were all good at plowing. When it came to picking cotton, my brother Hezekiah and I were the best in the family, and among the best cotton pickers in the county. We often competed with each other to see which could pick the most cotton. One day we carried "grab" rows all day. Each had his own row of cotton to pick and the middle row between us was the "grab" row. The fun came for the one who could pick fast enough to be getting more of the cotton on the grab row than the other. Hezekiah, "H. H." as we called him, and I competed all day, from sunup to sundown. We picked cotton steadily and fussed just as steadily, each claiming that the other was getting all of the cotton off of the grab row. We both exaggerated, for when father weighed the cotton that evening, H. H. had picked 424 pounds and I had picked 425.

I did not mind being hired out to pick cotton at forty or fifty cents a hundred. Picking only 300 pounds earned me $1.20 or $1.50 a day, whereas I could make only forty or fifty cents a day plowing or hoeing cotton. Unfortunately, I did not always get to keep the money I made after being hired out. If Father needed it, he got it.

I loved the farm. To this day I enjoy seeing a beautiful crop of green corn blowing in the wind, or a patch of growing cotton, especially when nature has cooperated with the right amount of sunshine and rain and the cotton has been well tilled.

The few Negroes in my county who owned their land—and they were rare—were looked up to by other Negroes but had to be exceedingly careful not to be accused by white people of being "uppity," or of trying to "act like a white man." Both were serious charges. The more a Negro owned, the more humble he had to act in order to keep in the good graces of the white people. When a landowning Negro, living in a nice-looking, painted house decided to buy an automobile, he had to get permission from the leading white people in Ninety Six before he dared purchase it.

We wanted Father to buy land, but we did not succeed in persuading him to do so. I wanted him to be like Tom Waller, perhaps the wealthiest Negro in the county, despite the fact that he was illiterate. He had Negro sharecroppers and wage hands just like the landowning white farmers. His land was owned, not mortgaged; and he was a solid citizen. As I look back, I feel sure that it was just as well that Father never owned any land, because there would soon have been no one to work it. My oldest brother, James, was killed by a brother-in-law who was envious because his sister, whom James had married, had fallen heir to their father's home place. When the sister, my brother's wife, died and he married again, the brother-in-law couldn't endure having two "foreign" people in his parents' home, so he followed James into the field one day and shot him down. And since nothing in the racial situation in my county was conducive to encouraging sensitive Negroes to remain, my brother John soon left, ending up in Cleveland, and H. H. made his home in New York. I was "called" or driven to do something other than farming.

I cannot say that my home life was pleasant. Quarreling, wrangling, and sometimes fighting went on in our house. I got the impression early that Father was mean to our mother. He fussed at her; and when he drank too much he wanted to fight and sometimes did. All too many times we children had to hold him to keep him from hurting Mother. He would take out his knife and threaten to cut her. Often at night, we were kept awake by Father's loud and abusive raging. I think if Mother had said nothing, there would have been fewer arguments. But Mother had to talk back. Our sympathy was with her.

Father did his trading and buying in Greenwood, and it was there that he bought his liquor. We knew when he was "high," as he would come roaring home in the wagon, beating the mules (normally he was very careful about keeping the mules in good condition) for no other reason than that he had been drinking too much. When we heard him coming at such times we knew that there would be fussing and feuding that night.

Father's drinking embarrassed me, especially so when he did it at church. Largely under the influence of my mother, I made a vow at twelve years of age that I would never drink liquor. I have kept that pledge, not because I felt this made me better than those who drink but because I never discovered any good reason for breaking it. My decision was not based on religious or moral grounds but on what I saw drinking do to my father and our family. I claim no virtue for keeping this pledge. For the same reason, I never developed the habit of smoking. Father smoked and chewed tobacco, and was not always careful where he spat. Here again I claim no special virtue; I was repelled and disgusted by my father's indulgence in these habits and I never found any reason to follow his example. At Christmastime, we used to share a little toddy, a mixture of whiskey, sugar, and water. After I was twelve, I didn't take any more of the toddy.

As I look back over the years, I am convinced that my father was not a heavy drinker. He simply could not hold his liquor. I believe that a little whiskey "did him up." When he was under the influence of drink, his eyes sparkled and became bloodshot. At most times he was a very kindly man, but when he was otherwise one would shiver in his presence and feel like running for safety. I was afraid of my father until I was past eighteen. I was then ready to defy him when he scolded me or said harsh things to me. But he was not really an alcoholic. He lived to be eighty-two years old, and in his older years he stopped drinking altogether. When he lived with me in Washington, D.C., during the time when I was dean of the School of Religion at Howard University, he never took a drink.

My mother was very religious. Every night she called the children together for evening prayer before going to bed. She always led in prayer. Occasionally all the children said short prayers, too. Father usually prayed with us. Any one of us who got sleepy and went to bed early would say prayers alone. Often I read the Bible before evening prayer, and when

Father was in good humor he would read. Frequently I would read the Bible to my mother, especially certain consoling passages in the Psalms and sections of the Sermon on the Mount. How often I read to her the Thirty-seventh Psalm after one of Father's tirades!

There was no doubt in Mother's mind that God answered prayers. She believed this to her dying day. When I made a trip around the world in the latter part of 1936 and the early months of 1937, Mother "knew" that it was her prayers that brought me safe home. Shouting in church was common in my youth, and Mother did her share. The preaching was usually other-worldly, and the minister often stirred up and exploited the emotions of the people. This fact, along with her somewhat turbulent home life, accounted for Mother's emotional outbursts in church. The depth and sincerity of her religious faith had great influence on me.

In later years, my wife was shocked when she first saw the Brickhouse School, for she had expected to see a real brick building. It was named the Brickhouse School after a large brick house nearby owned by a white man. It was a frame, one-room building with a wood stove in the center of the room, with boys seated on one side and girls on the other. The school ran for four months, from the first of November through February. When we moved from the Childs' place to the Mays' place, the round trip to school was increased from about six to approximately seven miles.

It was a happy day for me when I entered the Brickhouse School at the age of six. I discovered on that eventful day that I knew more than any of the other children who were entering school for the first time. Susie, my oldest sister, had taught me to say the alphabet, to count to a hundred, and to read a little. Since I was the only one in the beginners' class who could do these things, I was praised and highly complimented by the surprised teacher. As we put it, she "bragged on me." The next church Sunday, the second Sunday in November, my teacher sought my parents and told them, with other people standing around, "Bennie is smart." From that moment on, I was the star of that one-room school. The experience made a tremendous impression on me, so much so that I felt I had to live up to my teacher's expectations. I became Exhibit A when visitors came around and I was called upon to recite, which I was always eager and ready to do. I dearly loved the spelling class, where the best speller stood at the head of the class. If the boy or girl at the head of the class missed a word, the one who spelled the word correctly moved to the head of the class. I had been so impressed with myself that first day that I always strove thereafter to occupy the first place in class. I loved school so well that when the weather was bad and Mother kept me home I would weep. The student who was out of school a day had to go to the foot of the class, even though he had been standing at the head. When it did happen that I had to go to the foot for being absent, I took great delight in working my way up from the foot to the head.

I fell in love with my teacher, and I am sure I studied hard to please her as well as to learn. My first teacher was Ellen Waller, daughter of Tom Waller, the wealthy Negro farmer. Miss Waller was a high school graduate from Benedict College in Columbia, South Carolina. Very few Negroes went to college from my county. I can think of only four, before my time, who went to college and received degrees. A fair number went to high school and were graduated.

At the close of the school year, we had what was called an "Exhibition." Students sang, took part in dialogues, and made speeches. I was always one of the students to say a little speech of some kind, and whether or not I deserved it, the people applauded generously. I was a "great" baseball player at school in those days, and I recall two events in connection with the Exhibition which were somewhat unpleasant. Once, beautifully dressed in a white suit to give my Exhibition speech, I got pretty dirty sliding bases and had to speak in soiled clothes, much to my mother's disgust. Another time, when I was tagging a runner, he fell and his shoe hit me in the mouth, breaking off a piece of one of my front teeth, which naturally didn't improve my appearance when it came time for me to speak.

Like any normal, healthy boy I had my fights with a few of the tough guys in the community. I recall one fight when I was cut by one of the two boys with whom I was fighting. I was cut on the hand, the arm, and the head. When I got home, I was bloody. Before I could explain to my father what had happened, he kicked me off the porch and proceeded to beat me thoroughly. He never let me explain what had happened, that the two boys had "laid" for me when I passed their house returning from the store. They had jumped me. I had only two choices: run or fight. I chose to fight. I still think that I did not deserve the whipping my father gave me. I had other fights in school, but none as serious.

Father gave me another whipping which I did deserve. Although I never owned a pistol, my brothers did, and most of the boys in the county carried pistols. The young men who called on my sisters usually had their pistols. Since the firearms were a little heavy, they would put them on the table while visiting my sisters. One night one of the visitors left a loaded pistol on the table in one of our rooms. I found the pistol, assumed it was empty, and pulled the trigger. It went off with an awful noise, the bullet hitting the fireplace. I was so frightened that when Father asked me what the noise was about I told him I didn't know. H. H. showed Father the pistol. The whipping I got was indeed impressive. It has been vivid in my memory ever since.

Old Mount Zion was an important institution in my community. Negroes had nowhere to go but to church. They went there to worship, to hear the choir sing, to listen to the preacher, and to hear and see the people shout. The young people went to Mount Zion to socialize, or simply to stand around and talk. It was a place of worship and a social center as well. There was no other place to go.

This was my church, six miles from the town of Ninety Six and four miles from our house. Preaching was held every second Sunday, the pastor having other churches. If all of us were to go to church, we had to ride in a two-mule wagon, seated either on chairs or on wheat straw in the bottom of the wagon. As a rule, however, someone stayed home, and then two buggies were ample for the rest of us.

On the farm, we worked hard six days a week. Father wanted the mules to rest on the Sabbath; but he never tried to keep them rested on the first and second Sundays when there were services at Mount Olive and at Mount Zion, our own church. Mount Olive, though not our church, was closer, and we usually worshiped there on the first Sunday in each month. Fairly often on the third and fourth Sundays, however, Father would insist that the mules needed rest, so if we wished to go to Sunday school at Mount Zion on those Sundays we had to walk—round trip, eight miles.

Although the members of Mount Zion were poor and most of them were renters, they were a proud lot, and many of them owned good-looking buggies and at least a couple of fine-looking horses or mules, although it is highly probable that most of them were in debt. As a youngster, I watched them driving up in beautiful rubber-tired buggies drawn by fine horses or mules. I think some of them came late to church just so they could be seen. This was the one place where the Negroes in my community could be free and relax from the toil and oppression of the week. Among themselves they were free to show off and feel important. My brother John was the sporty one in our family. He worked and saved until he could buy a white rubber-tired buggy and a beautiful white mule which he named Kate. John and Kate created quite a sensation in the community and at Mount Zion. When the boys came to church alone, they were expected to take their girl friends home—a duty which they did not find at all burdensome.

Fighting and heavy drinking on church property were common practices in many churches, but not much of this went on at Mount Zion, thanks largely to the man who pastored Mount Zion for fifty years or more.

The Reverend James F. Marshall was hardly more than a fifth-grade scholar, but he knew the Scriptures, at least so far as knowing where certain passages were to be found. He could quote almost any passage of Scripture from memory. He accepted the Bible as it was printed and held it was "wicked" to doubt any part of it. We thought he was the best preacher in the world (our world was Greenwood County). He was eloquent. He could moan, and did. Almost invariably he made some of the people shout. If he did not moan a bit and make the people shout, his congregation felt he had not preached well. The intellectual content of his sermons was not nearly as important as the emotional appeal.

The Reverend Marshall set a good example for the people. I believe no one ever accused him of any dishonesty or immorality. Wives and daughters were safe in his presence. He did not touch liquor. The same could not be said of all the ministers who pastored in Greenwood County. The Reverend Marshall, who lived twenty-four miles away from the church, usually held Conference on the second Saturday afternoon and stayed overnight with a family of the church. It was a rare privilege to have the pastor spend the night in one's home. The house was spic and span when the preacher came, and the best food was served. He was the only hero we had around Zion to worship. So impeccable (or discreet) was the Reverend Marshall's conduct that the only story circulated about him was that once he got up in the middle of the night and left a certain woman's house because she had approached him in an immoral way. The young people heard all the gossip the old people talked, and if there had been any scandal about Marshall, the young people would have heard and no doubt circulated it. He was accused of loving money too well, but he was never accused of stealing it. Why shouldn't he have loved it? Why, indeed, should he not have lusted for it? He had ten children or more; and from his four churches he received a total of only $800 a year.

The Reverend Marshall's preaching was highly other-worldly, emphasizing the joys of heaven and the damnation of hell. He preached funerals according to the life the deceased had lived. He didn't hesitate to preach the dead "smack into heaven" or into hell, according to the life he or she had lived. The church was usually full at funerals, especially if the deceased had been well known; and when a man of bad reputation died the church was jammed. The people wanted to hear what kind of funeral sermon Marshall would preach. I am sure that a burning hell and a golden-streeted heaven were as real as their farms to a majority of the people in Mount Zion and in the community at large. They believed the trials and tribulations of the world would all be over when one got to heaven. Beaten down at every turn by the white man, as they were, Negroes could perhaps not have survived without this kind of religion.

There was no doubt in the minds of some that Marshall had special power with God. Even when he prayed for rain and it didn't come, they still believed he had influence with God. If he prayed for rain on the second Sunday in the month and it came the next day, it was obviously in answer to Marshall's prayer.

Members who had done great wrongs were brought before the Church Conference on the second Saturday in the month. Frequently they were turned out of the church if the Conference proclaimed them guilty. But a person could repent, or make a pretense of repentance, and be taken right back into the fold. I was present at a Church Conference when a young couple appeared who had been sexually intimate; the young woman was pregnant. They admitted what they had done. Marshall advised the young man to marry the girl. With his right hand lifted toward heaven, Marshall told the young man that if he didn't marry the young woman and live with her, fulfilling the duties of a husband, something unspeakably bad would happen to him. The young man married the girl on the spot, but then went on his way, never assuming any responsibility for his wife or child. Not long afterward, he was killed one midnight, so viciously beaten to death with a club that his brains were spattered all over the ground. In the summer of 1968, my sister told me Negroes believed that this young man had been killed by a certain white man because he was hanging around a Negro woman with whom the white man was having relations. Neither whites nor Negroes did anything to apprehend the murderer. The apparent fulfillment of Marshall's prophecy in this case skyrocketed his prestige in the community. Thereafter nobody wanted Preacher Marshall to "put bad mouth" on them.

Although Marshall taught the people to be honest and upright, the Gospel he preached was primarily an opiate to enable them to endure and survive the oppressive conditions under which they lived at the hands of the white people in the community. I never heard him utter one word against lynching. If he had, he would probably have been run out of the community—or lynched. When a visiting minister attempted to condemn white people, Pastor Marshall stopped him. I was there. I saw it and I heard it. I am not necessarily condemning the use of religion as an opiate. Sometimes an opiate is good in medicine. Sometimes it may be good in religion. Certainly religious faith has helped me in my struggles.

As my pastor accepted the system and made no effort to change it, so it was in other churches—Negro and white—in my day. Of the 118 persons interviewed who could remember what kind of sermons were being preached around the turn of the century, fifty-nine (50 percent) said that their ministers taught them nothing about white people. Twenty (17 percent) reported that their ministers instructed them to obey white people, be submissive and humble, and get along with whites. Twenty-one said their ministers taught them to be respectful to whites. Nineteen did not answer the question on the church and race. Only four said that their ministers taught them to demand their rights. One woman said that her pastor was bitter about the racial situation. The vast majority of them said the church was helpful to them.

Pastor Marshall "stayed in" with the local white Methodist preacher, although Marshall believed that all who were not Baptists were hellward bound. When certain elements in the church wanted to get rid of Marshall, he invited the Reverend Pierce Kinard, a white Methodist, to come to Zion and advise the Negroes to keep Marshall, which of course effectively ended the incipient move to have Preacher Marshall removed.

The Reverend Marshall baptized every member in my family, including Mother and Father. Father did not join the church until after the earthquake in 1886. My parents told me that, after the quake, the Reverend Marshall baptized a hundred men at one session. "God moves in mysterious ways!"

Mother believed, as Marshall did, that only Baptists could get to heaven—that is, she did until my brother, H. H., joined the Presbyterian Church! When I teased her about this, Mother replied, "All things are possible with God." As a small boy, I really felt sorry for the Methodists who passed our house going to the Methodist church. Not for long, however, could I believe that they were all bound for hell, for some of my best friends were non-Baptists; some of the girls I began to like were not Baptists; and indeed I ended up marrying a member of the CME Church.

Though the people of Mount Zion, for the most part, were poor and unlettered, nevertheless they did much for me. As I sat as a boy in Sunday school, discussing the Sunday school lessons with the adults, asking questions and making comments, they encouraged me and gave me their blessings. Each Sunday in June, we had what was called "Children's Day." I do not remember exactly how old I was—possibly nine—when I participated, having committed to memory a portion of the Sermon on the Mount. After my recitation, the house went wild: old women waved their handkerchiefs, old men stamped their feet, and the people generally applauded long and loud. It was a terrific ovation, let alone a tremendous experience, for a nine-year-old boy. There were predictions that I would "go places" in life. The minister said I would preach; and from that moment on the Reverend Marshall manifested a special interest in me. All of this was part of the motivation that had started with my oldest sister's teaching me how to count and read and write, thereby winning for me the encouragement and praise given me by my first teacher, Ellen Waller. The people in the church did not contribute one dime to help me with my education. But they gave me something far more valuable. They gave me encouragement, the thing I most needed. They expressed such confidence in me that I always felt that I could never betray their trust, never let them down.

After the Phoenix Riot, never a year passed in my county that there were not several brutal incidents involving Negroes and whites. In the months following the Phoenix Riot, I had seen bloodhounds on our land with a mob looking for a Negro. I saw a Negro hiding in the swamps for fear or being caught and lynched. Negroes always got the worst of it. Guilt and innocence were meaningless words: the Negro was always blamed, always punished. Among themselves, Negroes talked much about these tragedies. They were impotent to do anything about them. They dared not even mention them to whites.

I was twelve years old when I read about the Atlanta Riot in the Greenwood *Index* and the Atlanta *Journal,* the two papers to which we subscribed. As I recall, the papers played up the fact that the Atlanta Riot was the result of a series of attacks that Negro men were supposed to have made on white women. It was not until I was older that I realized that Hoke Smith, who campaigned for governor of Georgia on a white supremacy platform, and the four Atlanta newspapers which played up the accusations against the Negroes, not only struck the match but supplied the combustible material to ignite the flames that produced the Atlanta Riot.

It was in this connection that I received a stern lecture from the man who was later to marry my sister Susie. He was an unlettered but highly intelligent man. Like Susie, he would have done well in anybody's college had he been given half a chance to go. He often walked miles to see my sister, and frequently if he left before dark he would invite me to walk a distance with him. During one of our walks, the Atlanta Riot was mentioned. I was old enough at the time to hear what my parents talked about in the home. I heard the gossip about things that happened in the community. My older brothers and sisters learned all the rumors of the county and talked freely about them at home and in the cotton fields. We knew that a beautiful, light-brown-skinned Negro woman was living in the house with a white man, and that Negro men knew enough to leave her alone. It was common knowledge that "Hamp," the mulatto Negro who lived in a house a white man built for him in his backyard and whom the white man kept there to work in his house and to drive his daughters around, was really the white man's son, born to a Negro woman, and therefore half brother to the white daughters. It was an accepted fact that "Polly," a beautiful Negro woman, was the paramour of "Lowden," a white man. Once Polly was caught in a buggy with a Negro man, and rumor had it that Lowden made her get out of the buggy and threatened to shoot the Negro man. This story was so deeply believed that fifty years later Negroes living in that community were still talking about Polly and Lowden, who both lingered ill and suffered for years before they died. Negroes say even now that God punished them for their sins. It no doubt was a comfort to believe that God would mete out the punishment that Negroes were powerless to inflict. Occasionally, too, a white baby turned up in a black home.

In the Atlanta Riot, which began on Saturday night, September 22, 1906, and extended through Tuesday, September 25, many Negroes were killed and many more wounded. One or two whites were killed and several wounded. The riot was allegedly caused by black men attacking white women. It was in this context that I asked my brother-in-law-to-be why it was that white men could do anything they wanted to Negro women but Negro men were lynched and killed if they did the same to white women or even if they were merely accused and innocent. My prospective brother-in-law stopped by the side of the road and gave me a stern lecture. He told me in positive language never to discuss that matter again. It was dangerous talk, and if I said such a thing in the presence of a white person it would not be good for me.

Years later, when I thought it necessary to do some research on both the Phoenix and the Atlanta riots for this autobiography, I discovered that the four Atlanta papers—the Atlanta *Constitution*, the Atlanta *Journal*, the

Georgian, and the *Evening News*—played up the reported attacks on white women out of all proportion to the facts; and that John Temple Graves, editor of the *Georgian*, really whooped it up. I learned as recently as the summer of 1968 that an analysis of the twelve alleged attacks on white women, ***committed six months before the riot***, showed that two were cases of rape, three were cases of attempted rape, three were cases producing no definite proof of attempted rape, three were purely cases of fright on the part of white women, and a final one said at first that a Negro had assaulted her but finally confessed that she had attempted suicide.[6] Attacks were made on Negroes indiscriminately in the Atlanta Riot with as many as five thousand white men participating. Charles Crowe, associate professor of history at the University of Georgia, writing of the Atlanta Riot in the April, 1969, issue of the *Journal of Negro History*, says:

> As a result of the riot, one white person died and several dozen were hurt. Twenty-five black men perished, about one hundred and fifty suffered serious wounds, hundreds had less critical injuries, and more than a thousand black men, women and children fled the city. For several months to come white leaders busied themselves with public apologetics as black people concentrated on the restoration of "normal" patterns of work and life. The Atlanta race riot was not soon forgotten by black people who remembered with particular vividness the evening of September 22 as the terror-ridden night of the white assassins.[7]

Another incident happened in my county two years after the Atlanta Riot of 1906, which I remember vividly—I was fourteen at the time. Jack Johnson, a Negro, defeated Jim Jeffries, a white man, in Reno, Nevada, and became the first black heavyweight champion of the world. White men in my county could not take it. A few Negroes were beaten up because a Negro had beaten a white man in far-away Nevada. Negroes dared not discuss the outcome of this boxing match in the presence of whites. In fact, Johnson's victory was hard on the white man's world. Race riots broke out in a number of places and many Negroes were killed. Jack Johnson committed two grave blunders as far as whites were concerned: He beat up a white man and he was socializing with a white woman—both deadly sins in 1908.

This was the pattern during slavery and long after the post-Reconstruction years. In this relationship, white men and Negro women were free. Perhaps the best portrayal of the relationship between white men and Negro women, and, in the colonial days, between the Negro male and the white female servant, is to be found in E. Franklin Frazier's *The Negro*

Family in the United States.[8] Writing of the relationship that existed between white men and Negro women, Frazier says: "cohabitation of the men of the master race with the women of the slave race occurred on every level, and became so extensive that it nullified to some extent the monogamous mores."

I cannot close this chapter without words of commendation for my parents. My father was bitterly opposed to my efforts to get an education; and yet I owe much to my parents. I shall mention only two things:

My parents were industrious. There wasn't a lazy bone in their bodies. They didn't sit back and make the children do it. They did their part on the farm. In addition to cooking, seeing that our clothes were washed and ironed, and keeping the house clean, Mother hoed and picked cotton, and Father worked equally hard. I must have caught their spirit of work. To this day, I am impatient with lazy people. Father believed that a man should earn his living by the sweat of his brow, and that, to him, meant working on the farm in the blazing hot sun. And my parents were honest. I never heard them scheming how they might get something for nothing. I never suspected them of stealing anything from anybody. They taught their children honesty. I believe that not a single child in our family expected to get anything except through honest channels and by his own efforts. I am reminded of what John Hope, president of Morehouse College in Atlanta, once said. He admitted that Morehouse was poor, but added, "We live in respectable poverty!" The Mays family was poor and lived on the ragged edge of poverty, but we lived in "respectable poverty."

The rugged honesty of my parents has stuck with me through all these years. I am intolerant of dishonesty, particularly intellectual dishonesty, wherein men ignore or distort the truth and plot to take advantage of others for their own indulgence. My parents did little or no ethical philosophizing, but they *lived* their ideals of industry and honesty. I am indebted to them for their living example, and I am grateful.

There were only a few books in the Mays' house and no magazines. We had the Bible, a dictionary, picture books about Booker T. Washington, Frederick Douglass, and Paul Laurence Dunbar, and Sunday school books. We read the Atlanta *Journal* and the Greenwood *Index.* And we had the school textbooks from which we learned to read, spell, and figure to a certain level. This was about it. Nobody in the family had gone beyond the fourth or fifth grade. I didn't seem to have much to go on. But I had learned industry and honesty from my parents. I had been inspired by my county teachers, encouraged by the Reverend Marshall, and motivated by the people in the church who made me believe that I could become something worthwhile in the world. These are the things that drove me on and, when they are summed up, I guess they amount to quite a lot.

1. According to local legend, the town of Ninety Six, South Carolina, got its name from an event during the Revolutionary War when a Cherokee Indian maiden rode from the Cherokee reservation to Old Star Fort, then occupied by the British, to warn the British that the Americans were approaching. The distance was ninety-six miles; the warning was not successful; the Americans overcame the British; but the name Ninety Six was born.

2. South Carolina Constitution, 1895. *States' Laws on Race and Color*, compiled and edited by Pauli Murray (Cincinnati, Ohio, 1951), p. 407.

3. Negroes in the United States, U.S. Bureau of the Census, 1900.

4. Negro Population in the United States: 1780-1915, U.S. Bureau of the Census, p. 746.

5. A team of interviewers composed of teachers, senior and graduate college students, using a carefully prepared schedule of questions, conducted in-depth personal interviews of 118 selected persons living in the Atlanta area and born in the South just before and after the turn of the century.

6. Glenn Weddington Rainey, *Race Riots in Atlanta in 1906* (Master of Arts thesis, Emory University, Atlanta, 1929), p. 8.

7. Charles Crowe, "Racial Massacre in Atlanta, September 22, 1906" (*Journal of Negro History*, LIV, No. 2, April, 1969), p. 168.

8. E. Franklin Frazier, *The Negro Family in the United States* (The University of Chicago Sociological Series, Chicago, 1939), p. 482.

Chapter II

"Be Careful and Stay out of Trouble"

There wasn't much going for the Negro in the world in which I was born. The shades of darkness were falling fast upon and around him. The tides of the post-Reconstruction years were being turned deliberately and viciously against him. The ballot was being taken away. Segregation was being enacted into law. Lynching was widespread and vigorously defended. Injustice in the courts was taken for granted whenever a Negro was involved with a white man. Discrimination and inequity in education were accepted as morally right. Books and articles were being published, sermons preached, and anti-Negro speeches made, all saying in substance: *The Negro is a different breed. He is inferior to the white man. At any cost he must be kept down.*

The North and the South had reached an agreement about the Negro's role in the South and in the nation. It was to be a subordinate role, with the Southern white man free from Northern interference, whatever might be his treatment of Negroes. Poor whites, former slave masters, and the warring political factions among the whites shared one determination: the "inferior" Negro was not to be allowed to become a political threat to white supremacy. At every turn the black man was being dehumanized. In fact, the Negro was being enslaved again.

In this perilous world, if a black boy wanted to live a halfway normal life and die a natural death he had to learn early the art of how to get along with white folks.

The Negro's economic or educational status in no way modified the problem. It was always the Negro's responsibility to find ways and means to get along with white people; never need white people concern themselves with getting along with Negroes. Were a Negro slightly above the county poverty level, with a few dollars in the bank and the ability to read, write, and figure, it was all the more necessary for him to behave well and "walk humbly" among the white folks. Strange as it may seem to most Negroes and whites today, it was literally true, when I was a boy, that it behooved Negroes to be humble, meek, and subservient in the presence of white folks. It is even true in some backward sections of the South in 1970.

When my parents admonished their children, "Be careful and stay out of trouble," they had only one thing in mind: "Stay out of trouble with white people!" My parents were not more cautious or fearful than others; virtually all Negro parents tried in some way to protect their children from the ever-present menace of white violence. The meaning was unmistakably clear. It was dangerous to argue with a white person. No matter how false or stupid, his word was law and gospel. It was not to be disputed even in court. "Stay out of trouble" meant that if the white man cursed you, you were not to curse him back. Even if he struck you, it was not safe to strike back. The occasional few who did strike back either ran out of town under cover of night or sought the protection of some "boss" or other influential white man. No matter how they acted, it was not always possible for Negroes to "stay out of trouble"; the many who cringed and kowtowed to white people the most were in just as much danger as the few who did not. How could a Negro avoid trouble when his "place" was whatever any white man's whim dictated at any given time? Hundreds of innocent Negroes were insulted, cheated, beaten, even lynched for the sole reason that they had incurred the displeasure of some white man. The situation was the same in essence throughout the South, though the degree of brutality varied from one section to another. Inevitably, some Negroes decided to fight back and suffer the consequences. One in my area, in self-defense, killed two white men and tried to escape. He took refuge in an empty house. A mob burned the house down and shot the Negro to death as he ran out.

The recollections of the 118 of my contemporaries who were interviewed confirm and validate my own interracial experiences. Asked how their parents taught them to behave toward white people, sixty-three of the 118 (53 percent) replied that they were taught to show respect to white people at all times. Some added, however, that they were taught to treat all adults with respect, not just white people. Twelve of the 118 (10 percent) said that their parents taught them to be submissive to white people, to "stay in your place!" Ten told interviewers that their parents admonished them to avoid white people. Thirty-three (28 percent) fell into various categories: Several said their parents taught them nothing about their behavior around white people; one said his mother taught her sons to fight whoever attacked them —black or white—and to allow no one to run over them. Another, son of a railway mail clerk, said his mother taught him to try to outsmart white people in every area. Two women said that their mothers taught them to be bitter toward white people, to think of them as treacherous. Still another person was taught by her parents never to feel inferior to whites.

I was anxious to learn, from the persons interviewed, if the early contacts between Negroes and whites were cordial, cold, or hostile. The answers varied. Most of the 118 said that their early childhood contacts with whites were cordial. However, almost all of them admitted that social distance was rigidly maintained and Negroes knew their "place." Forty-two persons (36 percent) expressed negative attitudes—hostility, distrust, fear—toward whites. Of the forty-two negative attitudes expressed, 56 percent was based on experience or having witnessed some cruelty inflicted upon Negroes, such as police brutality, race riots, beatings and lynchings; on learning of the rape of a Negro woman; and on being cheated. One woman's fear and hate had been aroused by the hanging of a cousin. Another was bitter because she taught school for $25 a month whereas the white teacher got $50 a month. Her school ran three months out of the year; the white school ran nine. Bitter though she was, she had not protested the situation because she "had to get along." Fifty-two persons (44 percent) expressed positive or friendly attitudes toward white people. Even in this group, however, twelve women said they had seen a lynching or had seen a Negro beaten to death. One woman's close relative had been lynched, and one person had witnessed the castration and lynching of a twelve-year-old Negro boy.

The appearance of a friendly relationship between Negroes and whites was no guarantee of its existence. My brother-in-law lived on the place of a white man who seemed friendly toward him. The landowner had expressed great fondness for my parents who at the time were living with my sister and her husband, and on one occasion, on his return from Europe, he brought gifts for them. He seemed proud, too, of what I was doing. One day, my nephew had a slight misunderstanding with a neighboring white man, and my brother-in-law had to straighten it out to keep my nephew from being beaten. When he told his supposedly friendly landlord what had happened, he was told in no uncertain tones what was expected of him. Despite the landlord's pretended affection for my parents, his expressed admiration for me, and the rent which my brother-in-law was paying, the edict was final—get along with the white neighbors or move!

It was customary in Greenwood County, and throughout the South, for Negroes to call white men and boys in their teens "Mister." The whites called Negroes, no matter what their age, "John," "Charlie," "boy," "Jane," "Sallie," "girl," "Uncle," "Aunt," and often "nigger." Among the 118 contemporaries interviewed, 107 (90 percent) said that they and members of their families always addressed white people formally, by titles such as "Sir," "Boss," "Cap," "Mrs," "Miss." So, as a technique of survival, most

Negro parents in my community and elsewhere taught their children servility. Even here, however, there were a few exceptions. One Negro interviewed said that in her town Negroes and whites who grew up together called each other by their first names. She stated that it was not until she moved to Atlanta that she encountered the "Miss Ann" practice. "I was on my first nursing job in this exclusive Atlanta area," she said, "when I addressed a sixteen-year-old white girl as 'Nancy.' Her mother quickly informed me that I was to call her daughter '*Miss* Nancy'!" There were other cases where Negroes and whites grew up and played together, but at a certain age the white boy or girl demanded that his Negro playmate call him or her "Mr." or "Miss."

I am not wise enough to say categorically what this system did to Negroes in Greenwood County. I can only speculate on the basis of what I saw and observed. It certainly "put the rabbit" in many Negroes. They were poor, inadequately trained, and dependent on the white man for work. Few dared to stand up to a white man. When one did, he got the worst of it. It was not unusual to hear that a certain Negro had been run out of town, or, fearing he would be, had left the county before "they" could get him. Most Negroes grinned, cringed, and kowtowed in the presence of white people. Those who could not take such subservience left for the city as soon as they could—with or without their father's permission. They went to Asheville, Columbia, and Washington, and some went North. As a Pullman porter, I met several hundred of these boys who had fled the South. I often heard them say, "I would rather be a lamppost on Lenox Avenue in Harlem than be the Governor of Mississippi!" There were others who, though they could not get away, never quite accepted in their minds the role they had to play. Some parents, thinking that they themselves were too old to adjust in a new place, permitted their sons and daughters to go away, with their blessings.

Negroes lived under constant pressures and tensions all the time in my community. They knew they were not free. They knew that if attacked they dare not strike back—if they wanted to live. To be at ease, to be relaxed, to be free were luxuries unknown to Negroes in Greenwood County and in most sections of the South. Some Negroes grew bitter and hated white people—all white people. Ralph, a high school roommate of mine from Florida, was one of those who hated white people; and Ralph was not afraid. He was graduated from State College, from Lincoln University in Pennsylvania, and from Cornell. Though he did not return to Florida, he did teach in the South. I was always afraid that he would be killed. If he had been attacked, he would have fought. I believe to this day that Negroes in my county fought among themselves because they were taking out on other Negroes what they really wanted but feared to take out on whites. It was difficult, virtually impossible, to combine manhood and blackness under one skin in the days of my youth. To exercise manhood, as white men displayed it, was to invite disaster.

At revival time in August, people could go from one church to another for a whole month if they chose because there were churches within an eight- or ten-mile radius of our house that held preaching one Sunday each month, and August was "Big Meeting" month. For the church that held worship on the first Sunday in August, the Big Meeting, or Revival, was held the first week in August, and so on through the month. Many buggies and wagons were on the road. There were no paved roads; when it was dry the roads were very dusty, and when it rained they were very muddy. As a rule, Negroes did not pass white people on either a dusty or a muddy road. If a Negro did pass a white person, throwing dust on him, the Negro was supposed to apologize for passing. I have been with my father when he apologized for passing a white driver by saying, "Excuse me, Boss, I'm in a hurry." Did this mean that my father mentally accepted or emotionally approved this cringing behavior? I doubt it. It was a technique of survival. But I have always wondered how long one can do a thing without eventually accepting it. I believe my father rebelled against the system as best he knew how. Dozens of times, I heard him tell, in gleeful tones and with a sparkle in his eyes, how when he was young he had whipped two white men. He knocked one of them down and, while that one was getting up, he knocked the other man down. Every time he told the story, he would laugh, and laugh, and laugh. It was his prize story.

I never had a white playmate; but seventy-two (63.7 percent) of those interviewed for my study said that they had had white playmates. The vast majority of them admitted that such shared play ceased in the pre-teen or early teen years, usually at twelve or thirteen. When play stopped, so did friendship.

My parents advised us further, especially my mother. They admonished my brothers and me to stay clear of white women. My mother told us that white women were dangerous and would surely get us into trouble. Whenever we met them on the road, or on the street in town, we were to "give them space and the time of day." If there were white women in the community whom we knew, we tipped our hats to them and passed on. Although Negroes were lynched for minor offenses as well as for major ones, real or trumped up, the white press tended to give the impression that Negroes were lynched only when white women were involved. A careful review of the Southern newspapers published at the turn of the century reveals that scores of articles on lynching carried statements such as: "Lynched for the Usual Crime." However, all well-informed people knew that this was a cover-up, a false front to justify the lynching of Negroes. *Thirty Years of Lynching in the United States, 1889-1918* (NAACP: New York) discloses that of the 3,255 victims of lynching during this period only 19 percent of the cases involved rape or any alleged sex offense. The white press deliberately created the myth that lynching was necessary in order to protect white womanhood.

The false pretense of protecting white women expressed itself in ways other than lynching. Even a very young, innocent Negro boy could be beaten up—even killed—if by mere accident he touched a white girl. Not long ago, Arthur L. Johnson, deputy superintendent of the Detroit public school system, a graduate of Morehouse College during my presidency, told a representative of the Civil Rights Documentation Project what happened to him on a street in Birmingham, Alabama, when he was only thirteen years old. Through no fault of his, he accidentally put his hand on the shoulder of a white girl of about five or six, for which he was immediately almost murdered. This incident is best told in Mr. Johnson's own words:

> When I was thirteen years old, I was downtown with an uncle who was young at the time—he may have been in, I think, his early twenties—and the two of us were walking in downtown Birmingham behind a white man, his wife, and their young daughter, who appeared to me, if I can remember now, to be about four or five years old at that time—maybe five or six. At some point along the way, the young daughter of this white family stepped across—they stopped, apparently to look in the window—she stepped across in front of me and I dropped my hand on her shoulder. It was the kind of thing that a thirteen-year-old-boy, conscious of his being thirteen years old, would do to a younger child. The moment I dropped my hand on that child's shoulder, her father—I don't really remember anything else until I was on the ground—I was wearing glasses then—I had lost my glasses. This man attacked me so violently on the street that I—and so quickly—that I didn't really know what happened until it was all over. The thing, however, which stands out in my mind as a definite indicator of what that experience involved from the race viewpoint is that my uncle stood frozen in fear in the face of that attack. I wondered about that many times afterwards. I couldn't understand it. You know, it was natural for a boy to assume that an older adult in his family would come to his defense in a

> situation like that. But he didn't do it. And it was some time before I came to realize the meaning of this. In the few days, immediate days, after that experience, as I thought about it, I just surmised that he was afraid because this was a white man and he was a Negro.

How in the world could a thirteen-year-old Arthur Johnson stay out of trouble?

While white men used physical force to protect white women or to avenge alleged attacks on white women by black men, Negro parents had to contrive other methods to protect their daughters, often without success. My parents did what they could to prevent exposure of my sisters to white men. My sisters were never allowed to work for white farmers unless one or more of their brothers worked along with them. When one of my sisters went to the store, one brother always went with her. As a rule, Father never permitted my sisters to cook for white families. Only my oldest sister, Susie, cooked out; and this was for the Childs family. We lived on their place, and Susie has told me that Dr. Childs was very kind to the family, particularly when all of us, except me, were ill with typhoid fever. I was two years old when the fever epidemic struck the family, and I never knew Dr. Childs. My brother Isaiah, whom I also never knew, was the only one of my family who died in the epidemic. Dr. Childs and God shared the credit for saving the other members of our family!

It is not my intention to give the impression that all white men made sexual overtures or advances to Negro women. Such an indictment would be far from the truth. But there was more than enough evidence to instill caution in Negro parents who cared about their daughters. Nor would I be so naïve as to imply that all Negro women were paragons of virtue at the turn of the century. Human nature and desires are essentially the same the world over. People are people regardless of race. But Negro parents knew during those difficult years that their daughters—irrespective of their feelings—had little or no chance to resist, let alone refuse, the sexual demands of any lecherous white man. *Any!* One of the persons interviewed for this study told of a Negro father who, hard up for money, hired out his daughter as a maid in a white man's home. Soon she complained of being pestered by one of the white males in the family. The father, accusing her of laziness, of trying to dodge work, insisted that she keep her job. Later on his daughter gave birth to a white baby. The Negroes in the community blamed the father. The following statement, written by one of the women interviewed, shows how little protection some Negro girls received: "I will never forget one Sunday evening in a little town in South Carolina. I was standing on a friend's porch. His sister asked their mother if she might go and buy some salt. She went into the woods and a white man followed her. Later she had a white baby."

The cautiousness of careful parents was understandable. In the thinking of all too many white people, Negroes "didn't count," so that if white men invaded the sexual privacy of Negro women, no moral code had been violated. Chastity was a virtue "for whites (white women, that is!) only" and had to be protected at whatever cost. It was rumored and believed by many Negroes in my county that white men sought to cohabit with Negro women in order to get experience in the sexual act before marriage to white women. Perhaps this self-righteous attitude of the white man in protecting the virtue of white women was an abortive atonement for the sins he committed against defenseless Negro women, with and without consent, during slavery and throughout the Reconstruction and post-Reconstruction eras.

I have sought to compare and contrast my personal experiences with those of others in my age group who were born and grew up in the South, even though some lived in cities, in other counties in South Carolina, and other states of the South. Experiences and therefore conclusions vary according to environment. When asked what parents had taught their sons about white women, fifty-six of the 118 (48 percent) said their parents taught their sons nothing about white women. Sixteen did not respond to the question. Forty-six (39 percent) said parents advised their sons: "Avoid white women, show them respect, *leave them alone.*" A farmer stated that his parents taught him that white women were troublemakers and by all means to keep away from them. A woman domestic said that her brothers were taught to "honor" white women. Three said that their mothers told their sons that white women were "poison." My wife, who was among those interviewed, relates that when her aunt observed one of her two sons, at the age of six, with his arms around a little white girl who lived in the block, she told both her sons that white girls were "poison," and she didn't want them ever to put their hands on a white girl.

On the specific question of how Negro parents protected their daughters from white men, sixty-four (54.9 percent) said that their parents kept their daughters from coming in contact with white men by various means, such as refusal to let their daughters work in white families, and by having them accompanied by other members of the family whenever they went out. Several said that their parents imposed strict curfew for the girls of the family. In this group, there was found considerably deeper hostility toward whites. Twenty-eight (24 percent) said that nothing was done to protect the daughters in their families. In this group, it was found that the respondents' families had friendly attitudes toward whites, or had had very little contact with them. Fifteen of the 118 did not answer this question, and eleven made such statements as: "Daughters were taught to protect themselves;" "Defend yourself against improper approaches." One woman wrote, "When my sister and I would go to the well, we would carry a two-by-four with a nail in it. We slashed fellows' shoulders several times when they tried to attack us. They were never successful. My sister shot a white guy once when he broke into our house and tried to rape her." She added, "When sexual activity between white and colored took place, it was usually forced, or young Negro girls were taken advantage of. The attitude of Negroes was that they were trapped and helpless. They felt this way because often the guilty (white) person would be the sheriff, a school teacher, or some other supposedly respectable, law-abiding citizen. They would take advantage of young Negro girls who worked in their homes. If the acts were reported, the defendants would swear that they would "never think of touching a 'dirty nigger' much less going to bed with one." Other persons interviewed said that their parents simply advised their daughters, "Be careful."

Despite the protection that many Negro parents tried to give their daughters, fifty-eight (49 percent) of the 118 interviewed expressed the belief that sexual relations took place frequently between white men and Negro women. Only rarely did one hear of relations between a Negro man and a white woman. One interviewee said, "Once a white lady had a colored baby. The father of the baby was run out of town; and after that the white people in the town would have no dealings with this lady. She had to socialize with the colored."

In concluding the views on the racial problems of my early years, as expressed by the 118 respondents, my wife's experience and testimony are relevant. Many times in the past forty years we shared our interracial experiences. Since we have both always been sensitive to injustice based on race, we made every effort to improve Negro-white relations in this nation. But before recording my wife's experiences and reflections, a word about her family.

Like my father, my wife Sadie's father, James Gray, was born a slave. Her mother was born in 1865, and my mother in 1862. Unlike my grandfather on my father's side, Sadie's grandfather was white, and her great-grandfather on her mother's side was also white. Though by no means wealthy, Sadie's father owned his farm. So did her grandfather on her mother's side. From her report, Negro-white relations in Georgia were essentially the same as those I knew in Greenwood County. There were four brothers and five sisters in my wife's family, a total of nine children: Madison Blount, Julia, Emory S., James Madison, Cecil, Elizabeth, Emma C.W., Lucia, and Sadie. Although Sadie's father never attended school a day in his life, he could read, write, and debate issues. Her mother, Emma Frances Blount Gray, attended the high school of Atlanta University. Her sister, Emma Catherine Ware Gray, did her college work at Paine College in Augusta, Georgia, and earned a Ph.B and M.A. from the University of Chicago. Sadie's second oldest brother, Madison Blount Gray, completed his college work at Oberlin after completing two years of college at Paine. Another brother, Emory S., completed his high school work and freshman college year at Paine, went to the army, studied at Fisk, and earned a D.D.S. from Northwestern University. A sister, Julia Gray Burton, finished high school at Paine. The oldest sister, Elizabeth Gray Blount, attended high school at Haines Institute in Augusta; James Madison Gray studied at Georgia State College in Savannah; Cecil died young, and Lucia was never well enough to go to school. My wife, Sadie, after completing her high school work and two years of college at Paine, went to the University of Chicago, where she earned her Ph.B. and M.A. degrees.

One can readily see that this was an unusual family. Few Negro families, coming along so short a time after Emancipation, can boast of as much education and training. Emma was professor and dean at Paine College; Madison Blount taught at Paine, but spent most of his career teaching in the high schools of St. Louis, Missouri; and Emory practiced dentistry in Chicago. Sadie was a social worker in St. Louis, Washington, and Atlanta, and taught in the Atlanta University School of Social Work. James Madison (Mack) was a carpenter and farmer. Julia and Elizabeth taught in the county schools and married. James Madison, Elizabeth, and Lucia were children of Sadie's father by his first wife. Sadie's father was the son of James Madison Gray, for whom the town of Gray, Georgia, is named. On a roadside plaque, in front of a school just as one enters Gray, Georgia, by way of Highway 18, these words are inscribed:

James Madison Gray

Gray, Georgia, was named for James Madison Gray, regarded as Jones County's most outstanding citizen. He clothed the Gray Infantry, Company F. 45th Regiment, C.S.A., and during the war fed the soldiers and homeless families from his smokehouses. At death, he left the bulk of his estate to Mercer University, the "Gray" Fund, to provide a better college for local boys. The railroad ran through the center of Gray's property surrounding the present town. Though he never married, he was liked by all, slaves, sharecroppers, and plantation owners alike.

Although James Madison Gray never married, he was the father of three boys by a dark-brown-skinned Negro slave (perhaps the reason he never married!). Sadie's father was one of the three sons. In those days, white men could father Negro sons "without benefit of clergy" and still be respected and respectable pillars of society.

Before recording Sadie's statement, I must add a word about her grandfather on her mother's side. Of him, Sadie's sister Emma wrote: "Madison Blount, son of a slave owner and a slave mother, was the plantation carpenter. He was harshly treated by his master-father. They hated each other. He had learned his trade so well that he was able, after Emancipation, to provide for his family better than the average; and his ideals, his sternness, and his absolute fearlessness, were always a protection for them. He bought a farm, built a house, and reared a large family." These brief backgrounds of my wife's father and of her maternal grandfather add relevance to her statement on what her parents taught her and her sisters about white men. I shall relate it as she told it to me:

> I had advice from three people: my mother, my father, and my maternal grandfather. My grandfather, Madison Blount, was born a slave. His wife, my maternal grandmother, was also born a slave. My grandfather did not get along with his slave-holding father because of the injustices he inflicted on the slaves. Grandfather told his grandchildren that he hated his father, and that he was afraid of him until he was eighteen. After that, he told us, "I have not been afraid of God nor the devil!" He often said, "I am an Ebo!" He resented the fact that his slave-holding master took advantage of his enslaved mother. He told us that he was a bastard. I think Grandpa Blount really hated white people. I remember his lecture to me when I was sixteen. It seems he would give this lecture when his daughters and granddaughters reached a certain age. He told me that I was growing up, almost grown up to be a lady. He told me, "You must take care of yourself. You know your Dad and I are bastards, but we must be the last bastards in our families. Our mothers were slaves; they could not protect themselves. But you do not have to take insults from anybody. Your Dad and Granddad will spill every drop of blood in their veins to protect you little girls. I am not afraid of anybody; so if you are ever molested by a white man, you let me know. Remember, no more bastards. You must be as fine and clean as any family alive." Grandpa Blount died at the age of ninety-two. He never joined the church because he did not believe that God exists. Though unlettered, he arrived at this conclusion after seeing the injustices of slavery. When I tried to get him to see that it was the justice of God that enabled him to escape from slavery, he reminded me

> that many slaves, better men than he, died in the system, and some slaves were killed. "If there is a God, He is not just!"
>
> My father also wanted his daughters to tell him if they were molested; but Mother advised us differently. She told me and my sisters that if we were approached in an indecent manner by white men, we should handle it ourselves because "you will only get your father and grandfather in serious trouble, for they will raise hell if they know anything about it." When the principal of a white high school made overtures to my mother by writing her an inviting letter, my grandfather told the superintendent, and told him that if it happened again he would kill the man. It never happened again. It may be that my grandfather got away with a lot of things because he was absolutely fearless. Once, when a trap was laid for me by a group of white men at the railroad station, I was tipped off by a Negro man who heard them making the plot. When I told Mother about it, she advised me not to tell Father for he would get himself into trouble. Mother told me to be prepared to protect myself, to carry a hatpin in my bosom, and, if attacked, use it. As I recall, I carried a hatpin with me for a year or more.
>
> My father did not hate his father. He adored him. When I asked my father one day how he could love his father, who left his property to Mercer University to educate white boys, and left him nothing, my father cried. He said, "Daughter, you do not understand. My father was a good man. I was a slave in the system, and he was a slave to the system."

As bad as things were in Greenwood County when I was a boy, I hear from others that they were worse in some other sections of the South, and even in certain other sections of South Carolina. We could walk on the sidewalks when we went to Greenwood, the county seat. But Negroes by and large were a subdued lot and they showed their abject condition by the way they moved around on the sidewalks and the servile way in which they behaved when they went into the stores to trade. Negroes were always careful never to brush up against a white person. Negroes in my county tried to stay out of trouble, with little success; and it was circulated that there were towns in South Carolina where Negroes coming to town on Saturdays walked in the streets and left the sidewalks to the whites. A white friend of mine, Mrs. Elizabeth Jonitis, who now lives in Maine and Florida, wrote me in June, 1968, that such was the case in Walterboro, South Carolina, in 1943, when she stopped off there; that Negroes meeting her would step off the sidewalk rather than share it with a white woman; and that this custom differed from that of Chestertown, Maryland, where she had once lived, where Negroes and whites by custom used different sides of the sidewalks.

I never felt completely at home in my native county. The experiences

I had in my most impressionable years, hearing and seeing the mob, observing the way my people were treated, noting the way in which they responded to this treatment, never having developed any white friends in the county, and living all my early years in a rented house—all this left me with a feeling of alienation from the county of my birth. The chasm was so wide between black and white in my day that I never felt that any white person in Greenwood County or in South Carolina would be interested in anything I did.

It was surprising and delightful, therefore, when years later—1968—I visited the offices of the *Index-Journal* in Greenwood, South Carolina, to meet editor J. E. Chaffin and hear him express great satisfaction in my career. He gave me a copy of a most enlightened address on race which he had delivered at Erskine College. He carried a good story about me in the *Index-Journal.* I was equally surprised, shocked, and delighted when I received the Man of the Year Award from the Greenville Chapter of the Society for the Advancement of Management that year. My rapport had been with Negroes—not whites.

We always lived on the highway, a thoroughfare connecting Greenwood and Saluda and other small towns. When there was trouble, such as the Phoenix Riot, and when drunken men rode by at night cursing, using profane and obscene language, and sometimes shooting, it was not so good.

I trembled in my bed at night as white men passed by making the night hideous with their wild behavior. But there was also a pleasant side to living by the side of the road. Frequently people would stop for a few minutes to chat, en route to and from church and Greenwood. It was known that our spring water, about one-sixth of a mile away, was fresh and cool. Often we were sent to the spring to get fresh, cool water for a thirsty wayfarer. Some of these people who stopped to get water were white. In the country, we did not drink out of glasses. Dippers and gourds were used. And our white travelers drank out of our dippers and gourds. However, when we worked for white farmers by the day, if whites were working in the field with us, they maintained their "superior" status by drinking first.

The thing I remember best about our house by the side of the road was the handsome, big oak tree where we put up our swing. It was so close to the road that if we were swinging full blast it often proved frightening to the people on their way by. I loved that oak tree. For years, in passing by the place of my birth, I always looked for the oak and was glad to see it—still strong, stately, and handsome.

Chapter III

Frustrations, Doubts, Dreams

As a child my life was one of frustration and doubt. Nor did the situation improve as I grew older. Long before I could visualize them, I knew within my body, my mind, and my spirit that I faced galling restrictions, seemingly insurmountable barriers, dangers and pitfalls. I had to find answers to two immediate and practical problems: 1) How could I overcome my father's immutable opposition to my insatiable desire to get an education; and 2) Even if I succeeded in changing Father's attitude, how could I get the money to go away to school? I knew that my father had no money to give me, but I longed for his sympathetic approval, or at least his consent.

There was a third problem which, though not so immediate, was even more urgent—more frustrating, more confusing. This was a "white man's world." How could I be free in this world? How could I grow to my full stature as a man? The white boy born in Greenwood County knew that the county, the state, and the nation belonged to the white world and therefore to him. As one of the disinherited, one of the black boys, how could I know that a part of the county, the state, and the nation belonged to me too? How could I exist, let alone live, without cringing and kowtowing to white men as I had seen my elders do? How could I walk the earth with dignity and pride? How could I aspire to achieve, to accomplish, to "be somebody" when there were for Negroes no established goals? Moreover, aspiring was dangerous. It was all right for a Negro to "hitch his wagon," but he'd better not "hitch it to a (white) star." My teacher in the one-room school, my pastor, and the church people at Mount Zion had inspired me to want an education far beyond what the four-month Brickhouse School could offer, and away beyond what my parents could possibly provide. How then could I get to a better school? How could I manage to remain in school more than four months out of the year?

My greatest opposition to going away to school was my father. When I knew that I had learned everything I could in the one-room Brickhouse School and realized how little that was, my father felt that this was sufficient

—that it was all I needed. Weren't there only two honest occupations for Negro men—preaching and farming? My father must have repeated this dictum a thousand times. What did schooling have to do with farming? Would reading all the books in the world teach a man how to plow, to plant cotton and corn, gather the grain, and harvest the crop? Since my father saw no future for his sons except farming, education was not necessary. It was equally superfluous for the ministry. God "called" men to preach; and when He called them, He would tell them what to say!

Father had another reason. He was convinced that education went to one's head and made him a fool and dishonest. One of my cousins, a bright sixth- or seventh-grade scholar who taught at one of the county schools for the miserable salary paid Negro teachers during that period, forged a note on a bank, skipped town, and was never caught. He never returned to his home community. Later he joined the Ninth Cavalry. He wrote me occasionally, telling how much better the racial situation was in his part of Kansas than it was in the South. Whenever I pressed my father about further schooling, he would always remind me of what my cousin had done. The more education, the bigger the fool and crook! Though less literate than my father, my mother was far more understanding of my problems, and was a sympathetic listener to my hopes and dreams, my fears and plans. She had only two things to give me—her love and her prayers. She gave both with an open heart.

My mother believed that God answered prayers. Though not so credulous or optimistic about prayer as she, I was nonetheless greatly influenced by her prayer life. I sought a way out through prayer. I prayed frequently as I worked in the field and many nights alone in the moonlight. I often plowed to the end of the row, hitched the mule to a tree, and went down into the woods to pray. On moonlight nights, I would leave the house and go into the field and pray. My prayers were all variations of the same theme: a petition to God to enable me to get away to school. My desire for an education was not only a dream but a goal that drove and prodded me, day and night. I left the farm not to escape it but to find *my* world, to become myself.

I accepted the prayer jargon of the older people. I asked God to move out of my way "every hindrance and cause" which kept me from getting an education. Afterward I was sorry that I had prayed that way, for if God had answered my prayers as spoken, Father would have been the first obstacle to be moved out. Since presumably God is not particularly interested in semantics, he probably knew that had I been wiser I would have asked for the will, the wisdom, the tenacity to overcome the obstacles that lay in my way. My father died in 1938. I am glad that he lived long enough for me to be graduated from the high school of the South Carolina State College, to earn a degree from Bates, to receive M.A. and Ph.D. degrees from the University of Chicago, and to become dean of the School of Religion at Howard University. While living with me in Washington, Father admitted his error in fighting my desire for an education, saying that he had opposed me only because he didn't know any better. But I had long since forgiven him; and it was my joy that from 1921 until his and Mother's deaths in 1938, in an atmosphere of mutual understanding and appreciation, it was possible for me to insure their comfort and well-being.

When I was fifteen, Pastor Marshall persuaded my father to let me go to a small Baptist Association School in McCormick, South Carolina. It was little, if any, better than the Brickhouse School. Once more I was spending four months a year in school; and after two years at McCormick I had to go back to the farm. I was then seventeen and I had never had more than four months a year in school. At the end of my second year, I had to break with my pastor. He knew I was not satisfied with his school; but he wanted me to return the third year and be a student-teacher. Though I refused as politely as I could, he never really forgave me for not coming back.

McCormick is twenty-four miles from Greenwood; and it was a wonderful day for me when I got on the Charleston and Western Carolina Railroad and rode those twenty-four miles. It was a new experience. It was at McCormick that I decided that if I could not continue my education I would be a mail clerk on the railway. The job had no particular glamour for me, but it seemed better than nothing in case God did not see fit to remove the obstacles or I could not overcome them! The idea of being a railway mail clerk came to me because there was a Negro mail clerk on one of the trains that ran through McCormick, and just seeing him at work made a tremendous impression on me. It was something new under the sun for me, and many a day I met the train merely to see this Negro in action.

There was nothing more for me at the Brickhouse School, and the McCormick school had only a little more to offer, so I wanted to go to Benedict College in Columbia, South Carolina, or to State College in Orangeburg. Once more the battle with Father would have to be fought! Nevertheless, I wrote to Benedict and to State College (their high school departments). I chose State College because it was less expensive. I could go there for six dollars a month, and the fare from Ninety Six (nearest railroad to my home) to Orangeburg was $3.05. I knew that I could earn this much even if Father sent me nothing. When Father saw that I was determined to go to a better school, and knew that I had to have money in order to do so, he angrily threw a ten-dollar bill at me. So I made my way to Orangeburg without Father's blessing but with my mother's prayers. On my arrival, Miss Julia Mae Williams, teacher of the seventh grade, gave me an examination and then took me to Professor N. C. Nix, telling him that I belonged in the eighth grade.

For the first two years at State College I was called home at the end of February, according to custom, to work on the farm. I was vividly aware that time has swift wings. I was nineteen and not once in my life had I been able to remain in school more than four months in any year. In my third year, after my four months stay at State College, when my father again sent for me to come home to work on the farm, I was determined that—at whatever cost—I would remain at State for the full term. I invoked the help of Professor Nix, my high school mathematics teacher, who wrote my father asking him to let me finish the school year. Father was adamant. I wrote Father explaining that I could never get anywhere if I continued to go to school only four months a year. I told him, too, that I would not come home until school closed in May. So the break with my father came and it was final. I disobeyed him without regret and with no pangs of conscience. It was now crystal clear to me that I must take my education into my own hands and that I could not and must not permit my father to dictate or determine my future. Father threatened to send the sheriff for me; but fortunately he did not carry out his threat. Had he done so, I would have been compelled to go home.

Six dollars a month isn't much money, but it was a lot for a boy who had none, who indeed had nothing but a consuming desire to be somebody worthwhile. My brother John, who had a farm of his own, promised to send me three dollars a month for the next two months. The other three dollars I would have to earn, plus a little extra for laundry and so on. Professor Jones, called "Big Time" by the students, gave me a job. It was not a pleasant one. It was cleaning outhouses at midnight after everyone else had gone to bed. There was no indoor plumbing in the dormitories in those days. This was nauseating work, but it paid six dollars a month. With what my brother sent me, and what I earned, I could pay my expenses. I could stay in school for the full term.

Now I was on my own; never again would I have to depend on my father; my future was in my hands. Luckily for me, the Pullman Company was coming South each spring to recruit students for summer jobs. If a student was tall enough, strong enough, and had seventeen dollars to buy his cap and uniform, he had work for the summer. The Pullman Company paid the fare to New York and deducted it from the first money the student earned. I jumped at the opportunity to earn my way and to go North for the first time. Orangeburg, 125 miles from home, was the farthest I had ever traveled.

How was I to get seventeen dollars? Since I was the ranking student in my class—once more Exhibit A when visitors came!—I thought it would be easy to borrow seventeen dollars. Not so. It was necessary for me to approach five teachers before I found one who was willing to lend me seventeen dollars. This experience, and one which I had in Chicago years later, made me vow that once I got a job and held it, I would never again be broke—a vow that since 1921 has not been broken or even bent.

I have always been grateful to Professor Bollie Levister who without hesitation said he would be glad to let me have the money. He told me that he was making the loan to me without requiring me to sign a note, but advised that if ever I had any money to lend to be sure that the borrower signed a note. The realization that Professor Levister trusted me was as great a lift to my spirit as his money was to my practical need. I was proud and happy when I got my first paycheck to send a seventeen-dollar money order to Professor Levister. Several years ago, I met his two daughters, who were small girls on the campus when I was at State. I told them of their father's gracious generosity to me and assured them that if ever I could do anything for them it would be my pleasure to do so. When my book *Disturbed About Man* was published in April, 1969, I was happy to send one of Professor Levister's daughters an autographed copy expressing appreciation for what her father had done for me.

I spent the summer of 1915 and several more as a Pullman porter, working out of Grand Central Station in New York and South Station in Boston. I did fairly well. Indeed, I felt that I had done extremely well for I was able to return to school in the fall of 1915 all dressed up. I had two suits. Never before had I owned two good suits—or even one! I knew then the thrill that comes to a boy who earns his own money and spends it as he chooses.

New York was a bit disappointing to me. I had heard so much about it that it never quite came up to my expectation, not even to this day. Then, too, I found prejudice in the North; not the depressing, terrifying kind I knew in South Carolina, but in some situations just as ego-wounding, just as embarrassing. There were restaurants that would not serve Negroes and hotels where Negroes could not stay. In Detroit, one hot day, I went into a place to buy a cool drink. The attendant sold it to me, but smashed the glass on the floor as soon as I placed it on the counter.

For graduation, the high school at State College required the completion of thirteen grades. Having entered in the eighth-grade class, I expected to stay in the high school six years. Partly by accident I made it in five, completing the last four years in three. Professor Nix sometimes left me in charge of the class. One day, when I told a classmate that he had not worked a problem correctly, he went into a rage and pulled his knife on me, and a friend from his hometown came to help him "do me in." The fight did not develop; but when I related the incident to Professor Nix he said, "Mays, you can do the work in the next class. I am promoting you now to that class. It is nothing but jealousy, so I am taking you out of there." The next day I went into the junior class and I was graduated from high school in 1916 as valedictorian. In a tough Northern school this would have been impossible. In the sixteen years since I entered the first grade at the age of six, I had spent only seventy-three months in school—the equivalent of eight nine-month years of schooling. Had I been able to complete each year without being taken out for farm work, I would have been graduated at fourteen instead of at twenty-one. I regret those "lost years."

Although the high school teachers at State were excellent, I am well aware that there are gaps in my education which I was never able to overcome, despite the fact that the years brought me membership in Phi Beta Kappa, a Ph.D. from a great university, and honorary doctorates from twenty-eight distinguished colleges and universities. There are many things that one must learn and read in elementary and high school; otherwise it is too late, for each passing day makes its own new demands. Even if one had time to catch up on the reading he missed as a child, the end result would be different. I am sure that I would have read many books in my childhood had they been available. They were not. Not in the Brickhouse School, not in my home, not in the community. No library was available.

I studied hard and long in high school, not because I had to in order to keep up with my classmates but because I really wanted to learn. I was aiming for something; I did not know what. Vaguely, yet ardently, I longed to *know*, for I sensed that knowledge could set me free. The vast majority of the students at State in my day did not really apply themselves; few students had any desire to learn. The boys had their minds on the girls; the girls had their minds on the boys. The boys would sit on campus looking at their girl friends for hours at a time; for hours at a time the girls would parade the campus, the better to be looked at. Study or no study, however, most of them passed their work. The few students who did apply themselves and studied were considered odd and called bookworms. I was an "odd bookworm."

I can recall the names of almost all the students who did serious work. Then, as is ever true, they were the ones who succeeded best in after years. They, rather than the "don't care" boys, were my friends.

It did my soul good in 1911 to find at State College an all-Negro faculty and a Negro president. They were good teachers, holding degrees from Benedict College, Biddle University (now Johnson C. Smith), Lincoln University in Pennsylvania, Fisk University, and other colleges. President Robert Shaw Wilkinson was a graduate of Oberlin. His wife, Marian Birnie Wilkinson, was one of the finest women I have ever known. She fought racial injustice and discrimination, and the white merchants who sold to the school paid her the unusual tribute of calling her *Mrs.* Wilkinson. She had a proud carriage, and I enjoyed seeing her walk across the campus. The inspiration which I received at State College was and is of incalculable value.

All my teachers were lavish with their praise and encouragement, primarily I suppose because I studied hard and made good grades. Perhaps the one who inspired me most was Professor Nelson C. Nix. He had an interesting way of challenging the students. When virtually the whole class was stuck on a problem in mathematics, Nix would say, "You boys can't work these problems? The white boys at the University of South Carolina are eating these problems up!" All the forces in my environment had been designed to make me accept the fallacy that the quality of my mind was different from that of white boys; but Nix challenged us with his talk about the white boys at the University of South Carolina once too often for me. He said it one day just after he had returned a test paper to me marked "100." After class I asked Professor Nix how much more than 100 would the white boys at the University of South Carolina make on the test. His patting me on the back and saying, "Ah, my boy, they wouldn't beat *you!*" did not quite reassure me. The very fact that Nix kept saying it made me wonder sometimes if he himself did not believe there was a difference in mentality between black and white.

Professor Nix had an A.B., and I believe a degree in theology from Benedict College. I believe he had not earned an M.A. in mathematics, but he knew high school mathematics and he was a good teacher. He had studied at least one summer at the University of Chicago, and, from the proud and proprietary way he talked about the university one could believe that he had earned a Ph.D. there. It was he who made me want to attend the University of Chicago someday. One summer, working out of Grand Central Station in New York as a Pullman porter, I was delighted to be assigned to a car to Chicago. While there, I took the streetcar and rode to the South Side to see the University of Chicago. I was impressed. I wrote a card to a classmate, Mattie Mae Fitzgerald, telling her that someday I would be a student at the University of Chicago. This prophecy came true on January 3, 1921, when I enrolled there.

As already implied, I was not the most popular student socially at State. It seemed to me that it was the "dumb" boys, the lazy loafers, who caught and kept the prettiest girls. There were two girls in my high school years I liked very much, but they were snatched up by the "swift," well-dressed boys who never even knew that they were my "rivals." I couldn't afford the time to loaf on the campus flirting with the girls, or to hang around the halls waiting for them to come by. As I look back over my social life at State, I realize that I had an inferiority complex where girls were concerned, especially if they were city girls. I was reared ten miles from the railroad and was sure that city boys and girls had more sophistication than the "greenhorns" from the country. I was a bit reticent, a bit shy. I doubt that I would have been a bright and shining social light even if I had not been obsessed by the importance of study.

Despite my limitations as a "playboy," I did meet a beautiful, well-balanced, charming girl before I was graduated from high school. Her name was Ellen Harvin. Ellen was the kind of girl who could understand a boy like me—lured by a dream, driven to try to accomplish something worthwhile in life. She agreed with my resolution not to marry before completing college, and we became engaged. We remained engaged during my four college years, and were married in Newport News, Virginia, in August, 1920. She was then a Jeanes* teacher in Clarendon County, South Carolina. She was teaching Home Economics at Morris College in Sumter, South Carolina, and I was teaching at Morehouse when she died early in 1923, after an operation in an Atlanta hospital.

State College was the finest I had ever seen for Negroes, but it was obvious that, though "separate," it was not "equal" to the University of South Carolina, from which Negroes were excluded. State College was not designed to prepare Negroes for literary and professional careers. It was said that it was established in 1896 to get Tom Miller, a militant Negro

*Jeanes teachers: Supervisors of Negro rural schools from the million-dollar Rural School Fund established in 1907 by Anna T. Jeanes of Philadelphia.

leader, out of politics. Miller became the first president of State. It was thoroughly understood that Negroes were to be prepared in agriculture and trades. The emphasis was in these areas. At commencement, if the valedictorian had majored in English or history, the president saw to it that some boy or girl always gave a speech extolling the glories of agriculture and the trades. I heard Professor Butler once say that the teaching of Latin was allowed because they called it "agricultural Latin"! The spirit if not the letter of this allegation was true.

At any rate, every student had to take a trade whether he liked it or not. One day a week was set aside for the trades, and a student could work at his trade on Saturdays and in the afternoons. I started out in the harness making and shoe repairing trades, but after the first year I turned to painting. Professor Lewis encouraged me to change because he knew I had no aptitude for repairing shoes and less than none for making harnesses. I did well as a painter; I can still handle a paint brush artfully. (My wife, Sadie, more often than I, rejoiced that I acquired this skill.)

For white students, South Carolina had the University of South Carolina, Clemson, The Citadel, and Winthrop; all four denied entrance to Negroes. Only State College at Orangeburg was for Negroes, and State College had students enrolled from the third grade up. Negro high school pupils in South Carolina, as in Georgia and other Southern states, had to depend largely on the high schools attached to the Negro colleges—mostly the high schools of private colleges. It was not possible for my college to be as good as those for whites. When I was at State College, each of the four colleges for whites in South Carolina usually received more appropriation than State, although more than 50 percent of the population of South Carolina were Negroes. The excuse for this blatant inequity and discrimination was usually that white people paid most of the taxes. This argument never took into account the fact that the taxable properties and wealth of the whites were the result of the starvation wages paid Negroes. Moreover, in a democracy the poorest and the richest child are entitled to the same training at public expense. Poor whites, who paid no direct taxes, had access to the public schools without any form of discrimination.

In the year 1900, the total amount of the general cost of maintaining the five state schools in South Carolina, which included the Negro state college, was $627,574. Of this amount, $8,012 or less than 2 percent, was appropriated for the Negro state college. In 1910, the total amount appropriated for the general cost to maintain four of the five institutions was $424,198. Of this amount, State College where I was entered in 1911 received $9,298, or little more than 2 percent. The gross inequity reflected by these figures is more dramatically stated thus: *Fifty-five percent* of the population (Negroes) received *2 percent* of the appropriation for higher education; *45 percent* (whites) received *98 percent.* Things were a little better in 1920. Of a total of $549,272, the white schools received $485,399 and the lone Negro school received $63,272. Negroes received 12 percent of the appropriation. They were 51 percent of the population.

I was graduated from the high school of State College in 1916. In 1915, John E. Swearingen, South Carolina Superintendent of Education, queried: "Is it too much to hope for a minimum of $25 per white child and $5 per Negro child?" It is this attitude of unquestioning acceptance of discrimination that causes Harlan, in his book *Separate and Unequal,* to entitle Chapter VI "South Carolina: Inequality as a Higher Law." This kind of inequality did not bother Mr. Swearingen and the other South Carolina school officials one iota. To spend five times as much on the white child as on the Negro child was quite all right. Harlan points out that even Swearingen's wish was not carried out: "The average expenditure that year was $16.22 for each white child enrolled and $1.93 for each Negro child enrolled, a discrimination amounting to a ratio of 8.4 to 1. The ratio was even more disproportionate on the basis of the population of school age. According to the Federal Commissioner's estimate of population five to eighteen years of age, the amount for each white child was $13.98; for each Negro child, $1.13, a discrimination of 12.37 to 1."

When I started to school at the age of six in 1900, South Carolina spent $6.51 on each white child in school; on each Negro child, $1.55. Fifteen years later, in 1915, when I was a junior in high school, my state spent $23.76 on each white child in school as compared with $2.91 on each Negro child. In those years, the dollar increase for the white child was $17.25; during the same period the increase for the Negro child was $1.36. Not until Negroes began to sue in the federal courts was there any appreciable change in this situation. After decades of such discrimination in educational opportunity, it is almost miraculous that Negroes do as well as they do on national tests.

It would appear that during the twenty-two years between my birth (1894) and my graduation from high school (1916) one area of savagery had improved somewhat. In 1894, 192 persons were lynched in the United States; 134 of them were Negroes. In 1916, fifty-four persons were lynched, fifty of them Negroes. So far as the plight of the Negro was concerned, the improvement was only seeming: In 1894, 69.8 percent of those lynched were Negroes; in 1916 the percentage was 92.6.

I have mentioned earlier that the two demon problems with which I wrestled in my childhood and youth were 1) the practical one, how to get an education, and 2) the more fundamental one, how to become and remain a man of pride, dignity, and integrity in a society determined to rob me of all of these qualities. If a man is to be robbed of self-respect, death would be more rewarding.

It was during my junior year in high school that I encountered my bitterest and most embarrassing interracial experience. A young white medical doctor, Wallace Payne, had the reputation of beating up Negroes —for no reason. He was mean, and deeply prejudiced against Negroes. He hated them. It was our custom to stop at Epworth post office for mail, especially on Saturdays after going to Mount Zion, which was less than a half mile from Epworth. On this particular Saturday, which was to remain forever hideously imprinted in my memory, I had left my mother in the buggy while I went to the post office to ask whether there was any mail. I was standing outside the gate through which one entered the post office, waiting for someone to hand me the mail if we had any. Dr. Payne came up, evidently to get his own mail. He opened the gate and went in; but before going in he struck me a mighty blow in the face, saying, "Get out of my way, you black rascal. You're trying to look too good anyway." I was stunned, momentarily blinded by the force of his blow.

The racial attitude of Wallace Payne and others like him was summed up in that sentence: "Get out of my way, you black rascal; you're trying to look too good anyway." I was black; and a black man had no rights which he, Wallace Payne, was bound to admit, let alone respect. My life meant no more to him than that of a rabbit. I was black and he was white; accordingly, with or without provocation, he could—with impunity—do to me what he wished. A rascal is one who is unprincipled and dishonest, and I suppose that Dr. Payne's conception of all Negroes was that they were unprincipled and dishonest. My greatest sin, of course, was that I was "trying to look too good." I was standing erect; and I am sure that I had on clean clothes, however cheap they may have been. Mother saw to it that we were neatly and cleanly dressed whenever we went out. But a Negro was not supposed to look neat or intelligent, or to stand erect around Dr. Payne. Maybe he had expected me to start to grin and cringe when I saw him or to jump when he spoke to me. At any rate, he really let me have it. This humiliating experience is as vivid in my mind today as if it happened yesterday.

Why did I take it? Why didn't I hit back? What would I have done if it had been another Negro who had struck me? All of these questions went through my mind in those agonizing moments. Maybe I had already been conditioned by Mother's admonition, "Stay out of trouble." Maybe I was afraid. It was Saturday afternoon; the store was filled with white men dressed in overalls, smoking and chewing tobacco, some drinking. There is no doubt in my mind that had I struck back I would have been shot dead on the spot, and I am also sure that nothing would have been done about it. Dr. Payne would not even have been arrested. All he would need to do would be to say that I attacked him first. No white man in the store would have testified in my behalf; and the few Negroes in the store would have been afraid to testify against any white man, let alone Wallace Payne. Although my brothers carried pistols, I had never done so. I had nothing for defense. Some days later, when I was in the store, I asked the white store clerk, whom my parents thought a "fine fellow," why Dr. Payne had hit me. His face red, he snapped, "Ask him; he struck you." I was not as nonviolent then as I am now. For several summers afterward I worked out of New York and Boston as a Pullman porter; and for two or more summers I watched eagerly for Wallace Payne to get on my car. I intended to get him if he did. I am glad now that he was never a passenger on my car; and I guess he should be glad, too, because if I had ever met him in a place where the odds were not all against me I certainly meant to repay him in kind and more.

But strange things happen. In 1950, I was invited to give a major address before a national convention of Methodist women in Cleveland, Ohio. Evidently the address was well received because scores of persons came up to express appreciation. I noticed a small group of four or five persons standing a little distance away waiting for others to finish speaking to me. Finally, they came to make themselves known and one woman said that she undertood that I was from Epworth, South Carolina. When I confirmed this, they all chorused, "So are we!" I was startled for I would never have thought that a white person from Epworth, South Carolina, would appreciate the straightforward message I had given to the Methodist women that day. Another woman asked whether I knew Dr. Wallace Payne, and when I admitted I did, she told me that he was her husband and that they were now living in North Carolina. She probably knew nothing of what her husband had done to me and I did not tell her. Maybe I should have. I saw no need of spoiling what had been a pleasant few moments. She was not the guilty party; and it may have been that being married to and living with such a person as Wallace Payne was unpleasant enough.

My second unforgettable racial experience during my high school years took place in Orangeburg, South Carolina. I was always eager to earn a little money by working for someone in town, or by assisting Mr. Davis, my painting instructor, on one of his jobs in the city. A friend of mine, Isaiah Kearse, was leaving his job and I wanted it, so I went to apply for it. I knocked on the front door and the man of the house came to the door and angrily asked me what I wanted. I told him that I had come to ask for the job that Mr. Kearse had had. I had made two grave mistakes: I had come to his front door, and I had called my friend Mister. The man of the house called me a "black s. o. b." and warned me about ever coming to his front door. He made it clear that no *Mister* Kearse had worked there, but "Isaiah worked here; and if you want to see me go to the back door." I didn't go to the back door. I left.

It was not enough for this man to refuse to call any Negro Mister; he wanted to dictate to me what I should call members of my own race. It is degrading enough to deny a man a title of civility because he is black; but to deny him the right to give titles to members of his own race is just going too damn far! I left that man's house in a hurry, no more fearful of what he might do to me than of what I might do to him. Once I realized that Negroes were frequently expected to go to the white man's back door, I never went to see anyone if the back door was a requirement. One has to rebel against indignities in some fashion in order to maintain the integrity of his soul.

I hadn't known how I was going to find a way to go to State College, but I had managed it. Now the problem haunting me was how I could go North to School. It was depressingly clear to me that being the valedictorian of my class did not prove that I was good. I really wanted to compete with white students. Since I couldn't do so in South Carolina, I wished to go to New England. President Wilkinson, anxious to build up his college department, wished me to take the college course there. When he learned that I was determined not to return for college work, he told Mr. Davis, my painting instructor, to give me no more work. This meant cutting off the little money I was earning by painting on Saturdays in the city. When I learned of the president's orders, I was deeply hurt. Professor Nix learned about what happened and insisted that I talk with the president so there would be no ill will between us. President Wilkinson was at the station the morning I left Orangeburg, and I did speak briefly with him about the matter, expressing my disappointment that he had instructed Mr. Davis to give me no more work. The president, as I recall, said very little. Shortly afterward, I wrote him to explain why I wished to do my college work elsewhere. He did not reply. His attitude seemed strange to me since he sent his own children away to college and was himself a graduate of Oberlin. I know that one of his daughters went to Atlanta University and one son to Dartmouth. President Wilkinson and I met again in the fall of 1920 after I had been graduated with honors from Bates College and had been chosen Class Day orator by my classmates. The president was pleased with my address to the students, and our friendship continued from then until his death in 1932. He never explained. I never understood.

My oldest brother's wife had spoken encourangingly to me about my education. However, when I completed my high school work, she advised me to stop school, teach, and help my parents who were growing too old to run a farm by themselves. Father was sixty-two years old at the time and Mother was fifty-six. The girls had all married. H. H. had left home a few years before; James and John were married and had their own family responsibilities. What my sister-in-law said made sense; but it would have been a tragic mistake if I had followed her advice. I would have had to give up further training and would have been able to earn very little with only a high school education. The only thing I could have done with that high school diploma was to teach a school in the county, which at one time had been my mother's ambition for me. I knew it would have made her heart glad to have her youngest child near her and teaching, perhaps at the Brickhouse School. Nevertheless, I had to pursue the goal I had felt rather than seen as I prayed on my knees in a cotton field in South Carolina.

It is interesting to speculate what my salary might have been had I accepted a teaching job in the county in 1916. A guess can be made based on the average salary that was being paid for public school teaching in 1915. In that year, the average yearly salary paid white teachers was $383.39; the average paid Negro teachers, $112.31. There wasn't much I could have done with $112.31. Then, too, the racial climate of South Carolina was not conducive to developing manhood in anyone wearing a black skin. I might have heeded the Booker T. Washington call to "cast down (my) bucket" in Greenwood County, but I don't believe that I or my bucket could have survived! The time had not yet come for any Negro, or any white man for that matter, to try to change the racial pattern in Greenwood County. Fortunately for me and for my parents, just at the time they really needed my help I was going to my first job in Atlanta, in 1921, and from that time on I was able to give them adequate assistance.

It was a great thing for me to have my mother at my high school graduation. Orangeburg was 125 miles away from Ninety Six, and this was the farthest she had ever traveled up to that time. She saw in my graduation an answer to her prayers. She saw and heard me give the valedictory address on the subject "Watch the Leaks." Father did not come. This was the only one of my graduations my mother attended. We were not able to pay her way to my graduation from Bates in 1920; and it was not possible, because of her advancing years, to have her come to my two graduations from the University of Chicago, one in 1925 and the other in 1935. After my high school graduation in 1916, I left South Carolina and did not return for three years. Mother was one of those persons who would cry for joy as well as for sorrow. When I greeted her after being away for three years, she put her arms around me, "crying for joy," saying that if I stayed away that long again I would come to her funeral. Fortunately, she was mistaken, for she lived nineteen years after that. She had made this remark so often by 1919 that I told her then that I didn't believe her, that only her God knew how long she was to live.

To sum up, those first twenty-two years had made their impact on me in several ways:

I had come to the conclusion that the Southern white was my enemy—not only my enemy but the enemy of all Negroes.

Everything I had seen, and most of what I had heard, should have convinced me that the white man was superior and the Negro inferior. But I was not convinced; I was bothered; I was haunted night and day. I once startled my saintly mother by telling her that if I thought that God had deliberately made me inferior I would pray no more. I did not really believe that God had done this to me; but I knew I could never find out in South Carolina.

Since my earliest memory was of a murderous mob, I lived in constant fear that someday I might be lynched. Not that I need be guilty of any crime. The flimsiest excuse manufactured by a white mob would suffice to insure a Negro's being brutally beaten or lynched. So, whenever I saw a crowd of whites together I was ill at ease and, if possible, I avoided contact with them.

I certainly didn't know what, when, how, or where, but before finishing high school I hoped that someday I would be able to do something about a situation that had shadowed my early years and had killed the spirit of all too many of my people.

I came to the conclusion that I could never do what I hoped to do or be what I aspired to be if I remained in the state of my birth. I had to seek a new world.

Chapter IV

Finding Out for Myself

Within a year I was to go to Bates College against the advice of President George Rice Hovey of Virginia Union University, and against the advice of friends. Certainly I was growing in self-confidence and self-reliance, but my problems were far from solved. Financially, I still had to "make bricks without straw." There was so much that I had to discover, to demonstrate, to validate.

I wanted to go to New England primarily for one reason: My total environment proclaimed that Negroes were inferior people, and that indictment included me. The manner in which white people treated Negroes; the difference in school buildings; in the length of time the schools ran; the difference in salaries paid Negro and white teachers; the inability of Negroes to vote; the brutal treatment of Negroes, including lynching; the economic dependence of Negroes upon whites; the way in which news about Negroes was handled in the press; and, most of all, the manner in which Negroes accepted their denigration tended to make each new generation believe that they were indeed inferior. Although I had never accepted my assigned status—or lack of it—I knew that I had to prove my worth, my ability. How could I know I was not inferior to the white man, having never had a chance to compete with him? Since such competition was impossible in the South, the arena had to be elsewhere. I had the notion—fallacious, of course—that the Yankee by nature was intellectually superior to the Southern white man, and that if I could compete in New England with the naturally superior Yankee I would have *prima facie* evidence that Negroes were not inferior. It did not take me long to discover that Yankee superiority was as mythical as Negro inferiority. In my early years, however, the conviction was strong; the challenge very real. Yankee superiority was the gauntlet thrown down; I had to pick it up.

During my senior high school year, I tried hard to make a connection with a Northern school. I wrote for and received catalogues from several Northern institutions, among them Dartmouth and Brown. I knew that Dartmouth was Daniel Webster's college, and that John Hope, the first

Negro president of Morehouse College, was a graduate of Brown. But the catalogues from Dartmouth and Brown frightened me and convinced me of two things: Financially I could not afford either institution; and judging by the curricula I was not academically prepared to attend either of them. I learned, after going to Bates, the folly of making final judgments without thorough investigation, solely on the basis of reading catalogues. I finished Bates in four years after high school graduation. At the time, however, having been frightened away from trying to enter Brown or Dartmouth, I decided that I would spend a year in a Northern prep school and then seek admission to some New England college. So I wrote to several such schools, but I received little or no encouragement from any one of them. The one positive reply which I received had the virtue of honesty but nonetheless was disappointing, dispiriting. The Reverend Lorin Webster, L.H.D., rector of Holderness School in New Hampshire, stated clearly that he could not take me because of my race. Quite often Northern schools "put it on the South" when they refused to accept Negro students, but the rector of Holderness School "told it like it was." I have kept Mr. Webster's letter:

Camp Wachusett
Holderness School
Portsmouth, New Hampshire
The Reverend Lorin Webster, L.H.D.
Rector

Mr. B. E. Mays
107 West 132 Street
New York City July 31, 1916
My dear Sir:

I wish I could help you in your laudable desire to get an education, but if I should admit a boy of your race to Holderness School I should lose several students. So I am obliged to decline to receive you.*

Very truly yours,
L. Webster

I had already met Northern prejudice in a small way in New York in 1915 and also in Detroit. Now I had met it in the Holderness School in New Hampshire, in a letter which banished all hope that I might be able to enter a Northern college in September of 1916. When Professor F. Marcellus Staley of State College, who knew of my desire to go North for my college work, learned that I had not been accepted by a Northern school, he recommended that I go to Virginia Union in Richmond, Virginia, although

*Holderness School has long since abandoned the policy of racial exclusiveness.

he had done his own undergraduate work at Morehouse and further study at Cornell. I accepted his advice and entered the freshman class at Virginia Union in September, 1916. I was amused, when I got to Richmond, to find that many Virginians considered themselves "Northerners"; and some of them referred to me as "my friend Mays from the South"!

I found a more serious-minded student body at Virginia Union than I had previously known. The college course was firmly established there although, like other colleges for Negroes, Virginia Union had its academy or high school department. There were a few seniors in the college, and one or two in the seminary, who could be respected for their scholarship and character. There were a few students, too, in my class whom I admired and who were worthy competitors in the pursuit of academic excellence. I got the impression that the faculty at Union was able. It was a racially mixed faculty and, for the first time in my life, I came to know a few white persons who expressed an interest in Negroes. This was a wholly new experience for me. The one thing that impressed me most at Virginia Union was the fact that in the opinion of the students the Negro professors were just as able as the white ones. The Negro teachers presented a good image to the Negro students, an image which was perhaps quite as important as the content of their courses.

I did well academically at Virginia Union. I took college mathematics, English, German, and Latin. At the end of the first semester of my freshman year, approximately half of my classmates had flunked college algebra, and I was chosen to teach mathematics to those who had failed. The money for teaching the course came as a boon, for I had not saved enough money as a Pullman porter the previous summer to carry me through the year. A dining-hall job and the student-teaching job enabled me to pay my bills for the year.

Despite the claim that Virginians were Northerners, I found the same racial pattern in Richmond that I had experienced in South Carolina. Orangeburg and Greenwood did not have streetcars. We walked where we wanted to go or rode in buggy or wagon or on mule back. Richmond had its segregated steetcars, with Negroes sitting in the back. I was seeing segregation in a large Southern city for the first time, but it was the same old segregation that I had known since infancy. We freshmen had heated arguments about whether Negroes should or should not patronize the segregated theaters in Richmond. I went to a segregated theater just once during my school year at Virginia Union, and I decided then, in the academic year 1916-17, that never again would I go to a segregated theater. I have kept that vow. I held then, as I do now, that there is a difference between voluntary segregation and compulsory segregation. One has to accept compulsory segregation or pay a penalty; but one does not have to accept voluntary segregation. I had to accept Richmond's segregation on the streetcars if I wanted to get where I had to go. But it was in no way necessary for me voluntarily to accept an embarrassing seat in a Jim Crow theater. Another situation which we students at Union discussed was the fact that all the Negro schools in Richmond had white principals. We could discuss this, but we couldn't do anything to bring about a change. Richmond Negroes generally did not even discuss it very much. They accepted what "had always been."

Before leaving Virginia Union, I had an important decision to make. I was old enough to be a soldier in World War I. In November, 1916, Woodrow Wilson had been re-elected President of the United States, partly on the slogan "He Kept Us Out of War." But despite Wilson's intentions, on April 6, 1917, the United States entered the war against Germany. I can still hear the silence of that Richmond audience when William Howard Taft spoke there, ending his speech with the statement, "The United States is now at war with Germany."

A Jim Crow officers' training camp was set up in Des Moines, Iowa, and college Negroes were being recruited to go to Des Moines to be trained to become officers in the United States Army. Wilson coined a phrase that became famous: "We are fighting to make the world safe for democracy." Many of my friends were making applications for a place at the camp in Des Moines. What was I to do? I had known everything but democracy in South Carolina. I was finishing my freshman year in college and would be twenty-three my next birthday—easily five years retarded owing to the crippling educational circumstances imposed upon me by my native state of South Carolina. So I registered for military service, but did not volunteer to go to Des Moines. I decided to go on to Bates and wait to be drafted. Nor did I join the SATC at Bates, as President Chase advised. When the draft forms came, one question on them was, "Do you claim exemption for any reason?" I replied, "No, except that I am a student for the ministry." I was classified 4-D, and the war ended before I was reclassified. If I had been visibly present in Greenwood County, I might not have been deferred.

I enjoyed my year at Virginia Union and left only because I was still determined to go to a New England college. My mathematics teacher, Roland A. Wingfield, and Charles E. Hadley, the YMCA faculty adviser, who also taught chemistry, were both graduates of Bates. Learning of my desire to study in New England, they wrote to President George Colby Chase of Bates in my behalf. As a result, I was accepted as a sophomore on probation, with the understanding that if I did passing work in the first six weeks' tests I would be a full-fledged sophomore. I passed my tests successfully.

President Hovey of Virginia Union did not take kindly to my going to Bates. The friends with whom I worked out of Grand Central Station as a summer Pullman porter were even more insistent that I remain in Richmond. Their argument was that I would freeze to death in Maine; and that Maine was too far away from South Carolina in case I had to go home in an emergency. I was grateful for the interest in my welfare that prompted their advice, but once more I had to make my own decision. I entered Bates in September, 1917.

My friends were almost prophetic in their prediction about my freezing in Maine. Since I was too far away to go home at Christmastime, I stayed on the campus through the 1917 holidays. On Christmas Day, it was forty-four below zero—one of the coldest Christmases in Lewiston's history, and my first winter out of the South. I remember well that it was a clear day, the Maine sky beautiful, and the ground sparkled with snow. I accepted the job of clearing away the snow at President Chase's residence. I had not been working very long when the president's daughter invited me to come inside and get warm. I assured her that I was quite comfortable, not knowing that I had reached the point of numbness where I could not recognize how cold I was. When I finally did go inside, my fingers, toes, and ears were aching most painfully. I was told that had I remained out in the cold much longer my toes and fingers would probably have had to be amputated. For several months thereafter my toes felt numb. Even now, more than fifty years later, my feet are still very sensitive to cold. I wear two pairs of socks in winter, and when I am sitting indoors I can tell when the temperature is dropping outside. My feet are my thermometer. I say jokingly that my feet got cold in Maine in 1917 and they have never been warm since!

The weather was cold but the hearts at Bates were warm. It was a dreary day and a lonely ride from New York to Lewiston, Maine, that day in September, 1917, when I was traveling to a strange land where I didn't know a single soul. The Bates brand of friendliness started on the train. As I recall, I was the only Negro aboard. A Bates student, returning to school, introduced himself and asked where I was going. When I answered, "Bates College," he told me he was a student there and would be glad to help me find housing. This he did, and I have never forgotten, nor can I ever forget, his warm friendliness. Shortly after arriving in Lewiston, I met Julian Coleman, a Negro in the senior class, from Pawtucket, Rhode Island. That first night when he offered me shelter marked the beginning of a close friendship that lasted until his death a few years ago. He was one of the finest men I have ever known.

There were only a few other Negroes at Bates my first years there. I was living in a predominantly white world, and how different a world it was from any I had known before! The teachers and students were friendly and kind. I was treated as a person, as a human being, respected for what I was. Faculty and students, men and women, greeted me when I met them on campus and on the street. We met and mingled as peers, not as "superior" and "inferior." This was a new experience for me. I was getting another view of the white man—a radically different view. They were not all my enemies. For the first time, whether on campus or in the town of Lewiston, whether alone or in a group, I felt at home in the universe. I do not mean to give the impression that there was no race prejudice at all at Bates in my time. We Negro students quickly spotted and knew the few students who gave evidence of prejudice, but their number was negligible and didn't exercise any influence on the Bates College family as a whole or on us in particular. The one time I was called "nigger" by a white student waiter, the white students handled the situation so decisively that there was no need for me to speak. On three other occasions when I fancied there was discrimination, I think now that I was mistaken. There were only a few Negroes in the whole state of Maine; and in the small towns and rural areas a Negro was really a curiosity. White children stared at me, their eyes wide with curiosity, but there was nothing mean, nothing offensive in their curiosity. To the great embarrassment of a friend, his small daughter once tried to rub off my dark skin and asked me why I didn't have skin like her daddy's. Once in Lewiston, a small white boy saw me and called to his mother, "Here is a nigger!" Such incidents were rare; there really was very little manifestation of prejudice in Maine.

When I arrived at Bates, I had ninety dollars in my pocket. A year's expenses totaled about $400. Without Bates' concern for me, I would never have been able to meet my financial obligations for my three years there. Bates had a rule not to give scholarships to transfer students, not even to one with a "straight A" record such as I had brought with me from Virginia Union. For the first year, I was able to borrow some money from the college's loan fund. In my junior and senior years, I was on scholarship. I worked in the dining hall for a while; was a student helper in the library; served as janitor of a small academic building; washed dishes in a restaurant in downtown Lewiston; worked as a Pullman porter during summers and holidays; and painted floats one summer in a shipyard in Boston. My brother, who was farming in South Carolina, sent me fifty dollars while I was at Bates, and a friend in South Carolina sent five or ten dollars occasionally. Obviously, I did not suffer from affluence!

I had read in the Bates catalogue that very soon after the opening of the college year the sophomore declamation contest would be held. I had won two prizes in public speaking during my high school years at State, so I made up my mind that I was going to try to win the contest at Bates. I didn't know whether one could choose his own declamation subject, but I decided to take a chance. I had been mightily impressed with an oration entitled "The Supposed Speech of John Adams." I committed it to memory; and all summer long I rehearsed it before the mirror of a Pullman car on the New York Central Railroad. When the announcement of the sophomore declamation contest was made, I presented myself, asking permission to use the speech which I already knew quite well. I was permitted to enter, and was chosen as one of the six to compete in the finals.

Someone had told me that Mrs. Fred Pomeroy, wife of Professor Pomeroy who was head of the Biology Department, was good in speech and drama. She had studied speech in Boston. I was taking a course in biology and asked Professor Pomeroy to find out whether his wife would train me for the contest. He assured me that she would be happy to help me and indeed she was most gracious in coaching me. Campus gossip had it that I could not hope to win because of my Southern drawl. This was news to me, since I had always assumed that the Southern drawl was uniquely the possession of Southern whites. However, the rumor intensified my determination to win, and I did, by unanimous decision of the three judges. This victory gave me campus recognition by both faculty and students. After only eight weeks at Bates, I had won first prize in the sophomore declamation contest, and I was elated to win over my five white competitors. That contest was won on the Pullman cars of the New York Central Railroad, and through the coaching of Mrs. Fred Pomeroy and "Professor Rob," as Grosvenor May Robinson, professor of Speech at Bates, was affectionately called.

I have always been deeply appreciative when people did things for me that they were in no way obligated to do. I shall never forget Mrs. Pomeroy, and as long as she was alive I went to see her whenever I was in Lewiston. In the same way, I shall never forget Professor Levister at South Carolina State who lent me seventeen dollars to buy a cap and uniform for my first job; Professor Nix who made it possible for me to be graduated from high school in three years; Professors Wingfield and Hadley of Virginia Union, who interceded for me at Bates; the student who befriended me on the train while I was en route to Bates; and Julian Coleman who extended himself to help me adjust at Bates and who was as ecstatic as a child with a new toy when I won the declamation contest.

My victory in the declamation contest also attracted the attention of A. Craig Baird, professor of English and Debating coach. The same afternoon that I won first prize in the contest, Professor Baird visited my room to urge me to try out for the debating team. At first I refused on the grounds that I needed all my time for study, particularly since I had to do other work in order to meet expenses. But Baird did not accept "No" so easily. He went away, but in a day or two he was back. On the third time around, he convinced me that I should try to make the varsity debating team. He told me of the fine record Bates had made, the finest in the nation, having won in recent years forty-two decisions out of fifty-two debates. Accordingly, I went out for the tryouts and made the team, although I did not participate in intercollegiate debate during my sophomore year.

Until I entered Bates, I had always been a "straight A" student. During my first semester at Bates, I made only one A, and was embarrassed and chagrined to receive the first and only D in my whole academic career. In the second semester, I made three B's and three A's. In my junior year, my record was ten A's, five B's, and three C's. In my senior year, I received eight A's, two B's, and one C. I was one of the fifteen to be graduated with honors.

Amusingly enough, that solitary A that graced my first semester record was made in Greek, the subject that was most difficult for me and troubled me most. Paul Tilden, who was a student in that class, made me the object of his rather unkind amusement. I had particular difficulty with pronunciation, and whenever I recited Paul Tilden had a good chuckle or laugh at my expense, so much so that Professor Chase rebuked him. His obvious contempt for my efforts was painfully embarrassing to me; but perhaps I should be grateful to him for intensifying my determination to master Greek. I can recall that once, after his amusement had been especially exasperating, I studied Greek until midnight and got up at three A.M. to study more. I asked Professor Chase for a conference to discuss the difficulty I was having. He invited me to his home, analyzed the problem, made some suggestions, and assured me that I had the ability to do the job. Immediately I began to improve, and by the end of the semester I had made an A. I was just plain curious to find out what my fun-making friend had made; and I was mean enough to gloat because he had made a B. I must admit that that B never did become a source of sorrow for me! Later my heckler became much more friendly and wanted us to study Greek together. It was a subject that was never easy for me; but by consistently diligent work I was able to make one B and five A's in the six semesters in which I studied Greek at Bates. These good grades, however, did not endear the subject to me—they had been too hard-won—and I refused to teach Greek at Morehouse when I went there in 1921. While President at Morehouse, I always urged every student to seek an early conference with his teacher if he was having difficulty with a subject.

I confess I was disappointed when I was not elected to Phi Beta Kappa at graduation—that honor came fifteen years later. It did not lessen my disappointment when several students and three professors expressed surprise that I was not among those elected. Two professors predicted that I would make PBK in the future, another that I would do quite as well in life as any of my Phi Beta Kappa classmates—or better. Their predictions were cold comfort at the time. At first I was inclined to blame racial prejudice for my failure, but I could not really justify that position. Five of my six semesters at Bates might well have been considered outstanding, but not the first one. I was objective enough to admit that though the fact that I was adjusting to a new physical and spiritual environment might well explain those low grades, it could not erase or change them. Moreover, things had gone too well for me at Bates to make excuses by ascribing prejudice and discrimination to the Phi Beta Kappa Committee. In order to be accurate on this point, I have reviewed the official transcript of my Bates record. In summary, I made twenty-two A's, thirteen B's, six C's, and one D. Though possibly these grades represent an A-minus or B-plus average, I am sure that the six C's and the one D spoke loudly in that Phi Beta Kappa Committee meeting. Then, too, I had spent only three years at Bates, and my "straight A" record at Virginia Union was not taken into account. It may appear that I attached undue importance to my grades. They were tremendously important to me, but not just for themselves. They were the evidence I had promised myself to produce, the proof that superiority and inferiority in academic achievement had nothing to do with color of skin. Only in New England, I had felt, could I get the evidence; in New England I had produced the proof.

I made the debating team my first year at Bates (sophomore year), but there were enough experienced debaters so that I was not used then. That was just as well, because it enabled me to strike my academic stride during the second semester. The junior year, however, was a great disappointment to me, for not once in that year did I get to debate. It was customary at Bates for a varsity debater to try out each fall in order to make the team, but this was not an ordinary fall. Bates was eager to debate larger and more prestigious colleges, and the chance came in the fall of 1918 when Cornell agreed to debate a subject of their own choosing. Since they gave us only three weeks, there was no time for tryouts; but there were four of us carried over from the year before, so the rules were waived and three of the four carry-over students were chosen to debate Cornell. I was not one of the three. Immediately after the Cornell debate, which Bates won, the opportunity came for Bates to debate Harvard, again on short notice. The debating committee chose the same three men who had defeated Cornell. This apparently deliberate exclusion from both debates made me furious. I believed then, and I believe now, that if all four debaters had been white, all four would have been used in the two debates. It may be that race had nothing to do with the selections. It is difficult to prove that it did. It is even more difficult to believe that it did not.

Since my three debating colleagues had not had to participate in the tryouts that fall, I stubbornly refused to participate in them, on the ground that my status was identical to that of my associates who had debated Cornell and Harvard. I won the battle and was continued on the squad without having to try out. However, the college against which I was scheduled to participate in debating that year withdrew from the contest; so my junior year passed without my participation in intercollegiate debate. In my senior year I was the last speaker and captain of the Bates debating team that defeated Tufts College in the spring of 1920.

Besides being a varsity debater and winner of the sophomore declamation contest, I was among the finalists in both the junior and senior oratorical contests. My classmates elected me Class Day Orator. I was a member of the YMCA Cabinet and represented Bates at the Northfield YMCA Conference in 1919. The members of the Bates Forum and the Philhellenic Club also elected me their president.

The social life at Bates was no particular concern of mine. I had gone there primarily for academic reasons. Then, too, when I entered Bates I was engaged to be married and was corresponding almost daily with Ellen Harvin, who had become my fiancée before I was graduated from high school and whom, as I have mentioned before, I married two months after my college graduation. There were fewer than fifty Negroes in Lewiston and only one Negro girl whom the Negro men at Bates seemed to like very much. Unfortunately, she was the girl friend of a jealous Portugese, so we kept our distance. Nevertheless, I became friends with several of my women classmates and have kept in touch with some of them through the years.

There was only one time during my three years at Bates that I experienced physical fear. Thomas Dixon's novel, *The Klansman*, had been made into a motion picture and released under the title *The Birth of a Nation*. Along with other Negro students at Bates, I went to see it. It was a vicious, cynical, and completely perverted characterization of Negroes. Even in Maine, the picture aroused violent emotions and stirred up racial prejudice. Certain parts of it evoked violent words and threats from the audience. My fellow Negro students and I were not sure we would be able to get back to the campus unmolested. This was my only experience with a prejudiced and hostile audience during my years at Lewiston. As those of us who are older may recall, this vile picture, despite protests by Negroes, was shown throughout the United States. The author of the book, Thomas Dixon, was a minister in North Carolina on Sundays; at other times he devoted his mediocre talents to writing books designed to inflame prejudice between Negroes and whites and between whites and Asians as well.

I spent three wonderful years at Bates. I have related some of my disappointments; but they were as nothing compared to the rich harvest I gleaned from my association with the Bates faculty and students. I still knew no white Southerners whom I considered my friends, but I had made many friends at Bates and my racial attitude was undergoing a tremendous change. Most of my professors are dead, but as long as they were alive I delighted in calling on them whenever I returned to Lewiston.

One of my dreams came true at Bates. Through competitive experience, I had finally dismissed from my mind for all time the myth of the inherent inferiority of all Negroes and the inherent superiority of all whites—articles of faith to so many in my previous environment. I had done better in academic performances, in public speaking, and in argumentation and debate than the vast majority of my classmates. I concede academic superiority to not more than four in my class. I had displayed more initiative as a student leader than the majority of my classmates. Bates College made these things possible. Bates College did not "emancipate" me; it did the far greater service of making it possible for me to emancipate myself, to accept with dignity my own worth as a free man. Small wonder that I love Bates College! It was a moving and wonderful experience to return there in 1970 for my 50th class reunion.

Although I had been licensed for the ministry in 1919 (I was ordained two years later, in 1921) I came to my senior year in college still undecided about my future plans. I was not as sure as I had been in my earlier years when the pastor and church people at Mount Zion had predicted that I would preach. Professor Halbert Haine Britan told me he could get me a fellowship at the University of Chicago in the Department of Philosophy. I had done well in mathematics and had given some thought to doing graduate work in that field. And knowing my interest in religion, Professor Herbert Howell Purinton was ready to speak for me at Newton Theological Seminary and the University of Chicago. Religion finally won out over both philosophy and mathematics.

Although I had set my sights on the University of Chicago during my high school days, I was interested in hearing about Newton Theological Seminary. When the Newton "scout" came to Bates recruiting in the spring of 1920, he made it quite plain that Newton was not interested in Negro students, and advised me to go for my theological training to Virginia Union University, where I had spent my freshman college year. So it was not only Holderness School that didn't want Negroes; the famous Newton Theological Seminary was similarly prejudiced. Professor Purinton assured me that I need feel no concern over Newton's racially closed doors because the University of Chicago was superior.

My choice of the University of Chicago for graduate work was largely determined by the influence of N. C. Nix, one of my high school teachers at State College. My bride, whom I had married in Newport News, Virginia, in August of 1920, returned to South Carolina to teach. I returned North to work as a Pullman porter that fall, hoping to earn enough to pay a few debts, and to save enough to enter the Divinity School of the University of Chicago in January, 1921. When January came, however, I was no more financially able to matriculate in the University of Chicago than I had been to enter Bates in the fall of 1917. I had arrived at Bates with $90 in my pocket; I landed in Chicago with $45.

Though I had worked in the Pullman service for several summers and had a good record, I was fired in Boston in December, 1920. I had hoped to work my way to Chicago as a Pullman porter, so that I would have at least forty or fifty dollars on arrival. Two things were responsible for my being fired.

Boston was my headquarters and the district out of which I worked. It was customary not to pay a porter when he was being held for service in his home district. If things were slack and a porter couldn't get an assignment, he received no pay, even if ten or more days passed before any work developed. But a New York porter in Boston would be paid. Porters not regularly in the employ of the Pullman Company resented this partiality. Some local officials would try to save the Pullman Company money by detaining their own men for special service while giving assignments to porters from other districts.

Either in October or November, Harvard played Yale one Saturday afternoon in New Haven. The Boston porters who came into Boston any day of that week, Monday through Friday, were held in Boston to guarantee that there would be enough porters to service the parlor cars which would be needed for fans going to the Harvard-Yale football game. Several Boston porters came in on Monday, and instead of being sent out again they were told to report on Saturday to go to New Haven. Porters from other districts who came into Boston were assigned out. The Boston porters protested to no avail. So a group of us decided to make out our own time slips and sent a letter to the Pullman superintendent in Chicago explaining the situation and requesting pay for the week. Chicago authorized Boston to pay us. Our signatures had appeared only on the time slips; however, since I was the only college man in the group the Pullman officials in Boston immediately suspected me of initiating the appeal to Chicago. The porters had previously agreed that the group was responsible rather than any one person, and although no one was fired for this incident, my name was suspect.

Later, I had an altercation with a Pullman conductor. Early one morning, around six o'clock, I was to discharge a passenger at Syracuse. While he dressed, I put his bed away so he would have a place to sit until arrival in Syracuse. Just as my passenger got off, a gentlemen came up and asked me whether I had a seat to Buffalo. I said "Yes." When I told the conductor, he replied that I had no space. I explained, telling him that his diagram would show that I had put one passenger off at Syracuse. The conductor kept insisting that I had no space; and even if I had discharged a passenger, the berth had not been put away. I was equally insistent because it was I who had put the berth away. The conductor and I exchanged hot words. He said that he was going to report me. Since the conductor was the porter's superior officer, a black mark from him could spell disaster—and did. The conductor carried out his threat; he reported me to the Boston superintendent.

Christmas was close, and I had to make the trip to South Carolina to see Ellen, my wife, whom I had not seen since our marriage in August. I had it all planned. From Columbia, South Carolina, I expected to work as a porter to Chicago to save what little money I had and to pick up a few tips en route. My plans fell apart. I was unable to get any work out of Columbia. Instead I was given an assignment on a "deadhead" car (when a Pullman car is not in service a porter is sent along to protect it) which was hitched to a slow-moving freight.

In Richmond, I learned that my deadhead car had been assigned to Pittsburgh and not Washington. I tried to get an assignment to Chicago out of Richmond. No success. I decided to beg the train conductor to let me go from Richmond to Washington on my Pullman keys. Kindly conductors occasionally permitted this, and luckily this conductor consented. Cheered by his consideration, I had hopes that Washington would assign me to a car bound for Chicago. I almost made it. The slip assigning me to Chicago had been put in my hand, and then I was told "Wait a minute!" and the assignment clerk went through some letters and told me that since I was wanted in Boston he would have to send me there. As soon as I got to Boston, the man in the yard office told me that the superintendent wanted to see me. I knew what was coming. It took few words for the superintendent to tell me that I was fired and to demand the return of my keys.

This was on Friday, December 31, 1920. I had forty-seven dollars in my pocket and a thousand miles separated me from the University of Chicago. I told Bryant, another porter and my friend, my plight and how much I wanted to enroll in the University of Chicago on Monday, January 3, 1921. I was talking to the right man. Bryant and I had had adjacent cars going to Buffalo one summer day. However, he got sick and was unable to care for his passengers, so I took care of his car as well as my own. In Buffalo, Bryant had to be taken to a hospital. After putting away his car and mine, I went to the hospital to see my friend and took him the $13.60 his passengers had given me in tips. When I explained my predicament to Bryant, he was eager to help me, again expressing his appreciation for my earlier kindness to him. Bryant had an assignment out of Springfield, Massachusetts, for Cleveland, on New Year's night. First he offered to give me his assignment to Cleveland, but we both realized that he would lose his job if he did so. Next he offered to take a chance and let me deadhead with him to Springfield, Massachusetts, and from Springfield to help me hide from the conductor until we got to Cleveland.

I was to join Bryant on his deadhead car at Back Bay Station. But Bryant's deadhead car was hitched to a fast train which did not stop at Back Bay. When the train came whizzing through Back Bay, it was literally flying. Bryant was on the platform of his car waving frantically and I was left standing on the platform of the station holding my bags. This was on Saturday night, January, 1, 1921. I was due to register at the University of Chicago on Monday morning, January 3.

I decided to pay my way on the next train from Back Bay to Springfield and look for my friend, who was not to leave Springfield for Cleveland until late that New Year's night. My ticket cost me $3.17. When I found Bryant in Springfield, making down his beds, I put on a white coat to help him finish the job and receive his passengers. This was all very well; but how was I to get to Cleveland without the conductor's discovering me and pulling me off the train? Bryant and I agreed that I would evade the conductor by getting behind him as he went through the train checking his passengers and collecting tickets. When a conductor checks his passengers, he usually takes a seat somewhere and makes up his record. While the conductor was preparing his records, Bryant hid me in a vacant upper berth, and there I slept until late the next morning. Somewhere between Rochester and Buffalo, when Bryant was sure the conductor was not around, he awakened me.

I dressed and Bryant stowed me away in the linen closet. To keep me from suffocating, he put a cord on the door so that it wouldn't slam and lock. To protect me further, he placed the soiled linen bag in front of me. Twice the conductor came to that closet for something, but I was securely hidden. Thus concealed and barricaded, I rode into Cleveland, where Bryant's car terminated. This was Sunday night, January 2. Registration at the University of Chicago was less than twelve hours away—and I was still three hundred miles away.

Luck was still with me. When I got to Cleveland, the Pullman man in charge was short of porters. He needed someone to man a car to Toledo. I explained that I had to register the next morning at the University of Chicago, and pleaded with him to send me to Chicago. I had been fired and was no longer in the employ of the Pullman company but, fortunately, another set of keys was in my pocket. How I got them, I do not now know. (My mother, perhaps, would have considered them an answer to her prayers!) The Cleveland man was sympathetic and told me that he had a porter coming in who was really too tired to go to Toledo, but if I would make down the car and put the passengers to bed so that the tired porter, due thirty minutes before the Chicago train was scheduled to leave, could go to bed and get some rest, he would send me to Chicago as a swing man (a porter sent along to help, but not in charge of the car). I was only too happy to accept his offer. I arrived in Chicago at eight A.M. on January 3.

Luck was still in my pocket. I had my forty-three dollars. Thanks to Bryant, I had eaten between Springfield and Cleveland. I registered on the day of my arrival in Chicago, found a place to live a few blocks from the university, and secured a job washing dishes in the Commons. There was virtually no tuition in the Divinity School. I got my meals in return for washing dishes and, if I remember correctly, got paid something besides.

Finally, at long last, I was registered at the University of Chicago, about which N. C. Nix had bragged so much and of which I had dreamed so often. Moreover, I was to come in contact with some of the university's great scholars. Despite my extremely conservative background and orthodox religious upbringing, the ultra-modern views of the University of Chicago scholars did not upset my faith. What they taught made sense to me. After three quarters of stimulating and rewarding work, I went to Morehouse College to do my first teaching.

I found more prejudice at the University of Chicago and in the city of Chicago than I had found at Bates and in the city of Lewiston. Less, of course, than I had found in Greenwood County. At the university, Negro women could not occupy the dormitories. Negro men could live in Goodspeed Hall, but only because Goodspeed was the dormitory reserved for graduate students in the Divinity School. Most Southern students, and some Northern students, would not eat at the same table with Negroes. Negro students therefore took great delight in increasing the physical activity of the prejudiced. In the university Commons, where the majority of the students ate, the service was cafeteria style, so that persons went through the line, selected food, and sat wherever they chose or where there was space. Those persons who would not eat at a table with Negroes were soon spotted. Many times I saw white men and women, halfway through their meals, take up plates, silver, and glassware and move to a table where there were no Negroes. Some of us took pleasure in plaguing these people by deliberately seating ourselves at a table where some white person had fled to escape eating with Negroes. I recall one man who moved three times to avoid the Negro students, who followed him from table to table, and finally, with ill-concealed disgust, he left without finishing his meal.

At Bates, teachers spoke to Negro students on campus and downtown, especially if the Negro student was in the professor's class. I knew one or two professors at the University of Chicago in 1921 who never recognized a Negro student when off campus or on. We sometimes saw one of them with his wife, and whenever we did we spoke, calling him by name, bowing and tipping our hats. Of course, he had to return the courtesy. We enjoyed that response. Lewiston restaurants were open to Negro students without discrimination. Not so in Chicago in 1921. Most of the restaurants, perhaps all, in the vicinity of the University of Chicago denied service to Negroes. Interesting and stimulating though the University of Chicago was, it was not quite the "heaven" Professor Nix's fond recollection had painted—at least not with regard to racial discrimination.

Chapter V

Atlanta, 1921–1924

How fortuitous is the life of man! A simple contact may be decisive in determining one's career. It is highly improbable that I would have spent thirty years at Morehouse (three as teacher and twenty-seven as president) had it not been for that summer day in 1921 when John Hope, then president of Morehouse College, came to the library of the University of Chicago and invited me to teach college mathematics and high school algebra in his college.

John Hope tempted me by offering me the "lucrative" salary of $1,200 for a teaching year of eight months, to begin in September, 1921. However, too much was involved for me to grab his offer. I no longer planned to do graduate work in mathematics, for Ellen and I had decided that it was in the field of religion that I would seek my career. Even if going to Morehouse did not mean changing my ultimate course, it certainly necessitated delay in my pursuit of a doctorate in some phase of religion or theology. Wisely, Mr. Hope did not ask for an immediate reply but suggested that he would see me after I had had time to think.

This was my first job offer since my graduation from Bates. The more I thought about that $1,200, the bigger it looked: 10.7 times larger than the $112 I would have received had I accepted a teaching position in Greenwood County after finishing high school in 1916; and fourteen times as much as the forty cents a day I had made chopping cotton from sun to sun. It was not difficult to find other reasons why I should accept President Hope's offer. I had no money and it was not clear to me how I was going to be able to continue my work at the University of Chicago. Moreover, if I went to Atlanta I would be closer to my wife who was teaching at Morris College in Sumter, South Carolina. Our continued separation was difficult but was an economic necessity. From Atlanta I would be able to visit her once or twice a month. Finally, the decision was made: I would go to Morehouse.

The decision to go to Morehouse created the immediate problem of where to get the money. I needed at least eighty dollars. I had to buy a ticket to Atlanta; I needed a few items of clothing; and I wished to buy a diamond ring. When we had married the year before, I had been unable to buy Ellen a ring. Eighty dollars would buy a ticket to Atlanta, some cheap articles of clothing, and a diamond ring. I had seen "the" ring in a pawnshop window for $37 and I wanted very much to get it for Ellen.

For three days I walked the streets of Chicago trying to find somebody who would lend me eighty dollars. No fairy godmother appeared to grant my three wishes; no good Samaritan seemed about to haul me from my ditch! A friend suggested that I wire Mr. Hope for railroad fare to Atlanta, but I firmly rejected the idea for I had no intention of going to Morehouse under obligation to my employer. Rather than borrow money from Morehouse or the president of the college, I would have walked to Atlanta! Finally a South Carolina lawyer named Williams who practiced in Chicago came to my rescue by signing a note for me. It was due in ninety days and I was only too happy to pay when I got my second salary check; but as grateful as I was to the lender for trusting me, I resolved never again to find myself in this position. I had not forgotten my Orangeburg difficulty in borrowing seventeen dollars. I have never broken my vow.

With my ticket, a few clothes, and my ring for Ellen, I took leave for Atlanta. By the time this book is published, I shall have lived in Atlanta thirty-nine years, more than half my life.

I made history at Morehouse by teaching the first course in calculus ever to be given there. The times do change! Never during my twenty-seven years as president of Morehouse did I even consider hiring anyone to teach mathematics unless he had an M.A.—preferably a Ph.D. in that field.

Going to Atlanta meant entering a new world in Negro-white relations. My earliest relationship in South Carolina had been largely rural and depressing. My one year in Richmond, Virginia, was largely limited to my school associations. Negro-white relations at Bates were pleasant; and during my three quarters at the University of Chicago, not too bad. It was in Atlanta, Georgia, that I was to see the race problem in greater depth, and observe and experience it in larger dimensions. It was in Atlanta that I was to find that the cruel tentacles of race prejudice reached out to invade and distort every aspect of Southern life. The picture was not pretty:

Since 1891, the Negro in Georgia had been segregated on streetcars and railroads.

Since 1908, he had been bereft of his ballot.

In 1906, the Atlanta Race Riot ravaged the city.

In 1915, the Ku Klux Klan had been reborn on Stone Mountain, in a suburb of Atlanta.

Less than two years before my arrival in Atlanta, the return of Negro soldiers from Europe at the end of World War I had created a situation of explosive tension. Negroes who had been exploited, demeaned, and segregated all their lives had been sent to Europe to fight to "make the world safe for democracy," a democracy they had never known. Southern Negroes, who had fought the "war to end wars," had never been allowed to vote in their native land. Many of them had relatives who had been lynched. (A few, on their return to the United States, were themselves lynched.) But they had gone to Europe to fight for democracy.

As soon as the war was over, November 11, 1918, racial tension rose all over the nation. Writing on this point, Wilma Dykeman and James Stokely say in *Seeds of Southern Change* that "the winter following the armistice of World War I spread a chill across the South more penetrating than any blast of wind or snow." Will Alexander, who had worked hard for interracial cooperation, and who headed the Interracial Commission in Atlanta for twenty-five years after World War I, was amazed to discover how rapidly the tension increased, all over the South, within forty-eight hours after the peace treaty was signed.

In many a local community, Negro soldiers were told, "Take off those uniforms and act like a nigger should." Around this time, lynching increased in the United States. In 1918, the year the war ended, sixty Negroes were lynched. In 1919, the year following the war, twenty-six riots broke out in the United States, the worst of them occurring in Chicago. I saw the aftermath of that riot when I went there as a Pullman porter in the summer of 1919. The escalating of racial tension in the postwar years seemed inevitable. John Hope Franklin (*From Slavery to Freedom*, p. 482) tells us that thirty-eight persons were killed in the Chicago Riot (fifteen whites and twenty-three Negroes), 537 were injured, and more than one thousand families, mostly Negro, were left homeless. The riots were also very bad in Washington, Omaha, Philadelphia, Knoxville, and Elaine, Arkansas.

Negro leaders and the President of the United States wanted to reduce the mounting racial tension, hoping against hope that race riots could be avoided. Rumors that Negro soldiers had been cowards and that they raped

French women were widely circulated, adding fuel to the fires of hatred and distrust. Dr. Robert Russa Moton, of Tuskegee Institute, was sent to Europe to investigate and to publicize his findings to the United States. On April 19, 1919, the Birmingham *Pipe* carried this headline: NEGRO SOLDIERS WIN LASTING FAME DESPITE THE WHISPERING GALLERY SHOUTS R. R. MO[R]TON OF THE TUSKEGEE INSTITUTE. In brief, Moton discovered that the number of French women raped by Negro soldiers had been highly exaggerated, that of the seven charged with rape only two were found guilty and convicted, and that the percentage of rape among Negro soldiers was no higher than among white soldiers. Furthermore, Moton's investigation showed that the courage of Negro soldiers was equal—neither inferior nor superior—to that of all other soldiers. Although his document did not stop the riots, it was good to have the record set straight. I heard dozens of Negro soldiers tell how white American soldiers had tried to discredit them by telling the French that Negro soldiers were rapists, that they had tails, that they were not human. The Birmingham *Pipe* in its April 19, 1919, issue quoted Dr. Moton as saying:

> . . . Your record has sent a thrill of joy and satisfaction to the hearts of millions of black and white Americans, rich and poor, high and low. Black mothers and wives, sweethearts, fathers, and friends have rejoiced with you and with our country in your record.
>
> You will go back to America as heroes as you really are. You will go back as you have carried yourselves over here—in a straightforward, mannerly and modest way.

Dr. Moton advised the soldiers to find work, buy a home, save money, marry and settle down. They were urged to do nothing in peace to spoil the grand record they had made in war. In the same issue, Dr. Moton made this appeal to white soldiers:

> . . . The men of my race who will return will have many unnecessary hardships and limitations, and along many lines. What a wonderful opportunity you have, therefore, and what a great responsibility to go back to America resolved that as far as it in your power lies, you are going to see that these black men and the twelve million of people whom they represent in our great country, who have stood so loyally by you and America in peace and in war, shall have a fair and absolutely square chance with every other American citizen along every line—this is your duty and your sacred

obligation. They ask only fair play and as loyal Americans citizens they should have it.

Dr. Moton further pointed out to the white soldiers that the Negro soldiers and officers had done a heroic job in spite of hardships and discriminations. But despite the soldiers' fine performances and the eloquent rhetoric of Dr. Moton, twenty-six riots broke out in the United States and the Negro was re-locked into his pre-war status. Throughout the country, the Negro was so enmeshed in a tangle of segregation, discrimination, and disfranchisement; his physical safety and emotional well-being so constantly assaulted that a visitor from Mars would have believed that from the dawn of creation Negroes had been segregated and lynched—kept in their inferior "place," that the condition was somehow a fixed fact of nature, as irreversible as the tides.

How grim it is that when bad laws are enacted to degrade Negroes, they are implemented instantly and enforced vigorously. Law and order are maintained with clubs and guns, or whatever force is necessary. But when good laws are passed to remove the crippling constrictions placed upon Negroes, then "the mills of the gods grind slowly" indeed! As I write this, fifteen years after May 17, 1954, date of the monumental decision of the United States Supreme Court, the decision backed by Congressional law, the nation is still resisting the complete desegregation of the schools. Many sections of the country are evading the court decisions and Congressional law guaranteeing Negroes the right to vote. Their name is legion who are determined to set aside the law on open occupancy. How quick we are to implement evil laws; how loath to accept, let alone enforce, just laws. Was there even a whisper of protest when the Supreme Court made segregation the law of the land in 1896? But what a deafening chorus of angry defiance when it ruled that segregation is unconstitutional!

When I came to Atlanta to teach at Morehouse in 1921, two opposing organizations were in full swing, one vociferously, the other quietly, almost secretly; the first, the Ku Klux Klan; the latter, the Atlanta Commission on Interracial Cooperation.

The first Ku Klux Klan organization came into being as a result of the tense racial feeling which developed in the South during the Reconstruction era. The second KKK organization was founded on Stone Mountain, very near Atlanta, in December, 1915, by William Joseph Simmons, a preacher and promoter of fraternal organizations. Simmons called his organization the "Invisible Empire, Knights of the Ku Klux Klan," and he acclaimed himself the Imperial Wizard. He boasted that the leading white citizens were members of the Klan: senators, representatives, governors, mayors, city councilmen, sheriffs, chiefs of police, and policemen. He advertised the Klan as a high-class, mystic, social, patriotic society, devoted to the protection of womanhood (meaning, of course, white womanhood) and the maintenance of white, Protestant supremacy. It was anti-Catholic, anti-Jewish, anti-foreign born, and, most of all, anti-Negro.

The tension that developed between Negroes and whites when Negro soldiers returned from Europe in 1919 furnished grist for the Klan's mill. Simmons estimated that in the six years, 1915 to 1921, the Klan had grown to 100,000 members; and by 1926 the Klan claimed a membership ranging from 2,500,000 to 4,000,000.

Atlanta was the headquarters for the Klan, and the Imperial Wizard lived in Atlanta. Negroes were the chief objects of their venom; after all, Jews were at least white-skinned and most Catholics were white. Negroes were black; and the Klansmen knew well that if they attacked Negroes the law-enforcement bodies in the South would do little if anything to stop them. So when I came to Atlanta in 1921 Negroes were quite aware of the Klan, and its activities were much talked about. Fresh in memory and much discussed was the case of two Negro landowners, Asbury McClusky and Willie Peters, who had suffered the Klan's wrath. They lived on the Dixie Highway, between Winder and Athens. Both their cases confirmed what I had already learned in South Carolina: the humble Negro, if well-to-do, who tried to get along by "staying in his place," had no better chance of surviving and was liked no better than other Negroes. More about the McClusky-Peters story later.

The quiet organization, the Commission on Interracial Cooperation, was not organized until 1920, although efforts at organization were in process throughout 1919, the year of the great riots. Will Alexander, a Methodist minister, was a moving spirit in the organization of the Commission.

In 1921 it was mainly concerned with counteracting the malicious work of the Ku Klux Klan. The Commission's program soon developed to the point of bringing together Negroes and white people in local communities throughout the South for the express purpose of working to ease racial tensions and to solve some of the problems confronting Negroes and whites. This effort was something new under the sun. Heretofore, white folks had not attempted to get to know trained Negroes, had made all the decisions, and told Negroes what to do. The Commission sought to have people in the local communities, including State commissions, work together to solve local problems. Legal justice, educational equality, sanitation and housing, economic opportunity, the prevention of lynching, adequate travel and recreational facilities, and child welfare—all these were on the agenda of the Commission on Interracial Cooperation. In its early years, the Commission fought the Klan on four fronts: It publicized the churches' denunciation of the Klan; encouraged a Congressional investigation of the Klan; gathered and made available data on the Klan's activities; and fought the Klan on specific situations. Under the leadership of Will Alexander, the Commission also worked with the Southern press to persuade it to handle Negro news in a constructive manner. Later, the Commission made a major effort to stop lynching in the South and in the nation. As early as 1920, at Tuskegee, the National Association of Negro Women's Clubs urged Southern white women to take a strong position against lynching. They urged those responsible for administering the law to put down lynching and punish the lynchers. An Interracial Conference was held in Blue Ridge in August, 1920. There the women made an appeal to Christian people of the South to use the pulpit, the religious press, and denominational literature to speak out against lynching. They uncompromisingly condemned all mob violence and declared lynching a crime against the nation. It was not until 1935, however, that the Commission on Interracial Cooperation called for federal law against lynching. Heretofore it had relied on an appeal to local and state authorities.

Judged by the criteria of the 1960-1970's, the Commission was a conservative organization; it followed the segregated pattern. But in 1920, and for the next two decades, it was considered a liberal, progressive organization. The Commission never sought to abolish segregation; it worked to improve conditions between the races *within the segregated system.* If Alexander had set out in 1920 to abolish segregation, the Commission would never have been allowed to function; and Will Alexander would have been considered insane had he insisted on it. If he had tried to abolish segregation, the Ku Klux Klan would have had the support of most white Southerners who would have abolished the Commission. And yet this conservative organization was regarded as dangerous by the people "on the right," and the members of the Commission had to sneak and hide when they held meetings. Only a few white ministers would allow the Commission to hold its interracial meetings in their churches. Negroes and whites could not eat together in the churches; and for Negroes to eat in downtown restaurants was out of the question. Most of the Atlanta meetings had to be held at the Negro colleges—Atlanta University, Morehouse, Morris Brown, Spelman,

Gammon Theological Seminary, and Clark College. The Commission did its work quietly and secretly, with no fanfare.

When I came to Atlanta in 1921, the Ku Klux Klan and the Interracial Commission stood at opposite ends of the pole. The Klan was encouraging hostility and brutality. The Commission was trying to bring Negroes and white people together to solve their differences and to get rid of their prejudices. The McClusky and Peters cases illustrate vividly how wide apart were the Klan and the Commission, both with Atlanta headquarters located not far apart. To dramatize the philosophies of the two organizations and to do full justice to what each aimed to do, I rely heavily on the following stories told by Will Alexander (*Seeds of Southern Change*, p. 105) about what could happen and often did happen to prosperous Negroes, however law-abiding they were and regardless of how hard they tried to get along with white people.

In the 1920's, several Negro landowners lived on the Dixie Highway between Winder and Athens, Georgia. One was Asbury McClusky, owner of 380 acres of very good land. Asbury, who had no formal training but was intelligent and a successful farmer, not only owned his land but kept his money in two banks so that white people would not think he had too much money for a Negro. He was so anxious to get along with white people he wouldn't buy a car for fear of antagonizing them, but rode to town in a wagon, and he lived in an unpainted frame house. In hard times Asbury is reputed to have bought fertilizer not only for black neighbors but for white neighbors as well. Poor man! He thought he knew how to get along with white folks, but something terrible happened. According to *Seeds of Southern Change*:

> A Negro neighbor of Asbury's bought a piano or organ from a white man on the installment plan. Eventually there was a disagreement as to whether the installments were all paid. The white man insisted they were not and came with legal papers to repossess the organ. The Negro appealed to the courts and . . . someone had to sign the bond for the safety of the organ. This Negro . . . came and asked Asbury to sign the bond. Taken off guard, he signed the bond. That was one Negro taking the side of another Negro against a white man, and in those days that wasn't done in the South. The Klan heard about it.
>
> That night a hooded gang appeared at his house. Asbury blew out the lights and put his wife and children under the bed. He bolted the little thin front door and took his stand behind a doorstop a few feet down the little hall, armed with a single-barreled shotgun. The mob began to knock on the door.

"What do you want with me?" Asbury asked.

"Well, we're going to *show* you what we want with you."

They got an ax from the woodpile and hammered his door down. They had some torches and they thrust these in so they could see. "The son of a bitch is back of that doorstop." They began to fire.

After they had shot thirty-two bullets at him, Asbury let them have the one load of shot in his gun. They withdrew, and Asbury got away. He reached Atlanta and came to us for advice and protection. We had him locked up in the tower, a safe prison in Atlanta, for fear the crowd would come and pick him up. The next day, when we investigated, there were thirty-two bullet holes in that doorstop, and some of them in Asbury himself. One arm was completely torn up.

Angered by their failure, the mob the next night decided to go after another Negro landowner. This time the victim was Willie Peters, a little, bullet-headed fellow with considerable energy, whose wife, Odessa, had inherited a small farm from her white father. The Peters put out their lights, and Willie struggled with the mob. In some way he got hold of the pistol of one of the mobsters and pulled the trigger, emptying most of the contents of the gun in his antagonist's stomach. He then escaped and fled. The crowd beat Odessa unmercifully. She was pregnant. They left her unconscious in a roadside ditch in front of the house.

Odessa got to feeling better in a day or two, and she got word through the grapevine that Willie was in Atlanta. We had him in the tower, purely for safekeeping so that he wouldn't be taken back down there and lynched. Odessa went to the tower and found Willie locked in jail. She had never been to the city before, and she didn't understand why he was in jail. Willie couldn't explain very well . . . she thought she had to get him out.

While she was standing there a friendly white man came up and asked if she was in trouble. She certainly was, and told her story. He suggested the need of a lawyer. She didn't know any lawyer. It turned out that he was a lawyer and was willing to take her case. She finally agreed to employ him, and he presented her with a paper to sign. Odessa could not read or write, so she made her mark. In a short time Willie was out of jail, through no efforts of her attorney; but we found that the paper she had signed with her mark was a deed to her land. We had to get Willie and Odessa and the children together, and we called Governor Hugh Dorsey, this good governor that Georgia had, and told him about the case. Governor Dorsey took them down to one of his farms and put them in a house. . . .

We . . . tried to get the lawyer who had tricked her disbarred, but the other lawyers wouldn't do it. Once I told this story in the presence of a very distinguished and benign member of the Supreme Court of Georgia. After the meeting, he called me aside and said, "You oughtn't to have told that story. We oughtn't talk about those things . . ."

The judge in the county where all this happened was an honest and courageous man. He convened a special grand jury free of Klansmen, and they found true bills against a number of the mobsters whom the Negroes had recognized. For twelve months, then, we had to keep these Negroes and their witnesses together while we waited for the slow process of the law.

. . . . .

The case finally came to trial. We had to carry the witnesses in a car every day down to Winder, Georgia, and bring them back at night because we didn't dare leave them down there. The Klan had a very tough man at the head of their secret service, and he was trying to get at these people and scare them away. He did reach one or two of them, but Dr. Woofter was in charge of the situation, and he knew his way around in that atmosphere. We went to trial after many difficulties. The jury refused to find their neighbors guilty. They went scot-free.

All the things that were going on in Atlanta to degrade Negroes when I "discovered" the city in 1921 cannot be attributed to the Ku Klux Klan. The foundation upon which the Klan stood had been laid in laws and customs decades before the second birth of the Klan in 1915. Not only in major areas—the right to vote, the right to economic security, the right to education, the right to decent housing—was the Negro deprived. But these basic denials proliferated also in countless ways to guarantee that every Negro should be consistently subjected to humiliating injustices and insults calculated to destroy his self-respect, his pride, and his sense of manhood. Here again I wanted my own recollections and responses validated, so I questioned a number of representative Negroes who were adults in Atlanta in 1921 and who still live here. My own experiences and observations coincide with theirs almost one hundred percent; therefore, as I tell what I experienced and observed in Atlanta in the early 1920's, I speak for every black man and woman who was alive at that time. The experience of one black man was the experience of every black man whether he was a college professor, doctor, minister, janitor, or maid.

Riding coach on the railroad was always a humiliating experience from the time I took my first twenty-four-mile segregated ride from Greenwood to McCormick, South Carolina, and including the segregated rides I had to take from Ninety Six to Orangeburg during my high school years. So the segregated coach ride during the later part of my trip from Chicago to Atlanta was no new unpleasant experience. What was new was the fact that I had to move into a segregated coach on arrival in Evansville, Indiana. Going from Orangeburg to New York, I recall, Negroes changed to a non-segregated coach in Washington, but since they usually changed trains in Washington, moving from a segregated coach on one train to a non-segregated coach on another train somehow did not seem so embarrassing as being hustled from a non-segregared coach to a segregated coach on the same train.

Buying a ticket at a segregated window in a segregated waiting room in Atlanta and riding in a segregated coach on a train out of Atlanta was a most humiliating experience, especially when the waiting rooms and the trains were crowded. Everything was done to degrade Negroes. Usually the segregated window to serve Negroes was neglected as long as white people were waiting to be served on the other side. Often the ticket sellers were mean and rude to Negroes, making it painfully clear that they did not want to serve them. If Negroes were not able to get tickets before the train left because white people were waited on first, they could either wait for the next train or pay their fares to the conductor on the train, who was just as brusque and discourteous as the ticket sellers in the station.

Pullman tickets were not sold directly to Negroes; they could be purchased only through a certain Pullman or railroad official. Jesse O. Thomas of the Urban League was well known as the one Negro who could get Pullman reservations for Negroes. For many years after my arrival in Atlanta, any Negro who secured a Pullman ticket through a special channel was given space in the drawing room and, ironically enough, for the price of a lower berth. I know of no other situation in which a Negro got more than he paid for under the segregated system. The insult was appallingly obvious—segregation had to be maintained, and the Negro had to be hidden away even if it meant giving him a costly accommodation at a loss. Whenever this was done, the "quarantined" drawing room sold to a Negro was marked on the ticket as "Lower 13."

In and out of Atlanta, as elsewhere throughout the South, Negroes occupied the front coach on the train, half passenger car, half baggage car, next to the engine—the dirtiest, sootiest, noisiest, roughest location on the entire train. When the few seats in this coach were filled all other Negro passengers had to stand, even though the conductor was using four seats for his "office" and the white butcher was using four seats for his "store." Sometimes a "benevolent" conductor would permit an overflow of Negroes to occupy the front section of a coach reserved for whites.

Traveling was always very unpleasant and the atmosphere was usually tense. Many Negroes got into trouble, were beaten or put off trains because they protested the conductor's using four seats and the butcher's using four seats while Negroes who had paid their fares had to stand; or because they protested Negro passengers having to stand while there was space in an adjacent white coach. Listen to Dr. Hugh M. Gloster, now president of Morehouse College:

> I was traveling by coach on the "Frisco" from Atlanta to Memphis in late 1941, soon after joining the faculty of Morehouse College in Atlanta. The Jim Crow coach in which I was seated was divided into three sections by an arrangement of rods probably four to five inches apart, going up from the back of the seats at one-third intervals to the ceiling of the coach. The coach had not been designed as a three-part coach; and the rod arrangement was a device used so that if the white coach became overcrowded white passengers could be brought into the Jim Crow coach but still kept separate from the Negro passengers.
>
> When the train reached Amory, Mississippi, a large number of Negroes, mostly small town and farming people on their way to Tupelo to shop, boarded the train and took up all of the seats allotted to them, leaving many standing. They were afraid to go into another section because this would mean sitting in front of the conductor and the baggage man who were occupying the third section engaged in their usual occupation of smoking, spitting, cursing, and drinking. This meant that one-third of the coach was jammed with Negro passengers while two-thirds was not in use except where the conductor and baggage man were holding forth. The conductor got up, took up tickets from the last passengers to get on, and went back and took his seat, leaving Negroes standing, some of them women and children, rather than give up any of the unoccupied part of the coach. When he got up again a few minutes later and walked toward the baggage car, which was the next car, I said: "Conductor, these people are not taking seats because they don't want to sit in front of you and the other gentlemen." The conductor said, "You have a seat, don't you? That's what's wrong now. Too many niggers trying to run the train." I told him, "I'm not a 'nigger,' and I'm not trying to run the train. I was simply trying to make a suggestion for the comfort of the other passengers." The conductor did not reply, and although he did go back and open up the other section, I knew I was in trouble. I could see him talking to the baggage man, and I knew they were planning something for me. I told the man sitting next to me that if anything happened to me to get in touch with Dr. Benjamin E. Mays, President of Morehouse College in Atlanta, or with Attorney A. A. Latting in Memphis, Tennessee. The man did not think anything was going to happen. I knew it was.
>
> When the train stopped at Tupelo, the conductor went into the station and either called or had somebody call the police. Three, maybe five minutes later, the police boarded the train, came into the coach and demanded, "Where's this nigger who's trying to run the train?" Not one of the Negro passengers would point me out. The conductor then squeezed

into the crowded section in which I was seated and pointed me out. The police ordered me out of my seat. I refused to move, and told them that my fare was paid, I had done nothing wrong, only asked the conductor to give seats to standing passengers. When I did not get up, I was snatched out of my seat, kicked down the aisle between the two rest rooms, and thrown off the train onto the station platform. Then they started beating me. I tried to cover my face and head as best I could. They beat me for what was probably only a few minutes but which seemed like hours and then they took me off to jail. At the jail they looked into my billfold, found I was a teacher at Morehouse College, and that I had a brother who was a medical doctor at Tuskegee Institute. After that, they didn't beat me any more, but by that time I was in pretty bad shape. Although I had tried to protect my head and face, I was badly mauled; and I had suffered the most excruciating agony when one of the brutish policemen had put all of his two hundred fifty pounds into a hard kick into my groin. Even now, after many years, I can still feel the pain of that kick, and I still have aches and twinges in that part of my body.

I was thrown into a cell with four bunks. The upper bunks were pull-down affairs, which sprang back flush with the wall when the weight of the body was removed. In my semiconscious condition, it was hard for me to figure out how to pull down an upper, but I finally managed, crawled in, and there I stayed for the night. There was no medical aid whatsoever for the bruises and contusions which literally covered my entire body.

Early the next morning, I could hear the telephone ring every few minutes; and I knew somehow that these calls were about me. Later I learned that calls had come from Atlanta (Dr. Mays); from New York (the NAACP); from Memphis (Attorney Latting and my family); from Washington, D.C., and other places where the news had reached so early. Attorney Latting and Leo Zenn came from Memphis to rescue me, as did some of my wife's family from Atlanta, and the Frisco agent came to apologize. Later I sued the railroad and although I did recover some damages there was no amount which could compensate for the horror of my near-brush with death at the hands of Mississippi goon policemen.

In 1921, and for many years thereafter, servants, redcaps, and porters were the only Negroes allowed in the white waiting room in the train station in Atlanta. The white waiting room was spacious and clean; the Negro waiting room, small and dirty. The white person in charge saw to it that a porter kept the white waiting room clean; but no such demand was made of him concerning the Negro waiting room. Once, when I asked a Negro porter "Why the difference?" he told me plainly that he was expected *not* to keep the Negro waiting room as clean as the one for whites. The differential had to be maintained!

As recently as the 1940's, the station policeman threatened to shoot the late Dr. Rufus E. Clement, president of Atlanta University, for the heinous crime of having *walked through* the white waiting room to the train to avoid walking outside in the rain as would have been necessary to get to the Negro waiting room. When the weather was stormy, Negroes were forced to walk a hundred feet or more in the rain or cold to get from the entrance of the white waiting room on Spring Street to the Negro waiting room on Mitchell Street, whereas white passengers could step out of their cars or taxis directly at the entrance of their waiting room. It took a lot of doing to get the terminal officials to provide steps so that Negroes could more easily get to their little dirty segregated waiting room. The station policeman was no respecter of persons; he treated all Negroes with equal disrespect, whether it was Marian Anderson, world-famous singer, or Florence Reed—herself white but "contaminated" because she was president of Negro Spelman College. "They shall not pass" through fair Atlanta's white waiting room—this was his high and holy responsibility, which he fulfilled with great zeal.

Negroes, who were not permitted to go to the Western Union office at the train station because it was located in the white waiting room, had to send their telegrams through the Negro Travelers Aid worker stationed in the Negro waiting room. Once, when the Travelers Aid worker was absent, I went to the Western Union office in the white waiting room. While I was writing out my telegram, a white man came by, knocked off my hat, and kept going. He had *his* hat on.

The streetcar situation was much worse. On the train, Negroes did have a separate coach, but in Atlanta, in 1921, Negroes boarded the streetcar from the front, where each passenger paid his fare, but only after all the white passengers had gotten on. If all seats were taken by whites while Negroes were waiting to get on, Negroes had to stand; but even if they were standing in the aisle near the front door, where they had boarded, they had to leave by way of the back door. The law was inflexible; there were no exceptions even on lines where almost all the riders were Negroes. If white people spread themselves over most of the seats, as some did, Negroes still had to stand because a Negro could not sit beside a white man, nor could he sit in front of a white man. If a white man sat on a seat beside a Negro, the Negro was supposed to get up. On one occasion a white man plunked himself down beside a Negro educator. When the conductor insisted that the Negro get up and he refused, the conductor had him arrested. A Negro nurse, a friend of mine, was arrested because at the end of the line she got off the front of the streetcar, thinking that the front had now become the rear since the car would be headed in the opposite direction. Another friend, still living in Atlanta, saw a motorman take off his iron steering handle and strike a Negro woman with it. If the distance I had to go wasn't prohibitive, I usually walked rather than ride the streetcars in Atlanta during the years 1921-1924.

When the intercity buses started operating, the travel situation worsened. The bus driver was armed. Negroes were required to seat themselves at the rear of the bus. White passengers could sit wherever they chose, except in the very last row. More than once, I saw bus drivers refuse to permit Negro passengers to board the bus until all white passengers with tickets had gotten on. If all seats were taken, Negro passengers had to wait for the next bus whether it was due in a few hours or the next day. It mattered not to the bus company. Two or three experiences of "equality" as interpreted by the bus companies in Atlanta in 1921 sufficed—no more bus rides for me! At least on the train Negro passengers were not left to take the next train; and when a Negro went to the segregated train he could get on. But when the bus driver would not allow any Negro to get on until every white person had secured a seat, he strutted around with his pistol on his hip, and several times Negroes were beaten, shot, or arrested when they protested. Although no law gave the conductor and the butcher authority to use four seats each as "office" in the segregated Negro coach on the train, and no law gave a white bus driver authority to keep Negroes off the bus until whites were on and seated, such was the universal practice in the South. They did it, and they got away with it. Protesting to the train and bus companies evoked no response. Status made no difference. Black doctors, professors, businessmen, ministers—all felt the scourge of discrimination and segregation in travel just as did the black butler, maid, cook, and janitor. All Negroes were equal and equally inferior, so far as the white man's law was concerned.

When I came to Atlanta in 1921, and for a long time afterward, I always knew that when I went to downtown stores I stood more than a fifty-fifty chance of being insulted as soon as I entered. Before my hair became obviously white, I was greeted as "boy." "What do you want, boy?" "What can I do for you, boy?" When I became prematurely gray, I was called "Uncle" or "George" or "John." *Anything* to be offensive. How could one fail to resent such terms, knowing that they were meant as a denial of his manhood? One could walk out, as I often did. In some instances, a clerk would attempt to force me to say what I had come in for. To walk out without responding was considered impudence, a sin in Negroes. If one made it unmistakably clear that he did not consider himself a boy, he would sometimes precipitate a row, or be told, "to me you are a boy!" If one said he resented being called "Uncle" since that implied kinship, then he was really in for trouble! Here again was the constant theme: A Negro was a Negro; position or status meant nothing. For the average white man, the terms "Negro" and "status" were mutually contradictory. And the battle had to be fought all over again when a Negro went to buy shoes. After white customers had been served, the clerk would try to put a Negro buyer in a special corner, hand him the shoes, and walk away. Indeed, it was hard to find a store that would fit shoes on Negroes. If one did not fit them for himself, he had no choice but to walk out unserved. I had to buy shoes under such conditions, order them by mail, or buy them elsewhere when I would luckily be in New York or some other Northern city.

It is terrible enough for Negro men to be robbed of their essential manhood, but to deny dignity and respect to a woman merely because she is black has never been understandable to me. For this reason the phrase "Southern chivalry" rings hollow, is a "sounding brass, a tinkling cymbal." In Atlanta, in 1921, few white men or women were courteous—or was it courageous?—enough to call a Negro woman "Miss" or "Mrs." Highly educated, presumably well-bred white men were slaves to their environment. The superintendent of the Atlanta Public Schools would address a white teacher in public as "Miss"—whoever she might be—and a Negro teacher as Jane or Sallie or Mary or whatever her first name was. Demonstrations and teacher strikes were unheard of in those times. Negro teachers were afraid of losing their jobs, so they swallowed their pride and accepted this humiliation. Age and status didn't matter. When reading the Atlanta *Constitution*, the Atlanta *Journal*, and the Southern press generally, one would know that the woman referred to was Negro if no title was used. In the press, the Negro man was often referred to as "Professor," "Reverend," or "Doctor," but never "Mr." To call a Negro "Miss" or "Mrs." or "Mr." would imply social equality and such heresy the South could not tolerate.

How lyrical was the South about its "chivalrous gentlemen," but rarely, if ever, did one of these chivalrous white gentlemen remove his hat when he went to a Negro woman's house to sell something or to collect a bill, or in the presence of Negro secretaries when he went to a Negro's office. Many Negro women accepted this; others did not. Some husbands and wives did not allow collectors to come to their homes; they paid by mail, or had some male member of the family go to the office. Some Negro housewives would pay at the door, giving the collector no reason to enter the home. A few Negro women requested salesmen to take off their hats, and objected whenever any white man used their first name or "claimed kin" by the term "Auntie." However, there were thousands of Negro women in Atlanta and the South who accepted this disrespect and did nothing about it except complain to other Negroes. Some even accepted this as a matter of course and did not object. I know of one case in which a white man, rather than remove his hat in a Negro home when requested to do so, went to the porch to transact the business. The Negro housewife had the courage to ask him to move on.

Sensitive Negro women had a difficult time when they went to buy a dress, hat, or shoes. White women could try on as many dresses and hats as they wanted before making a selection. In most cases, Negro women had to buy first and *then* try on the dress or hat. When purchasing shoes, they received the same brand of Southern attention as Negro men—the inconspicuous seats in the back of the shoe section, the all-white-folks-first routine, and no individual service. It was amazing, too, how white clerks would fish to get a Negro woman's first name to avoid calling her "Miss" or "Mrs." It was equally amazing how expert Negro women became in *not* giving their first name. Many would say, for example, "My name is Mrs. J. W. Johnson." The clerk would continue to probe; and if the article were delivered it would be sent to "J. W. Johnson" even though a woman's dress or hat was obviously in the package. Both my first wife and my second met these embarrassing experiences in South Carolina and in Atlanta and dealt with them in their own way, never capitulating.

The shabby Southern custom of denying Negroes the dignity of titles persisted for many years and lingers on even now in some parts of the South. As recently as the 1940's, I was awaiting my turn in an outer office on a matter of income tax. The white receptionist, obviously in her teens, took great care to call each white man, waiting as I was, by the title "Mister." When she reached my name, she called out "Benjamin." When I expressed my resentment, she reported me to a superior as being discourteous. I think I was able to convince her superior that it was his employee, not I, who lacked courtesy. During the second World War, I volunteered to give blood. The fact that I was president of Morehouse College meant nothing to the white technician who drew the blood. I was "Benjamin" to her. I reported the incident to the Red Cross and received a feeble apology.

Until I came to Atlanta in 1921, I had never had to use an elevator in the South, segregated or otherwise. As far as I know, there were then no buildings in Greenwood or Orangeburg, South Carolina, tall enough to require elevators. I had no business to transact in downtown Richmond when I was a freshman at Virginia Union.

In Atlanta, I soon learned about segregated elevators. Elevators for Negroes were usually the freight elevators or the ones used for janitor services. Regardless of their business or its urgency, Negroes had to wait for the freight elevator. Idiotically enough, in some buildings in downtown Atlanta, Negroes could ride down on the "white" passenger elevators but could never use them going up. If for any reason the white man elected to ride on the freight elevator with Negroes, he was free to do so. In the elevator, Southern chivalry languished and died: a Negro man must remove his hat if a white woman were present; never did a white man extend the same courtesy to a Negro woman. More than once I saw white men, wearing their hats in an elevator with a Negro woman present, snatch them off with military precision when a white woman got on, only to replace them with finality if the white woman got off before the Negro woman. No opportunity to show the Negro woman that she was unworthy of respect must be missed! If a Negro man kept his hat on in an elevator, he was told to take it off; if he refused, his hat was knocked off.

In the last conversation I had with him before his death in 1969, Mr. A. H. Yancey, a former mail carrier and one of the most intelligent men in Atlanta, told me how Negro mail carriers had circumvented the requirement to use segregated elevators. They protested to the federal government that they could not finish their work on time if they had to wait for the segregated elevator to deliver mail in office buildings in downtown Atlanta, and that they could not handle the mail efficiently if they had to keep cap in hand on elevators and when distributing the mail. The government handed down a decision that the mail carrier was like a soldier serving his government and therefore was not subject to the segregation requirement. Mr. Yancey said that segregated elevators began to operate in Atlanta in 1903 and that by 1921 only mail carriers were exempt from the segregation demand.

Segregation in hotels was rigidly enforced in Atlanta in 1921 and until the 1960's. The only Negroes permitted in hotels were employees: maids, porters, waiters, and elevator operators. No one registered in a downtown hotel could entertain Negro friends in his room, or even in the hotel lobby. The colleges as a rule provided for white guests on their campuses. I remember the experience of E. Franklin Frazier, famed sociologist, back in 1923. He had spent a year or more studying cooperatives in Denmark. He was a professor of sociology at Morehouse, and one of his friends from Denmark upon visiting Atlanta invited Dr. Frazier to the downtown hotel where he was staying. Dr. Frazier was not even permitted to get to the desk to let his friend know that he was there. Rather than be arrested or beaten, Dr. Frazier went away and phoned his friend to meet him on the street. For decades, Negroes with white friends who were stopping in white hotels while visiting the Negro colleges would agree to meet on the street in front of the hotel at a stipulated time. It was dangerous for a Negro to call for his guest at the hotel desk.

The Negro in Georgia was robbed of the ballot in 1908. He did not get it back until 1946 when a federal court, in the Primus King case, declared the white primary in Georgia unconstitutional. Prior to 1946, therefore, blacks had no vote in local and state elections. Only in bond elections could they vote.

Besides being deprived of the ballot, Negroes had no public high school in Atlanta in 1921. High school education was provided by the private colleges: Atlanta University, Clark, Morehouse, Morris Brown, and Spelman colleges. It was not until 1924 that Atlanta's first Negro high school (Booker T. Washington) was built, and then only after Negroes had helped to defeat a bond issue because no provision was made in it for the construction of a Negro high school. The second bond issue passed, with Negro support, after the city officials had promised to build them a high school. Prior to 1924, some high school grades were taught in the Negro elementary schools.

According to figures in the Fiftieth Annual Report of the Department of Education of the State of Georgia, discrimination was rampant in Atlanta in 1921. The average monthly salary paid the white male in grammar school was $175; that of the Negro male was listed as zero—evidently only Negro women were teaching in the grammar schools in Atlanta in 1921. The white female teaching in the grammar schools received an average monthly salary of $113; the black female was paid an average of $67.50. The white male and female teaching in high schools received an average monthly salary of $168.50, whereas the average salary paid Negro women teaching high school grades in Atlanta in 1921 was $80. For the state as a whole in 1921, the white male in the grammar schools earned an average of $85.35 per month; the average for the white female was $66.80. The average for the Negro male was $43.20 per month; and for the Negro female $33.66.

The same pattern of discrimination was in operation in 1924, for we find that the monthly high school salary of the white male in Atlanta was $168.50 and that of the Negro male teaching high school grades was $95; the white female in Atlanta received a monthly high school salary of $168.50; the Negro female teaching high school grades received a monthly salary of $95. In the same year, the State of Georgia paid white teachers a total of $9,-460,842.49 and the Negro teachers a total of $969,666.27. This glaring discrimination is highlighted when we consider that the U.S. Census shows that the total population in Georgia in 1920 was 2,895,479, and of this number 1,206,365, or 41 percent, were Negroes.

Even the most fanatic segregationist could not control the water supply, but he could and did label the public water fountains, some "For Whites" and others "For Colored." This practice could never be completely enforced, for even the most zealous and bigoted policeman was not wise enough to tell if light-skinned John Hope or Walter White was Negro or white! Then, too, there were a few devilish ones like me, who, though unmistakably black, just had to have a sip of "white water" once in a while just for the fun of it.

There were other ridiculous manifestations of segregation: Negroes paid taxes and made their returns at a segregated window and used paper of a different color. Their money was the same color as that of whites; it was never rejected; it was wholly acceptable. Only *they* were not! According to one member of my research team, this practice of segregating Negroes as they made returns and paid taxes dates back to February 28, 1874, when the Georgia Legislature passed "An Act to Require the Receivers of Tax Returns and Tax Collectors to make separate Returns of all Taxes Returned and Paid by colored taxpayers, and to Require the Comptroller General to Exhibit the Same in his Report, and for other purposes." Only recently was the segregated window abolished.

Certain banks, for example First National, did not allow Negroes to deposit and receive money from the same window with whites. There was a black line for Negroes. B. C. Baskerville, now of Newark, New Jersey, believes to this day that he was dropped from the employ of the Southern Bell Telephone Company in 1932 because he wrote an article in the Atlanta *Independent* condemning the First National Bank for having a segregated window for Negroes. Mr. Baskerville writes me that those "untouchable" Negroes in the segregated line had, according to a top bank official, seven million dollars deposited in the First National Bank at that time. Baskerville worked for Southern Bell from April 1, 1929, through March 31, 1932. As a ranking salesman, he had earned a 10 percent increase in salary; but shortly after his article appeared in the *Independent* he was dismissed. Reason given: the depression made it necessary for the company to reduce the number of employees.

City parks, except Grant Park, were for whites only. Policemen were diligent in making certain that no Negro relaxed or rested his bones in these parks. If there were any rest rooms at all for Negroes in the downtown stores they were in the basement, and were rest rooms set aside for Negro help. Many stores in downtown Atlanta had no toilet facilities for Negroes. If nature called, it was just too bad. Theaters were so rigidly segregated that in the one or two which accepted Negroes at all, they not only had to sit in the topmost balcony but also had to enter and leave from a back or side door or from a side street. All downtown restaurants were closed to Negroes. Filling stations gladly sold gas and oil to Negroes but either denied them the use of rest rooms or provided inferior and filthy ones. Churches were tightly segregated. Salvation, presumably, was for "whosoever will"—but not in the church pews! Until recently, only Negro taxi drivers in Atlanta could carry Negro passengers, and only white taxi drivers could carry white passengers. All too frequently, white taxi drivers sternly lectured white women passengers coming to visit one of the Negro college campuses in the Atlanta University Center. White men—any white man—felt a duty to *protect* white women against associating with Negroes for any reason, however praiseworthy.

In the courthouse, a certain section was set aside for Negroes. Even when there was space in the white section, Negroes had to stand if there were too many Negroes for the space allotted. Let Attorney T. J. Henry tell about the court situation in his early years of law practice in Atlanta:

> The conditions that surrounded Negroes in general (1923) were the most disturbing element confronting Negro attorneys. First, Negroes were poor and unable to pay adequate fees. This caused the colored attorneys to take on more work than was feasible in order to eke out a living, and very likely miss some points in a case because of being unduly rushed. Negroes who were able to pay adequate fees for the most part were loath to trust colored attorneys and were loath to leave their good white friends.
>
> Then there was the general disrespect of white people, who were the judges, jurors, prosecutors, and court attendants. . . .

Negroes were not addressed by the court or attendants, all of whom were white, as Mr. or Mrs., and neither were Negro lawyers, although they called colored lawyers "Captain," or "Colonel," never "Mister."

Unfavorable decisions were rendered against Negroes not because of their colored lawyers but because they were Negroes, whose rights they were not bound to respect.

The Negro lawyer could sit in the seats provided for lawyers in general, but woe to the unknown colored lawyer who strayed in. This is from personal experience. Confusion and arguments followed until the judge presiding could straighten out the matter.

Shortly after I came to Atlanta in 1921, a Negro who was working for a white woman fell from a ladder and broke a leg. The woman, not knowing that in the South pain is segregated, called a white undertaking establishment to send an ambulance to take the man to a hospital. When the white ambulance driver arrived and saw that the suffering man was a Negro, he drove away leaving the Negro lying in his own blood and pain. The white woman had to call an ambulance from a Negro undertaking establishment. Years later I knew of an even worse case which happened in North Augusta, South Carolina. My first wife's sister, Mrs. Julia Palmore, was struck by a hit-and-run automobile driver. A white person, not knowing the custom, called a white undertaker to send an ambulance. When the white driver came and saw that the injured woman was a Negro he drove away and left her there to die. A Negro ambulance was called, but by the time my sister-in-law was taken to the hospital she was pronounced "dead on arrival."

Negroes were required to sit in segregated waiting rooms, inferior to those reserved for whites, in the offices of white doctors. In some cases, Negro patients had to use back-door entrances in order to see their white doctors. Negro patients, as a rule, had to wait until white patients had been attended to. I have always patronized Negro doctors and have gone to white doctors only when referred to them by my Negro doctor. Even then, I always made an appointment with the white doctor so that I could see him on arrival without waiting in his segregated waiting room.

I have never believed that a white doctor who segregates his Negro patients and thus demonstrates that he considers them inferior could give me the same professional care as his white patients. I have had personal experience to confirm my suspicion:

Years ago, one of my sisters, living in Greenville, South Carolina, had to see a white doctor in his segregated office. After calling her "Auntie" and giving her a perfunctory examination, he concluded that she had a growth in her right breast and suggested immediate surgery. When she wrote me about this, I immediately wrote the doctor for details. He never answered my letter. Later, on my way to Europe, I took my sister to New York to be sure that she needed the operation and, if so, that she got it. A schoolmate of mine at South Carolina State College, Dr. Robert Shaw Wilkinson, Jr., a graduate of Dartmouth and Harvard Medical School, was my New York physician. He found no growth in my sister's breast and she lived twenty years after that with no signs of breast cancer.

In Atlanta, in 1921, as I soon found to be the case throughout the South, segregation was god—the absolute—and was worshiped not only in secular life but in the "House of God." On His altars were sacrificed the bodies, minds, and very souls of Negro men and women and little children. This was Atlanta in 1921, the city in which Morehouse College was and still is located, the city in which I have spent most of my years. The conditions I have described did not change in any significant way until after the middle of the twentieth century. The Atlanta of 1970 is a new creation.

Chapter VI
Morehouse and Shiloh

When I first came to Atlanta there were, besides the public elementary schools, six institutions of learning for Negroes: Atlanta University; Clark University (now Clark College); Morris Brown University (now Morris Brown College); Morehouse College; Spelman College; and Gammon Theological Seminary (now a member of the Interdenominational Theological Center, made up of the Morehouse School of Religion, Turner Theological Seminary, Phillips School of Theology, Gammon, Johnson C. Smith Theological Seminary, and The Charles Harrison Mason Theological Seminary).

Of necessity, each of the colleges, and even Atlanta University, had an academy or high school. Atlanta itself did not provide a high school for Negroes until 1924, and then only after Negroes had defeated a bond issue because a high school for them was not included in the proposal. When the authorities agreed to build a high school for Negroes, the next bond issue was passed. In 1921, the enrollment in four of the college high school departments was much higher than that of the colleges themselves. The total high school enrollment in the four (Clark, Morehouse, Atlanta University, and Morris Brown) was 1,139 as compared with 527 in the colleges. The total college enrollment in Morehouse, Spelman, Clark, and Morris Brown in 1968 was 4,358, nine times the college enrollment in the four colleges in 1921. Between 1921 and 1967, the Morehouse student body had grown from 136 college students to 1,037. Good—but not good enough. There were too few Negroes in college—approximately 260,000. Though we comprise 10 percent of the total population, we represent barely 4 percent of the total college enrollment of the country.

Remember the grim, the ugly picture of Atlanta in 1921: the closed doors, the barriers, the ever-present threat of physical harm, the strangling miasma of emotional assault, or spiritual attack? What did Morehouse College do about the degrading conditions its students were expected to endure? There seemed little anyone could do to change the system; that is, to introduce either democracy or Christianity to the South. White America had stamped its approval upon the segregated way of life. John Hope, Morehouse's first Negro president, was working with W. W. Alexander of the Commission on Interracial Cooperation to bring more justice to Negroes *within the segregated pattern.* Hope was a staunch foe of segregation in every area of life; but he was trapped by the system, and any overt plan of his to overthrow the segregated system would have made his work at Morehouse wholly ineffective and possibly would have brought physical harm to him. Most of the older Negro leaders were supporting the Commission. The more courageous Negro leaders were also contributing to the work of the National Association for the Advancement of Colored People. John Hope supported the NAACP from its inception in 1910, and was part of the Niagara movement out of which the NAACP sprang. The National Urban League, organized in 1911, had several programs designed to improve conditions of Negroes. But nothing happened to change the social order during my first three years at Morehouse, nor for many years thereafter.

What did Morehouse teach her students about the injustices that bore down upon them every minute of every hour, every hour in the day, and every month in the year? Did Morehouse teach her students to prepare themselves for active attempts to change society, to accept segregation submissively, or to protest against it with the hope that someday the situation would change? Morehouse certainly did not teach students to accept, let alone gloss over, the environment as they found it. Though no one at Morehouse taught submission, neither did anyone encourage Morehouse students to attempt by force to overthrow or change the system. At least, by precept and example, the Morehouse student was taught never to accept the system in his own mind as being inescapable or right. Never was his intelligence or his pride insulted by his being asked to believe that the cruelty and injustice of racism were the "will of God." Perhaps Morehouse could and should have done more. However, judging from the harvest, she must have—however indirectly—planted good seeds, and the field was unquestionably fertile. For many Morehouse men of this period have made, in the decades since then, such valiant, and frequently such successful, efforts to change the ugly world in which they were born. Even in 1921 Morehouse did not encourage voluntary patronage of segregated facilities, nor follow the custom of providing special seats for white visitors. Little things? Yes. But perhaps they were the first faint whisper of the mighty winds that today are sweeping away the debris and trash that for so long have buried the altars of freedom, justice, and equality.

It is hardly an accident that so many students I knew and taught and from whom I learned so much have done so well in the world despite the crippling circumstances of racial discrimination which they faced in Atlanta, in the South, and in the nation. They were motivated by inspired men, men like John Hope, Samuel Howard Archer, Benjamin G. Brawley, and later C. D. Hubert. The Morehouse tradition is a proud and honorable one, one to evoke the best from its students, one that provides a lifelong goal. At Morehouse the A.B. has never been considered a terminal degree. The Morehouse man learned well that "a man's reach should exceed his grasp" and never accepted the idea that the ceiling was the limit of his striving. Rather, the sky was his goal, even though, all too often, his wings were clipped at the ceiling level.

When I was graduated from Bates in 1920, it was possible to become an instructor or even a professor with an A.B. degree. Negro college graduates were so rare that a man with an A.B. was esteemed as highly then as is a man with a Ph.D. now. Moreover, it was assumed that a college graduate could teach many subjects. At Bates, students were graduated with honors in science, the humanities, or philosophy. I had been graduated with honors in philosophy, which included psychology. However, for four years I had studied college mathematics; so I went to Morehouse to teach mathematics. My teaching program turned out to be not only mathematics but psychology, one course in religious education, and, for two years, coaching the debating team!

During my first year I had my first clash with President John Hope. At the end of the first semester, my final examination questions in psychology were stolen, duplicated, and passed to some of my students. I learned about the theft after the examination. I had only two clues. Miss Maggie Howard, one of the teachers, had seen a group of students examining a sheet of yellow paper and then tearing it up. Being curious, she picked up enough of the pieces to determine that the handwriting was mine and that the questions were in psychology. Of the sixty or more students in the class, sixteen had failed the four monthly tests. I concluded that if these sixteen passed the finals, something was "dead up the creek." When I graded the papers, I found that fifteen of the sixteen had passed the final examination. This seemed to me sufficient evidence that the examination questions had been stolen and studied by at least some of the failing students. In addition, about an hour before the examination I had discovered a shortage of copies, which I had to replace hastily. I announced to the class what had happened, told them that I would have to give another examination, and would set the time for it.

When some students complained to the president, he forbade my giving another examination on the ground that it was unfair to the innocent. I argued that it would be unfair to both innocent and guilty if a second examination were not given. I protested that he had no right to interfere with my academic freedom. At first, I refused to grade the papers. The argument continued throughout the second semester until May. In our last heated argument, I promised to grade the papers and give each student what he made, including the fifteen who had failed the monthly tests but passed on the finals. I capitulated to avoid the charge of insubordination. I did not wish to resign my position, as otherwise I should have had to do. I graded the papers.

I had gone to Morehouse College to stay only one year, with the plan of returning thereafter to the University of Chicago for further study. I was convinced that John Hope would not want me around after the semester-long "battle of the second exam." So I could hardly believe my ears when he called me and urged me to stay at Morehouse a second year. My surprise was no greater than my respect for this man. I think that he had equal respect for me, as a teacher who believed that students came to college to get an education. The academic discipline I had received at Bates had become a part of me. I had tried to apply this discipline of thoroughness to my Morehouse students. Most teachers want their students to pass; certainly I did; yet a goodly number failed my courses. I was considered hard but, I think, never unfair. I believe John Hope understood this.

President Hope surprised me again by requesting me to stay for a third year, at the end of my second year, this time to serve as acting dean. I was pleased and gratified by this proof of his confidence in me. Nevertheless, to remain at Morehouse for a third year was a hard decision for me to make. I needed and I wished to get back to Chicago for further study; but there was tempting bait in Mr. Hope's offer—my salary would be increased from $1,200 to $1,800 per year! This was an astronomical increase and I was duly flattered. I rose to the bait—I stayed the third year. During that third year the student to whom I had given a job cleaning my room confessed to me and to President Hope that he had stolen copies of that famous psychology examination and sold them at twenty-five cents a copy! This student was never disciplined.

One part of my reputation as acting dean I did not deserve. I was accused of being against intercollegiate sports—a wholly false accusation. I was against students who, though failing in their work, went on a basketball tour for two or three weeks. And I did insist that the men who played football should be up in their studies. This reputation persisted throughout the twenty-seven years of my presidency at Morehouse because we didn't buy players and didn't produce championship teams.

The question of what President Hope really thought of me was finally settled in my mind and heart in 1928 when I was leaving Tampa, Florida, to go again to the University of Chicago. I had three offers: a General Education Board Fellowship; an offer to go to Fisk; and an offer from Channing Tobias to join the staff of the National YMCA as student secretary. Dean Augustus Farnham Shaw of Fisk wrote John Hope for a recommendation, and, in extending the invitation to me to come to Fisk, he wrote: "John Hope's recommendation of you is so commendable that there's no need for us to write anybody else." I still believe that the second examination should have been given, but I am glad that I had the opportunity to learn the "bigness" of President Hope.

In the spring of 1923, I went with my team—Howard Thurman and Jim Nabrit—to debate Fisk University in Nashville, Tennessee. I made a painful discovery on that trip. Professor Isaac Fisher was away with one of the Fisk teams, so I was to deal with President Fayette Avery McKenzie. It was customary for the visiting team to submit a list of names from which the host college would choose three judges. I submitted ten names—an integrated list, Negroes and whites. McKenzie went down the list and about every unfamiliar name he would ask, "Is this man white or colored?" If I replied "colored," he would scratch his name. He did that with every name of a Negro until all had been eliminated. I protested this display of rank discrimination, but to no avail. Once I had submitted my list, I was bound to accept any three names chosen by the host college: there was no higher court of appeal. I was furious, but I was powerless. I told Thurman and Nabrit that they had no choice either: they *had* to win that debate! When the judges gave the decision to Morehouse, I was (and still am!) accused of making one flying leap from the first floor of the Fisk University Chapel to the rostrum to congratulate Nabrit and Thurman.

Ellen, my first wife, while still teaching in South Carolina, died early in 1923 after an operation in an Atlanta hospital. During that year, in addition to teaching and serving as acting dean at Morehouse, I was pastor of the Shiloh Baptist Church. Toward the end of the year, I began to visit friends and attend meetings. I was delegate to the Omega Psi Phi Fraternity Conclave which was held in St. Louis during Christmas week. On my way there, I stopped in Birmingham, Alabama, to visit friends, and decided that when I left I would make the remainder of the trip riding first class. My friends pointed out the danger of such a venture, assuring me that no Negro could purchase a Pullman ticket in Birmingham. Unconvinced, I went with a friend to the city ticket office. When I requested a ticket for a lower berth to St. Louis, the ticket agent asked, "Who wants it?" I replied, "Mr. Mays." No more questions. I have always had a preference for telling the exact truth, and I had done so. It was not my responsibility that the agent assumed that Mr. Mays was a white man. Remember—Negroes were not supposed to call themselves Mister, Miss, or Mrs., when speaking to a white man. Indeed, it was dangerous in many sections of the South for a Negro to call another Negro "Mister."

I boarded the train for St. Louis around noon. My friends' forebodings had not been idle. It was sheer chance that I reached St. Louis safe. No other Negroes were riding Pullman, and every white person who walked through the car in which I was seated looked at me in consternation. The train was crowded; and it seemed to me that hundreds of persons passed me on their way to and from the diner. Each person looked daggers at me; many, after passing my seat, turned around for an additional glare of hatred. Frankly, I was scared to death. I felt certain that something terrible would happen any minute.

Finally, the Pullman conductor came to me and told me that passengers were objecting to my presence and he feared for my life. My reminder that I was a passenger and that it was his and the train conductor's responsibility to protect me fell on deaf ears. He urged me to leave my berth, go back to the "deadhead" Pullman car (a Pullman car without passengers), and remain there with the porter of that car until he arrived in Nashville. I did not obey immediately. When the train got to Columbia, Tennessee, I got off to greet Professor J. W. Johnson, a Morehouse colleague of mine. When I told him that I anticipated trouble, he attempted to reassure me, but I decided that it would be wise to take the Pullman conductor's advice. I got on the deadhead car and sat in the drawing room with the porter behind a locked door. Almost instantly after the train left Columbia, there was a knock on the drawing-room door. Three men demanded to see the "nigger" who was riding Pullman in the car ahead. When I went to the door, two of them, aiming their pistols in my face, wanted to know why I was riding Pullman and who had sold me the ticket. Before I could reply, they ordered me to get my bags and move as fast as I could to the segregated Negro coach. I obeyed.

The three men followed through several day coaches and Pullman cars, placing their pistol barrels on my back at the end of each. As we moved along, many white men and boys jumped up to join the parade. As I opened the doors between coaches, I could see that the crowd following me was getting larger and larger all the time, gathering recruits in each coach. When I reached the Negro coach, I wasn't a bit sure they were not going to get me after all.

Shortly after I took my seat in the Negro coach, a white man, possibly representing the Pullman or railroad company, brought me a document to sign to the effect that I acknowledged my error in riding Pullman since it was illegal in Tennessee for a Negro to do so. I reminded him that I was an interstate passenger; I did not sign. He attempted to find out who had sold me the ticket. He did not learn. At Nashville, the Pullman conductor came running to invite me to return to my berth since the people who had driven me out had gotten off the train. I did not return, but instead took a place in the drawing room with other Omega men en route to the Conclave.

Neither the Pullman conductor nor the train conductor did a thing to protect my person and my right to ride as a free man in a so-called free society. Not one white passenger protested my treatment. It is my considered judgment that if I had been killed or thrown off the running train, absolutely nothing would have been done about it. The conductors would not even have lost their jobs.

I had to decide in St. Louis whether I would return to Atlanta in a day coach or in a Pullman car. This question troubled me all through the Conclave. Wouldn't I be a coward if I did not at least try to purchase a Pullman ticket? Scared as I had been, I hated to admit to myself that fear could prevent my exercising a right which I knew was mine—to ride comfortably in a Pullman car if I so desired. It was possible to buy Pullman accommodations in the North, going South, but virtually impossible to buy one in the South going North. I had proved, just a few days earlier, that having a Pullman ticket did not guarantee a safe and comfortable ride.

I have always been glad that I did buy the Pullman ticket and, with my friend Jesse O. Thomas of the Urban League, made the trip from St. Louis to Atlanta. Trouble could easily have developed again, but this time the Pullman conductor was not afraid. When the white passenger in the berth next to J. O.'s and mine complained that he could not sleep in a coach with "niggers" and insisted that we be put out, the conductor refused and hushed the complaining passenger by offering to give him space in a car in which there were no Negroes. The man accepted. The next morning the same man looked in the men's room of our car and snarled, "Goddamn it!"

A beautiful thing happened on that return trip from St. Louis. One often finds courage and principle in unexpected places. We returned to Atlanta on the Dixie Limited, a crack train which carried Negro maids to give special service to women Pullman passengers. The maid on our car was neatly dressed and beautiful. She came to J. O. and me to tell us that some white passengers were grumbling about our presence, but that we were not to fear and not to move; that if anything ominous developed she would keep us informed. I never saw her again after that trip; I do not remember her name, but I have never forgotten her.

I related my Birmingham to St. Louis experience to President Hope and sought his advice about what steps I might take in seeking redress. He made an appointment for me to see Will W. Alexander, executive director of the Commission on Interracial Cooperation. I was aware of the "ideal" aims of the Commission and so was deeply hurt and disillusioned when Dr. Alexander advised me to drop the case. A Chicago lawyer, hearing about the case, offered his services. Some four years later, he claimed he could get only $200 from the Pullman company and mailed me a check for $100.

Remember, Southern chivalry was "for whites only." It was dangerous for a Negro of either sex to ride Pullman in the 1920's. In a speech to an interracial group of women at the Memphis YMCA in October, 1920, Dr. Charlotte Hawkins Brown, eminent educator and president of Palmer Institute, related the harrowing experiences of her Pullman travel en route to Memphis, in which *twelve* white men surrounded her, threatened her with bodily harm, and forcibly escorted her out of the Pullman car to the day coach although she had been assured by the ticket agent in Greensboro, North Carolina, that she would be allowed to use a sleeper without being molested. A full account of this disgraceful incident appears in *Seeds of Southern Change* (p. 94). The meeting which Dr. Brown addressed with such passion and eloquence had been called by W. W. Alexander to bring together Negro and white women, which in itself was something new in those days.

Going Pullman remained dangerous for Negroes for a mighty long time. It made no difference how important the person was—if he was black, he had no right to sleep on the train at night. Even a Negro United States Congressman was not supposed to ride first class in the South. The May 22, 1937, issue of the *Journal and Guide* (Norfolk, Virginia) carried a front-page item about the suit filed by Congressman A.W. Mitchell because he had been denied first-class accommodations although he had purchased a first-class ticket. Using well-laid legal strategy, Congressman Mitchell was able to win his case.

Shiloh, a small Baptist church three blocks from Morehouse and across the street from Spelman College on Greensferry Avenue, asked me to consider being their pastor. Before I could accept, I had to be ordained. Dr. C. D. Hubert, a professor at Morehouse, was also minister of a church in Darlington, South Carolina. At Christmas time, 1921, I had arranged to spend the holidays with Ellen; so her pastor, J. P. Garrick, and Dr. Hubert arranged for my ordination in the Reverend Garrick's church in Sumter, South Carolina. Thus in January, 1922, I assumed the pastorate of Shiloh Baptist Church in Atlanta.

Shiloh Baptist Church was a small church of 125 members. Most of its congregation were unschooled—common laborers and domestic workers. Oddly enough, I had no difficulty preaching to these people who, though untrained, were highly intelligent. Needless to say, I felt no compulsion to preach to them about the historical methods prevalent in the Divinity School of the University of Chicago! I attempted to speak to their needs, and they responded warmly and well. There wasn't much money in the church. I think I was paid $100 a month, and from that I paid my choir director twenty-five to forty dollars a month. Students and teachers from Morehouse and Spelman were frequent visitors during my three years at Shiloh. Forty-five years later, I have many vivid memories which I cherish.

The people of Shiloh grew very dear to me. I loved them and they loved me. Several of my members are still alive and have a warm spot in my heart. The membership accepted me wholeheartedly, despite my inexperience, and some of them rebuked me kindly when they thought I needed it. Despite their poverty, a member would come up after services once in a while and press a quarter, a half dollar, and occasionally a dollar bill in my hand and say, "This is for you." Though I knew they needed the money more than I, I could not hurt their feelings by refusing it. I could only accept it and hope to be as generous as they in my own giving. I especially remember Sister Reddick, a domestic worker in a white family's home. She lived in a servant's house built at the back of the white man's house. I have never known a finer person than Mrs. Reddick. Her husband was dead and she had no children. Frequently, she would invite me to her house for dinner. She had to work during the day on Sunday, but she never missed a Sunday-night service, unless she was ill, and never failed to make her contribution. There were many like Mrs. Reddick in my church—warm, generous, open-handed and open-hearted. Small wonder that I cherish their memory.

It was at Shiloh, too, that I learned that a thief will steal from a church as readily as from any other place. One Sunday morning, someone stole my winter overcoat from the study during the eleven o'clock worship service. After visiting a dozen or more pawnshops, I was able to re-purchase my overcoat.

I smile when I recall an act of mine that created a stir in the community. I went to an Omega picnic one Saturday and danced with the young woman I had escorted there. I heard rumors shortly afterward that the church was going to dismiss me for this "sin." Another rumor was that I would be called before the officers and reprimanded. I was not dismissed, nor was I ever reprimanded.

My church services were much shorter than was customary in most Negro churches. They began at eleven in the morning and we were out by twelve-fifteen, or by twelve-thirty on Communion Sunday. This innovation made Shiloh a popular church, and I am sure that many visitors came there to worship because they knew that they would be out before one, one-thirty, or two o'clock in the afternoon.

At Shiloh, we treated white visitors just as we did Negro visitors. Many Negro churches segregated white visitors by giving them choice seats, but such a practice was unthinkable for one who felt as I did that segregation was a denial of dignity and manhood.

My three years at Shiloh concluded my career as a pastor. Thereafter, social work, research, YMCA work, and education were to command my energies. My first three years' experience in Atlanta had come to an end: a rich and rewarding experience, a period that validated old convictions and opened new vistas.

Chapter VII

Chicago to Orangeburg to Tampa

Dropping out of school to work before completing graduate or professional study is risky business. I went to Morehouse in September, 1921, expecting to stay one year. I stayed three. I was eager to return to the University of Chicago to complete the requirements for the Ph.D. degree. When I enrolled at the university again in September, 1924, I still was thinking of the church as my vocation and decided to qualify for the master's degree in the New Testament. A Ph.D. was still my goal, but I had decided that it was the better part of wisdom to acquire my M.A. degree along the way. That degree was conferred upon me in March, 1925.

Interracially, things had not changed much at the University of Chicago during my three years' absence. Dormitories were still closed to Negro women; only one or two were open to Negro men. Many white students were still running when Negroes sat at table with them in the Commons. Most of the restaurants in the university community still refused service to Negroes. The Reynolds Club was first opened to Negroes in 1924-1925. However, Negroes were denied admittance as guests in the downtown hotels and restaurants.

Because Negroes were discriminated against in the United States, Oriental students at the university looked upon them as America's "untouchables" and sought to avoid them. Negro students were convinced that Indian students wore their turbans to make sure that they would not be mistaken for Negroes. In those days, a Negro wearing a turban could ride through the South unsegregated and unmolested. All foreign colored peoples (except Africans) fared better in travel. They could ride unsegregated.

Eager to do something to bring Negroes and other racial and ethnic groups together, a few of us organized a forum for discussing the race problem at the university—in Chicago and in the nation. The forum, of which I was chairman, and which was the only place at the university where problems of race were frankly and openly faced, grew rapidly. Speakers were members of the university community and visitors who had come to the university on other business.

It was in this forum that I developed my first real friendship with a Southern white man. During my first twenty-one years in South Carolina, I had no Southern white friends; indeed, the relationship between Negroes and whites in my county was such that I had no confidence whatsoever in *any* Southern white man. Nothing had happened to me in any part of the South to mitigate the impression that the mob had burned into my heart before I was five years old. I did not particularly or aggressively hate Southern whites, but I feared them and completely distrusted them.

That Southern whites were the Negroes' worst enemies was my firmly established conviction at the time when a graduate student in sociology, a Texan by the name of W. O. Brown, addressed the forum. He talked about segregation and discrimination as they related to Negroes. He said in essence that segregation and discrimination against Negroes were based upon 1) the false conviction of white people that the Negro was biologically and inherently inferior to the white man, and 2) their assumption that they were therefore free to treat—or mistreat—any Negro as they saw fit. Segregation was a badge that the white man forced the Negro to wear so that he could be disregarded and exploited. Segregation was also designed, said Brown, to make the Negro accept his inferiority so that he would feel and behave like an inferior, cringing and kowtowing, expecting little, asking for less.

Of course, I knew everything that W. O. Brown talked about, as did every intelligent Negro, but I was really startled and amazed to hear such words from a Southern white man—and in public! As I listened, I felt that I, who knew too well what segregation meant, was in the presence of a miracle: a Southern white man who was aware that the doctrine upon which segregation rested was false and who believed it was wrong.

W. O. Brown and I became friends; and my horizon began to expand. I stopped generalizing about Southern white people. He was only one Southern white man, but I felt that there must be others just as honest, just as decent, just as trustworthy. Subsequent years proved that I was right. W. O. Brown was my "first," but he was not the only one. Before receiving my Ph.D. from the university, I had made friends with other Southerners, students in my department. Previously, of course, I had met Will Alexander of the Commission on Interracial Cooperation, but I had known him only casually and had been thoroughly disillusioned when he advised me to drop my efforts to bring suit against the Pullman Company. Today my friends are many and varied, including people of all races and ethnic origins and of many religious faiths. I only wish that I could have known W. O. Brown earlier. It is sad that I had to wait until I was thirty years old to develop a saner view about the Southern white man; sad that I had to leave South Carolina and the South to have my first experience of a good Southern white.

While I was at the University of Chicago, I was on leave from Shiloh Baptist Church. But now it seemed best to give up the pastorate of this small church which I had grown to love so well. After earning the M.A. degree in the spring of 1925, I continued at the university through the summer quarter, expecting then to study straight through for the Ph.D. degree. However, temptation proffered an alluring face: President Wilkinson offered me a position at South Carolina State, my high school alma mater. Flattered by the offer to teach English at the college where the president and I had disagreed so completely about where I should attend college, I accepted his offer and went to Orangeburg, South Carolina, in September, 1925. Mabel James, President Wilkinson's secretary, urged me to accept the position, and her words carried weight for me. I had not forgotten that she was the only person in my class who had written a note of congratulations when I was promoted from first to second year and was thus able to finish high school in three years.

In the nine years since I had been graduated from high school at South Carolina State, the college department had enlarged, but there was little if any improvement in the level of academic interest and achievement. The few teachers who had high academic standards were not the most popular, especially if they flunked a large number of students, as I did. I was dumbfounded when a senior student, who had failed all qualifications for graduation, was nonetheless voted graduation by the faculty. I led the opposition against this degrading of a college degree, but I lost by one vote.

It was customary in all Negro state colleges, whenever trustees or members of the State Legislature ate at the college, for them to eat alone, without the company of the president or any faculty member. The law of segregation had to be obeyed even in a totally Negro environment, and despite the fact that President Robert Shaw Wilkinson, a graduate of Oberlin, was probably better educated and better trained than the Governor or any visiting member of the Legislature or the Board of Trustees.

As far back as 1896, the United States Supreme Court had ruled that segregation was constitutional, provided the separate facilities were equal.

It was blatantly and painfully obvious, however, that there had never been the slightest intention of providing equality of education so far as Negroes and whites were involved—nor was there equality in any other area of life. (Although Negroes in South Carolina in 1925 constituted half the population, the appropriation for State College, for the school year 1924-25 and for the fiscal year ending December 31, 1925, was $106,625; whereas the appropriations for the four state institutions for whites amounted to $1,057,324.71, ten times more for the whites than for Negroes.) This inequality was an ingrained way of life. Negroes and whites alike took inequality for granted. Nobody dared question it. Negroes might whisper their complaints among themselves, but there was no public outcry. All the president of a Negro state college could do was try to get from the state authorities as much money as possible for his college.

Acceptance of inequality existed in every area of Southern life in 1925. Even a top official of the Commission on Interracial Cooperation espoused this outrageous doctrine. Mrs. Marian Birnie Wilkinson, wife of President Wilkinson, was South Carolina's outstanding Negro woman; indeed, in programs designed to help the poor and improve racial relations, in my opinion she was *the* leading woman in South Carolina. She invited me to attend a meeting sponsored by the State's Commission on Interracial Cooperation at which Mrs. Jessie Daniel Ames of the Commission on Interracial Cooperation of Atlanta was to speak. Negroes considered any official of the Commission "liberal"; most white people called him "radical." I was shocked and sickened to hear Mrs. Ames say that the only way to advance the Negro child one step was to advance the white child two steps. She assured her listeners that this formula must be accepted if there were to be any better educational opportunities for Negroes.

When I returned to South Carolina, inequality between Negroes and whites was taken for granted—unprotested, unquestioned. Segregation with equality would have been wicked enough; segregation with built-in inequality was adding insult to injury. Segregation and inequality are inseparable twins, equally evil in origin, equally evil in manifestation. If there could be equality in a legally segregated society, the reason for segregation would disappear. If Jim Crow cars, Negro waiting rooms at railroad stations, segregated Negro schools, and all the other accessories after the fact of segregation had been as good for Negroes as for whites, there would have been no need for separation. But to the distorted thinking of Southern whites of that time, providing equality would have been tantamount to admitting equality of worth, and such admission was never even contemplated, let alone implemented. So widely accepted and practiced was the infamous doctrine of separate and unequal that no doubt Mrs. Ames felt wildly and daringly liberal and magnanimous when she proclaimed: "In order to advance the Negro child one step, the white child has to be advanced two steps."

I was becoming increasingly aware that in the interracial meetings Negroes and whites did not communicate. In the careful effort not to hurt each others' feelings, Negroes and white people alike rarely were honest when they met. As much as Negroes resented segregation, with its implicit and inevitable injustice, they never said that it was the Commission's duty to try to abolish it. Negroes and whites often sat on different sides of the table, and as often lied to each other. People truly communicate only when they tell each other the truth.

I was only too well acquainted with this silence. I remembered that the minister of my childhood, the Reverend Marshall, never touched on social questions in his sermons and would stop any visitor who tried to do so. White people did not have to be present to hear any "radical" remark any Negro made. It would be reported to them before the day was over. To curry favor, to stay in the good graces of the white bosses, some Negroes would "tattle" anything that had been said about the unjust way in which Negroes were treated. There was always a leak. Self-preservation dictated that Negroes make no public utterance that savored of criticism of white people.

Through an invitation from Ralph Bullock, Boys' Work Secretary of the National YMCA, I spoke to the Negro Older Boys' Conference at Benedict College on February 26, 1926. The invitation came to me in an odd manner. Mr. Bullock and I were on the same train, going from Atlanta to Columbia and Orangeburg, South Carolina. Bullock heard me request a Pullman berth to Orangeburg. Of course, I received the usual answer: "All space has been sold." Bullock introduced himself, saying, "I want to meet a Negro who has the nerve to ask for a berth in Atlanta, Georgia." A few days later I received a letter inviting me to be the banquet speaker at the Conference and suggesting that my topic be "The Goal."

I accepted the invitation, and I worked hard on that speech because I knew that Negro high school students from all over South Carolina would be there. I knew, too, that these Negro boys needed inspiration as surely and as sadly as I had needed it when I was a frustrated lad in Greenwood County only a few years before. It was tremendously gratifying to me that when I finished speaking, those Negro boys, hungry as they had been for someone to speak to their souls, sprang spontaneously to their feet and applauded long and loud. Actually, I felt that it was a mild, moderate speech —so much so that I said in the course of it, "Forty years from today, a youth reading my speech will perhaps call it 'old-timey' and out-of-date." There is no doubt that many of the black radicals of 1970 would say that I was prophetic—the speech *is* "dated." In 1926, however, some of my elders considered the speech so radical, so explosive that they expressed fear for my life. They fully expected that at the least I would be run out of town. Because a few white people had been present, some Negroes, wholly unaccustomed as they were to a Negro's speaking so forthrightly in the presence of white people, were genuinely afraid for me. The reader will no doubt smile as he searches in vain for the "wildly radical," the "dangerous" statements in these short excerpts as reprinted in *Sketches of Negro Life and History* in 1929:

> . . . Were I white, and held a professor's chair in the University of South Carolina; were you white, and represented the best white schools of this commonwealth; my task would not be so difficult. We would then be clothed in that skin that gives perpetual protection. We would represent that group that presumes to hold the destiny of this nation in its hand, and to whom the doors of opportunity are never closed. Were this true, I would define the goal without limitations. I would recommend that you aspire to be governor of your native state. I would point the way to the president's chair. As it is, Americans though we be, I must speak to you not as an American to Americans but as a Negro to Negroes. It is this regrettable fact that makes the goal most difficult for me to define. . . . Young men, you must strive to be an agriculturist, not a Negro agriculturist—just an agriculturist! Strive to be a doctor, not a Negro doctor—just a doctor! Seek to serve your state, not as a Negro, but as a man. Aspire to be great—not among Negroes, but among men! God knows I want to be a great teacher; not a Negro teacher—just a great teacher. I want no racial adjective modifying it. I want to preach the gospel of peace, good will, justice, and brotherhood—not to Negroes and for Negroes, but to men and for men. I want to act so that each tomorrow will find us farther than today—not the Negro race, the human race. It seems to me that this is our goal. . . .

That many Negroes considered this a radical speech indicates how cautious Negroes were even when only a few white persons were around. I have known Negro speakers to change the tenor of their remarks when just one white man was present or when one showed up unexpectedly. I suffered no ill consequences from this speech, however, even after it was printed in full in a Negro paper.

South Carolina State College at Orangeburg is very dear to my heart. This is true not only because the Negro teachers there gave me great inspiration and encouragement, but also because it was there that I met my first wife and, later, Sadie Gray who was my second wife until her death. Sadie and I met in September of 1925 at State College, and during the summer of 1926, while both of us were doing graduate work at the University of Chicago, we decided to get married. Since there was a rule at State College that both a man and his wife could not teach there, I wrote to Dr. Wilkinson immediately after Sadie and I married asking whether the rule could be set aside in our case. Sadie's father, in his advancing years, was about to lose their home place because of a two-thousand-dollar mortgage. Sadie and her sister had assumed the mortgage, and it was obligatory that Sadie have an income. The full situation was explained to Dr. Wilkinson, but he did not feel an exception could be made. His decision left us no choice but to seek a place where both of us could work. Fortunately Jesse O. Thomas, field director of the National Urban League, was looking for two persons to go to Tampa—one as executive secretary of the Tampa Urban League and the other as a case worker with the Family Service Association, with offices in the headquarters of the Tampa Urban League. He offered the positions to us. When a second attempt to persuade Dr. Wilkinson failed, Sadie and I signed contracts and went to Tampa in September, 1926.

Chapter VIII

The Tampa Story

Tampa was not the "city of our dreams"; we went there because we had to have jobs. I have never seen blacker clouds than those that hovered overhead as we rode on the train from Jacksonville to Tampa, wondering whether we had made the right decision. It was a dark and dreary day when we arrived, but the picture brightened somewhat when John Hall, a distinguished Negro citizen, met us at the station and gave us a glowing account of life in Tampa. A few days later a reception given in our honor seemed to confirm his sanguine report.

The St. Paul AME Church was packed to capacity as we were introduced to the Tampa public, including the mayor, other city officials, and newspaper editors. Negroes and whites were there, and all the talks—both the speeches and the conversations—were variations on the theme: "Negro-white relations in Tampa approach the ideal." The theme was somewhat tarnished by the fact that the white people present occupied a special section! Mrs. Ruth W. Atkinson, the executive secretary of the Tampa Welfare League and Community Chest, referred several times in her address to "our good Negroes"; and over and over again one of the leading Negroes spoke of her as "our little white angel." The implication was unmistakable: Negro-white relations in Tampa were "good," and would so continue as long as the "good Negroes" and the "little white angels" maintained their respective fictions and illusions. Despite the disquieting undertones, it was a friendly and cordial reception.

Each new day in Tampa confirmed our South Carolina and Georgia knowledge and what we had begun to suspect at the reception: All too often "good relations" between Negroes and whites meant no more than reciprocal flattery, superficial "mutual admiration societies." Sadie and I had tried to assess the welcoming reception; we tried to assess our present roles. We were not happy over the phrase "our good Negroes"—it betrayed a patronizing, albeit benevolent paternalism. Tampa Negroes seemed to have great faith in Mrs. Ruth Atkinson, and some, perhaps, even shared Father John

E. Culmer's vision of "our little white angel." Were "our good Negroes" good only so long as they stayed in their places, accepting the status quo without complaint—preferably with gratitude? Did the phrase "little white angel" express sincere affection, or was it an echo of the plantation praise designed to get things from white people? (Tell Mr. Charlie how beautiful his wife is; tell Mrs. Charlie how pretty she *and* her daughters are!) Fine as the reception had been, we could not escape the feeling that they "protest too much"; there was too much "sweetness and light." Convinced that true understanding and mutual appreciation can exist only in an atmosphere of honesty, Sadie and I resolved that we would serve with integrity rather than expediency.

Physicians, ministers, schoolteachers, and mail clerks were the Negro leaders in Tampa. The most prestigious position for a Negro in Tampa in 1926 was that of Executive Secretary of the Tampa Urban League—*I* was expected to be both the chief spokesman on Negro affairs and the liaison man between the black and white worlds: an almost impossible job. At Morehouse, I had known my role: to teach mathematics and psychology; at State College in South Carolina, to teach English. Sadie was a social worker, so her job was fairly well defined. But as liaison man between the black and white community, what was *I* to do? There was no paucity of problems, no dearth of needs: juvenile delinquency; a lack of recreational facilities; underpaid jobs and unemployment; police brutality; poor housing; inferior educational facilities for Negroes. In every area of existence and of life, the Negro had been short-changed, pauperized. Theoretically, at least, the executive secretary was free to map programs for improvement and relief. Hercules himself might well have been daunted in the face of this Augean stable!

We did make a few dents; we did take a few steps forward. Not long after our arrival, Arthur Raper, of the Commission on Interracial Cooperation in Atlanta, and I, as executive secretary of the Tampa Urban League, made a study of Negro life in Tampa. On the basis of our findings, the Tampa Urban League attempted to project a program for its future.

Arthur Raper, a Southerner on the order of W. O. Brown, my first Southern white friend, was an admirable man, aboveboard and honest. Working with him was a pleasure. My respect for him and his for me grew to a fine proportion. I shall never forget, however, two experiences I had with him. Mr. Raper refused our invitation to a dinner at which we launched the study on Negro life in Tampa. Not realizing his reason for declining the invitation, we pressed him to accept, which he did. At the dinner he was seated next to me, and when we had finished eating, he turned and said, "I didn't feel funny!"—thereby admitting that was the first time he had eaten with Negroes and at the same time inadvertently explaining his initial hesitancy about accepting our invitation.

Another time, Mr. Raper and I had rented a car for our use in collecting data. The rental company had to put on a temporary cardboard license plate. One day we were stopped by a policeman who inspected the license plate, angrily snatched it from the car, and spoke sharply to Raper, incensed that a white man should be acting as chauffeur for a Negro. Had I been driving, it would have been all right. This incident reminds me of a Booker T. Washington story: Mr. Washington had to make a train, but the white taxi driver (in the only taxi available) refused to drive him to the station. They changed roles: Mr. Washington got into the driver's seat and the white taxi driver became the passenger!

The study completed, Mrs. Atkinson arranged to present it to the leading white people of Tampa. It was appropriate that I, as executive secretary of the Tampa Urban League, give the report and Mr. Raper insisted that I do so. A quite exhaustive and comprehensive document, it revealed many things about Negro life in Tampa. Eager to know what the press had to say, I hurried to read the Tampa papers the next day, only to find that the (white) press had given Mr. Raper alone credit for having made the report. Even in Tampa in 1926, I was a bit puzzled. Perhaps the same old belief prevailed: If a white man gave the report, it was true; white Tampa would accept its authenticity only if it came from a white man. No explanation was ever made, no apology offered. That a white man's word carried more weight than a black man's was part of the racial pattern. It still is, though to a lesser extent.

It was essential that the executive secretary of the Tampa Urban League know some of the judges in the city. Fortunately we were able to establish good contacts with the judges of the Juvenile Court. As a result, many Negro boys, first and sometimes second offenders, were placed in the custody of the Urban League rather than being sent to the home for delinquent boys. They made weekly reports to me at the Urban League. In the evenings during the week we used vacant lots to provide recreational programs for them. When Negro boys were scheduled to appear in Juvenile Court, either Sadie or I was there. It is a good feeling to know that we helped many boys during our brief two years in Tampa.

Quite often when Negroes fell into the hands of the law, the Urban League helped them get legal aid. Our outstanding case was that of a Negro woman from St. Petersburg, Florida, whose car struck and killed a white man who was, I believe, a Doctor Parks, a white educator from Georgia. We read that Mrs. Allen had been arrested and charged with manslaughter, so we went to the jail to talk with her. She denied the police charge that she had been speeding, and said that she had stopped instantly after the man was hit. After hearing her account, we concluded that the accident had been unavoidable. We went to see Mrs. Atkinson of the Tampa Welfare League and Community Chest, explaining that we sought only justice for the Negro woman and asking whether she would recommend a lawyer. Mrs. Atkinson sent us to Judge W. Raleigh Pettiway. Judge Pettiway was a courteous man who rose when Sadie and I entered his office and addressed her as Mrs. Mays. Such courtesy was new in Tampa, and in the South for that matter.

We explained our mission to Judge Pettiway and asked him to recommend a good lawyer, one who could and would be fair where a Negro was involved with a white person. We emphasized that we wanted a fair trial and nothing more. Judge Pettiway told us that as a judge he could not recommend a lawyer, but he did give us a lead by saying, "If I were on trial for murder, I would get Attorney Cody Fowler to defend me." So we went to see Mr. Fowler.

Mr. Fowler agreed to take the case with $150 retainer fee. The accused woman's husband was reluctant to part with the money without a guarantee that his wife would be freed—he didn't trust "white" justice. We were able to convince Mr. Allen that even if his wife were convicted and sentenced, he still had to try to get justice for her if he cared for her. We told him that his wife knew she was not guilty; that we as well as he believed her, but that only the court could decide her guilt or innocence.

Mr. Fowler's chief task was to find the white woman with whom the accident victim had been talking just before he stepped off the sidewalk into the street and directly into the path of the car driven by Mrs. Allen. Fowler spent many hours trying to find this witness, and it was only shortly before the trial that he informed us he had succeeded and that the woman would appear in court. She did testify. Questioned by Attorney Fowler, she told the judge that Dr. Parks had turned around and without looking had stepped into the street in front of Mrs. Allen's car. On further questioning, she told the judge that the defendant had stopped immediately, had not run away, and had offered to do whatever was possible to help. I recall Mr.

Fowler's final question: "Was it her fault?" The witness asserted that under the circumstances it could have happened to anybody. "It could have happened to you, Judge, or to me." In a dramatic fashion, Attorney Fowler said, "Judge, I move that the case be dismissed." Mrs. Allen went free.

Not too many years ago, I was speaking in Tampa and Attorney Fowler was present. It was my delight to express to him again and in public my appreciation for what he had done to free an innocent Negro woman. I do not know whether Mrs. Allen is still living. I do know that through the Tampa Urban League justice was obtained for a woman who otherwise would have had little chance of acquittal. Dr. Parks' family did not press the case. Whether it would have been different if the family had done so, I do not know. But knowing as I did that Negroes seldom got justice in court, particularly in cases involving white persons, it was a revelation to me to find even one instance where the charge was not pressed. It was even more remarkable to witness both a Southern lawyer and a Southern judge dealing with the defendant not as a Negro woman, but simply as a person, a citizen, a human being entitled to justice. I have often wondered what the outcome would have been had the witness been a Negro. The policeman's accusation, I am sure, would not have been so readily set aside. We cherished this experience to set against other less rewarding experiences in Tampa. That we could have been so grateful for a simple act of justice is a sad commentary on the accepted formula: "Due process—for whites only."

My rapport with the Tampa police was not particularly good. They had a reputation for beating Negroes for little or no reason, and for shooting and killing them on the least provocation. Much of this mistreatment of Negroes took place within a dozen blocks of the Urban League. Negroes complained bitterly among themselves about this police brutality, but nobody was willing to report it to the mayor or chief of police. Instead, they felt that the Urban League should try to change the situation. I agreed. But before I could do anything I needed proof, specific information. A number of Negroes who had themselves been victims of police brutality or had been eyewitnesses to such brutality agreed to go with me to the chief's office to testify.

I spent one Saturday morning taking Negroes to the office of the chief of police to testify against certain policemen who patrolled the Negro section near the League. No policemen were fired, but several were removed from the Negro area. I was well aware that my activity in the matter of police brutality would not endear me to the police force, yet I felt it had to be done. Thereafter the police made no secret of the special hostility they felt for me. On one occasion, when I went to police headquarters, every officer fairly bristled when I came in. Several standing around with clubs in their hands and pistols on their hips called, "Boy, take off that damned hat!" No women were present—only policemen in uniform. Thereafter, when I had reason to go to police headquarters, I went bareheaded. I had developed the habit of going without a hat in frigid Maine, so I saw no reason for not doing the same in tropical Florida.

One night when Sadie and I were returning to Tampa from St. Petersburg, I missed my street and was turning on a red light when a police officer yelled at me. In explaining what had happened, I said "Yes" to him. He came around on my side of the car, swinging his club, and bellowed, "You say 'Yes, sir' to me!" I had never minded saying "Yes, sir" to both Negroes and whites—I still don't mind—but to do it under duress and on command is quite another thing. I was silent for a few seconds; then he asked me whose car I was driving. I replied that it belonged to the Tampa Urban League, of which I was the executive secretary. He had never heard of the Urban League and wanted to know what it was and who owned it. When I explained that it was owned by the board of trustees, of which the mayor of the city was chairman, and gave him the names of the other board members, prominent Negro and white leaders in the community, he apparently decided to forget his demand to be yes-sirred.

So long as there were relatively few articulate leaders, it was customary to have one Negro speak for the whole group, or even for the entire race, as with Booker T. Washington from 1895 until his death in 1915. With my appointment to office as the executive secretary of the Tampa Urban League, I automatically assumed the role of spokesman for my community.

It was taken for granted that I would follow in the footsteps of my predecessor, Mrs. Blanche Armwood Beatty, an able woman, whose leadership was accepted by both Negroes and whites. Mrs. Beatty had endorsed a subdivision for Negroes so designed that in time all Negroes would live within its confines, with none in the other seven sections of Tampa. Lots were to be sold, houses built, streets paved, lights provided, sewerage put in, police protection given, and transportation installed. Soon after Sadie and I assumed our duties at the League, a delegation of white men called to get my approval for the subdivision. They extolled all the advantages of the new site for Negroes; reminded me that not only my predecessor but also the leading white people so thoroughly approved of it that they had promised to provide all facilities to make it a most desirable subdivision; and, finally, told me that I was to have, free, two spacious lots of my own choosing. A meeting was set up for me, city officials, the executive secretary of the Tampa Welfare League and Community Chest, and owners of the subdivision—a dozen or more white persons and one lone Negro. I was to represent all the Negroes of Tampa. Realizing the magnitude and the significance of the decision I must make, I requested a postponement of the meeting in order to confer with some of the Negro leaders of Tampa.

It should have been glaringly clear that a new man in the community, and one who owned nothing, had no right to make a deal with anybody without the full knowledge and consent of the Negroes themselves. How could I match a dozen white and powerful community leaders? The mayor alone represented ten times the power I had. At the next meeting, I was accompanied by a dozen Negroes—all property owners, all property tax payers. One Negro, Doctor M. J. Anderson, was paying $2,000 a year in taxes, which represented considerable ownership in 1926. These men made it clear that the idea of the subdivision was highly undesirable, impracticable, unwise and unsafe for Negroes; that the facilities would be too long being provided; that in case of racial conflict Negroes could be located and abused too easily for comfort. Happily, the "ideal" relocation plan for Negroes was abandoned.

Such decisions are not easy. Such "bait" as the "two choice lots" is too obvious to elicit more than a wry smile, but it is pleasant to be liked, gratifying to be approved. Moreover, it is astonishingly easy to rationalize in a situation like this—to say, "Perhaps it would be better to go along with them. If I play ball with them, maybe they will play ball with me, with us. Maybe in the long run it would be better for all of us." But I could not believe that "ultimate good" could come from immediate evil, from conscious betrayal of what I believed to be right.

My decision against sponsoring deliberate segregation won me few friends among white Tampa citizens. It may have won the respect of a few. Far more important, it did not mar my self-respect. Long ago, I learned to say to myself, "I do not have to live with these people—whoever they might be—but I do have to get up with myself every morning and I do have to go to bed with myself every night. I want to be able to look at myself. I'd better keep on good terms with me!"

The following pages are important only because they reveal once more how deep the roots of prejudice penetrate; picture once more the wounds and hurts which the prejudiced inflict upon those whose human sensitivity they ignore or deny.

Dr. J. R. E. Lee, president of Florida A & M College, sent his singers to Tampa where they were to give a private concert in the home of Peter O. Knight, one of Florida's wealthiest and most distinguished citizens. I was happy to honor President Lee's request that I make the necessary arrangements for the program. The concert was to last about thirty minutes, and, as the program began, I sat down in the chair in front of which I had been standing. Immediately, Mrs. Knight came and asked me to stand, telling me not to sit down in her house. Shades of my back-door experience in South Carolina where a Negro was not good enough to enter a white man's front door! One does not sit in the presence of "royalty"; one does not tramp with muddy feet into the "Holy of Holies." I am not sure whether Mrs. Knight was protecting her self-assumed royalty or the sanctity of her parlor!

Perhaps no one should sit down in anybody's house without being invited to do so. I had not even considered the question of etiquette. By request, I was doing a favor for a friend, Dr. Lee, and for the Knights. I was in charge of the program, and I had simply taken it for granted that by ordinary courtesy I would not be expected to stand for thirty minutes.

Spiritual assaults of this kind make an indelible impression. The question always arises, "What should I do?" Clearly I could not sit down in Mrs. Knight's house. Just as clearly I had to show my attitude to her grossly rude and insulting behavior. So I simply left the house and stood outside in the yard until the program was over. How to live in a segregated society without accepting that society is a constant battle, a battle that is won only by steadfast and continuous refusal to admit as inevitable or right that which is ugly and mean, stupid and cruel. Trivia? Only to one who has never known the bitter taste of humiliation, the galling pain of day in, day out denigration.

I had great admiration for Mr. J. J. Henry, affectionately known as "Old Man Henry." I met him soon after our arrival in Tampa. A long-time resident of Florida, Mr. Henry so resented the introduction of segregated streetcars in Tampa that he vowed never to ride on them and he never did. A carpenter by trade, he would rise early enough to walk to his job, carrying his tools on his back, often walking several miles. He was quite old when I knew him, and by then he was riding in his own Ford. Mr. Henry had little formal education but his was a rare and cultivated spirit. He never bowed and scraped; he never kowtowed or knuckled under. He was one of those rare Negroes who are free despite the system.

Refusal to give a woman the title of Miss or Mrs. is an expression of the belief that the person is unworthy of being so addressed. In the South, in 1926, calling a Negro woman Mrs. or Miss was equivalent to granting her social equality with white women—an intolerable admission. Many Southern whites even objected to Negroes using titles among their own people. Not satisfied with their own degradation of Negro women, they wished Negroes themselves to confirm their "inferiority" by showing the same lack of respect for each other and for their womenfolk.

If Sadie and I were ever on the verge of losing our jobs in Tampa—an ever-present possibility—it was on the battleground of titles. We could not control what white people called Negro women. Nor could they restrain us from using titles in referring to black women. We met the problem of titles head-on, almost at the beginning of our short career in Tampa. What should we do when people who did not know my wife, who were not close friends, phoned and asked to speak to "Sadie" or "Catherine," the employment secretary? Certainly it would not help to get angry, or for me to yell indignantly, *"Don't call my wife Sadie, call her Mrs. Mays!"* Our solution was simple—and effective. When someone called and asked to speak to "Sadie" or "Catherine," whoever answered the phone would say, "Just a moment, please, Mrs. Mays (or Miss Romar) will be with you in a minute."

The battle of the titles extended to the Family Service Association where Sadie did her social work. Sadie insisted on writing Mr., or Miss, or Mrs. before the names of her clients. Her supervisor objected to Sadie's giving such respect to Negroes, but Sadie, believing that giving titles to her clients helped build their self-respect, not only continued to write the proper titles before their names but also used these titles when she talked with them. The supervisor considered Sadie insubordinate and made it a point to take her records and erase the titles. Sadie continued to write them; the supervisor continued to erase them! Finally, we were reported to our "boss," Mrs. Ruth Atkinson, executive secretary of the Tampa Welfare League and Community Chest, the "little white angel." We were charged with insisting on being identified as Mr. and Mrs., and Sadie with writing titles before the names of her Negro clients. We had heard that we were to be called in, so we were not surprised when it happened. We did not know what the outcome would be. We knew that our behavior was right —and knew equally well that it was not the way Negroes in the South were supposed to behave. We had resolved to be so efficient on our jobs and do our work so well that no one could honestly say that we were incompetent or neglectful. If we were dismissed it would have to be because we insisted on practicing the principles which were more precious to us than any job could ever be.

We pleaded guilty to the charges that Sadie had continued to write titles before the names of her Negro clients and that we did indeed use the formula, "Mrs. Mays (or Miss Romar) will be with you shortly," in answering the office telephone. It was a long conference, but there was no meeting of minds. Mrs. Atkinson proposed a compromise: If Sadie would agree not to resent being called "Sadie" by white people, she would be permitted to write titles before the names of her Negro clients. This compromise we could not accept. Mrs. Atkinson said that there was resentment also because I referred to Sadie as "Mrs. Mays" when I introduced her to white people in Tampa. My reply was that if the time ever came when I was afraid to call my wife Mrs., I hoped she would file suit for divorce immediately, for at that moment I ceased to be worthy of her.

We left the conference not knowing what would be the consequences. Mrs. Atkinson was a kindly woman and really wanted to do the right thing. She wanted to satisfy Negroes and please whites. She was liberal within the status quo. She wanted to keep everybody happy and not "muddy the waters." When no other white person was present, or in the presence of white people she knew to be liberal enough to endure hearing her give titles to Negroes, she did not hesitate to do so. But when in doubt, or when she knew white people would object, she became an artist of evasion. She would introduce me as "our executive secretary" and Sadie as "our executive secretary's wife." Even at that, she was way ahead of most Southerners on the race question. White she was; "our little white angel" she was not. But she tried, and I write of her not to condemn but to reveal further how prejudice enslaves the spirit.

Fairly soon after the dead-end conference, Jesse O. Thomas, field secretary of the National Urban League, came to Tampa. He had been sent for because he was responsible for our coming to Tampa, and moreover he was the person who would recommend our successors—if there were to be any. We were not fired. Mr. Thomas took the position that we had done nothing to be fired for. A man of lesser character might have gone along with the Tampa "establishment," in which case we would have been dismissed on the spot. In his autobiography, *My Story in Black and White* (Exposition Press, New York, 1967), Mr. Thomas tells the story. We did not know that Mrs. Atkinson and others had intended to fire us for our insistence on dealing with Negroes in the same way that we dealt with other human beings until we read Jesse O. Thomas' autobiography more than forty years later.

An article, "It Cost Too Much," which appeared in the April 7, 1928, issue of the Tampa *Bulletin*, dealt with a pageant entitled *From Darkness to Light* which had been staged in the Tampa Bay Casino by students from the Booker T. Washington High School. The pageant was designed to portray the progress made by Negroes from slavery up to 1928. The Tampa Bay Casino was city-owned, but was rented to the U.S.S. Tampa Post No. 5 of the American Legion. The Legion rented the Casino to the Booker T. Washington High School, on the condition that the laws of segregation would be strictly observed and rigidly enforced. These conditions were so meticulously followed that the result was ridiculous.

The main floor orchestra and dress circle seats of the Tampa Bay Casino were reserved for whites, the balcony for Negroes. When the balcony was filled and Negroes were forced to stand, it took an absurd amount of time and persuasion to obtain permission for them to sit in the empty dress circle seats, to say nothing of the seats on the main floor, also largely unoccupied. The situation aroused my most indignant "righteous indignation." The segregated seating made a complete travesty of the title *From Darkness to Light. Let Darkness Reign Forever* would have been far more appropriate. Once more the question: What should be done about it? Should the executive secretary of the Tampa Urban League make this his concern? If he was supposed to speak for Negroes in Tampa, should he not speak now? Must he not at least speak out for himself and his wife?

Sadie and I went home from the pageant deeply concerned about what had happened. We sat a long time discussing what to do. That we must do something, we knew full well. What would be most effective? We decided that an article must be written to be published in the Negro paper, the Tampa *Bulletin*—an article so censorious of what had happened at the Tampa Bay Casino that it might mean our days in Tampa were over. We weighed the possible consequences: Would we be run out of town? Fired? Given so many days to pack and leave? We felt that any one of these could happen, but we felt even more strongly that the article must appear.

We consulted with the Reverend M. D. Potter, editor of the Tampa *Bulletin*, who agreed to print the article. Potter, a courageous though mild-mannered man, assured me, "I will not only carry your article; I will support it with an editorial," and he did. That the article would not go unremarked, we were certain, but we were not prepared for all the commotion and repercussions it elicited. Most of it, as it appeared in the Tampa *Bulletin* (long since out of business), and the various reactions to it are given below. Unfortunately, the very first and last parts of the article cannot now be found; but the major portion is still in a scrapbook which I have kept these forty years. To the white Tampa public, this was a radical document. Some considered it dangerous, even incendiary. I think most Negroes agreed with the contents of the article, but probably many also agreed that its publication was unwise, Negroes as a rule being overanxious to say what was pleasing and acceptable to white ears. To me, it was and still is a sanely restrained, objective expression of my attitude toward segregation; and it was an article which I had to write:

> . . . Evidently it was bargained or agreed that Negroes would use the balcony and that the white people would take the orchestra and the dress circle seats. This is evidenced by the fact that well-informed ushers from the Booker T. Washington High School politely exclaimed, as Negroes entered, "Upstairs, please," and no Negro was allowed to sit downstairs until the balcony became overwhelmingly crowded. The intelligence has come to me that when the balcony was filled and Negroes went downstairs in quest of seats, they were not allowed to sit and had to return upstairs to stand and wait for further adjustment. The crowded balcony seemed to present a difficult problem to the colored officials. They hardly knew what to do. Finally, the good news came that Negroes would be allowed to sit in the dress circle to the right. This section filled up rapidly. Negroes were then allowed to occupy the seats in the left dress circle.
>
> Were it not pathetic, it would be laughable that out of 800 or 900 seats reserved for white people, only 68 were present, including little children. Excluding the seats to the sides, which were eventually occupied by Negroes, there were 576 seats in the orchestra or main auditorium reserved for white friends. Sixty-eight of these were taken. There is no denying the fact that these are the best seats in the house. To be mathematically exact, 508 of the best orchestra seats were vacant all during the pageant and Negroes could not sit in them. The writer, wanting a good seat, attempted with his wife and a friend to sit in orchestra seats in the rear. The usher went up in the air and insisted that we crowd ourselves into the side seats. Our seats were so inconvenient that at times we could not see the performance. The balcony and sides were crowded while 508 of the best seats in the house remained vacant. Had I been allowed to sit in the rear of the main auditorium, I would have been fully 14 seats from the nearest white man (one) and much farther from the other 67. . . .
>
> . . . It cost too much. It cannot be justified by law; cannot be justified by tradition. Neither justice nor money can justify it. . . . It sets a bad example before the ambitious youths of our city, does not help the Negro

in developing group self-respect, and does not increase the white man's respect for him.

As promised, the Reverend Potter wrote a strong editorial in support of my article, in which he said, "The thoughtful mind, the logical mind, the mind that reasons soundly and meets arguments with arguments will not attempt to defend what happened at the Casino. It cannot be defended."

In a long letter to the editor of the Tampa *Bulletin*, the Negro Ministers Alliance endorsed the article "It Cost Too Much." Speaking for the Alliance, Father John E. Culmer wrote, ". . . If Negroes responsible for the 'bargain' knew that those rules were unalterable even though Negroes were renting the auditorium to present a Negro show to Negroes and which Negroes supported, why should Negroes *WANT* the Casino. Perhaps it was all thoughtlessly done. But if that is the way we go from "Darkness to Light," Heaven knows "IT COST TOO MUCH!"

Thomas H. Davis, chairman of Tampa Post No. 5 of the American Legion, wrote a hot reply to my article in which he said, ". . . The agreement between the Legion and the school officials was well understood and . . . satisfactory to the Superintendent of Public Instruction and I see no need for such radical statements as appeared in your paper. Such statements do not tend to increase the feeling of mutual respect between the races and . . . do much to hinder the progress of the Negro race. . . . All who meet in the Casino will be subject to our rules and should they dislike said rules they need not meet here."

My article was the talk of the town in Tampa for several weeks. J. G. Anderson, Jr., chairman of the Board of Education, did not like it and sent word he wanted to see me. Consequently, on May 16, 1928, Mr. Anderson and I had a conference in his office where, after a lukewarm greeting, he pulled the article from his desk drawer and began to criticize me for what I had said.

From Anderson's point of view, this was not a conference between equals but rather one between a man and a boy. His purpose was not to seek understanding through an exchange of ideas but to give me a lecture on how I should behave as a "leader" among my people. The chairman of the Board had not done his homework: He accused me of being a "northern" Negro who did not know the ways of the South and said I had come to Tampa to stir up trouble between the races. I had to remind him that I was born north of Florida in the secessionist state of South Carolina.

In my article I had drawn a distinction between obeying unjust laws through sheer necessity and the voluntary acceptance of a law which one did not have to accept. Mr. Anderson did not understand how any Negro could be dissatisfied with segregation. He saw nothing amiss with the humiliating experience to which the principal of the Booker Washington High School had subjected Negroes when he accepted the American Legion's condition that he could use the Tampa Bay Casino provided that Negroes sat in the balcony. In discussing my reasons for opposition to segregation, I discovered that Chairman Anderson did not even know the depth of inequality in the accommodations for blacks and whites on train coaches between Tampa and Jacksonville and throughout the South. He was unaware that frequently the conductor and the butcher occupied eight seats while Negro passengers stood, and that often there was one toilet for both Negro men and women. He was naïve enough to believe that a letter from me to the Interstate Commerce Commission calling attention to these inequities would bring about the abolition of inequality in train travel.

Mr. Anderson's chief complaint about my article was that it would stir up Negroes, incite them to riot by "leading them to believe that segregation was unjust and therefore should be abolished." Our discussion took many turns. He accused me, and rightly so, of believing in mixed schools. He said that this would never happen in the South, and that the mixing of the races in the schools would be detrimental to both races. This statement gave me an opportunity to tell him that I had faith that someday the race problem would be solved precisely because of the contacts I had and the friendships I had made with a few white Southerners at the University of Chicago. Mr. Anderson never did grasp the fact that Negroes did not want to go to school with white people simply because they were white, but because Negro schools, such as those in Tampa and throughout the South, were inferior to the white schools and the school officials had shown no intention of making the Negro schools equal.

Chairman Anderson made mention of the fact that white people could not get out of the Casino on the night of the pageant without Negroes rubbing up against them. I pointed out that this was unavoidable unless several hundred Negroes had been required to remain seated while sixty-eight white persons passed out. Mr. Anderson said that all the white people with whom he had talked were enraged over what I had said in the article and felt it was an attack on the Southern way of life. He advised me that if I had grievances I should not publicize them. "You cannot cure a sore by rubbing it," he said. "You should go to the proper authorities and see about them and not incite and stir up bitter feelings . . . for your article did just that. We may have a duplication of the riots they had in Chicago, Washington, and Atlanta." I tried to assure Mr. Anderson that he had overestimated my ability to incite a riot and that I had done only that which my conscience dictated, but I left his office without having convinced him that I had taken a valid position, and certainly I went away more confident than ever before that I was right in publishing the article "It Cost Too Much."

It is significant to observe that the four comments quoted above are divided along racial lines: The two comments favoring the article came from Negroes and the two opposing it came from whites.

We were not fired from our jobs in Tampa. After refusing a Rockefeller-endowed General Education Board fellowship, we resigned. I became student secretary of the National Council of the YMCA, with headquarters in Atlanta, and Sadie accepted a position with the Georgia Study of Negro Child Welfare. There was never any doubt in our minds that had we not resigned we would eventually have been fired. The Tampa atmosphere was not as warm and cordial as it had been upon our arrival. We would have been fired, not for incompetence on our jobs, for we did our work; not because we were urging Negroes to disobey the laws, because we did not do that. We would have been fired eventually not because we were drunkards or dope addicts; these sins were not ours. We could not be charged with sexual immorality. We were decent citizens. Probably any one of the above charges could have been more easily forgiven than could our real sin: our refusal to accept the status quo, our determination to elevate the level of Negro pride and self-respect. We were engaged to work to improve the lot of Negroes in employment, recreation, housing, health, education, and juvenile delinquency, and, if possible, to reduce the friction between Negroes and the police. Black and white Tampa agreed that we were to perform our tasks in these areas. But in addition I saw our role as one of helping Negroes build respect for and pride in themselves despite the strangling chains of segregation. I did not see our roles as merely the ones defined by the Tampa Urban League. Mr. Anderson had said that the article I had written was dangerous and could incite a riot. Was it "dangerous" because it bolstered the Negro's dissatisfaction with and his resentment of segregation? It surely was not smart to resent that Negro women were called by their first names, such resentment encouraging them to feel that they were as good as white folks. It was nothing short of heresy to oppose a segregated subdivision for Negroes, thereby rejecting instead of being grateful for what the white people had planned for Negroes. Not for much longer could white Tampa have tolerated "uppity" Negroes who were introducing new rules by which to play the game. Yet we did not run away. We gladly responded to invitations to work in Atlanta at better salaries than we were receiving in Tampa.

We anticipated that the recommendations of white people under whom we had worked in Tampa, and others, might not be overly laudatory. We had not accepted the status quo without some protest. We had protested politely and, we hoped, with dignity, but protest we had. Reports of our "radical," our "subversive" behavior in Tampa did follow us, but we never failed to receive many offers of new positions.

Miss Louisa Fitzsimmons, head of the Georgia Study of Negro Child Welfare, wanted Mrs. Mays to join her staff in Atlanta, and asked for a recommendation from Mrs. Atkinson. Mrs. Atkinson was so long in replying that Miss Fitzsimmons requested me to speak to her. Mrs. Atkinson was quite frank when I talked with her. She told me that she had not answered Miss Fitzsimmons because she did not want to say anything that would hurt Mrs. Mays, but "you know your wife objects to being called 'Sadie' so what am I going to say to Miss Fitzsimmons?" I suggested that she just tell the truth, say that Mrs. Mays objected to anyone other than a close friend calling her by her first name. I made it clear to Mrs. Atkinson that being respected as a human being was more important than the job, much as we both would like Sadie to have it. Mrs. Atkinson wrote Sadie a good recommendation, pointing out, however, that although my wife was a splendid, competent worker, she wanted to be called Mrs. Mays. She added that Sadie's attitude made it difficult for her to work in the South. Oddly enough, Sadie got the job and she and Miss Fitzsimmons became good friends. After forty years, they still exchanged greetings at Christmastime.

Twelve years later, I was being investigated to determine my worthiness to become the president of Morehouse College in Atlanta. I had been checked out thoroughly, including my record as a young teacher at Morehouse and South Carolina State; my performances as national student secretary of the YMCA; and my six years as dean of the School of Religion of Howard University, Washington, D.C. The only question mark was my record with the Tampa Urban League; and Mr. Jesse O. Thomas, acting executive secretary of the National Urban League, was asked to answer this question. After Mr. Thomas' endorsement of my work in Tampa, I was unanimously elected in 1940 to serve as president of Morehouse College. The Tampa experience never kept us from getting jobs, which might have been because our work stood on its merits, no matter how suspect our "radical" attitude.

Despite our belief that we would have eventually been fired from our positions in Tampa, Sadie and I were particularly pleased and somewhat amazed that we received several letters of praise and recommendation from white people of Tampa, including a splendid letter from my "boss," Mrs. Ruth Atkinson.

I concluded my final report to the Board of the Tampa Urban League, in August, 1928, with these observations:

> No part of the work is dearer to our hearts than that of interracial relations. In our dealings with white people, we have been ever mindful of the possibility of an entire group being appraised through us. We have endeavored to have the respect for the Negro raised rather than lowered. We have struggled to have him judged in the light of his possibility, his opportunity and the depths from whence he comes rather than in the light of finality. We have striven to pursue a policy that differs widely from that of the average Negro who chances to come in frequent contact with white people. In substance, we have carried one message to Negroes and whites alike. We believe that any Negro who has one message for white people and another message for Negroes is a hypocrite, dangerous to both groups, and retards the growth in interracial good will and understanding. We believe that honesty is the best policy in interracial affairs, as in all others; and that interracial foundations built on anything other than honesty and fair play are destined to crumble. To this end, we have tried to be fair to our white friends; we have been careful not to sell the Negro in an unfavorable light.

The depth of the race problem was revealed throughout our two years in Tampa. Mr. Anderson of the School Board had no understanding of the Negro problem, and no sympathy whatsoever for a Negro who did not accept—and preferably lovingly embrace!—the insult which law and custom placed upon him. What I had tried to say to Mr. Anderson was as difficult for him to understand as if I had spoken in Hebrew or Arabic. My article was equally unintelligible to Mr. Davis of the American Legion. Even Mrs. Atkinson, euphemistically called by some Negroes "our little white angel," had no empathy with our desire to be given dignity and respect such as all people are entitled to by virtue of the fact that all are born in the image of God. We could not communicate with them. We spoke a foreign language. Over and over again I was reminded of these words of Countee Cullen, the great Negro poet:

Yet Do I Marvel
I doubt not God is good, well-meaning, kind,
And did he stoop to quibble could tell why
The little buried mole continues blind;
Why flesh that mirrors Him must some day die;
Make plain the reason tortured Tantalus
Is baited by the fickle fruit; declare
If merely brute caprice dooms Sisyphus
To struggle up a never-ending stair.
Inscrutable His ways are, and immune
To catechism by a mind too strewn
With petty cares to slightly understand
What awful brain compels His awful hand.
Yet do I marvel at this curious thing:
To make a poet black, and bid him sing!

And to paraphrase the last lines of Cullen's poem:

Yet do I marvel at this curious thing:
To make a man black, and bid him aspire!

Exhausted and weary from finishing our work and preparing for a major move in our lives, we left Tampa in a drawing room. A dozen friends came to the train to see us off, and their presence dramatized the fact that we were leaving in a sleeper. It was obvious that we were being discussed by the white passengers who were traveling to Jacksonville in the same car, and by their friends who had come to see them off. We paid little attention to their mutterings and glowering looks until the Pullman and train conductors came to get our tickets. On leaving our drawing room, the Pullman conductor said, "Lock your door, and don't you open it for anybody." The next morning when we arrived in Jacksonville our porter told us that the train conductor had done his best to stir up something; that at every station stop between Tampa and Jacksonville he had told every white man standing on the platform, "We have two niggers in that drawing room." The porter had been afraid that someone might phone ahead and have a mob take us off the train. The Pullman conductor must have thought this could happen when he instructed us to lock the drawing room door and not to open it for anybody. The porter also told us that a representative of the Pullman company had slept in a berth next to our drawing room in order to protect us if anything threatened us.

So ended our days in Tampa—not a very happy interlude, but one rich in friendships, and one about which we have no regrets.

Chapter IX

Two More Detours

I had fully intended to go straight through for a Ph.D. once I entered the University of Chicago in 1921, but one detour after another detained me: Morehouse, South Carolina State, the Tampa Urban League; thereafter, the National YMCA, and then the Institute of Social and Religious Research.

My detours were made easy, for I always had good positions offered me. My problem was not "what job can I get?" but "which shall I choose?" Leaving Tampa, I had to choose between a General Education Board Fellowship and a position in Atlanta with the National YMCA as student secretary serving Negro colleges in South Carolina, Georgia, Florida, Alabama, and Tennessee. There was no doubt I was to serve Negro colleges —the sky would have fallen, the world collapsed if the National Board had tried to have a Negro service the YMCA in the white colleges in these five states in 1928. The YMCA, like the church (and everything else) was rigidly segregated in the South—in the North, too, for that matter. Both complacently accepted the status quo of segregation.

Many memories of associations with the YMCA in high school and college impelled me to choose the offer of the National Board. Moreover, I knew that the Negro leaders in the YMCA, such as James Moreland, Channing Tobias, J. H. McGrew, William Craver, and Ralph W. Bullock, were able and admirable men, each demonstrating manhood and dignity in a highly segregated organization. So in 1928 I joined the staff of the National YMCA with headquarters in Atlanta and remained in that position for two years. Sadie joined the staff of the Georgia Study of Negro Child Welfare and later she joined the faculty of the Atlanta University School of Social Work. For the next six years we kept residence in Atlanta.

In those days, the Negro student secretary was highly respected on Negro college campuses. Negro students then, as now, needed to be encouraged and inspired to aim high and to reach for the "unattainable goals." There was little for them to look forward to in the late twenties except preaching, teaching, social work, and possibly medicine and law. Any speech or informal discussion brought terrific response when it broadened their horizons, assured them that they were "somebody," and held out hope for the future. So many were hungry for the motivation to aspire beyond what seemed available to them. The YMCA conferences brought Negro students something special, something deeper and more spiritual than the colleges could provide.

The National YMCA had established Kings Mountain in North Carolina as the segregated site of the annual conference for Negro college students of the Southeast who met at Lincoln Academy. Blue Ridge was the segregated conference ground for white students. Although Blue Ridge was truly a segregated conference, a "closed society," Kings Mountain was in reality an open society, segregated but never segregating. From the beginning, the Kings Mountain conference was all-inclusive. White people who came to Kings Mountain were never segregated. This was not true at Blue Ridge. It was highly segregated—the "Christian" in the name Young Men's Christian Association was non-operative when it came to the races. Even W. W. Weatherford, who was in charge of Blue Ridge, and who was one of the pioneers in breaking down barriers between the races in the days of the Commission on Interracial Cooperation, was trapped in the miasmic tradition of a segregated "Christian" society.

The Negro leaders of the Kings Mountain conferences, supported and encouraged by Channing Tobias and his Colored Works Department, brought together each summer the ablest black and white leaders of the nation to speak to Negro students. The invited speakers were carefully screened and picked—men who were not afraid to grapple with the religious, social, economic, and racial problems of the South and the nation. Only men with a message that spoke to the needs of Negroes, and who had a point of view that enabled Negro students to look hopefully beyond their circumscribed plight, were invited to speak at Kings Mountain. No other organization, except the Young Women's Christian Association, was providing this kind of leadership for Negro students. They found identity at Kings Mountain. It was an oasis in a desert of segregation and discrimination. It could do these things because the conference was under the auspices of Negro executives and administrators.

It has always been true that when a suppressed group wants change it must take the initiative to bring it about. Moreover, it must be armed against stubborn resistance, for there is no length to which people will not go who are determined to perpetuate an evil. The Blue Ridge YMCA Conference carried their segregation policy to the point of absurdity. The two conferences were supposed to exchange delegates. Blue Ridge would send a delegation to bring segregated greetings to the Negro students; and Kings Mountain would send a delegation to carry similar greetings to their white "brothers" at Blue Ridge. The white delegation came to Kings Mountain as fraternal delegates, entitled to and receiving all the rights and privileges of the Negro students without embarrassment of any kind. However, Negroes who went to Blue Ridge could not go as fraternal delegates. They had to go as program participants. The reasoning behind this absurdity was that if Negroes were accepted as "fraternal" delegates the inference might be that they were regarded as equals—a shocking and revolting thought! Surely the leadership of the YMCA must have felt a furtive blush of shame to label their segregated God "Christian"! The idea of "program participants" was in character, for it was traditionally quite acceptable for Negroes to "entertain" white people. The Negro students who went to Blue Ridge were segregated at meals and in housing.

Frank T. Wilson, the senior Negro secretary in the National Student Division, and I decided that we would no longer cooperate with Blue Ridge by sending our students there as "program participants" to be segregated and humiliated. We could not control what Blue Ridge did, but we could control what we did. We agreed, further, that fraternal delegates from Blue Ridge would still be welcome at Kings Mountain, and that they would never be humiliated or segregated. Commenting on the action we took, I quote from a letter Frank T. Wilson wrote Miss Celestine Smith on July 11, 1936, in connection with research she was doing to write the history of Kings Mountain–Blue Ridge YMCA Conference relationships:

> You might be interested in having this item of history from the point of view of the action of Kings Mountain men: In 1928, the men at the Kings Mountain Conference did not accept the invitation to send fraternal delegates to Blue Ridge because of unsatisfactory living provisions. But in 1929 Kings Mountain men voted against sending fraternal delegates [actually program participants] to Blue Ridge until conditions for the accommodation of these delegates could be worked out without limitations. The Council further requested the staff of traveling secretaries to refrain from going to Blue Ridge and not to encourage Negro leaders to go to Blue Ridge until more satisfactory arrangements could be provided for the accommodations of such staff members and adult leaders.

The Negro Student YWCA was also having its problems with segregation at Blue Ridge. Not until 1928 did the Negro YWCA Conference vote to put an end to eating and sleeping at Blue Ridge under segregated conditions. The last fraternal exchange of delegates between Negro women and white women was in 1930. In that year, the white women students meeting at Blue Ridge and the black women students meeting at Kings Mountain voted simultaneously to discontinue the exchange of fraternal delegates.

The YMCA and the YWCA establishments clung to Blue Ridge despite its policy of segregation. As late as 1949, the Blue Ridge assembly had a rule limiting Negro delegates to five in number, or five percent of the Conference delegates, whichever was greater. Long before 1949, however, the YWCA had broken with Blue Ridge and held interracial conferences at Berea, Kentucky, while also holding conferences at Blue Ridge for those "pure" souls who feared contamination from attending interracial affairs at Berea or any other place. Even after the YMCA of the Southeast Region purchased Blue Ridge in 1943, the segregated policies continued. As a member of the Board of Directors of the Southern Area Council of the YMCA, I protested the segregated policies of that body. I wrote a strong letter to the Board condemning the YMCA for continuing to segregate Negroes at Blue Ridge. I went further. I urged all the Negro secretaries of local YMCA's in the South not to go to Blue Ridge until the segregated policy was abandoned. Finally, in 1951, the color bar was broken at Blue Ridge. The Southern Area Council of the YMCA not only had power in setting racial policies of the YMCA in the South, but the Southern secretaries and executives (white) wielded considerable influence in the National Council and on the National Board in racial matters. The National body always moved very cautiously so as not to offend their Southern colleagues on the race problem.

In 1929, my colleague, Frank Wilson, was in India representing the Student YMCA. We wished to invite white students to Kings Mountain when he returned but were not quite sure how to do it. We knew that no white student would be allowed to come on behalf of his college. However, Howard Kester of the Fellowship of Reconciliation was so vitally interested in the problems of labor and race that defenders of the status quo labeled him a radical and dangerous; hence we turned to him for help. He gave us the names of twenty-five or thirty liberal white students who might come to Kings Mountain as Christians on their own.

We wrote them, explaining in detail what the Conference was all about and why we wanted them to come, making it clear that they would have to come on their own, and that they would be expected to worship, participate in the programs, eat, and sleep in the same quarters with Negroes, with no special provisions for their being white. To our delighted surprise, twelve young men came, and everything worked out beautifully! We had been wise enough not to seek permission from our superiors for fear they would not grant it, and we were prepared to accept full responsibility.

Two other incidents connected with Kings Mountain are vivid in my memory: One of the twelve white students was accompanied by his father and introduced me to him as "Mr." Mays. The father could not bring himself to call me Mister, so he just said, "How do, Mays." The atmosphere of the Conference was so cordial and friendly, the worship services so outstanding, and the leadership at the Conference so superb that when the young student and his father were leaving, the father expressed appreciation for what the Conference had meant to him and accorded me the supreme accolade by calling me "Mr." Mays. Something had happened to this man. It had been a new experience for him, and he admitted he had never seen anything like it.

The next incident concerned Ruth Lockman, a beautiful white girl who had just joined the staff of the Intercollegiate Association in Washington, D.C., which sent her to the Conference at Kings Mountain. Miss Lockman had been in one conference in Detroit where a few Negroes were present, and had been on the campus of Wilberforce in Ohio, but Kings Mountain provided her first experience of intimately sharing life with a large number of Negroes. It was the first time, too, that the Negro students at the Conference had seen a Southern white woman moving in and out among them, displaying no prejudice, acting as if she really "belonged," as if she were one of them. It was such a rare event in the South in 1929 that the students wondered why she had come, what she was "up to."

Ruth Lockman told me how pleased she was that her father agreed to her participating in the Kings Mountain Conference. She said that when she told him she was going to a men's conference, he expressed no surprise; when she told him it was a conference of Negro men, he still displayed no shock, simply saying, "That's all right. You can help a great deal." I have never forgotten this story. Just why this white father did not explode, as I believe most white fathers in the South would have, I do not know. Miss Lockman recently told me that her father, a Methodist, had come in contact with Negro Methodists in South Carolina in a money-raising effort for Claflin University, a Negro Methodist institution in Orangeburg. Perhaps that association may partially explain his attitude. Miss Lockman may never have heard her parents discuss Negroes adversely. Many persons, not themselves prejudiced against members of other racial groups, are so enslaved by "the system" that they do nothing that might make them unacceptable to their own "kind." They move quietly along, saying nothing.

It is sad but not surprising that the Negro conference students at Kings Mountain had misgivings about Southern white women who were human and liberal on race and who had the courage to break with the "sacred" tradition of the South on segregation. As late as the 1940's, when Lillian Smith spoke at Morehouse and was a guest in our home, the Morehouse students were amazed and bewildered. Some wanted to know whether Miss Smith really stayed in the president's residence and actually dined with us. When they heard her speak, many could not believe their ears. Such straight talk on race was hard to believe, especially coming from a Southern white woman, one born in Florida and living in Georgia. Most of them doubted her sincerity.

These two events, more than a decade apart, reveal how deep and wide was the chasm of misunderstanding between two peoples who lived side by side in the same geographical areas. Even while this chasm existed, the white South was enjoying its most prestigious delusion, claiming with great confidence, "We know our Negroes!" Negroes were never so unrealistic. They never even pretended "We understand the white man!"

A white woman visiting a Negro men's conference in the sixties or seventies would go unremarked. In 1929, it was a daring venture. If publicity had been given to the fact that a Southern white woman was practicing "social equality" by attending a Negro conference, it would have been as strongly condemned by the white South as was President Roosevelt's inviting Booker T. Washington to the White House for dinner.* After all, it was not until 1925, at the University of Chicago, that I met and developed a friendship with a Southern white man. It was not until 1929 that I came to know and appreciate a courageous Southern white woman. My mother had warned me to avoid Southern white women: "They will get you into trouble." If the Kings Mountain experience was something new to Miss Lockman and to the Negro students, it was equally new to me to meet a Southern white woman on a level not known to me before.

Despite my genuine desire to return to my graduate study, I had already yielded to four delaying tempatations. Now there was another one. In the summer of 1930, the Institute of Social and Religious Research, a Rockefeller-financed agency, invited me to direct a study of Negro churches in the United States, and I accepted. The human mind, I rationalized, can be most

*See Appendix A.

accommodating. It can usually find justification for the decisions it makes. I was interested in the church and religion; ergo, I should welcome this opportunity to learn more about the Negro church (in modern terminology in some areas the "black" church) and at the same time gain a new kind of experience. In whatever I decided to do, I was accumulating much knowledge, practical and otherwise, preparing me for the years ahead. I had been a teacher of mathematics, psychology, and English; an acting academic dean; a pastor of a church; a social worker; and a student secretary of the National YMCA. Now I was entering into a new area.

Having thoroughly convinced myself that this job, if not heaven-sent, must surely be heaven-bent, I, and Joseph W. Nicholson, a CME minister, began the study in the late summer of 1930. We spent fourteen months collecting data and ten months writing the book, which was to be published in 1933 under the title *The Negro's Church.* It was the first study of its kind and was thoroughly representative of that institution at the time. It covered 691 Negro churches in twelve cities: Atlanta, Baltimore, Birmingham, Charleston, Chicago, Cincinnati, Detroit, Houston, Memphis, New Orleans, Philadelphia, and Richmond. One hundred eighty-five Negro rural churches were studied in four areas: Peach County, Georgia; Orangeburg County, South Carolina; Montgomery County, Alabama; and Fort Bend County, Texas. *The Negro's Church* was widely read and favorably reviewed. In many ways it was a revelation, for it unearthed hitherto unknown information about the Negro church. (It was reprinted as recently as 1968).

Our study showed that the most distinctive thing about the Negro church is its origin. We wrote:

> The characteristic forces underlying Negro church origins are thus seen to have been five: growing racial consciousness, individual initiative, splits and withdrawals, the migration, and missions of other churches.

The basic reasons the Negro church came into being are the same basic causes that keep them separate from the white churches today. The origins of the Negro churches could be summarized by saying that the Negro was segregated and discriminated against in the white church, prima facie evidence that he was not wanted; the white church did not speak to the needs of the masses of Negroes; and Negroes wanted to own and control their own affairs. Despite token integration in a few churches, the merger of Methodist bodies, which finally abolished Central or Negro Jurisdiction, and the existence of a few church bodies that organically include Negroes, the conditions that gave rise to the Negro church still hinder the development of an all-inclusive, interracial church on the local level, as well as on the national level, especially when it comes to such bodies as the Negro Baptists, the African Methodist Episcopal Church, the African Methodist Episcopal Zion Church, and the Christian Methodist Episcopal Church. Nowhere is the racial problem more acutely felt than in the church and in housing.

There is much said today about "Negro identity," that is, being related to what is black. In earlier years, the Negro related himself most completely to his church, finding his identity there. The following excerpts taken from *The Negro's Church* (Chapter XVII: "The Genius of the Negro Church") are not wholly unrelated to what black churchmen are saying today:

> . . . The opportunity found in the Negro church to be recognized, and to be "somebody," has stimulated pride and preserved the self-respect of many Negroes who would have been entirely beaten by life, possibly completely submerged. Everyone wants to receive recognition and feel that he is appreciated. A truck driver of average or more than ordinary qualities becomes Chairman of the Deacon Board. A hotel man of some ability is the superintendent of the Sunday church school of a rather important church. A woman who would be hardly noticed, socially or otherwise, becomes a leading woman in the missionary society. A girl of little training and less opportunity for training gets the chance to become the leading soprano in the choir of a great church. These people receive little or no recognition on their daily jobs. There is nothing to make them feel that they are "somebody". Frequently their souls are crushed and their personalities disregarded. Often they do not feel "at home" in the more sophisticated Negro group. But in the church on X street, *she* is Mrs. Johnson, the Church Clerk; and *he* is Mr. Jones, the Chairman of the Deacon Board.
>
> Langston Hughes' "Negro Servant," though related to Harlem, is somewhat illustrative of what is portrayed here, and if the Negro church is kept in mind as well as Harlem, the idea expressed in this poem becomes more universal in its application:
>
> All day, subdued, polite,
> Kind, thoughtful to the faces that are white.
> O, Tribal dance!
> O, drum!
> O, Veldt at night!
> Forgotten watch-fires on a hill somewhere!
> At six o'clock, or seven, or eight,

You're through.
You've worked all day.
Dark Harlem waits for you.
The el, the sub,
Pay-nights,
A taxi through the park.
O, drums of life in Harlem after dark!
O, dreams!
O, songs!
O, saxophones at night!
O, sweet relief from faces that are white!

Conditions have changed mightily since *The Negro's Church* was written in 1932, but the emphasis on ownership and control, having a voice in the policy-making in education, in the church, in civic affairs, in politics, in economic life and government, is what Negroes are saying today that they want. The identity Negroes have had in the church lo! these many years they now seek everywhere. They want a black church more relevant to the black community than the Negro church has been to date. They want an integrated church not in name only but one that is as much black as it is white. The December 1, 1968, issue of *TEMPO*, published by the National Council of the Churches of Christ, tells of what happened at the Second Annual Convocation of the National Committee of Black Churchmen held in St. Louis prior to the December issue. Kay Longcope states: "That search for identity has already led us to the establishment of black caucuses in predominantly white churches. Their main interest is to find out whether present church structures can be made to bend a little in order to give black churchmen more of a voice in church policies and practices." Longcope's article quotes Hayward Henry of Boston of the Black Affairs Council of the Universalist Association: "There is no justification for black churchmen to participate in predominantly white denominations if we can't address ourselves to basic conditions of black Americans. The question of whether we withdraw or not is still open, but we are faced with a historical decision."

These 1968 complaints do not differ significantly from the things that gave rise to the Negro church as portrayed in our book on the subject. Negroes have always wanted to own and control their churches. They have felt that the white church did not speak specifically to their needs. What black churchmen are saying in the present time is not wholly new. Their forefathers were struggling with this phase of racism decades ago.

After completing the study, Sadie and I vowed that there must be no more detours, no more yielding to the temptation of other jobs. My work for the Ph.D. had to be completed without further delay. So in September, 1932, I finally returned to the University of Chicago to complete course work, write a thesis, and seek to pass all the examinations.

Regardless of one's previous academic record, he takes a risk when he announces his intention to earn a Ph.D., especially at an institution like the University of Chicago. It was the prevailing opinion that the university made it difficult for those who sought the degree, and it was rumored that approximately half of those who started out in the department in which I was enrolled failed to accomplish their goal. I knew a few persons who had failed their Ph.D. work at the University of Chicago, and it seemed to me that they were never quite the same thereafter. A man who seeks a doctorate and fails to earn it seems to go through life either apologizing for his shortcoming or overcompensating for the failure. I am reminded now of what the Honorable James A. Farley said to me when we were en route to Rome in 1963 to attend the state funeral of Pope John XXIII. Mr. Farley and I were discussing politics and his role in it. He explained his break with Franklin D. Roosevelt over the third-term issue. Our talk turned to candidates who sought the Presidency and were defeated, and Mr. Farley said that any candidate, Republican or Democrat, who sets his mind on the Presidency of the United States and misses it is never the same again.

Though I knew the dangers and pitfalls of the long road I had to travel in quest of a Ph.D., I wanted to travel that road. My determination was all a part of my "finding out for myself," of seeking to prove something; of my resolution to overcome, in part at least, the wounding circumstances which had characterized my early life. I say "in part" deliberately, because I realize that it is impossible to compensate fully for inadequate and inferior training in early years. Other persons may be unaware of these inadequacies, but one directly concerned knows them all too well. Whether I would have done more and better if I had not been denied the opportunity to remain in school a full term until I was nineteen, and if I had been reared in a home where there were books and magazines, I do not know; and now it doesn't matter. It did matter tremendously then, however, that a high school teacher had inspired me to want to go to the University of Chicago and earn its highest academic degree, and that the dream was in the process of being magnificently fulfilled.

Nevertheless, there were still areas of prejudice and discrimination that I kept bumping into at the university, and it was not my nature to leave them alone. Negro friends advised me not to tamper with these problems. One man tried to convince me that I would never get an advanced degree if I protested discrimination, but I found it hard to believe that the professors in my department would penalize me for fighting injustice in a great university, especially when I was not asking them to get involved.

Both Mrs. Mays and I were in residence in August, 1931, when she received her A.M. degree from the university's School of Social Service. Tickets for the Convocation were then being issued: white tickets for seats on the main floor of Rockefeller Chapel; colored tickets for balcony seats. The usher was giving white people the white tickets and Negroes the colored. Sadie, her sister Emma, and I got in line for tickets for ourselves and friends. When we were handed colored tickets and we promptly asked for white ones, we were told that there were no more. Accepting the colored tickets, we stepped aside to watch. The white person just behind us was given a white ticket, a Negro following him a colored ticket. We got in line again and told the ticket lady that we were going directly to President Hutchins's office to report her discriminatory practices. She gave us white tickets, pleaded with us not to report her, and tried to justify her position by saying that in the past gallery seats had been reserved for Negroes. Her instant capitulation was proof that she was not following a university policy but rather the dictate of some subordinate, self-appointed to maintain segregation. We did not report the incident.

The next episode was far more serious. I was in university residence during 1932-1934. In the spring of 1933 my sister-in-law, Emma C. W. Gray, a teacher at Paine College in Augusta, Georgia, wrote that she was coming to the university the following summer and planned to stay through the year to complete her work for the master's degree in English. Miss Gray was handicapped, having had a leg amputated in childhood. Because climbing steps was difficult for her, she wanted a first-floor room in one of the dormitories only a few yards from the academic building where her classes would be held. Negro women, so far as we knew, had not been housed in the university dormitories—with the exception of a Miss Mabel Byrd; a white friend had told the housing authorities that she wanted Miss Byrd for her roommate. The battle for Miss Gray had to be fought with Mr. William J. Mather, a Quaker, who was in charge of housing at the university.

On the ground that Southern white women would not stand for it, Mr. Mather refused to house Miss Gray in the dormitory. He was deaf to my argument that my sister-in-law worked at Paine College, founded by the

Methodist Church South and the Colored Methodist Church, and that she taught daily with Southern white women. I further argued that a great university should not allow Southern white women to determine its policies. This line of reasoning was equally futile. Mr. Mather was adamant. I am sure I annoyed him greatly because I was as persistent in my requests as he was unbending in his refusals.

When I finally decided to take the case to President Hutchins, he was in Europe. His young assistant advised me to take the case to Dr. George A. Works, dean of students, assuring me that if necessary he would arrange an appointment with the president upon his return. It was good advice. Dr. Works listened attentively to my story and then asked whether I really wanted a room for Miss Gray. I assured him that I had no desire to put the university on the spot but that I very much wished my sister-in-law to have space in the dormitory close to her class building. He promised that he would do something—and did. A few days later Mr. Mather sent me an assignment for Miss Gray in the dormitory next to Cobb Hall. It was a good one, on the first floor.

I had planned to thank Mr. Mather the next day for his consideration, just as I had expressed appreciation to Dean Works. Before I could see Mather, however, he sent a reassignment for Miss Gray, this one on the top floor. I was sure that he had forgotten about Miss Gray's physical handicap, so I went to remind him and to request that her initial assignment be reissued. Mather stubbornly refused to do so. Miss Gray's difficulty with stairs concerned him not at all. I had not known any Quakers previously, but I had heard of their involvement in the abolition of slavery and their liberal policy on race. I was now learning the hard way that Quakers—like other groups—have members whose actions are a far cry from their professed religious beliefs.

Negro students at the university soon learned about the Mays-Mather "war." Some Communist students, wishing to help, urged me to bring pressure on the university by publicizing the incident. I resisted this suggestion both because I did not want publicity and because then, as always, I was wholly unsympathetic to the Communist ideology.

Our fears of how Emma would fare in the dormitory were premature. The white girls not only did not resent her presence, but indeed it was the Southern white women who were the most solicitous. It was they who ran errands for her and went to the basement to do her laundry and iron her dresses. As I look back at the past and around at the present, I realize that most often our greatest fears are of eventualities that never occur. Mr.

Mather's fear that the walls of Gates Hall would surely fall if a young Negro woman lived within them—particularly if her room was conveniently located—was groundless. Our fears that Emma's dormitory experience might be an unhappy one was never substantiated. My friends' fears that my fight against discrimination would jeopardize my Ph.D. degree remained unrealized.

Of course, my main purpose at the University of Chicago was to earn my doctorate. The housing episode was just another chapter in the mounting file of my interracial experiences. The last seven quarters at the university, between 1932 and 1934, were hard but exciting years. My one disappointment was my inability to complete the thesis in time to receive the degree before I went to Howard University in the fall of 1934 to become dean of the School of Religion. I had no difficulty with the final two-day written examination, and I passed the three-hour oral examination on my thesis in a manner that satisfied me and won the praise of my examiners. The doctorate was conferred in March of 1935.

Other dreams came true for me that year. I had come a long way from those brooding days on the farm in South Carolina, when I wondered whether Negroes were really inferior and whether God had made them that way, to a Ph.D. at one of America's best universities. The question of innate racial inferiority had been settled in my mind forever. In fact, it was settled when I was graduated from Bates College in 1920. Several in my classes at Bates and Chicago had keener minds than I and had much better educational backgrounds. Nevertheless, I had done better work, both as an undergraduate and as a graduate, than most of my fellows.

The year 1935 saw three hopes achieved, three dreams fulfilled: the Ph.D. from the University of Chicago; election to Phi Beta Kappa by the Bates Chapter; and election to Delta Sigma Rho by the Bates Chapter of that society. For many years a Negro could not be elected to Delta Sigma Rho. My colleagues in intercollegiate debating were elected to membership in the forensic society while still at Bates. At the time of my graduation, the national body forbade the acceptance of Negroes. For years Bates had fought against the policy of exclusion, but until the national policy was changed the college was helpless. As soon as the bars were dropped, however, Bates elected me. My Greek professor at Bates, George Millet Chase, who thought I should have been elected to Phi Beta Kappa in 1920, lived long enough to see me inducted into membership, and it was he who escorted me at the initiation.

My life at Bates and at the University of Chicago taught me, despite many unpleasant and humiliating racial experiences, that all white people cannot be categorized as enemies of the Negro, just as all Negroes cannot be classified in a single mold. My experiences at Bates and Chicago, and the friendships I developed with teachers and students at both places, are certainly among the most potent reasons why I cannot hate white people and why I am little inclined to generalize about them or any people.

Chapter X

In the Nation's Capital

Having completed all course requirements, I had no reason to remain at the University of Chicago beyond the summer quarter of 1934. I was ready now for work in a church, or in a college or university. I had had some correspondence with church officials about a pastorate in St. Louis. President Thomas E. Jones had offered me work at Fisk. A little later in the summer, Mordecai Johnson, president of Howard University in Washington, D.C., invited me to accept the deanship of Howard's School of Religion. President Johnson's offer came after I had accepted the offer to work at Fisk.

Although I was morally obligated to go to Fisk, I was strongly drawn to Howard, both because I felt that it offered the greater challenge and because I knew Mordecai Johnson very well. Money played no role in my preference: both offered salaries of less than $4,000 a year. I wrote to President Johnson telling him that I would gladly accept his offer provided President Jones would give me an honorable release from my commitment to go to Fisk. I felt that I could ask for such a release only in a face-to-face situation, so I went to Nashville for a conference. Thomas Jones graciously granted my release and I accepted the position at Howard.

I was eager to go to Howard for several reasons. I felt the challenge to make the School of Religion outstanding, to lift it, if possible, from its stepchild role to a place of respectability in the institution. Moreover, I had great admiration for Mordecai Johnson. He made a tremendous impression on me when I first heard him speak while I was a teacher at Morehouse, and thereafter I had followed his career. In 1926, when the news broke that Mordecai Johnson, a Negro, had been elected to the presidency of Howard University, a group of us had had a heated argument on the campus of the State College at Orangeburg, South Carolina.

Since its founding in 1867, only white men had served Howard as president, and Mordecai Johnson's election ignited the same old argument. Whenever a Negro was elected to a high position formerly held by a white man, the "doubting Thomases" would wonder loud and long, "Can a Negro do the job?" In the case of Howard University and Mordecai Johnson, the major question was, "Can he possibly get the necessary money from Congress?" Each year Southern congressmen fought the appropriation to Howard. The few of us who were convinced that there were several able Negroes who could do impressive work as president of Howard University cited as evidence that Booker T. Washington and Robert Russa Moton had built Tuskegee; that John Hope, a Negro, had been president of Morehouse College since 1906; and that Negroes were presidents of Negro state colleges. Such arguments, however, made no dent in the position of those who held that the presidency of Howard should be filled by a white man.

Much progress has been made in this area since 1926, but many Negroes still have a long way to go before they can rid themselves of the false notion that a white professional is necessarily better qualified than a black one. I once heard Bishop Hickman of the AME Church tell this story: A Negro woman, talking to her next-door neighbor, Mrs. B., told her that their mutual friend, Mrs. C., was ill. "How sick is she?" queried Mrs. B. "She's sick enough to have a white doctor!" was the reply.

Systematic undermining of self-confidence has done damaging things to black people. In 1956, when my wife had a serious illness and I was relying on the able skill and advice of the Morehouse College physician, Dr. J. B. Ellison, some of our close, highly intelligent, well-educated friends urged me to get a white doctor. I refused. I knew that if Dr. Ellison needed medical counsel, he would seek it. A year later, when Mrs. Mays was doing well, and we went to Mayo Clinic for our periodic check-up, it was the opinion of specialists there that Mrs. Mays had had the very best of care. When the State of Alabama was trying to put Martin Luther King, Jr., behind bars on an income tax charge, some Negroes wanted Martin to get white lawyers. But Martin insisted on having Negro lawyers defend him. After the wonderful accomplishment of Negro lawyers in winning the May 17, 1954, decision of the United States Supreme Court one would have thought that the issue of white lawyers would not have been raised in King's case. As one of the character witnesses for King, I was happy to see two Negro lawyers, Robert Ming of Chicago and former Judge Hubert T. Delaney of New York win the case. Unfortunately, all too many Negroes saw no good at all for Howard University in the election of Mordecai Johnson as president.

It would take no great power of divination for the reader to conclude that I had more than a casual interest in Mordecai Johnson's success at

Howard. I am basically a "race" man. I believe in the black man's ability, and my heart leaps with joy when a Negro performs well in any field. For me it was imperative that the first Negro president of Howard University be an unqualified and triumphant success. I had watched Howard's growth during Johnson's first eight years there; and I was eager to help him build a great university by making the School of Religion a first-rate institution. It was no prize that had been handed to Mordecai Johnson. Kelly Miller and two or three other Negro educators had given Howard University some prestige, but by no stretch of rhetoric could it be called an outstanding institution. It was a puny thing. Mordecai had accomplished wonders for Howard, and he had passed the acid test: He had demonstrated that a Negro university president could get money from the federal government!

According to data from Secretary Stanton of Howard University, when Mordecai Johnson went to Howard in the fall of 1926, the current appropriation from the government was $218,000 for the academic year 1926-1927. When Johnson relinquished the presidency in 1960, the appropriation for 1959-1960 was $4,617,000—twenty-one times greater than it had been when he went there in 1926—a dramatic increase of 1,800 percent.

Professor Walter Dyson, in his *History of Howard University: 1867-1940* shows that in the forty-seven years between 1879 and 1926, the federal government appropriated $4,376,875.50 to Howard University. During the first fourteen years of the Johnson administration (1926-1940), the government appropriated $12,068,268 to the university, almost three times as much in fourteen years as in the previous forty-seven years. From 1930 through 1960 (thirty of Johnson's thirty-four years at Howard), appropriations totaled $30,779,200 for the physical plant. Since 1960, the appropriations continued to increase under President James Madison Nabrit. In the eight years through 1968 of his administration, the government has appropriated $11,-784,600 for plant improvements; and whereas the appropriation for the current budget for Howard in 1959-1960 was $4,617,000, it had increased to $17,830,000 in 1968-1969! These figures prove that Negroes could and did get big money from the government, and, moreover, that those few who in 1926 expressed confidence in Negro leadership at Howard University have been vindicated a thousandfold.

When I first remember Howard as it was in 1926 when Johnson became president, then as it was when he left in 1960, and what it is under James Madison Nabrit and, James E. Cheek, the new President of Howard, I have a strong conviction, even if I cannot prove it, that it took Negro leadership to do for Howard what needed to be done. Had a white president been elected in 1926, he might not have had sufficient faith in the Negro's ability to achieve, might not have been adequately dedicated to the cause of Negro education to request and press the government for funds to build a great university devoted mainly to the education of black persons. Now, in the 1970's, with the current emphasis on blackness, and the tendency to swallow up top Negro leadership in education under the disguise of integration, it is more desirable that a national university like Howard, open to all peoples, be under the leadership of an able Negro.

My respect for Mordecai Johnson increased mightily during the six years I was at Howard. Despite his excellent accomplishments, however, a small group of Negroes was determined to get him ousted. Several of his enemies were Sadie's friends and mine. Yet we never allowed their animosity toward Johnson or our loyalty to him to interfere with our amicable relationship with all the people in the university community. I never really knew why a few people hated the man so intensely; and, as I think of it now, I am sure that Mordecai Johnson himself never was aware of how passionately a few faculty people disliked him. The only reasons I ever heard expressed were, "He is dogmatic!" "Dishonest!" "A liar!" None of my experiences with him gave the slightest confirmation of any of these. A man of conviction is often accused of being dogmatic. Dishonest? Deceitful? On the contrary, I always found him to be a man of honor and integrity. He was not, he is not, perfect. Who is?

When I went to Howard, a reporter signing himself "Unknown Correspondent" was writing weekly articles in a national Negro newspaper against the president of Howard University. Somebody in the university evidently was supplying "Unknown Correspondent" with material for his bitter, vindictive diatribes. I recall the circumstances at a Founders' Day Banquet at which Secretary of the Interior Harold Ickes was the speaker. As we went to the banquet, men looking like thugs darted from the darkness into the light, handing out leaflets entitled "The Case Against Mordecai Johnson." I learned, on good evidence, that someone had even gone to Charleston, West Viginia, where Johnson had pastored, and tried without success to dredge up evidence of immorality. He was falsely accused of using government material to build a home in West Virginia. No gossip was too petty or mean, no charge too preposterous or damaging; but against his would-be character assassins Mordecai Johnson never tried to defend himself, either on the platform or in the press. He never fired from the faculty persons known to be his enemies.

There was academic freedom at Howard, and Mordecai Johnson was one of the nation's number one critics when it came to economic injustice and racial discrimination. He did not easily yield to pressure. When a government official urged him to fire a university official, he refused. The greatness of Howard University today must in all honesty be ascribed to the magnificent leadership of two men: Mordecai Johnson for thirty-four years and Jim Nabrit for nine years.

I was glad to see the anonymous and cowardly attack on President Johnson boomerang to his benefit. Because the university at that time was under the Department of the Interior, of which Ickes was Secretary, Johnson's adversaries evidently thought that their tactics in distributing scurrilous leaflets the night of the banquet would elicit Ickes' support and turn him against Johnson. Apparently they understood the quality of Ickes' character as little as they did that of Johnson. Over-attack, more often than not, is self-defeating. Many persons who were not especially fond of Mordecai Johnson, and even some who actively disliked him condemned the episode at the Founders' Day Banquet. It made Secretary Ickes so skeptical of the charges that he determined their falsity for himself. As an expression of confidence, he gave a dinner at the Willard Hotel in Mordecai Johnson's honor.

That dinner was a triumph not only for President Johnson but for Sadie as well. The invitation read "Black tie." I had never owned a tuxedo. Reluctant to buy one, I asked Mrs. Avis Robinson, secretary to the president, whether she thought I would disgrace the party by attending it in a dark business suit. She gave me an unqualified, "Yes, it would be completely out of place and most embarrassing!" This was good news to Sadie, who had told me at the outset that I must buy a tuxedo. I meekly did as I was told.

In closing this particular phase of my recollections and reflections on Howard University, it must be said that the contributions of Johnson and Nabrit are by no means limited to the vast budgetary increases. In addition to their educational contributions, the mere fact that they are black should not be lost to sight—that is, their more symbolic contributions. They helped to shatter illusions about black talent and leadership. If Johnson and Nabrit had been white and had been able to get as much or even more money, the consequences would not have been the same. No white man could have done, in the same context, what these two men did. They inspired the minds, gladdened the hearts, and lifted the spirits of Negro youth and Negro people in ways white leadership could never have equaled.

When I went to Howard in 1934, I found the School of Religion to be the university's stepchild, and so it remains to this day. Prior to 1934, the School of Religion had been mainly an institution for graduating men with the Bachelor of Theology degree, one which required only two years of college and two years of theological training. In 1934 the B.Th. degree was being phased out with the goal of making the School of Religion a full-fledged professional school, accepting only college graduates. My predecessor, Dean D. Butler Pratt, was very apprehensive about making the School of Religion a professional school. President Mordecai Johnson had his misgivings also. They doubted that such a School of Religion could attract enough college students to justify its existence.

Other factors were status-deflating. The School of Religion was housed on Sixth Street in a shabby frame building. The library holdings were grossly inadequate. The school did not have the prestige of the other professional schools in the university community: medicine, law, dentistry, and engineering. The fact that the School of Religion was as old as the university itself added no luster to its reputation. Salaries were lower, partly because government money could not be used to pay salaries in religion, just as government money could not and cannot be used to erect a plant for the School of Religion. So it was not the glories of the Howard University School of Religion, but the challenge to improve it, and the opportunity to work with Mordecai Johnson which made our pilgrimage to Washington in August of 1934 an exciting one for both Sadie and me. I was eager to begin my new deanship, Sadie to start a new job as social worker in the District of Columbia.

The following excerpts from the history of the school are taken from a handwritten copy of minutes of a meeting held June 25, 1867, and of meetings on later dates:

> . . . A Committee was appointed by the Board of Trustees to take into consideration the organization of a Theological department, and pending this, the Trustees, Dec. 20th, 1867, requested Rev. Danforth B. Nichols to give instruction in "Biblical Interpretation and the Evidences of Revelation," to such students as proposed to enter the ministry. . . a Regular theological course was not determined upon until Aug. 1st, 1870, when reports and been received from the various Societies, to whom application for assistance had been made. The American Missionary Association being the only one that responded favorably to the appeal, it was resolved to accept its proposition and open a regular theological department.
>
> It was formally opened Sept. 15th, 1871, with Rev. John B. Reeves, D.D., as Instructor, with power to employ a teacher of Hebrew.

It is interesting to note that Howard University itself had its inception in a missionary prayer meeting of the First Congregational Church of Washington, D.C. The plan for a theological seminary was laid as early as November 20, 1866. Religious training, therefore, has always been an integral part of Howard University.

When I became dean in 1934, six urgent needs confronted me:

1. To increase the enrollment.
2. To improve the faculty.
3. To rehabilitate the physical plant.
4. To enlarge and improve the library.
5. To establish an endowment.
6. To seek accreditation by the American Association of Theological Schools.

I found an enrollment of twenty-eight students—fourteen with college degrees in the graduate school and fourteen who were combining two years of college with two years of theological work. It was mandatory, I felt, to increase the number of Bachelor of Divinity students. As a result, when I left Howard six years later, we had an enrollment of forty-three college students pursuing either a B.D. degree or an M.A. in Religious Education. The school had developed a good recruiting program; and the following year fifty-three students, all college graduates, were enrolled. This dramatic increase in enrollment must be attributed to recruitment and to a group of able teachers, Negro and white. Perhaps the most important factor in building a theological school restricted to college graduates was the number of Negro teachers who were well known nationally in the Negro community.

In my six years at Howard, five of my immediate objectives were realized: an enlarged graduate enrollment was made a reality; the faculty was strengthened; the library was made adequate; the School of Religion was accredited by the American Association of Theological Schools; and the school's plant was greatly improved. Really, only four objectives were fully achieved, because the improved plant of the School of Religion was expected to be only temporary as it was hoped that the university, president and trustees, would soon launch a campaign to erect an entirely new plant. This was not done during my tenure, nor in the thirty years since I left.

The government did appropriate money for a new library (Founders' Library) while I was in office. The Carnegie Library had long since proved inadequate for the university; but the building itself was quite ample for the School of Religion at that time. The dean and the faculty of the School of Religion were thus quick to bid for the Carnegie library building once the university library was housed in its new facility. All had high hopes that we would get it. But our hopes were temporarily shattered when we learned that the president was thinking seriously of giving the building to the law school, which also needed better quarters. I argued that in time the government would give Howard money for a law school building, but it could never support religion, under our present constitution, by erecting a building designed for this purpose. I argued further that the government had not given either the land or the money for the Carnegie Library building, and so had neither reason nor excuse for objecting to the proposed new location of the School of Religion. We won our debate.

It was a happy day when we learned that the Board had voted that the Carnegie building be used by the School of Religion. President Johnson, using private funds, had the structure renovated; and on October 20, 1939, we moved into our new quarters. We were so thrilled that one Saturday afternoon students and faculty happily transferred our library by hand from Douglass Hall to our new School of Religion building.

The year 1939 was really a banner year for me. In October, the School of Religion had a new home; two months later, on December 15, the school was placed on the accredited list of the American Association of Theological Schools, making it the second Negro seminary to qualify for such accreditation. (The other school was Gammon Theological Seminary in Atlanta, Georgia.)

The next big job before us was to increase the number and quality of volumes in the School of Religion library. Like an answer to prayer, my friend, John Moore, professor of philosophy at Swarthmore College, alerted me to the fact that Auburn Theological Seminary in Auburn, New York, was merging with Union Theological Seminary in New York City, and that the Auburn officials were anxious to sell the majority of their books. The Auburn Seminary had around fifty thousand volumes in its library, not more than eleven thousand of which were needed at Union. I could hardly believe my ears when I was told that the remaining thirty-nine thousand volumes could be purchased for $10,000. Two or three Presbyterian seminaries were bidding for the Auburn library, so I wired President Johnson from Auburn telling him that it would be a colossal blunder not to take advantage of this once-in-a-lifetime bargain. Mrs. Robinson, secretary to the president, dramatized the event by rushing into his office, waving the telegram, and exclaiming, "Mr. President, it will be a colossal blunder!" My urgency and Mrs. Robinson's histrionics did not sweep President Johnson off his feet. He wanted the library appraised by the librarian at Colgate-Rochester and the librarian from Union Theological Seminary.

Waiting until the President received his expert advice from Colgate and Union was a tantalizing ordeal. The man from Colgate-Rochester reported that the thirty-nine thousand volumes would not be worth $10,000 to Colgate-Rochester. The librarian from Union agreed with me that it was an excellent bargain and that the books were needed in any first-rate seminary. President Johnson was more inclined to agree with the semi-negative report from Colgate-Rochester. When he pointed out that the two experts did not agree as to the value of the collection, I was quick to remind him that *three* experts had examined and appraised the collection: the gentleman from Colgate-Rochester; the one from Union; and *his own dean!* It was two against one. In dealing with President Johnson, one had always to be prepared for debate, and this time I felt that I was in the catbird seat. I was able to argue that if Colgate-Rochester did not need the books, certainly they would not be worth $10,000 to them; but to an institution with fewer than ten thousand volumes the Auburn offer was a gift. I was able to show President Johnson that at the annual rate we were buying books, it would take the School of Religion seventy-five years to purchase thirty-nine thousand volumes.

After agonized days of waiting, I was finally rewarded when President Johnson approved my recommendation, just in time for us to close the deal one day before another school was ready to take the collection. The purchase was made in 1940, soon before I left Howard for Atlanta in midsummer. I am still jubilant that I was able to supervise the shelving of those hard-fought-for thirty-nine thousand volumes for the School of Religion before moving to my new job. The School of Religion might easily have missed the Carnegie building and the Auburn volumes if I had not kept putting pressure on the President of Howard University. Such persuasion, pressure, and persistence is the duty of every dean and every chairman of a department if he wants to get things done.

Several able men have served as deans of the School of Religion at Howard University since I left it in 1940: William Stuart Nelson, Frank T. Wilson, Daniel Hill, and Samuel L. Gandy. All four have done excellent jobs. Stronger faculties have been secured, and the enrollment has increased, though too slowly. I still feel, however, that despite the high quality of work the school is doing, the various administrators of Howard University have treated the School of Religion as of minor importance. Over a period of one hundred years, not one of the twelve presidents of Howard University has given the School of Religion top priority as has been done from time to time for the other divisions of the university. Thus the School of Religion always has been and still can be called the university's stepchild.

I said, when I went to Howard in 1934, that if in twenty years graduates of the School of Religion were not occupying significant places in religion across the country, the school should be closed. Hence, it is gratifying to know that the men who were graduated in the six years that I was dean, or were students of mine, and those who have graduated since, have made their significant contributions in religion and other fields. One can scarcely even dream what the record might have been if the School of Religion had had equal treatment with the other schools in the university.

Nevertheless, Howard University was kind to me during my six years there. Between 1936 and 1939, I was permitted to attend four World Conferences, three in Europe and one in India.

The author's birthplace, many years after he was born.

Sister Susie and her husband, Samuell Glenn, in front of the one-room Brickhouse School.

Mt. Zion Baptist Church where the author was baptized; the left and right wings were added later.

Above: Sister Susie at 92. She taught the author the alphabet and how to count.

Left: The author's mother, Louvenia Mays. Her prayers sustained him. (Drawn by Jenelsie W. Holloway of Spelman College)

The author won the sophomore prize declamation contest at Bates in 1917.

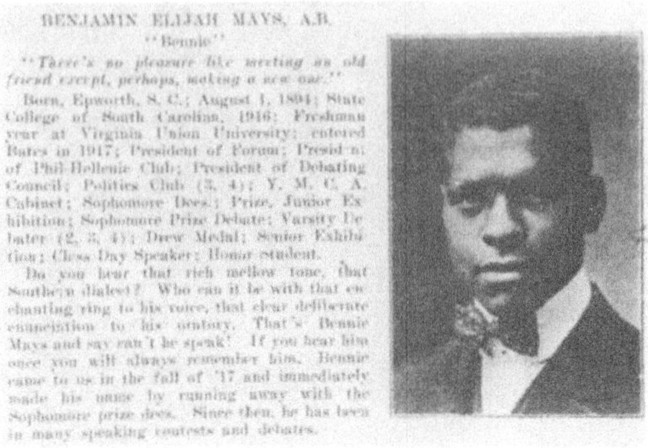

BENJAMIN ELIJAH MAYS, A.B.

"Bennie"

"There's no pleasure like meeting an old friend except, perhaps, making a new one."

Born, Epworth, S. C.; August 1, 1894; State College of South Carolina, 1916; Freshman year at Virginia Union University; entered Bates in 1917; President of Forum; President of Phil-Hellenic Club; President of Debating Council; Politics Club (3, 4); Y. M. C. A. Cabinet; Sophomore Decs.; Prize, Junior Exhibition; Sophomore Prize Debate; Varsity Debater (2, 3, 4); Drew Medal; Senior Exhibition; Class Day Speaker; Honor student.

Do you hear that rich mellow tone, that Southern dialect? Who can it be with that enchanting ring to his voice, that clear deliberate enunciation to his oratory. That's Bennie Mays and say can't he speak! If you hear him once you will always remember him. Bennie came to us in the fall of '17 and immediately made his name by running away with the Sophomore prize decs. Since then, he has been in many speaking contests and debates.

Bates senior football team, fall of 1919.

Bates honor students, 1920.

Bates yearbook picture, 1920.

Improvised recreation for delinquent boys, Tampa, Florida, 1927. The Urban League saved them from reform school.

A dream fulfilled—Ph.D. degree from the University of Chicago. (A later picture.)

With students during the author's last year as Dean of the School of Religion at Howard University, 1939–1940.

Central Committee of the World Council of Churches, Toronto, July 1950.

Reception for Robert Frost at Morehouse, January 30, 1955.

The author, vice president of the Federal Council of Churches of Christ in America from 1944 to 1946, shown here with Bishop G. Bromsley Oxnam, incoming president; and the Right Reverend Henry St. George Tucker, outgoing president.

Receiving the degree of Doctor of Humane Letters from Morehouse, June 6, 1967.

The author and Fred Patterson present letter of appreciation to Catherine Waddell for her great work for the U.N.C.F., 1960.

With President William V. S. Tubman of Liberia, who received Morehouse's honorary degree on November 5, 1954.

The Mayses on their twenty-fifth wedding anniversary, August 9, 1951.

Dining with friends in India, 1953.

With Sadie in Egypt in 1953.

With Sadie, dressed for the White House dinner honoring the Shah of Iran, April 11, 1962.

At the White House with President John F. Kennedy, early in 1962.

On the plane with Vice President Lyndon B. Johnson en route to Rome to attend the state funeral of Pope John XXIII, June 16, 1963.

Receiving the degree of Doctor of Laws from Harvard University, June, 1967.

Receiving the degree of Doctor of Laws from Morgan College, 1967.

Receiving the Amistad Freedom Award, May 15, 1968 (American Missionary Association)

Presenting the commencement address at Michigan State University, where he also received an honorary degree in June, 1968.

With Mrs. Mays and Mayor Ivan Allen, Jr., on May 30, 1967.

Presiding at a meeting of the Atlanta School Board of Education, early 1970.

The First Lady of Morehouse for 27 years was loved and admired by faculty and students.

Being hooded after receiving the degree of Doctor of Humane Letters from Emory University, June 8, 1970.

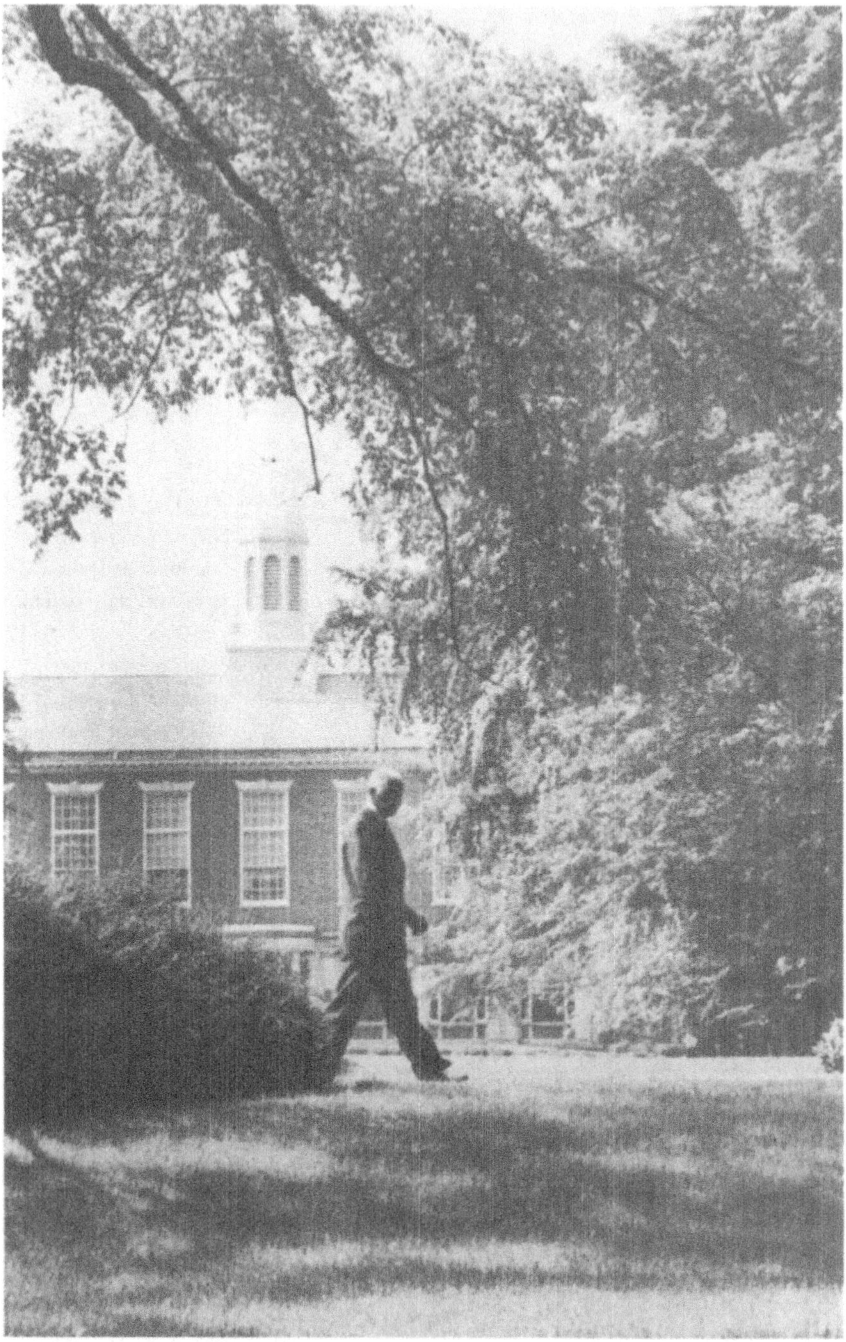

En route to Chapel at Morehouse on a Tuesday morning to address faculty and students.

Chapter XI

Race and Caste Outside the U.S.A.

All my life the race problem had been as close as the beating of my heart, circumscribing my thoughts, my actions, my feelings. A black man must not only meet the problem publicly, but invariably when Negroes are by themselves the conversation drifts to some phase of Negro-white relations. It is omnipresent; it creates a physical and spiritual climate from which there is no escape. I thought that for three and a half months, as I traveled around the world, I would be able to forget color, race, and prejudice; that I could be just a man among other men; that I would have a brief respite from thinking and talking about the race problem. I was mistaken. I did find, however, that it works both ways. The Negro dominates the thinking of white people as inescapably as whites are an inextricable part of the thinking of Negroes. There is no eluding the race problem anywhere on this earth.

I was one of thirteen Americans chosen to attend the World Conference of the YMCA which met in Mysore, India, in January of 1937. More than two hundred official delegates, representing thirty-five nations, assembled to study the complex problems confronting the youth of the world in 1937. "Race Relations" was one of the seven topics listed for study. Besides myself, there was one other American Negro, Dr. Channing H. Tobias (1882-1961), a very distinguished man.

I began the trip to Mysore, India, on November 18, 1936, leaving New York on the *Queen Mary* despite admonitions that I might meet more discrimination and prejudice on an English boat than on a French or Italian liner. My cabin was designed for two, but I was the sole occupant. Well schooled in the techniques of discrimination, I requested the steward to seat me in the center of the dining room. I did not wish to be tucked away in a corner. Quite graciously the steward granted my request—but I was seated alone. So this was discrmination, British style! Sitting there in solitary grandeur made me very conspicuous. I didn't mind too much, although I could not help feeling a bit queer. No one wishes to be isolated by design.

Not many persons spoke as they passed my table. Four seated across from me did speak, pleasantly and smilingly. They were Russians. Two had been sent by their government to study engineering in the United States; one, an elderly woman with beautiful white hair and a kindly face, was returning to Russia after a brief visit in the United States; and the fourth person, Mrs. Sara Horowitz, a Jewish American woman from New Haven, Connecticut, had come to the United States from Russia when she was six years old and was returning to her homeland for her first visit. They invited me to join them, so, after the second day, I ate dinner with these four. Since I could speak no Russian and the three Russian citizens spoke no English, Mrs. Horowitz was our interpreter. When they asked why I was seated alone, I replied, "I took the seat assigned to me." But they knew, as I knew, why I was seated alone.

I felt terribly alone the first two days from shore. People sat and stared at me. Yet such behavior does not always indicate prejudice or rudeness. Often people hesitate to take the initiative to be human, but once the barrier is broken they are eager to form acquaintances and want to talk. By the time we reached Southampton, friendships had formed and multiplied, and I felt that many persons were sorry when we reached journey's end.

But I did not escape having to talk about race. Not only foreign passengers but some Americans also wished to talk about racial conditions in the United States. I was a bit surprised when the English–South African woman, sitting at another table from the one at which three of us were having tea, requested me to sit on the other side of the table so that she could see my face as I talked because "I would enjoy looking at your face much more than at your back." Afterward she and I talked. I wished to know about the South African race problem, and she was curious to know how Negroes were treated in the United States. She did not try to justify what the English and the Dutch were doing to the Bantus, Indians, and Coloured people in South Africa, nor did she claim, as some South Africans whom I met later on did, that the Southern United States was as bad racially as South Africa.

On arrival at the Regent Palace Hotel in London, I was cordially received and encountered no prejudice. Perhaps the good treatment was the result of a letter written to the manager of the hotel by the Austin Travel Service of New York. (I make this observation because when—unheralded—I returned to London in the summer of 1937 I met undeniable discrimination.) In the letter, the Austin Travel Service had "promoted" me from the position of dean of Howard University to that of *president* of Howard

University. I am confident that had I been white the agency would not have felt it necessary so to identify me. This is what the courtesy-insuring letter said:

> Dear Sir:
> Please reserve a single room for the above passenger, who is a colored man, and the President of Howard University for colored people, at Washington, D.C. Doctor Mays is an educated gentlemen, associated with the activities of the Young Men's Christian Association. He is en route to Mysore, India, to attend the World Brotherhood Conference, and will afterward travel around the world to Washington, D.C.

Later, in an article, I wrote of my own reaction:

> I had occasion to tell the Austin Service people that I was not the president of Howard University, and that they had left no stone unturned in their apology to make me acceptable to the people of London. No one who wants to be fair can question the motive of the author of this letter. But it is more important that we live in a world where apologies of this kind have to be made. I believe no one loves embarrassments, and certainly no one would invite them, but I think I would choose to be embarrassed rather than to be the recipient of special privilege.

In no hotel in the United States would I have been so well treated as I was at the Regent Palace during my five days in London. Most of the hotels in the United States, in 1936, did not accept Negroes at all, certainly none in the South, and even in the North the hotels that received Negroes discriminated against them in some way. The dining rooms at the Regent Palace were usually packed and jammed at dinner time, and I was seated next to whites and they next to me without hesitation. Leaving London on November 28, 1936, I wrote in my diary, "In all places I visited in London, I have met no discrimination anywhere." I had to visit London again in 1937 to learn that such treatment was far from typical. Often a Negro must go on his own, unsupported, unrecommended, and unaccompanied by whites, if he wishes to learn what the racial score really is.

In my five days in England, I did what visitors usually do when they go there for the first time. I saw the historical sights and did some shopping. My shopping was limited by time and money, but on my way from Westminster Abbey to Westminster Cathedral I passed an army and navy store. A most beautiful black velvet dress was on display in the window. I gazed at it, and at the price, and counted my money. On my way back from the

Cathedral, I stopped at the store. I was so impressed with that black velvet dress that I went inside and talked with a clerk about it. I decided to buy it, but I had forgotten Sadie's dress size, so I had the clerk get several young women clerks to parade before me until I saw one about Sadie's size. My notes show that I paid $25.57 for that dress—a wild extravagance in view of my limited funds. I had planned to purchase something in each country I visited, and I did, but from London to Bombay I had to buy less expensive things to be sure that I could get back to Washington with a little money on hand. The dress reached Sadie in Washington on Christmas Eve, and only slight alterations had to be made.

My schedule called for six days in Paris after London. I expected no discrimination in Paris in hotels, restaurants, theaters, and other places, and I found none. On one of my tours there, I met a Miss Wolf of New York who was returning to the United States after a visit to South Africa. I had read of the racial conditions in South Africa, but I had not had the privilege of talking to someone who could give me firsthand data about the treatment of South African nonwhites. For six hours, including dinner, Miss Wolf and I talked of the hopeless condition of the Bantu in South Africa, as well as the treatment of Indians and Coloured people. Miss Wolf was sure that she had annoyed her hostess in South Africa by expressing her concern for the Bantu people. Hitherto I had thought that the black man's plight could not be as bad anywhere else in the world as I had known it in my native South, but I then concluded that South Africa was even worse than the United States. More extensive travel subsequently, and experience with South African delegates in World Conferences, confirmed that conclusion. And to this day, of all the persons I have known who have visited South Africa or lived there, I have yet to find one who could speak hopefully of the South African situation. Those who write about South Africa shed no ray of hope, not even my very good friend Alan Paton, who has incurred the wrath of the South African government because of his writings and sympathetic attitude toward the Bantu, Indian, and Coloured people.

My only encounter with discrimination since leaving the United States had been on the *Queen Mary* when I was housed and seated alone. The P. & O., another English line, was no better. It was hardly an accident that my three cabin mates on the *Kaiser-I.-Hind* were Indians, as were my tablemates. The steward was smooth, suave, and polite. The four tables he pointed out to me that were not filled were those where Indians were seated. My suspicion of deliberate segregation on the P. & O. line was confirmed by a cabin mate who had made the trip to England several times. He said it was the custom on English boats sailing east to separate Indians and whites at meals and in the cabins. There might be an occasional exception, but the rule was "separation."

I saw many things on the boat which I had read about, and many about which I learned a great deal more after my arrival in India. For example, there were a few Anglo-Indians on board, but I never saw them mingling with the Indians. Occasionally they were to be seen with whites, but usually they kept to themselves. Mr. W. J. Morgan, the English YMCA secretary, and I played deck tennis, and once he suggested that the two of us play against a white Englishman and an Anglo-Indian. Since ordinarily neither an Englishman nor an Anglo-Indian would play with a Negro, it amused Morgan to engineer such a foursome. However, when Morgan invited an Englishwoman to play with us, her answer was, "I would not be caught mixed up with that!"

Through Morgan's introduction, I met two Anglo-Indian women, one of whom spoke rather freely about the Indian–Anglo-Indian relationship. She said that though she did not share her father's attitude, there was nothing she could do to change it, and that he would die if she married an Indian. The Indian men kept constant company with English girls, but I never saw them associating with the two Anglo-Indian women, although one of them was undoubtedly the most beautiful woman on the boat. The two Anglo-Indian women were very pleasant to me, especially one who invited me to visit her home if I came to Calcutta.

When I observed the Indian–Anglo-Indian situation in India and talked with Indians and Englishmen about it, I had to think about the Negro-white relations in the United States. Although there were clusters of white Negroes in places like Charleston, Washington, and New Orleans, the wall between dark Negroes and white Negroes had never grown so wide or so bitter as that between Indians and Anglo-Indians. My first wife, Ellen, was fair-skinned. She told me that she had visited a Negro church in Charleston, South Carolina, (forty-five years ago) and that she was the darkest person in the church! Despite such an easily discernible difference, Negroes in the United States were forced to make common cause because the white man insisted that *one drop* of Negro blood in a person made him a Negro. So the war against discrimination in the United States has been and must be waged by all Negroes—black, white, tan—together.

Other interesting things happened on this trip. A North Carolina white man, en route to India as a missionary, had talked to me on the *Queen Mary*

—always, however, at my initiative. We talked two or three times when his wife was with him, but he had never introduced her. En route to Egypt, he was also on board a boat with me where Indians were numerous. This time he took the initiative to speak with me and shake hands. I interpreted this change to mean that once he was in an Indian environment the North Carolinian felt that he could afford to be more friendly. It is a grim commentary on man's inconsistency and his inhumanity that so many white men and women have gone to foreign lands to "save souls" who would not share the bread and wine of a communion service with a Negro in the United States, let alone sit down to share an ordinary meal.

While waiting at the Casino Hotel in Port Said, I sat down to watch an Egyptian do some tricks. An Englishwoman sat down in the seat next to me. She was friendly, and we talked for ten or fifteen minutes. She told me about her family; her husband was a retired engineer, having worked in Australia. When her husband appeared he beckoned for her to come to him; she beckoned for him to come to her, saying, "I want you to meet my husband." He kept urging her to come, and finally she did so. I passed the two of them twice after that and she gave no sign of recognition or of ever having chatted with me.

My greatest rebuke, however, came from a Moslem Indian, an archaeologist for one of the Indian states, who lectured me sternly because I looked away once while he was talking to me. He told me that he would not be ignored that way. He adored the British, and thought Negroes were a happy-go-lucky people. I think he had contempt for all Negroes, including me. It is not surprising that he loved England, because the maharajas dealt directly with the English government and many of them were exceedingly wealthy.

Before I left New York, my travel agency had arranged for me to spend a few days in Palestine. In addition to visiting the many sites in and around Jerusalem, I spent as much time as I could talking with Jews and Arabs. It does not surprise me in the least that the Israelis and the Arabs are still warring in 1970. The Jerusalem YMCA was serving a good purpose: In December of 1936 it was the only place in Jerusalem where Jews and Arabs could meet for any kind of friendly discourse.

When I returned from Palestine to Egypt, my cabin mates were Moslems. They were deeply interested in Negro-white relations in the United States. They asked whether white people lynched Negroes in the United States. I replied in the affirmative. They asked whether Negroes were segregated in the United States. Again I had to say "Yes." Then they wanted to know what was my religious faith; and when I told them that I was a Christian, they immediately inquired what was the religion of the American white man. Told that he, too, professed to be Christian, they were bewildered. How could Christians do these things to other Christians? They said that once a person embraces Islam there are no racial barriers. I told them that I did not understand the situation in the United States any better than they did. I still don't!

The poverty I saw in Egypt was surpassed only by what I saw in India. It gave me no comfort to realize that the plight of the poor in Egypt and India was even worse than that of poor Negroes in the United States.

When I arrived in Bombay on Christmas Eve, 1936, I must admit that I was lonely. I had planned my arrival at that time so that I could attend the All-India Congress which was meeting not far from Bombay. Jawaharlal Nehru was the president of the Congress, the sole purpose of which was to discuss ways and means to free India from England. I talked briefly with Nehru, who was to become India's first prime minister, and at greater length with Nehru's sister, Mrs. Vijaya Lakshimi Pandit, who was to play such a significant role in the political life of India. But I went to the Congress mainly in the hope of meeting Mahatma Gandhi. For a very long time I had wished to see and talk with this ninety-pound brown man who had done so much to make Indians proud of their history and culture; who had identified himself with fifty million untouchables, determined to lift them to a place of dignity and respectability in the life of India; and who had started a movement for India's independence which would eventually lead to the dissolution of the British Empire.

I had thought that I could arrange a conference with Gandhi at the Congress and have time to visit the Taj Mahal before the YMCA Conference in Mysore. However, the Mahatma's secretary assured me that although Mr. Gandhi wanted very much to see me, it was time for his evening prayers and that if he saw me then it could be for only a few minutes. However, if I would come to Wardha he could give me unlimited time. So he made an appointment for me to see Mahatma Gandhi on December 31, 1936. Later, when I told the Mahatma that I had preferred talking with him to seeing the Taj Mahal, he responded, "You chose wisely. When you come to India again, the Taj Mahal will be there. I may not be here." He spoke prophetically, for when I returned to India in late 1952 and early 1953 to attend a meeting of the Central Committee of the World Council of Churches in Lucknow, Gandhi had been assassinated. The Taj Mahal was as breathtaking as ever, and Sadie and I had the pleasure of seeing it together.

My ninety minutes with Gandhi were spent mainly in his replying to two of my questions. I asked him 1) to tell me in his own way what "nonviolence" meant to him; and 2) why he didn't declare war on the caste system as well as make an attack on untouchability. I shall give his answers as I recorded them in my diary at that time.

Mahatma Gandhi emphasized in his first statement that nonviolence is not passive resistance but rather is an active force. It is three-fourths invisible, one-fourth visible. Likewise, its results are likely to be invisible and not capable of measurement. Nonviolence must never be practiced as a technique or strategy because one is too weak to use violence. It must be practiced in absolute love and without hate. It is better to be violent than to be a coward. One may have to call off a nonviolent campaign if the minds of the participants are not pure; that is, if hate develops and love ceases to be the dominant motive for action. In nonviolence, the welfare of the opponent must be taken into consideration. If the method of nonviolence tends to destroy one's opponents, it is to be called off. If a nonviolent campaign becomes too arduous for one's adherents, it should be called off unless the participants are willing to die for the cause.

Gandhi argued that no temporary use of violence for what one considered to be for the good or welfare of others is ever justified. When violence is used, whether temporarily or otherwise, it is a concession to human weakness. When violence is used to kill dangerous insects and animals, it is a concession to human weakness, an admission that we do not know any other way to handle the situation. Violence is always self-defeating. The repercussions from nonviolence will never be hatred and revenge. When one retreats in a nonviolent effort, he must never retreat out of fear, nor because he believes the nonviolent technique will never win. His faith must teach him that nonviolence can never lose because three-fourths of it is invisible and cannot be measured. So it can never be said that the method is impractical, or that it has failed, if a campaign is called off.

When I questioned Gandhi on the charge that the nonviolent man who violates the law has no respect for it, Gandhi's response was that the nonviolent man is law-abiding in that he is willing to pay the price when he disobeys unjust laws. Later, this part of my experience with Gandhi was to give me a deeper understanding than most persons of the program of Martin Luther King, Jr.

In answer to my question as to why he didn't launch a program to abolish the caste system, Mahatma Gandhi made it clear to me that he was not fundamentally against caste. He believed in caste. He described it as an economic necessity. To him there was no "lower" caste. Caste was a division of labor. Society must have priests and teachers, politicians, warriors, merchants, and farmers. Someone must do the ordinary work. For the most part, it is a good thing for sons to follow in the footsteps of their fathers, for there are no inferior and no superior castes. He said he condemned caste as it was practiced and that he himself recognized no caste in his evaluation of people. Certainly Gandhi condemned the hard, rigid lines that had developed among the various castes in India, whereby one caste had no social concern for anyone outside its own group. Essentially, however, Mahatma Gandhi thought that caste was not an evil in itself. Caste does give status, he believed, but the untouchable had no status and no rights which any caste man was bound to respect. All caste men could with impunity step on and spit upon the untouchable. So Gandhi had cast his lot with the man farthest down, the untouchable.

Bad as Indian untouchability was in 1937, I predicted that it would be legally abolished before segregation was legally abolished in the United States. I was right. Untouchability was abolished when India became constitutionally independent in 1947. Segregation in the public schools of the United States was not struck down by the Supreme Court until 1954; and Congress did not legislate against segregation until ten years later.

Mysore was my first World Conference, and having been segregated and discriminated against most of my life, I found it most interesting to be in a World Conference where members of different races and nations met on a plane of absolute equality. The Conference leadership was distributed without regard to race. Indians, Germans, Americans, and Chinese were among those who gave principal addresses. The leaders of the commissions were men from England, Australia, Scotland, China, South Africa, Switzerland, and the United States. Channing Tobias, an American Negro, headed one of the commissions; and devotions were led by an Englishman, a Swiss, an Indian, a Chinese, a Russian, a German, and me—an American Negro. At Mysore I was elected to membership on the World Committee of the YMCA.

Housing was assigned irrespective of race and nationality. In one tent the occupants were a Swiss, an Indian, an African, and a white American; in another, a Japanese, an Englishman, an Egyptian, and a German; and in still another, a Chinese, a Frenchman, a South American, and a Filipino.

There were few places in the United States where a conference like this could have been held in the thirties, and nowhere in the South.

While at Mysore I was invited by the headmaster of an "untouchable" school in a neighboring village to speak to his students. I asked him why, since there were thirteen US. delegates, he had chosen me. He replied that he wanted a Negro; and when I told him that Channing Tobias was also a Negro, he answered that Tobias was too fair of complexion to do what he wanted done. "I want you." I accepted his invitation, and, on leaving Mysore, went to his school where I dined with his untouchable students. After dinner, I was introduced as an untouchable who had achieved distinction. The headmaster told them that I had suffered at the hands of the white men in the United States every indignity that they suffered from the various castes in India and that I was proof that they, too, could be "somebody worthwhile" despite the stigma of being members of a depressed class.

At first I was horrified, puzzled, angry to be called an untouchable, but my indignation was short-lived as I realized, as never before, that I was truly an untouchable in my native land, especially in the Southern United States. In my country, I was segregated almost everywhere I went, always in the South and often in the North. I was not permitted to sleep or eat in white hotels and restaurants and was barred from worship in white churches. I had been slapped almost blind because I was black and had been driven out of a Pullman car with pistols at my back. I—just as they—through the mere accident of birth, was indeed an untouchable!

Participation in the Conference at Mysore was a great experience. But I left this, my first World Conference, as I was to leave subsequent ones, feeling that our pronouncements on the various issues were much too mild —and had they been stronger the results might have been the same. Nothing had been done that would contribute to the solution of the racial situation in South Africa; nothing that would offset the rising hatred between Arabs and Jews; no commentary had been made on the subject of untouchability in India; and nothing accomplished that would aid greatly in eliminating segregation and racial discrimination in the United States.

The Commission on Race, of which Channing Tobias was chairman, condemned segregation based on race, but that censure did not change one iota the segregated practices of the local YMCAs in the United States; and this statement was opposed, though unsuccessfully, by a white man from South Africa. The Conference at Mysore did nothing that would help avoid the world catastrophe which broke out in Europe in 1939. The sad truth is that the governments of the world do not listen to the pronouncements of religious bodies. Perhaps it is small wonder, if the governments observe how little the religious bodies themselves practice what they preach.

As I made my way to Colombo from Bombay, I spoke to several YMCA and student groups in Madras, Madura, Trivandrum, and Colombo. Speaking to college students in India was much like speaking to Negro students in the United States. They, too, were groping for a better life and needed motivation and inspiration. They responded warmly to my speeches, expressing their appreciation by long applause. YMCA groups were very much interested in Negro-white relations in the United States. In the places I stopped between Mysore and Colombo, the word had been passed along that foreign delegates were paying brief visits to colleges and YMCAs on the way. To my surprise, the press and photographers were more interested in having a press conference with me than they were in having one with my white comrades. Their interest was not so much because I was a Negro but because as a Negro I had experienced discrimination in the United States, and they were eager to hear what I had to say about the race problem in my country. They had their own notions—often erroneous ones—but they wished to talk about nothing else. They were somewhat reluctant to talk about caste and the depressed classes right on their own doorsteps. As the train arrived in Madras, Madura, Trivandrum, and Colombo, the photographers were invariably there to take my picture and the reporters to interview me. Never before had I experienced preferential treatment over white people.

The caste system in India, and the presence of a depressed class (untouchables), revealed to me how cruelly inhuman and oppressive people of the same racial stock can be to one another. My impression in 1937 was that the caste system had done more to retard India than had approximately two hundred years of British rule. I thought caste was much worse than segregation in the United States, because in the States there was some social conscience across racial lines, whereas I could detect no such social concern across caste lines. Of course, Gandhi was an exception.

I traveled on the *Katori Maru* from Colombo to Shanghai; and on the *Chichibu Maru* from Shanghai to San Francisco. I expected no discrimination on Japanese steamers and I found none. Nor did I encounter it as I moved among the colored peoples of Egypt, India, Ceylon, China, and Japan. I found curiosity in China and Japan, but no discrimination. Some of my experiences on the Japanese boats may prove interesting.

Now and then, in the course of conversation, someone made a general statement about a race or ethnic group, such as, "Chinese are dishonest." "Japanese are sneaky." "White people lose prestige when they treat Indians of ordinary rank as their equals." "Negroes who accomplish much have white blood in their veins." The person who made this last absurd generalization attributed Paul Robeson's genius to the untraceable speck of white blood that may have been in his veins. Such a lunatic belief on the part of white people in the superiority of their blood is arrogance turned to insanity!

For a while on the *Katori Maru* I sat at the table with a white missionary and his wife who had spent forty years in India. They had been retired and were returning home to the United States. It wasn't long before I discovered that these two had no love for the Indian people. They proclaimed that Indians were unreliable, lazy, and dishonest. Under pressure they admitted that there were exceptions, but they held to their characterization as a general rule. Their appraisal of Gandhi was highly uncomplimentary. They were decidedly pro-British. And they didn't like Gandhi both because he had not embraced the Christian religion and because of his attitude toward the missionary enterprises. The attitude of these two representatives of the Christian faith was so hostile, so venomous, that I asked the steward to give me another seat.

When I got off the boat in Shanghai, on February 4, 1937, I was to go to the YMCA there. Some Americans in Shanghai persuaded me to take the streetcar to the YMCA rather than be overcharged by a Chinese taxi driver. They told me to get off the streetcar two blocks from the YMCA. I had not thought to ask whether I was to go two blocks north, east, south, or west. So there I stood, asking one person after another which was the way to the Chinese YMCA. None could speak English. In a few moments, a crowd began to gather to "behold the black man!" I stopped the better-dressed Chinese, because I thought they might be more likely to know some English. They shrugged their shoulders and laughed. I was feeling sillier by the minute. I went into a store to inquire, the crowd following, but no one there could understand me. Finally a well-dressed white woman came along and I felt that I was "saved" for, English or American, she would surely speak English.

When I spoke to the white woman saying, "Pardon me, Madam, do you know the address of the YMCA?" she was visibly a bit nervous. She said "Yes" and then remembered that she didn't really know where the Y was.

I asked if she spoke Chinese. She did not. Although she and her husband had been in Shanghai with an American oil company for twenty years, she was as ignorant as I of the Chinese language. It was most revealing—here was a woman living in Shanghai among English and American whites and she had never taken the time to learn Chinese. She invited me to walk with her about six or seven blocks to a shop where a Chinese spoke English. As we walked away, the crowd dispersed. When I finally found out how I was to get to the YMCA, I was advised to take a ricksha to be sure that I didn't miss it. I didn't want to ride in a ricksha because I had an aversion to being drawn by a human being. Nevertheless, it seemed the only way. As it turned out, the YMCA really was only two short blocks from the spot where I had attracted so much attention had I known in which direction to walk.

I disembarked in Kobe and went by train to Tokyo to spend a few days there before taking the boat at Yokohama for home. A youth delegate to Mysore named T. W. Currie was my cabin mate across the Pacific, and we went around together in Tokyo. Mr. Currie, a Texan, was almost seven feet tall and he was a blue-eyed blond. When we went into Tokyo's finest department store—comparable to, say, Bonwit Teller's in New York or Rich's in Atlanta—we almost disrupted the place. Pretty Japanese girls came running up to us from every direction, smiling and giggling. I insisted that they were curious to see the tall, blue-eyed blond Texan; Currie argued that they wanted to see, close-up, the big black man from Washington, D.C. We really couldn't settle the argument since neither of us could understand a word they were saying.

Tokyo impressed me greatly. I was glad to see a non-white nation accomplishing everything that I had seen white men achieve in New York, London, and Paris. Then, early in March, 1937, after stopping in Honolulu and San Francisco, I returned to my work as dean of the School of Religion of Howard University.

Chapter XII

Learning the Problem in Depth

I had been back in Washington only a few days when I was chosen to attend the Church Conference on Church, Community, and State to be held in Oxford, England, in the summer of 1937. I attended the Oxford Conference as a co-opted delegate, representing no particular denomination. Naturally, I was deeply concerned with the problem of race outside the United States. So my reactions to the Conference were largely in terms of what Oxford had to say about race. Most of the five sections dealt with race, but the section "Church and Community," to which I belonged, made the strongest statement. I quote here from what I wrote in the November, 1937, issue of *Crisis* magazine, for it is, essentially, my credo:

> Even deeper are the distinctions of race. The existence of black races, yellow races is to be accepted gladly and reverently as full of possibilities under God's purpose for the enrichment of human life. And there is no room for any differentiation between the races as to their intrinsic values. All share alike in the concern of God, being created by Him to bring their unique and distinctive contributions to His service in the world.
>
> Here again, however, the gift can be, and is, abused. The sin of man asserts itself in racial pride, racial hatreds and persecutions, and in the exploitations of other races. Against this in all its forms the church is called by God to set its face implacably and to utter its word inequivocally, both within and without its own borders.
>
> Moreover, it is a first responsibility of the church to demonstrate within its own fellowship the reality of community as God intends it. It is commissioned to call men into the church, into a divine society that transcends all national and racial limitations and divisions. In the services of worship, in its more informal fellowship, in its organization, and in the truly Christian home, there can be no place for discriminations of race or color. There is neither Jew nor Greek, bond nor free, for ye are all one in Christ. A church which allows her lines of action to be determined by racial discrimination denies the Gospel whose proclamation is her task and commission.

Here, as in Mysore, it was someone—a Scotsman—from South Africa who objected. He was insistent that such a declaration would not be accepted by the whites of South Africa. My somewhat pessimistic feelings about the whole Conference were summarized in an article which I wrote for *Crisis* of October, 1937:

> There is always a danger that in a world conference we will deal in glittering generalities and so water down our pronouncements that they will carry neither force nor conviction. In our efforts to speak to no situation that is purely national in character, and in our great desire to say nothing that will offend the powers or representatives of certain countries, and in our eagerness to have something that all can subscribe to, there is great danger that we will say and do less than we should and that prophetic actions and utterances will be sacrificed for the sake of unity. At many points, as good as the reports are, I felt that they had been so toned down that people reading them would not be convicted of sin and would not be sufficiently aroused to a sense of urgency and peril. . . .
>
> Nothing we did at Oxford will have any influence on the governments of the world with respect to their armament plans. Japan will look longingly at Chinese territory and if strong enough she will take it. The world in time will recognize Italy's conquest of Ethiopia and if Italy succeeds by building a few skyscrapers, paving a few roads and improving the telephone and telegraph systems for the government, the world will forgive Mussolini and it will give him credit for civilizing the heathens. Nothing we did at Oxford will change Hitler and Germany in their ruthless warfare against the Jews and nothing we did there will destroy Italy's ambition to reestablish the Roman Empire. The communists and fascists in Spain will continue to fight despite what we said at Oxford. . . .
>
> When the next world war comes, the church of God will bless it, and will claim to be fighting a holy war, as she has always done. I hope that when the next conference convenes, efforts will be put forth to have at the conference representatives of the various governments of the world and masters of industry and finance, for I cannot help but feel that the people who really determine world policies and who shape the destiny of mankind never attend a conference such as Oxford. If our repentance and conversions could really reach the people who make the decisions that change the world, our conferences would have far more immediate significance. Let us sincerely hope and fervently pray that as this fellowship develops and becomes all-embracing, it will be so powerful that wars and economic exploitation will cease and racial conflicts will be a thing of the remote past.

When I was in London in November, 1936, I had met no discrimination at the Regent Palace Hotel, and none elsewhere in the city. Even the barbershop at the hotel had received me and, to my surprise, had given me as good a haircut as any Negro barber in the United States could have.

My wife, Sadie, and her sister, Miss Emma C. W. Gray, were with me on the trip to Oxford in the summer of 1937. While I attended the Conference, they visited the historic sights of England. After Oxford, we planned to spend a few days in London before touring south Germany with friends, the Tracy Strongs. Tracy Strong was the general secretary of the World YMCA, with headquarters at Geneva, Switzerland.

I wanted to be on my own this time, with no intercession for me as had been the case in London in 1936, so by telephone I arranged for hotel accommodations in London. The man at the hotel took our names and told me he had space—two rooms, a single and a double. I told him that we would be there within the hour; we grabbed a taxi and were there in forty minutes.

When we arrived, the clerk denied having accommodations and denied having talked with me. We argued for several minutes, but to no avail. He recommended a small Swiss hotel not far away. However, I was schooled in such tactics. We stepped aside and waited, standing close enough to the desk to hear as others arrived and got rooms without having made any reservations at all. Lying to a black man and being openly caught in their lying did not in the least embarrass the hotel management. We had no choice but to go to the Swiss hotel. A porter standing by asked to assist us to the Swiss hotel. He said, "I heard what they told you. They have several vacant rooms. I'm Irish. I hate the British."

The next place where we met discrimination in London was at the station of the American Express which was arranging tours for foreigners. The American Express agent told us frankly and decisively that he could not book me, my wife, and sister-in-law on the same bus with whites. We argued this one out, too. The agent maintained that many Americans went on these tours and they would object to our presence. I admonished him to remember that it was his own British prejudice which was being exposed. This man really had nerve. He offered us a private car, with a driver, at a fee much higher than the bus would cost. Being in our right minds, we rejected his cynical proposal.

Two points stand out prominently in my mind about our trip through parts of south Germany after we left London: First we saw the Hitler Youth groups in action. We saw them "Heil Hitler" all over the place and on the trains. We found out that these children made even their own parents afraid to speak out against Hitler. In one German home where we stayed, the parents were afraid to talk about conditions in Germany when their twelve-year-old son was in the room and talked about the situation in whispers even when the boy was not present. This was two years before Hitler started the war. In 1938, when I stopped in Berlin en route to Stockholm to attend a meeting of the Central Committee of the World YMCA, the Baptist friends with whom I stayed were now also speaking in whispers about Hiter although their children were not around. In 1937 we saw signs frequently reading, *"Die Juden Sind Unser Unglück"*—The Jews Are Our Misfortune.

Another impression left with me by the 1937 trip was that the inhabitants of southern Germany were not accustomed to seeing colored people. I was definitely a Negro—black—and my wife and her sister might be mistaken for Japanese or Chinese. Even when we visited the Cathedral in Cologne, we almost blocked traffic as people slowed down to stare at us. My white friend, Tracy Strong, and I walked ahead. People we met on the sidewalks turned around to look at me, and when they turned back to continue their journey they were shocked again by seeing Sadie and Emma following. A similar episode occurred in a little town in south Germany, Eisenach, I believe, where we saw a statue of Martin Luther. We walked down the street to get a good look at it, and by the time we came back the stores were empty of people who were all on the sidewalk staring at us. Later, in Kassel, a boy about five years old was walking past hand in hand with his mother. The boy was so utterly amazed at seeing a black man that he kept looking back, his mother pulling him along. Finally he blurted out in German, "Such a man as that I have never seen before!"

In Sweden, the next year, a couple of waitresses in a restaurant in Stockholm touched my hand and rubbed it to see if the black would come off! Even in Scotland we found that many Scots were unaccustomed to seeing black people. Our friends, Mr. and Mrs. Lightbody, whom I met in Mysore, invited us to visit them in Edinburgh. The management in a hotel there made it clear that we were not welcome. While we were visiting a beautiful garden in that city, a woman saw me from several yards away, stared, and then started toward me, grinning. She came closer and closer, so close that her face almost touched mine. Lightbody, with good Scottish humor, exclaimed, "Kiss her, Doctor, kiss her!" Before I could carry out his order, she had fled.

As a leader in the Conference of Christian Youth held in Amsterdam, Holland, in the summer of 1939, I was able to see the problem of race in greater dimensions. One of the issues discussed at the conference was

"Christian Youth and Race." Fifteen hundred young people came from seventy-two nations to participate. The average age of the delegates was twenty-four and a half. In this section, every race problem throughout the world was represented. Members of black, white, brown, and yellow races were there, with delegates from five continents and more than twenty countries.

The Commission on Race spent most of its time discussing the racial situation in South Africa and the United States and the Jewish problem across the world. Although the Amsterdam Conference was a youth conference, the young people were just about as conservative on race as the older people had been in other world conferences. A small but articulate group of young people, led by a spokesman from the Dutch Reformed Church, defended segregation in every area of life. Once more I was hearing the same arguments in defense of a segregated society that I had heard all my life. This small minority were agreed that segregation and Christianity are compatible.

The Dutch argued that segregation in South Africa was not only the plan of God but the divine will of God. It was God's will that the Europeans and the Bantus remain segregated, separated in Church and state and in every other area of life. The two cultures must be maintained separately for the good of both. One of the spokesmen, in defense of a segregated Church, took the position that it was better for the natives themselves that they have their own churches. This argument, too, I had heard all my life: I had heard it abroad for the first time in India in 1937; and I was to hear it over and over again in every world Christian conference I attended through 1954.

In summarizing the position of my section on race, I submitted the following report:

1. A small minority held that segregated churches, though imposed on the weak by the strong, are not unchristian; that it is God's will that separation be maintained; and further that God is guiding the Dutch Reformed Church in dealing with the Bantu people;

2. A good many said that any system that denies fellowship across racial lines is unchristian and that the Church should move with dispatch to end discrimination in God's house;

3. A third group accepted the assertion that segregation in the Church is unchristian, but felt that we should face reality as it is; that there

is nothing that can be done about it, so it should be accepted as inevitable. We should, however, work cautiously and gradually toward the ideal of a non-segregated Church.

Although I am writing about this conference thirty years after it took place, there seems to be not one iota of change in the segregated church situation in South Africa; and thirty years after Amsterdam the churches in the United States are for the most part still highly segregated. If a World Conference of Christian Youth were called in 1970, the findings of the group would probably not differ in any real sense from those arrived at in Amsterdam thirty years ago. I take this position because I do not know of one large, thoroughly integrated church in the United States, one where Negroes are a part of the congregation in large numbers, and where the whites retain active membership. A few Negroes in a white church pose no problem. In some cases they are "showpieces," demonstrating the "liberality" of the church; but a large number creates a problem, the solution being that the white members usually move from the community in frantic haste and the church building is eventually sold to Negroes, often at great financial sacrifice to the fleeing "Christians." It is quite obvious that Christianity, as practiced by so-called Christians, has not solved the problem of race in the Church.

Amsterdam was the fourth World Conference I attended—all while I was dean of the School of Religion at Howard. These conferences enabled me to learn from experience, from observation, and from wide contact with people across the world that the black-white problem was a major problem (as it still is in 1970) and that our Christian people, Negro and white, have their work cut out for them if Christianity is to play a decisive role in solving the problems of race, war, and poverty and thus avoid world catastrophe.

Nowhere can a black man escape. On sea and on land, at home and abroad, the same stupid and cruel discrimination spreads its tentacles. In August, 1941, Mr. and Mrs. Jesse O. Thomas, Sadie, and I went to Havana, Cuba, for a brief vacation. We left Miami at night, and were shocked when we entered the diner the next morning to be politely told by the headwaiter that we could not be served with the white passengers. He suggested that we come back in an hour's time. We refused to do this, insisting on immediate service. It was not a matter of waiting for space. There was plenty. "The rule is that blacks and whites cannot be served together and I cannot break the rule." We were stubborn, and like a child who persists in asking the embarrassing "Why?" we continued to press for a reason.

We were told that Florida laws obtained on the boat between Miami and Havana. We wanted to know whether Florida owned the water; and when Florida legislated segregation for the state of Florida did the legislation include the body of water between Miami and Havana? By this time the steward, who had appeared on the scene, was getting redder in the face by the second. We made it clear that we were not going to wait and that if we were not served the company would be heavily sued. He asked whether we would accept service on the deck, assuring us, "It will be much cooler there." We accepted this compromise, and never have we eaten a more leisurely meal! Some of the passengers, having missed the first act of the drama, interpreted our eating on deck to mean that we were being favored and asked the management for the same preferential service. Faced with the possibility that too many passengers would make the same request, the management retreated in good order and thereafter we were served in the diner along with the other passengers.

We had made our hotel reservations in advance, but when we arrived in Havana the desk clerk said he had no reservations. It was the same puerile trick we had met in the United States and England. Dr. Mercer Cook, of Atlanta University, had met us at the boat and accompanied us to the hotel. Being fluent in Spanish, Dr. Cook succeeded in convincing the management that they would be in real trouble if our reservations were not honored. We were housed—in what I am sure were the most uncomfortable rooms they had. When we went to the dining room for our first meal, our food was so heavily salted as to be inedible. We complained to the management, and were then given palatable food. We subsequentely learned that though the management was Cuban, the hotel was owned by Americans.

We had been officially told that there was no discrimination based on color in Cuba. However, we unearthed two pieces of evidence, in addition to our hotel experience, that belied this assertion. We found that the colored Cubans had an organization designed to combat color discrimination in the country. In every store we visited the clerks invariably were white Cubans. Seldom did we see a white Cuban female entertainer on the street or in the eating places. Accident? Maybe, but highly improbable.

Despite these unpleasant experiences, Havana was delightful, reminding us somewhat of Paris. However, Sadie had not been well when we left Atlanta, and we had been in Havana only a short time when it became necessary to seek medical help for her. I went to the American Embassy, asking for the name of an American physician or of a Cuban physician who could speak English. After a sample of the typically rude "American" treatment especially earmarked for Negroes, I was given the name of a Dr. Nuñez Portuondo. I took Sadie to see him at once, only to be told at his office that he could not see Mrs. Mays until Wednesday afternoon. I told Dr. Portuondo's assistant that my wife was very ill and could not wait two days. After conferring with the doctor, the assistant told us that the doctor would see Mrs. Mays the next day. I then asked to speak to the doctor myself. After hearing firsthand of Mrs. Mays' condition, he agreed to see her after his other appointments.

The doctor's spacious office was filled with patients, possibly a hundred or more. We waited, I feeling more upset than Sadie. At the end of the afternoon, Dr. Portuondo examined Mrs. Mays and congratulated me on my insistence that he see her that day. Saying Wednesday would have been too late, he ordered her to the hospital for early Tuesday morning surgery. He told me again that two days' delay would have been fatal. After that, when my wife accused me of being hardheaded, I reminded her that my hard head saved her life in Havana in 1941.

To my great surprise, Dr. Portuondo would not accept pay for his services. He said that a man and wife on vacation in his country deserved the courtesy he had given us. This was twenty-eight years ago, and Sadie and I have never thought of Dr. Portuondo without deep gratitude, not so much for his free service as for his willingness to extend what had obviously been a long, hard day to act the good Samaritan. His consideration remained our most pleasant memory of Cuba.

Chapter XIII

So Much with So Little and So Few

In early 1940, when John Hervey Wheeler, a member of the Board of Trustees of Morehouse College, and now president of the Mechanics and Farmers Bank of Durham, North Carolina, interviewed me in my home in Washington, D.C., about the possibility of my coming to Morehouse as its president, I did not take him seriously. On leaving, Mr. Wheeler made it clear that I might hear no more about our conversation. I assured him that I understood, and added that I loved my work at Howard and was not looking for a job. Sadie, with a woman's intuition, predicted that the offer would surely come, and she was right. On May 10, 1940, a long-distance call from Trevor Arnett, a Board member, and former president of the General Education Board, informed me that I had been elected to the presidency of Morehouse College. I told Mr. Arnett that I would consider the offer, but that first I must talk with President Mordecai Johnson of Howard.

It took me three weeks to make up my mind. Salary was important to me, but it has never been a major determinant. To tackle a big job that needs to be done and succeed in doing it is for me the essence of happiness. My six years as dean of the School of Religion at Howard had been meaningful years. There was tangible evidence of success and progress. It wasn't easy to leave. Nevertheless, after talking several times with President Johnson; after holding conferences with President Rufus Clement of Atlanta University, President Florence Reed of Spelman College, Kendall Weisiger, chairman of the Board, and Acting President C. D. Hubert of Morehouse; after interviewing several members of the Morehouse faculty and getting advice from President Emeritus Samuel Howard Archer; after traveling to Michigan to see Trevor Arnett, to Durham to see John Hervey Wheeler, and back to Washington to talk with another trustee, W. W. Alexander; and after checking the condition of the physical plant and determining the financial status of the college, I accepted the offer to become the sixth president of Morehouse College.

There were some things I felt I should say in my letter of acceptance rather than waiting to say them after taking charge of the college. I had a point of view which I wanted known in advance so that the Board, if it so wished, could reconsider its offer. On May 31, 1940, I answered Board Chairman Kendall Weisiger's letter accepting the presidency of Morehouse College effective August 1.

In that letter I said:

> There are other matters, though not a condition of acceptance, which I do hereby present in the attached memorandum, requesting that the Executive Committee or the Board consider them as if they were conditions of acceptance.

The memorandum accompanying my letter of acceptance included the following points:

1. In accepting the presidency of Morehouse College, I am by that fact violating an agreement which I made sometime ago with the World Committee of the YMCA through its president, Dr. John R. Mott, whereby I agreed, Mrs. Mays and I, to give my sabbatical year, September 1, 1940, to September 1, 1941, to the World's Committee by serving the Bantu people of South Africa. I am therefore accepting the presidency as of July 1, 1940, knowing full well that I am obligated to carry out my contract with the World Committee of the YMCA. . . .

2. As I study the financial condition of Morehouse College, I am convinced that the members of the Board of Trustees were wise in not offering the president of the college more than $5000 and house. On the other hand, our coming to Atlanta is at considerable financial loss since it would hardly be expected that Mrs. Mays would engage in full time employment in Atlanta as was the case in Washington. . . . In view of this situation, I should hope that the Board would not consider the initial salary of the president as being adequate or static.

3. As I study the salary scale of teachers in Morehouse College, I am thoroughly convinced that on the whole they are too low. They should be raised all along the line. . . .

4. I request and urge that steps be taken immediately to do what we can to give Morehouse College equality of status in the system by electing the President of Morehouse College to membership on the Executive Committee of his own college and on the Executive Committee of Atlanta University. Since the two institutions have the same Board of Trustees, this request appears logical and reasonable. . . .

> 5. I am strongly of the opinion that it is unsound administrative policy to have the treasurer of Morehouse College outside of the administration of Morehouse. I am convinced that it would make for better working relationships and that the cause of Morehouse would be better served if the treasurer were within the administration of Morehouse. . . .
>
> 6. That we look forward very soon to having a Dean of Instruction. . . .
>
> These are some of the issues which I think should be set forth now in order to avoid possible misunderstanding later. . . .

In his reply, Mr. Weisiger wrote: "All points in your memo strike me as being pertinent to your new relationship with Morehouse, and I feel that each of them can be met and dealt with in time to your entire satisfaction."

Several factors influenced my final decision to go to Morehouse. I had not been asked, before receiving the offer, whether I would accept it if offered; nevertheless, the news broke in the press that I had been elected, and the news releases implied that I had accepted. In a way, this put me on the spot. To decline would lead the public to believe that I had made a commitment and reneged on it. A more persuasive factor was the challenge of the job. I thought I might get support from faculty, trustees, alumni, and friends to move Morehouse forward. And after all, this was *Morehouse* where I had begun my teaching career nineteen years before. Many of the students I had known and taught there were making their mark in the world. Many Morehouse men who were graduated prior to 1921 were making a unique contribution in their respective fields. I considered it an honor to be president of a college that had done "so much with so little and so few." I found a special, intangible something at Morehouse in 1921 which sent men out into life with a sense of mission, believing that they could accomplish whatever they set out to do. This priceless quality was still alive when I returned in 1940, and for twenty-seven years I built on what I found, instilling in Morehouse students the idea that despite crippling circumscriptions the sky was their limit. There is still this intangible something at Morehouse College. If it is ever lost, Morehouse will become "just another college."

The esprit de corps which characterizes Morehouse is certainly not there because the college has had adequate financial support. It didn't have it in 1940, and it doesn't have it now. The plant has never been adequate, and in the old days the faculty was very poorly paid. In 1923, when John Hope increased my salary from $1,200 to $1,800 a year to induce me to stay as acting dean for another year, he didn't have the money to pay me the extra $600. It was not until the following year when I had returned to the University of Chicago that I was paid the difference.

When I first knew the college in 1921, endowment was nonexistent. In 1940 it was only $1,114,000—one-third that of Spelman, and less than one-third that of Atlanta University, the institutions with which Morehouse was affiliated. At the time of the affiliations in 1929, the Morehouse endowment was $322,918.23; and in 1935, when the American Baptist Home Mission Society deeded the Morehouse land and plant to a private Board of Trustees, it was not in position to turn over much endowment to the college. The annual income on the $100,000 given to the college for endowment at the time of the transfer represented just about what the American Baptist Home Mission Society was contributing annually to the college. Morehouse shares with Virginia Union and Shaw University the income on approximately $900,000 which the Home Mission Board still holds for the three institutions. Grateful as Morehouse is to the American Baptist Home Mission Society for nurturing it through the years, it was wise for the college to operate under a private board and retain merely a church-related status with the Society. Changing to a private board of trustees opened up new possible sources of income.

So, it wasn't affluence that created and sustained the special Morehouse spirit and appeal. It was a few able, dedicated teachers who made the Morehouse man believe that he was "somebody." There were men like John Hope, Samuel Howard Archer, Benjamin Brawley, John B. Watson, C. D. Hubert, and others who widened the Negro's horizon and made him believe that he could do big and worthwhile things. This spirit, and the challenge to preserve and perpetuate it, clinched my decision more than anything else to accept the presidency. It was good for Morehouse that it had such inspiring black men on the faculty in the beginning of the twentieth century. Salaries were miserably low, but devotion was correspondingly high.

Not everybody was happy over the Trustees' choice. Even after my election and acceptance, there were a few who still wanted one of the other candidates. A few faculty people had predicted that I would wreck the school because, as acting dean of Morehouse, I had insisted that academic performance take precedence over athletic prowess and that a student who failed in his work should not be away two or three weeks playing intercollegiate athletics.

Some of the ministers thought that I was not orthodox enough to head an institution that was Baptist-born and now church-related. Conservative Baptists held no high regard for the University of Chicago Divinity School, considering it to be a "hotbed of heresy" and its professors to be agnostics, infidels, and atheists. Doctor D. D. Crawford, a Baptist minister and a Morehouse graduate, said of me in *The Georgia Baptist* of May 15, 1940, "The man they got is a notorious modernist. He believes in everything in general and nothing in particular. He is a scientific Christian, not a serious religious one." A few were opposed to me because they remembered that when I was pastoring Shiloh in 1924, I had gone to an Omega picnic and danced with the young woman I escorted. Whether my choice to go to Morehouse was a wise one is now history, and the record speaks.

A significant and far-reaching step had been taken in 1929 when Morehouse, Spelman, and Atlanta University affiliated in a university plan known as the Atlanta University System. Morehouse and Spelman agreed not to engage in graduate and professional study, and Atlanta University agreed not to carry an undergraduate program. This affiliation formed the basis of what is now known as The Atlanta University Center, which includes Atlanta University, Clark College, The Interdenominational Theological Center, Morehouse College, Morris Brown College, and Spelman College.

In the process, Morehouse, which could least afford it, gave more of itself to make the affiliation work than any other college in the Center. The front part of its campus, facing Chestnut Street (two and a fraction acres) was deeded to Atlanta University. Quarles Hall, now the home of the Atlanta University School of Social Work, was moved to its present location and given to Atlanta University. Also deeded to Atlanta University were a house and a lot and part of the land on which Quarles Hall is presently located. The Morehouse Infirmary was moved to Spelman. In exchange for the land and buildings ceded to Atlanta University, Morehouse was given administrative space in Harkness Hall, approximately 25 percent of the space, at no cost or maintenance. Without financial obligation, Morehouse students and faculty were to have full rights and privileges in the use of the Atlanta University library (given for the use of all four colleges and the university). Further cooperation between the two schools was shown in 1952 when Atlanta University contributed $100,000 toward the erection of the

$600,000 Morehouse chemistry building, in exchange for graduate facilities in biology and chemistry without cost of maintenance. That Morehouse gave more to make the affiliation succeed than did any of the other schools involved is understandable, since John Hope had been president of Morehouse for twenty-five years, including the two years he had been president of both Morehouse and Atlanta University.

Many factors contributed to the low morale which I found at Morehouse in 1940. Among them was the fact that Morehouse men were eating at another institution where Morehouse had no power to correct the things about which the students complained (and they surely did complain!). On the other hand, Atlanta University had no power of discipline over Morehouse men. When students complained of service and treatment at Spelman's MacVicar Hospital, Morehouse had no authority to investigate or make changes, though it paid for the services. In 1933, seven years before I came, Morehouse had been doing so poorly financially that the American Baptist Home Mission Society and President Archer had requested Atlanta University to assume financial direction and budgetary control of Morehouse. This the university had agreed to do, making it clear, however, that it would not assume financial responsibility for Morehouse. In 1942, this decision of the two boards was rescinded at my request.

Morehouse personnel were also complaining about the slowness with which requisitions were being processed, maintaining that urgent requisitions often lay neglected for days, awaiting approval of the president of another institution, who was the treasurer of Morehouse. The Morehouse faculty and alumni complained that the college was fast becoming a junior college because the juniors and seniors of Morehouse were being taught by teachers from Atlanta University and Spelman. I validated this complaint by ascertaining the number of faculty hired by Morehouse, by Spelman, and by Atlanta University in the decade between 1930 and 1940. In that period, Atlanta University's teaching staff had increased *220 percent*, Spelman's *78 percent*, while Morehouse's staff had *decreased* by 16 percent. For another thing, the alumni, faculty, and students of Morehouse could not understand why the front part of the Morehouse campus had been deeded to Atlanta University. Furthermore, the Morehouse faculty believed that they could hold their jobs at Morehouse only with the approval of the president of Atlanta University and the president of Spelman College.

Such, to mention a few items, was the situation when I came to Morehouse in 1940. Hence, it could hardly have been otherwise than that the morale of alumni, faculty, and students was low. I had moved from one stepchild to another—from the School of Religion of Howard University to Morehouse College of the Atlanta University affiliation. Circumstances had so converged that Morehouse was the weakest link among the affiliated institutions in the system.

I went to Morehouse with a conviction, and I left Morehouse on June 30, 1967—twenty-seven years later—with the same conviction: The strength of one institution in the affiliation is the strength of all, and the weakness of one is the weakness of all. There has been considerable talk about merging the institutions in the Center. I never opposed the affiliation of Atlanta University, Morehouse, and Spelman, nor a merger of the six institutions that now comprise the Atlanta University Center. But I have bitterly opposed merging the six institutions *without a thorough and unbiased study which could show that a single institution would improve the quality of education given in the Atlanta University Center as it now stands and make the Center stronger financially.* My first task, therefore, was to make Morehouse an equal partner in the Atlanta University system so that it could give as much as it would receive. Whatever was needed to restore the integrity of Morehouse had to be done; and in the course of the years it was done.

By far the most debilitating factor from the standpoint of good faculty morale, was the belief entertained by Morehouse teachers that their jobs depended upon decisions made by the presidents of Atlanta University and Spelman College. In late June of 1940, a Morehouse teacher had been fired by the acting president of Morehouse College and the presidents of Atlanta University and Spelman College. He appealed to me, as the new president of Morehouse, to protect his position. After thorough investigation, I decided that the man should have been fired, but not in late June or early July, when most academic appointments for the following year had been made. I sent him a letter stating that the reason for his dismissal was valid but that the timing was wrong; therefore, he had a one-year reprieve at Morehouse. Though I had acted only on what I thought was right, it clarified the situation regarding the Morehouse teachers and was a morale builder to the faculty and alumni of Morehouse.

Three more things had to be done immediately. We had to 1) secure more money; 2) increase the faculty in size; and 3) improve the quality of the faculty by hiring better trained teachers. I recall vividly how disappointed I was when my colleagues at Atlanta University and Spelman College showed little concern for Morehouse's position as "low man on the totem pole" in the affiliation. When I related the figures showing faculty increases of 220 percent and 78 percent, respectively, for Atlanta University and Spelman College for the decade 1930-1940 and the decrease of 16 percent in the teaching staff at Morehouse for the same period, and protested that Morehouse was being reduced to the status of a junior college, one colleague said, "That isn't so bad," and the other, "It doesn't matter who does the teaching so long as it is good teaching." I had thought they would be delighted to have a colleague who wanted a Morehouse strong enough to carry its own weight in the affiliation. I wanted the cooperation to be equal so that Morehouse teachers would be strong enough to teach courses anywhere in the affiliation on an exchange basis. If Morehouse had to pay for exchange teachers from Atlanta University and Spelman, I saw no reason why Morehouse should not so increase the size and strength of its own faculty that Morehouse teachers would be teaching all across the board in the affiliation. To accomplish this objective required money which, at the time, the college did not have.

There were only two ways of getting more money: 1) Raise it; and 2) do a better job of collecting students' fees. Morehouse had been so lenient with students that there was an accumulation of one hundred thousand dollars in unpaid bills. Many of the back debts were relatively small, but the range per student was from $50 to $800. It was common practice for each year to end with the student debt amounting to $12,000 or $18,000. The first responsibility facing the new president in 1940 was to insist that students pay their tuition and other charges.

My first official act when I arrived at Morehouse was to send a letter to each student who owed the college and acquaint him with our new policy. A student owing a comparatively small sum was required to pay the debt in full before being allowed to register in September, 1940. A student in debt for several hundred dollars had to reduce the amount before registering and pay the current fees for the academic year 1940-1941. The senior who owed the college $500 or $600 in September, 1940, had to pay all bills for the current year and sign a note indicating when the whole amount would be paid before he could be graduated. No transcripts were to be issued until debts were settled. The program worked exceptionally well, for we were soon able to close the academic year with only $2,000 or $3,000 outstanding, much of which was collected during the summer. This project earned me the name of "Buck Benny." Thereafter, when I made a speech that the students liked, or did something else that pleased their fancy, they exclaimed, "Buck Benny rides again!"

Salaries were low at Morehouse in 1940. One of our best teachers was receiving $1,800 a year, another $2,600, and still another as little as $900 a year. One teacher, jointly employed by Morehouse and Atlanta University, received only $3,000. I accepted the Morehouse presidency for $5,000 a year and house. To be able to collect $10,000 or $12,000 a year in student fees not previously collected made it possible to hire four more teachers, thus strengthening the Morehouse faculty and reducing the amount paid other institutions for exchange teachers. Each year thereafter the Morehouse faculty increased in number and academic quality.

The second way to increase our income was to raise it from friends and foundations. To raise endowment is an eternal labor for all colleges, and for colleges serving Negroes it is trebly hard. If salaries were to be raised, Morehouse had not only to increase the endowment, but it was imperative that current money be raised annually in order to make such increases feasible.

Sad to say, I was never able, despite nearly three decades of ardent toil, to raise the Morehouse endowment to a respectable figure for a college of its size. I admit failure in this. It took twenty-seven years to increase the Morehouse endowment from $1,114,000 to $4,657,610 ($6,000,000 in market value). Instead of the endowment's having grown four times over by the time we left, it should have been eight times larger. My aim was to leave an endowment of $8 million book value and $12 million market value. In this respect, I trailed far behind my fondest expectations. By slow but steady accretions, however, the Morehouse endowment did increase.

A college is no stronger than its faculty. The building may be ever so fine, but if the faculty isn't strong, the college is weak. Thus I gave first priority to securing and maintaining able teachers. I knew this could not be done by relying wholly on Negro scholars. Morehouse has a strong, traditional policy of cutting across sex, national, ethnic, racial, and religious lines. I have boasted of building at Morehouse an ecumenical, interracial community. Then too, there were then, as there are now, so few black scholars available. Even as I write this book, it is too generous to say that there are three thousand Negro Ph.D.s in this country, living and dead. Three or four years ago there were around two thousand. In 1970, twenty-five hundred might be a more accurate figure. The competition for the black scholar has always been terrific, since there are so few. Now the competition is much keener—white colleges and universities, government and industry are vying for their services. This is another reason why I sought to secure faculty members beyond the Negro community. The trustees left the matter of faculty strength to the administration and faculty. Teachers were usually chosen after a consensus had been reached by members of the department, the dean of the college, and the president. Today the Morehouse faculty has Jews, Negroes, Protestants, Catholics, Hindus, Africans, white Southerners, and white Northerners. We sought to hire men and women of high academic achievement and good character, teachers who had risen above prejudice. If they met these criteria, they were hired. Consequently, I was able to say, in the final address I gave at our Centennial Commencement on May 30, 1967:

> Perhaps the greatest success the College has achieved in twenty-seven years is the high academic quality of teachers who comprise the faculty. This was our choice despite pressures from many sources to direct our meager funds to other useful and interesting but non-academic pursuits. Not to provide the students with the ablest faculty available is criminal and irresponsible. In 1940, we had the equivalent of twenty-three full-time faculty members and the equivalent of two full-time teachers who had earned the Ph.D. degree, or 8.7 percent of the staff. In 1966-67, we have sixty-five full-time teachers and 54 percent of them hold doctorates. The number of doctorates on the faculty is seventeen times greater than it was in the academic year 1940-41. Excepting one or two, the rest hold master's degrees; and many have studied from one to four years beyond. Three hold the B.D. degree.
>
> In academic training, this places Morehouse above all predominantly undergraduate Negro colleges. . . . It has taken twenty-seven years of constant planning to build and maintain a faculty of this strength.

During my administration, many Morehouse teachers were Southern white men and women. It has been my belief that it is good to bring together Southern white teachers and black students, since the racial gulf which usually prevents meeting on a basis of equality is so wide—in fact, it is almost impossible to span. As far as I know, there has been surprisingly little harassment or ostracism of white teachers because they taught at Morehouse. One of our white teachers told me of a few nasty telephone calls she received; and one Southern white woman had to decline a position at Morehouse because her young husband, who had just joined a law firm in Atlanta, was told that if his wife taught at Morehouse he could not be affiliated with the firm. I thought all this had been cleared in our initial conversation, and so had she. Though a Southerner, she admitted afterward that I knew the racial climate in Atlanta much better than she did. At the start of our negotiations, I asked her how her parents, her husband's parents, and her husband's colleagues would regard her employment at a Negro college. She thought that one set of parents would not like it, but there would be no very stiff opposition; she and her husband had agreed that it was their business and nobody else's. Although her husband wanted her to keep the Morehouse position, she regretfully resigned even before she began to teach because she did not want to impede his career.

Another case is more dramatic. We were greatly in need of a teacher with a doctorate in mathematics. One day I received a letter from a young white Georgian born a hundred miles from Atlanta, a graduate of the Georgia Institute of Technology. He wrote me from MIT, where he was finishing work for his doctorate, saying that he wanted to teach at Morehouse. He explained he had known of Morehouse through monthly forums which Negro and white students had held years earlier when there was concern among them for a better understanding between the races. At that time no crack had been made in the wall of segregation.

On one of my visits to New York, I wired the young man to come from Boston to see me. I was soon convinced that he really wished to teach at Morehouse. When I questioned him about his wife's attitude and that of his parents, he said that he and his wife had decided that Morehouse was where he should go but that his parents were bitterly opposed to his teaching in a black college. He told me he had already embarrassed them on two counts: He had become a Quaker and was a conscientious objector! He was sure that they would *really* consider him a disgrace to the family if he taught at Morehouse, but he knew that this was what he wanted to do. We talked about housing, on and off campus, and we agreed that it might be wise for him to seek housing off campus to make it easier for his parents to visit him. I urged him to seek an apartment in the vicinity of Emory University, but he thought that area was too far away.

Finally, this courageous young Georgian and his wife rented an apartment in West End, not far from Morehouse, so that his black faculty friends and students could conveniently visit him. When the landlady saw Negroes going into the professor's apartment, she gave him forty-eight hours to get out of her house. She told him she feared being bombed out by whites if they knew she allowed a white family who had "nigger" visitors to remain on her place. We provided quarters for him on our campus. His parents' prejudice was so intense that the young professor never dared introduce them to Sadie and me or to any of his black colleagues.

I had great admiration for this man, for it took unusual courage for a young Georgian to defy racial prejudice in its own bailiwick in the 1940's.

Prejudice is a strange animal—and well nigh indestructible. Although Morèhouse has been on its present spot for eighty years, it has not to any appreciable degree reduced the prejudice which whites living in the West End area, only a few blocks from the campus, hold toward Negroes.

We never had a big problem keeping our faculty. The turnover during my twenty-seven years averaged hardly four persons a year. We lost a small number to Howard University, to Atlanta University, and to Meharry Medical College. The only explanations I can offer for this low turnover are that Atlanta is a good city in which to live, the working conditions at Morehouse were and are good, academic freedom was a way of life there, and salaries, though low, were increased each year. I really believe that the faculty thought, and rightly so, that their president was doing his best to step up the salary scale, and that he took advantage of every opportunity to provide ways for them to improve themselves academically.

Dozens of Morehouse teachers have been aided by the college to study for and receive their doctorates. Through Morehouse's great friend Charles Merrill, thirty-three Morehouse professors have been able to spend summers abroad. Most of them were married, and their wives were sent along with them. These are some of the factors that kept the faculty strong and stable during the years of my presidency. As for the salaries, there was an upward trend year by year. The lowest salaries paid in 1966-67 were six and two-thirds times more than they were in 1940—$900 against $6,000. The highest salaries paid in 1966-67 were more than five times as much as they were in 1940—$2,600 against $13,500. The budget for 1967-68, adopted before I left, carried the highest salary at $14,500, and the average at $9,000 for a nine-month period. Most teachers supplemented this with summer work.

As a college is no stronger than its faculty, it is equally true no college can be strong without a strong board of trustees—men and women enthusiastically interested in the college, who will work for it and give to it not only money but also their knowledge and wisdom. To a degree, a college can be judged by the caliber of men and women it can secure to serve on its board. In selecting board members, Morehouse followed the same procedure it followed in recruiting faculty: We sought good men, and race and religion were no barriers. Among the twenty-four trustees, as of June, 1967, were women as well as men—Jews, Catholics, Protestants, Negroes, Southerners, Northerners, educators, ministers, lawyers, doctors, and businessmen. These deserve much credit for the strength and stature that Morehouse developed during the twenty-seven years I was president.

Although strengthening the faculty was always our top priority, the physical plant was not neglected during my tenure at Morehouse. In my Centennial Commencement Address in 1967, I was able to report:

> Although the physical plant needs to be enlarged in housing, worship, and academic facilities, since 1940 the physical plant has been improved by increasing the number of buildings from eight to twenty-five. . . . Our laboratory equipment in physics, chemistry, biology, mathematics, psychology, and health and physical education is first-rate and adds to the healthy morale of our faculty and student body. Again, this was our choice despite pressures from many sources to direct our meager funds to other useful and interesting but non-academic pursuits. The land area has been increased from 10.6910 to 20.1771 acres.

The buildings added between 1940 and 1967 are: five small dormitories housing 115 men, a large dormitory housing 120 men, a physical education and health building, an infirmary, a dining hall, a small academic building, a chemistry building, a physics, mathematics and foreign languages building, a meditation chapel, a dormitory on the campus of the Interdenominational Theological Center for the Baptist students enrolled in the Morehouse School of Religion, a small music studio, and three faculty apartments. Expansion continues under my successor, Dr. Hugh Morris Gloster.

At Morehouse we believe that a Negro should be given an opportunity to do whatever he is capable of doing. One of the most prestigious building erected at Morehouse since 1920 is Merrill Hall, the chemistry building. Edward C. Miller, a Negro architect, applied for the job of designing it. Never before had a Negro architect designed a building of that magnitude in the Atlanta University Center. Dr. Fred Patterson, then President of Tuskegee Institute, gave Mr. Miller an excellent recommendation; but both the contractor and the chairman of the Morehouse Board argued that white subcontractors would refuse to take orders from a Negro. The building committee insisted that we could not permit prejudiced white men to keep a Negro from getting a job on a Negro college campus. Mr. Miller was awarded the job, and white subcontractors worked under him without complaint.

E. C. Miller has been the architect for Morehouse College ever since —one more proof that our greatest fears are often fears of things that never happen. If Morehouse had not given Mr. Miller his opportunity, it might have been a long time before he could have proved his worth in Atlanta.

The title of this chapter is accurate: "So much with so little and so few." Few, if any, colleges of the size of Morehouse have done so much to uplift mankind. The student body has never been large. In 1967 the college enrolled 910 students from thirty-two states, the District of Columbia, and eight foreign countries. The enrollment in the academic year 1968-69 was 1,036.

It is only in recent years that Negroes have been going to college in relatively large numbers. In September, 1968, the nation's colleges enrolled 6.5 million students, and the estimated number of Negro college students was 275,000, approximately 4 percent of the total collegiate enrollment. Negroes represent 10 or 11 percent of the population of the United States, but only 4 percent of the college enrollment.

Morehouse has graduated fewer than 4,000 men with the A.B. and B.S. degrees. It carried a high school department until 1930, as did other Negro colleges, because even high school education for Negroes was relatively new. It was not until 1924 that the great city of Atlanta built its first high school for Negroes. Most Negroes who are college graduates received their degrees since 1920. Between 1889 and 1920, fewer than 4,000 Negroes had been graduated from college. These are facts the public overlooks when it complains that so few Negroes are qualified for the jobs for which they are sought at long last.

Morehouse men, though few in number, have done exceptionally well. If a college is to maintain a high level of academic excellence, it must have not only an able faculty and a good plant but also a large number of able students. In the final analysis, a college or university must be judged by the achievements of its alumni. On this score, Morehouse College has a proud record.

Within recent years, a high percentage of the graduates of Morehouse have gone on to graduate and professional schools. In 1964, 52 percent of Morehouse graduates entered graduate and professional schools; in 1966, 51.5 percent. The ratio has been as high as 56 percent. These percentages may be reduced now that industry is making such good offers to black college graduates. In the six-year span between 1961 and 1967, Morehouse seniors were awarded eighty-nine fellowships and assistantships to graduate and professional schools. In 1967, Morehouse graduates were studying in forty-five of the best graduate and professional schools in the nation. It is also significant that between 1945 and 1967 Morehouse stood second among Georgia institutions in the production of Woodrow Wilson Fellows.

By 1967, 118 Morehouse graduates had earned Ph.D. degrees. In 1967, one of every eighteen Negroes earning doctorates had received the A.B. or B.S. degree from Morehouse. This figure is marvelous on two counts: Not more than 4,000 men have been graduated from Morehouse. Moreover, Earl J. McGrath, in his book *The Predominantly Negro Colleges and Universities in Transition* (Columbia University, 1965), reports that there are 123 predominantly Negro colleges in this country. In addition, Negroes have been graduating from white colleges since the first Negro graduated from Bowdoin College in 1826. The one to eighteen ratio has hardly changed; since 1967 eleven Morehouse graduates have earned doctorates, making a total of 129 Morehouse graduates who hold such degrees. These degrees have been earned in the last thirty-seven years, for it was in 1932 that Samuel Milton Nabrit, Morehouse '25, became the first when he received the Ph.D. from Brown University. Since 1932, Morehouse has averaged three and one half Ph.D.s a year.

Morehouse men have received doctorates from forty-five different universities since 1932. Such a record is hardly an accident. It is a tradition at Morehouse that an A.B. or B.S. is not a terminal degree; every outstanding student is encouraged to continue his studies. It should also be noted that many of the Morehouse men who have earned doctorates were early-admission students who came to Morehouse as freshmen after completing the tenth or eleventh grades of high school. Morehouse started its early-admissions program before the Ford Foundation initiated theirs. With Morehouse it was a method of survival. World War II was so diminishing enrollment that the chairman of the Board suggested closing Morehouse for the duration. Actually, nobody took the chairman seriously; but we did get busy recruiting bright young students who had not finished high school. Among those so recruited was Martin Luther King, Jr., class of '48.

Morehouse stands among the first four Negro institutions in the production of graduates who go on to medical and dental training and careers. By 1967, more than three hundred Morehouse men had earned M.D.s and D.D.S.s, and forty of the three hundred achieved distinction as medical specialists—diplomates in medicine. A high percentage of all Negro physicians are graduates of Morehouse. Combining the degrees in medicine and the Ph.D.s in education, one out of every nine Morehouse graduates has earned an academic or professional doctorate.

There are several reasons why many Negro men have chosen medical careers: Medicine is a prestigious field with Negroes. For a long time, only a few professions were open to them—preaching, teaching, and medicine. As a physician or dentist, a Negro could be his own boss. Negroes looked up to their doctors; and even prejudiced whites had respect for Negro doctors.

For many years, Morehouse men have been holding administrative and teaching positions in Negro and white colleges and universities. In 1967, Morehouse graduates were teachers and administrators in fifty-eight predominantly black institutions and twenty-two white institutions. Twenty-one institutions of higher learning have had or now have Morehouse men as their presidents; and these presidents have served these twenty-one institutions for a total of 309 years.

When Morehouse celebrated its hundredth anniversary in 1967, the college had assistant superintendents of public schools in San Diego, Detroit, and Gary, Indiana. Five of the seven principals of the predominantly Negro high schools in Atlanta were Morehouse men; and Morehouse men were and are teaching in the public schools throughout the nation. In the field of music, too, Morehouse training has been outstanding. Among the best choirs and glee clubs in the nation are voices which are now being trained or which have been trained by Morehouse men at Morehouse, Spelman, Clark, Morris Brown, Dillard, Grambling, and other Negro colleges.

The early emphasis on religion and the later emphasis on the arts and sciences did not lessen Morehouse's interest in preparing men for the ministry. The Morehouse School of Religion is one of the four institutions that make up the Interdenominational Theological Center. Today Morehouse graduates are pastors of Negro churches in twenty-one cities. In addition to these pastorates, Morehouse men have achieved distinction in other religious fields, namely: Howard Thurman, listed several years ago by *Life* magazine as one of the twelve great preachers in the United States, who was chaplain at Boston University for more than a decade; the Right Reverend Dillard H. Brown, Episcopal Bishop of Liberia; Dr. Thomas Kilgore, the first black minister to become president of the American Baptist Convention; George Kelsey, professor at Drew Theological seminary; and the immortal Martin Luther King, Jr., who was both a great civil rights leader and a compelling pulpiteer. The first Negro daily newspaper in the nation, the Atlanta *Daily World*, was founded by a Morehouse man, and its present editor is a Morehouse man. The associate editor of *Jet* magazine and the senior editor of *Ebony* are Morehouse men. Among Morehouse men who are authors of note are: Lerone Bennett, Jr., James Birnie, Benjamin Brawley, George Kelsey, Martin Luther King, Jr., Ira DeA. Reid, and Howard Thurman.

Morehouse men are serving admirably in responsible positions in banking and insurance institutions across the country, and its graduates are creditably represented among the ever-increasing number of young blacks now employed and sought for employment by white financial institutions. Although it is not possible to determine at this writing all the places Morehouse men are in industry, it is known that they are serving well in many of the nation's giant firms. One is a pilot with American Air Lines.

The leadership of Morehouse College never accepted the status quo in Negro-white relations. The first president of the college, Joseph T. Robert, was a white South Carolinian who left the South because he did not want to rear his children in the section of the country where slavery existed. After Emancipation, Robert was persuaded to return to the South, and he became the first president of what is now known as Morehouse College. This fact about the early leadership has not been widely publicized. It could have been expected that a Yankee from the North would have been Morehouse's first president, but it is paradoxical that the first president was a man from the state that led the secession. Throughout its history, Morehouse's leadership has rebelled against racial injustices.

It is hardly surprising, therefore, that Morehouse men have been active in the civil rights struggle. The District of Columbia case, one of the five cases involved in the May 17, 1954, decision of the United States Supreme Court to outlaw segregation in the public schools, was argued and won by a Morehouse man, James M. Nabrit. The Reverend Samuel W. Williams and the Reverend John Porter are responsible for the federal court's decision which abolished segregation on the buses in Atlanta. The Reverend Charles Kenzie Steele, another Morehouse graduate, played a mighty hand in getting buses desegregated in Tallahassee, Florida. The Reverend Kelly Miller Smith was given credit by *Time* magazine for playing a major role in negotiating a respectable peace between the races in Nashville, Tennessee, when that city was torn asunder by the sit-in movement in the early 1960's. The leadership of Martin Luther King, Jr., which led to his winning the Nobel Peace Prize, is well known in every corner of the globe.

At this writing, Morehouse has three state senators, six representatives in six legislatures, a municipal judge in Toledo, a judge of the Recorder's Court and three aldermen in Detroit, and a judge for the Court of Appeals for the State of Washington. The Secretary of Commerce in the Republic of Liberia was graduated from Morehouse in 1950. President Lyndon B. Johnson appointed a Morehouse alumnus to membership on the Atomic Energy Commission and another alumnus to a position in the United Nations with the rank of ambassador.

There are two significant things about the establishment of a chapter of Phi Beta Kappa at Morehouse College in January 1968, the first of which is that the school began in 1867 in the basement of the Springfield Baptist Church in Augusta, Georgia, with thirty-eight illiterate adult ex-slaves. There were at that time only a few persons who believed that the Negro was capable of doing college and university work. For a long time scientists, educators, statesmen, and even men supposedly called of God to preach, had been proclaiming the Negroes' inability to learn. Years before my day, a fellow South Carolinian, thinking that he was perfectly safe in making such a proclamation, declared that he would be willing to give the Negro citizenship when he mastered the Greek verb. It is indeed a long step from the basement of the Springfield Baptist Church to the tower of academic excellence that warranted the establishment of a chapter of Phi Beta Kappa. The other significant thing is that Delta of Georgia, the Morehouse Phi Beta Kappa chapter, was established on the site of a great battleground in the siege of Atlanta during the Civil War. On the very spot where Southerners had fought so desperately to keep Negroes in bondage, an institution for the education of blacks had flourished to the extent that in less than a hundred years it merited the right to install a chapter of Phi Beta Kappa.

It took from 1953 to 1966 to persuade representatives of Phi Beta Kappa to visit Morehouse to determine whether we qualified for membership. In August, 1967, the United Chapters of Phi Beta Kappa, meeting at Duke University, voted to admit Morehouse College to membership. Only seven other institutions in the nation were selected that year.

On January 6, 1968, Delta of Georgia was established at Morehouse College, thus rewarding fourteen years of effort. The Installation ceremonies were impressive. Phi Beta Kappa members from other chapters in Georgia, the presidents of the other five institutions in the Atlanta University Center, the trustees of Morehouse College, and some of the outstanding high school students in the public schools of Atlanta were present.

On Friday, May 17, 1968, Delta of Georgia was proud to initiate into Phi Beta Kappa the first Morehouse students to qualify for membership: Benjamin Ward, Michael Lomax, Frederic Ransom, and Willie Vann. The installation and the initiation of the first Morehouse students into Delta Chapter in May of 1968 were historic events which were the culmination of a journey which really began in the basement of a church in Augusta, Georgia. Each triennium we had sent our credentials, and after each "No" we worked harder for the academic excellence which would qualify us. Now the dream had come true.

If Morehouse has done "so much with so little and so few," it is because many factors converged to make it possible. Good students have been graduated and acquitted themselves like men after leaving college. The alumni have made noteworthy contributions to society. The faculty has been able and dedicated. Individual persons and foundations have given the money without which the college could not have survived. The trustees have been loyal. They always gave me the freedom to do my work, with no restrictions, on the platform or in writing. I was never uneasy about my job, even when I was maliciously and falsely accused of being a Communist fellow-traveler. In my twenty-seven years as President, I never ceased to raise my voice and pen against the injustices of a society that segregated and discriminated against people because God made them black. No trustee ever took me to task for what I said in public and wrote in books and articles. This may be hard for some people to believe, but it is a fact. Without this kind of confidence and freedom, I would not have remained at Morehouse all those years, particularly since I had seventeen opportunities to leave during that time. I pay high tribute to the men and women who served on the Morehouse Board of Trustees between 1940 and 1967.

I am equally grateful to the persons and foundations that contributed to the college during the years of my presidency. No grant ever came to Morehouse with strings attached. Of course, integrity demands that money be used for the purpose for which it is appropriated, such as for buildings, scholarships, endowments, and other projects. But never was any money given to Morehouse designed to silence my freedom of speech as I lashed out from time to time against social injustices. A few persons on my faculty never quite believed in my complete freedom from pressure, yet I say emphatically that I state the complete truth. So, after twenty-seven years, I salute the members of the Board of Trustees, the individual persons and the foundations who assisted Morehouse without trying to tell the college what to do.

It must be said that Charles Merrill did more to vitalize Morehouse than any other individual. No one else was more interested in the total program of the college. After the early-admissions program was discontinued by the Ford Foundation, which had sponsored it for eight years, it was Charles Merrill who took up the tab; and he has sponsored the program for more than a decade. During his sponsorship up through 1967, a total of 194 Merrill scholars had entered Morehouse on $500-each scholarships. Thanks to Charles Merrill, sixty Morehouse students have studied and traveled in Europe for a year. At the end of my presidency that year, he had financed travel in Europe for fifty-two faculty members, including their wives or husbands. For many years, Mr. Merrill has been making annual contributions toward faculty salaries. On an annual basis, this one Trustee has contributed approximately $75,000 a year for a decade and a half toward the various programs of the college. It is my considered judgment that without Charles Merrill's valiant support Morehouse would not have been able to qualify for membership in Phi Beta Kappa.

There are many headaches and heartbreaks in raising money. Once in a while, I was made to feel like a dunce when I tried to get money from certain people and foundations for Morehouse. Some with whom I came in contact made me feel very bad. Had it not been for the fact that I loved Morehouse dearly and knew that the cause was worthy I would have thrown in the sponge. Fairly often, however, I was able to secure money. My heart was made glad when one morning I received an unexpected long distance telephone call from Maxwell Hahn of the Field Foundation, informing me that the Foundation had appropriated a half million dollars to Morehouse. Moreover, I made good friends through those twenty-seven years of fund raising. I learned that, on the whole, people with money are fine, generous, human, and understanding. Not all the wealthy are so, of course, but enough are to make me respect and appreciate the rich and those who handle money for the rich. Among my best friends are persons I met when I was trying to raise money for Morehouse.

I shall always cherish the opportunity and the honor which came to me when I was invited to serve a term on the Board of Trustees of the Danforth Foundation, crowning a friendship with Mr. William H. Danforth which began in 1942 when I attended my first Associate Conference at Camp Miniwanca.

Largely as a result of this friendship, Mrs. Dorothy Compton (daughter of Mr. Danforth), accepted our invitation to serve as a member of the Morehouse Board of Trustees. Upon her retirement from the Morehouse Board, John Danforth (grandson of William H. Danforth and now the Attorney General of the State of Missouri) joined the Morehouse Board. I appreciated being on the Board of the Foundation, for few Negroes ever have the opportunity to sit on a Board where policies concerning them are determined. Foundations' educational policies involving Negroes are usually made in the absence of Negroes.

Not all the headaches and heartaches originated in fund raising. There were some that were "closer home." I felt that the Morehouse faculty members, though dedicated and able, were a bit too conservative. They were timid about experimentation, hesitant to find new ways of doing things. Too many new ideas had to start with the administration. They also tended to cling to outworn attitudes. For example, I felt that Morehouse was too isolated from the problems of the Negro poor in Atlanta. I was shocked when I came to Morehouse to find a few faculty members who were opposed to Morehouse men dancing at affairs on campus when they had been dancing at city affairs since there was a Morehouse. I was susprised again when I found faculty opposition to the idea of equal student participation on the advisory committee, giving students an equal voice with the faculty when another student was being tried for some violation. Fortunately, we were able to overcome this opposition in a year's time, and for a quarter of a century students had equal voice on this committee. The fear that students and faculty would line up against each other on the vote never did eventuate. It was disappointing, too, that so few faculty members carried their full responsibilities on the job without the need of constant follow-up by the administration. I never did completely lick this one. I wonder whether any college president ever has.

Nevertheless, my greatest disappointment was in fund raising. I must admit that I was hurt many times during twenty-seven years because I was never able to get white Atlanta to accept Morehouse College as an integral part of the higher educational structure of Atlanta and therefore entitled to significant support. Morehouse was regarded as a *Negro* institution, and therefore as needing less support than would a comparable institution for whites.

I think it cannot be denied that there was great improvement in the quality of education offered at Morehouse during my presidency. I was convinced that when I approached the moneyed people of the nation I would be able to get much larger support if I could tell them, truthfully, that the Morehouse faculty was able and interracial, that our best students did well in the most outstanding graduate and professional schools of the nation, and that our graduates were making finer contributions to the country's welfare than were the graduates of most schools of comparable size, black or white.

This conviction was not always confirmed. Colleges with academic programs not as good, whose students did not do as well in graduate and professional schools, and whose graduates were not making comparable contributions to the community, stood just as good a chance, and in some cases a better chance, of getting public support. This realization was disappointing to me, for I had always believed that a college not only *should* but *would* be judged by the quality of its faculty, the performance of its students, and by what its alumni contributed to mankind. The Morehouse record speaks loudly when I say again: few colleges, if any, have done "so much with so little and so few." Despite this fact, we were never able to command large support. Morehouse was labeled a *Negro* college. It was not until the last two of my twenty-seven years at Morehouse that I felt foundations were beginning to judge Morehouse on the basis of quality.

Long before I went to Morehouse, chapel was a special institution, and so it remained for twenty-five years of my presidency. Though like some classes—occasionally dull—it was nevertheless as much a part of the educational process as the classroom lectures and discussions. Student organizations, including fraternities, class programs, departmental conferences, panels, forums, and campus and outside speakers held forth in the Morehouse chapel. It was here that students and faculty assembled as a family. It was here that students could hear firsthand from the president about the state of the college. Here students could and did question the president about matters concerning the college. They often griped about chapel, especially the compulsory aspect of it; yet I have met no former students who do not look back on the Morehouse chapel as a place where they received something valuable which they would not have gotten elsewhere. As president, I took it seriously. If I were in town and not involved in some vital meeting, I always attended chapel—with the exception of student body meetings, which I left strictly to the students themselves. For fully twenty years or more, Tuesday was the president's day at chapel, and I usually spoke to the students or had charge of the service.

In a small college, where a president is too busy to teach classes, the chapel offers a fairly good substitute for the more personal forms of teaching. Here students can learn firsthand what the basic thinking or philosophy of the president is. I know I made many uninspired speeches in chapel over the years, but as a rule I prepared for them as carefully as I did for engagements away from Morehouse, and usually the students came when I spoke. I must admit that it is gratifying now when I meet Morehouse men who were graduated many years ago, men successful in their chosen professions, to have them voluntarily tell me how a particular chapel speech helped them. If a man can quote in substance something I had said twenty or twenty-five years before, I feel that I have done some good. In my last two years at Morehouse, the chapel was in process of dissolution. When students and faculty no longer want it, it cannot endure. So an era came to an end.

It is discouraging and disturbing to me that there are indications of a subtle move afoot to abolish black colleges. Prior to Emancipation and since, thousands of white writers have taken pride in their determination to brand Negroes as inherently inferior. Something similar has occurred regarding black colleges since 1954. Writers have pounced on the Negro colleges, not with the purpose of helping them, but rather, it seems, of destroying them. Numerous critics have made a crusade of tearing the black colleges apart, but no group of white colleges has been selected and set aside as targets for annihilation. White liberals and white conservatives alike have participated in this tragedy. Colleges that were good enough for brilliant Negro students prior to May 17, 1954, ceased to be so immediately after.

One white educator said on the Morehouse campus that Negro colleges should stop striving to be excellent institutions but instead should settle for mediocrity and send their ablest students to white colleges. This statement made my blood boil because through all its years Morehouse not only strove for academic excellence but achieved a notable and commendable degree of success. Unfortunately, this speaker was not arguing for himself alone: He was the voice of a multitude. After 1954, it became fairly fashionable for white colleges with outside support to provide scholarships for the best Negro scholars to attend their white institutions but never proffer a dime to the black colleges to enable them to compete equally for the black students, to say nothing of providing money to recruit white students! The meaning is clear: black colleges, in the thinking of many, are not academically strong enough to train bright-minded blacks, but a white college—*any* white college—is so qualified. So the money flows one way—to the white college. Automatically, *whatever is white is better!*

Along with this attitude goes the continuing debate as to whether or not black colleges should soon be phased out, kept on such short financial rations that they will die of malnutrition. And the debate, damnedly enough, goes on among those with sufficient power to accomplish their misguided purpose without Negroes themselves having a chance to participate in the determining the outcome. There is gross discrimination here—thinly disguised racism. With the new awakening on the part of Negroes as to their identity and their role in American life, it would be tragic indeed for a democracy to say that only white colleges deserve to be supported and that they alone should survive. During my years at Morehouse, I worried about the future of this small college on a red hill in Georgia which had to do so much with so little and so few. If its future is precarious, and if other Negro colleges similarly situated are on shaky ground, the reason is that they are in the hands and at the mercy of those who have little faith in the Negro's ability to develop and maintain first-rate institutions.

Although the Negro has helped to make the wealth of the nation, he has not been allowed to help shape the policies of how that wealth is to be distributed. And this inequity is largely true, too, in the use of government funds. Negroes constitute ten percent of the population of the country. It is my considered judgment that not one foundation, not one government agency, national or state, has ever thought in terms of allocating ten percent of all monies given for education to the support of black institutions or for the education of blacks. The heads of Negro institutions appreciate the support which white philanthropy and state and federal governments have given to the predominantly Negro colleges and universities, but white philanthropists and governmental agencies are bound to know—as we know—that black institutions have been heavily discriminated against and still are.

If McGrath's book, referred to on page 184 of this chapter, had been taken seriously, the foundations would have gotten together to do something substantial about the problem of Negro higher education. When it comes to the support of black institutions, it takes philanthropy a long time to make up its mind, even when the appropriation is relatively meager. Simply put, neither white philanthropy nor state governments, have decided what should be done with the black colleges and universities. For good or ill, the white people have in their hands the power of life and the power of death for black colleges, but they do not have the wisdom to determine whether to sustain or to kill. I do not agree with James Foreman's method of trying to force white churches to turn over a huge sum of money to his organization. But I do believe that white churches should invest more heavily in projects designed to help the Negro poor. White philanthropy has an obligation to make amends for its hundred years of neglect of Negro colleges. It is odd indeed that after a war, a country should willingly make reparations to the enemy and yet feel little or no moral obligation to compensate its own citizens for decades of shameful and savage treatment.

It is easy for white colleges to get money to establish courses in black studies, provide scholarships for brilliant Negro students and deprived black students, and, with outside help or from their own heavy endowments, lure black scholars and faculty away from black institutions. But it never occurs to them to say, "Let us bring Negro colleges up to such a standard of excellence that white students will not hesitate to matriculate in them." Even with the prestige of President John F. Kennedy behind the effort, the presidents of thirty-three United Negro College Fund colleges could not get anyone to head a drive to raise $100 million for all of these colleges. The goal we had to accept was $50 million, and we raised only $30 million. The University of Chicago recently raised $160 million in three years. The Negro is truly the "Invisible Man."

I do not believe that the solution to the Negro's plight in higher education lies in strengthening white institutions and paying the best Negro students to attend white colleges, while Negro institutions are apparently being reduced to mediocrity. With the weakening or abolition of the black colleges, the Negro's image in education will be blotted out, except for a few brilliant stars on the faculties of white universities. The emphasis now is on blackness, and the emphasis will not soon subside. We should know by now that all is not sweetness and light for the black students on the campuses of the white universities in the nation. If white America really wants to improve Negro higher education, it would do well to recognize the fact that it will not be adequately done by allowing black colleges to die the slow death of starvation.

Twenty-seven years is a long time to stay on a job, and more than three score years is an incredibly long time to remain in the South, especially in the South at its worst, in the South that Sadie and I knew all too well. Why didn't we go North to work, or go to serve the World YMCA in Geneva, as I could have done? For one thing, Sadie and I loved our work at Morehouse. It should be crystal clear by now that neither of us ever adjusted to a society of segregation and discrimination. This we could never do. But neither could we run away merely to gain larger personal freedom. We understood only too well why many Negroes did leave the South; nor could we find it in our hearts to blame them. However, so far as we were concerned, to run away rather than face the always embarrassing, always humiliating racial problems would be an act of cowardice. We wanted to be in the thick of the fight as long as there was a glimmer of hope that we could help ameliorate the racial problem by even the slightest degree, could change the Southern pattern of society by one whit. We believe that during our twenty-seven years we helped instill in many a Morehouse student a sense of his own worth and a pride that thereafter enabled him to walk the earth with dignity. We believe that long before the current emphasis on pride in being black, the Morehouse student had already found his identity.

Chapter XIV
Other Involvements

To be president of a college and white is no bed or roses. To be president of a college and black is almost a bed of thorns. The ever-present necessity of raising funds is particularly difficult for the Negro college, since money owned and controlled by whites flows more freely and more abundantly from white to white than it does from white to black. Moreover, the Negro president of a Negro college is almost daily confronted by stumbling blocks, hurdles, and personal embarrassments that rarely if ever clutter the path of his white counterpart.

The proud and sensitive Negro, if he is to be free in his own mind and soul, must forever be on guard against accepting conditions that will enslave his spirit. On countless Tuesday mornings in chapel I pointed out to the Morehouse students that the only way they could be free in a rigidly segregated society was by consistent refusal ever to accept subservience and segregation in their own minds. As long as a man registers some form of protest against that which is obviously wrong, he has not surrendered his freedom, and his soul is still his own. The struggle to maintain one's integrity is always difficult, but for a black man in a white-dominated world it is a continuous "trial by fire." How should the president of a black college behave when his sense of right and righteousness is assaulted by the interracial wrongs in the society in which he lives? There is no once-for-all, no final answer. This question must be answered over and over again in a world where the problem of race is omnipresent, as close to a black man as the beating of his heart.

Nineteen years after I was almost mobbed on a Pullman car in Tennessee I was again almost mobbed on a dining car in my native South Carolina on the Southern Railroad between Atlanta and Greenville. This happened in 1944, four years after I had assumed the presidency of Morehouse.

I have lived long enough to experience five stages in the changing treatment of Negro passengers in Pullman cars:

The first stage was one of flat refusal, with an angry ticket seller snarling that there was space available but not for "niggers."

The second stage represented verbal improvement, with the ticket agent assuring the black passenger that there was no space available.

The third stage presented a rare spectacle—the black man being given *separate but better!* The Pullman company would sell me and other Negroes a drawing room for the price of a lower berth.

In the fourth stage, Negroes could buy berths, but only at the ends of the coaches, never in the middle.

The fifth and present stage is one in which segregation has been eliminated from Pullman travel.

The changes have been slow and grudging, not given but forced. In the history of a century of segregation, the drawing-room experience is unique because it appears to be the only instance where white people would give the Negro the best for less money in order to preserve the segregated system by hiding the black man from view.

The evolution of dining-car service for Negroes followed a similar route. In the southern part of the United States, the black man was excluded from the diner and no other provision was made for him. There was an "upstairs waiter" who came through with his cart selling drinks and sandwiches. In the half coach occupied by Negroes there was the "butcher," confiscating four seats and selling drinks, candy, and sandwiches. Of course, the white passengers in the white coaches would be served by the cart before it reached the colored passengers. Negroes usually carried their lunches with them.

The second stage was the provision by which Negroes wishing to eat in the diner had to get up early enough in the morning so that they could be served and out before the white passengers appeared. Or they could come to the diner between nine and ten, provided every white passenger had left. They were also permitted to the diner late at night after the white folks had finished.

The "curtain" represented the third stage. One table (occasionally two), at the end next to the kitchen was set aside for Negroes. This table was partitioned off by a heavy, thick blue curtain so that white passengers need not be affronted by the sight of the "untouchable" Negroes. Despite the curtain, Negroes often had to stand and wait until white passengers being served in the "Negro" section had finished and left. Of course, the curtain was never drawn when white diners sat at that table!

Frequently, when Negro and white friends were traveling together and wished to dine together, the steward would not permit the white man to sit with his Negro companion, or, if he did permit it, he would seat them both at the curtained table and draw the curtain segregating both the white man and the black man. My sister-in-law, Emma C. W. Gray, took impish delight in tormenting the dining-car steward by pulling the curtains aside just to watch him rush up like a house afire to close them and so protect the delicate sensibilities of the white passengers.

On my way to New York on the Southern Railway in October, 1944, not far from Greenville, South Carolina, I went into the dining car for lunch. Eleven of the twelve tables were occupied, including the one behind the curtain, supposedly reserved for Negroes. It was war time and most of the forty-four diners were soldiers. On entering the diner I stood momentarily, expecting the steward to seat me. When he failed to do so, I took a seat at the vacant table near the center of the car.

Quick as a flash, the steward, a man named E. M. Hames, was there, protesting vociferously, insisting that I could not sit in that spot. I pointed out that if he did not wish me to sit there then it was his responsibility to move the four soldiers seated in the place reserved for Negroes. He refused to ask them to move and was becoming angrier by the second. Two passengers came rushing toward me with fists clenched, ready and eager to aid and abet the steward. Fearing to turn away from them, I walked backward out of the diner.

The steward and the whites who came to his rescue were the law. They could defy it, could fill the space reserved for Negroes with whites, and could refuse to seat me at the only table vacant in the diner. The law was not made for white men to keep but for Negroes to obey. I would have been a "good nigger" if I had stood humbly and waited for the segregated table which white men were occupying.

It is my belief that had I not backed out of that diner I would have been badly beaten and arrested on arrival in Greenville. It is also my belief that more than just these three men would have attempted to "put me in my place." It was the "sportsmanlike" custom throughout the South for a crowd of whites to go after one black man. There were forty-four passengers and the steward in that diner—all white. Not one hand or voice was lifted in my defense. What could I do about this? What should I try to do? Could I do anything?

A Negro friend was sure that I should do nothing. He felt that any public protest would be bad publicity for Morehouse and would militate against my efforts to get money for the college. I could not in good conscience accept his advice. I had to try to do something about it—not for myself alone but for the cause of justice. I was relatively certain that anyone who would refuse to contribute to Morehouse because of such publicity would not have given anyway. My plan was to take the Southern Railway before the Interstate Commerce Commission and, if necessary, sue the railroad in federal court. To refrain from this course because of fear would have been tantamount to accepting the path of expediency and inaction. This I could not do.

Through the NAACP's lawyers, Thurgood Marshall (now Associate Justice), Spottswood Robinson, and Robert L. Carter, we took the Southern Railroad before the ICC. The Commission reprimanded the Southern Railroad and, in a feeble apology, promised me it would not happen again. The Commission rejected my plea for $2,500 damages. So I did not take the advice of my friend after all. I at least tried to do something about what had happened to me.

My attorneys in the case argued that certain regulations handed down on August 6, 1942, by the Southern Railway, were not only invalid but had not been filed with the ICC and had not been published. These regulations instructed stewards to pull the curtain to hide the two tables reserved for Negroes, place a RESERVED card on each, and seat no white passengers at these two tables until all other tables had been filled with white passengers. If no Negroes had come in by that time, white people would be seated at the "Negro" tables—after, of course, the curtains had been drawn back and the reserved sign removed. If Negroes came in while white passengers occupied the tables set aside for Negroes, they had to wait until the whites finished their meals, even if there were vacancies in another section of the diner.

My attorneys argued further that I had been refused service because of my race and that the statutes relied upon to segregate first-class passengers did not apply to interstate passengers. Moreover, my lawyers pointed out that laws for interstate passengers had to be uniform, and that each state could not legislate in this area without creating confusion and chaos. Nevertheless, the Interstate Commerce Commission did not rule in my behalf. Before we could go on to sue the Southern Railroad for damages, Elmer W. Henderson had won a similar case in court, and the dining-car curtain became a relic for the museum. (*Elmer W. Henderson vs. United States, et al. #339 US 816-1950.*)

Even after the infamous curtain was gone, some stewards tried to maintain segregation by attempting to seat all Negroes at the end tables. I have been on Hames' diner several times since the days of the curtain. The first one or two times after the Henderson case had removed the curtain he tried to take me all the way through the diner to the end. When I got to a vacancy before reaching the end of the diner, I sat down. When he looked back and saw me, he was always visibly upset. He would come back, throw the menu at me, and say, "Damnit." Later, he was either "converted," resigned, or discouraged, for he stopped trying to segregate me on his diner. It was a wonderful feeling to go into the diner and have that very man, who at one time was ready to lead a gang to kick me out, now lead me to an unsegregated table!

It was in the 1950's that the *Reader's Digest* sent one of its roving editors, Blake Clark, and me to find out how much discrimination there was in hotels, motels, restaurants, and theaters in the North. Mr. Clark subsequently wrote the article, and I was pleased with it, but for some unexplained reason the *Digest* never printed it.

We visited the following cities and surrounding vicinities: Boston, Wilmington, Philadelphia, New York, Cleveland, Columbus, Detroit, and Chicago. If the experiment was to work it was necessary to get a Negro who was unmistakably Negro; so I was requested to travel with the white Mr. Clark.

We found discrimination mostly in motels and restaurants and in a few hotels in Wilmington and on the North Side of Chicago. The theaters were open. Of the motels we visited requesting accommodations, approximately 50 percent of them turned me down, as did also a few restaurants. The greatest discrimination came in motels. They were past masters in the art of lying!

Our plan was for me to go in first and request accommodations for two. If I was refused—and more often than not I was—Mr. Clark would go to the desk twenty minutes later and make the same request. Without exception, those who turned me down had reservations for Clark. Of the many, varied, and often absurd evasions, I will mention only four.

Although the sign outside read "Vacancy," more than once when I appeared the man in charge would deny that he had rooms. When I inquired about his "Vacancy" sign, he would say that a large group had previously phoned for reservations and that the sign had not yet been removed. When Mr. Clark appeared twenty or thirty minutes later, rooms were available. Despite his lighted "Vacancy" sign, another proprietor denied me on the grounds that he had housed an athletic team the night before and that the maids had not shown up to clean the rooms. Half an hour later, Clark found the rooms spic and span and available.

On the outskirts of Columbus, Ohio, there is an impressive motel and restaurant known as Lincoln Lodge. A fine picture of Abraham Lincoln beams down upon the guests, welcoming—one would assume—all races, creeds, and ethnic origins. When I asked for a room for two, I was told that I had to make a reservation in advance. Twenty minutes later, when my white colleague requested a room for two, it was available. Next, I went to the exceptionally splendid restaurant, only to be told again that without advance reservations no one could be served. Twenty minutes later Clark appeared, and while the hostess was escorting him to his seat, he declined to eat, having proved our point. Thereafter we stood around and saw many persons without advance reservations getting rooms and being seated for dinner. It seemed a pity then—and it still does—that so fine and impressive an establishment should flaunt the name, yet operate in complete violation of the spirit of Abraham Lincoln.

We found discrimination on both the North and South sides, and in a few restaurants in Chicago's Loop. The most shameless case was at Fiftieth on the Lake, a plush motel on the South Side of Chicago, on Lake Michigan. We had made up our minds to spend the night there if we could get rooms without any discrimination being shown me. When I went to the desk to sign for a room for two, the price quoted was forty dollars per night, so I returned to the car. Approximately twenty minutes later Blake Clark went to the desk to get a double room for two. The price had dropped to fifteen dollars. The prices were raised especially for me in other places, too. We even met discrimination of this kind in a motel not far from Boston. After such experiences, I can never take seriously the accusation by white people that Negroes are expert liars!

In 1939, I was traveling for the Federal Council of the Churches of Christ in America. After spending several days at the Washington State University, three of us were planning to spend the night in the Spokane Hotel, to which a new part had recently been added. One of us, Mrs. Grace Sloan Overton, decided to leave that night but was still with us when I attempted to register. The desk clerk insisted that he had no space in the new part of the hotel but could accommodate me in the old section, where the rates were cheaper. One who has lived all his days in a society that discriminates against him because he is black becomes incredibly keen at detecting when a man is lying. When I told Mrs. Overton and our other colleagues that the man was lying, she—much against my will—talked to the clerk.

The clerk convinced Mrs. Overton that he had no space in the new section of the hotel; and she reported to me that she was sure that the man had told me the truth. Mrs. Overton needed convincing, so I suggested that when she got to the station she call back and request a room in the new part of the hotel, then let me know what she was told. When she called she said, "Bennie, I was naïve; you are dead right. They have rooms in the new part of the hotel and at a price cheaper than they quoted to you." It was small comfort that I knew so well when I was being lied to in racial matters—my knowledge had been dearly bought and paid for in the coin of oft-repeated and humiliating experiences.

For many years, beginning in 1942, Sadie and I were frequently invited to participate in the Danforth Foundation Associate Conference at Camp Miniwanca, Michigan. Even in Michigan it was necessary to start looking for a motel long before sunset, for the possibility was strong that we would be turned down several times before we found lodging for the night. We knew that south of Cincinnati we would be refused everywhere.

One Sunday, on our way from Camp Miniwanca, we had planned to stop in Cincinnati where there was a good Negro hotel, but the sun was too high for us to stop for the night when we got there and we decided to drive on toward Lexington. When the sun had almost set, we started looking for a motel. The lies varied from place to place, but the refusals were constantly final. We decided to have some fun, albeit rather grim "fun." I questioned one "Kentucky gentlemen" about his religion. He proudly proclaimed that he was an ardent churchman, and he saw no inconsistency between his professed religion and his denying us accommodations in his motel. Another man, a deacon in his church, felt bad when I asked him how, being a deacon, he could turn us away. It got next to him and he wanted to find a way to take us. He looked at me and asked, "Are y'all colored?" I am sure that if we had told him we were not Negroes—American Negroes!—he would have taken us. Instead, we spent the night in a bug-ridden hotel in Lexington, Kentucky.

Well into the 1950's, motoring throughout the South was embarrassing for Negroes. For more than thirty years, I always made it a point to buy gas in the larger cities, where the station owners were less inclined to refuse rest-room accommodations. Many times Sadie and I, and those traveling with us, preferred to respond to nature in the woods by the highway rather than have a quarrel at some filling station. Many times I came close to getting into serious trouble because I stopped an attendant from filling my gas tank when he refused to let us use his rest rooms. Larger towns often had segregated rest rooms.

As recently as early 1960, a filling-station man on the outskirts of Augusta, Georgia, threatened to shoot me because I said I didn't believe him when he told me I could not use his rest room because the plumbing was out of order. I knew that he was not telling the truth because I saw a white man come out of the rest room and give him the key. He was very angry because a black man dared dispute his word and stop him from filling up the tank. He threatened to shoot me if I didn't move on. Had I continued to argue with him, I am sure that he would have shot me without hesitation and would have sworn that he killed me in self-defense. He did not know that I was a college president. Had he known, it would have made no difference to him: I was black. I was so well known in educational circles that had I been killed there would certainly have been an attempt to do something about it—with little chance of success. But I still would have been dead!

Several years before 1940 a grant of $400,000 was made by the Rockefeller-endowed General Education Board to Atlanta University for Morehouse, provided the university would raise a matching $400,000, thereby increasing the Morehouse endowment by $800,000. By 1940, a period of several years later, virtually no matching money had been raised. Badly as Morehouse needed buildings, it needed endowment even more. Government money was not then available for dormitories and academic buildings. The $400,000 had to be raised by Morehouse, and my first job was to do all I could to get it in the designated time.

Believing that we should take the lead, Sadie and I sold our house in Washington for $8,500 and contributed $1,000 in cash. I had the fond notion that if Sadie and I did so, it would be easy for me to get the Negroes of Atlanta to contribute, and that if Negroes themselves led the way it would be very easy to get white Atlanta to give to the Morehouse endowment. So, with our $1,000 as incentive, we attempted to persuade fifty Negroes to give $100 each. Though it was much more difficult than we had anticipated, we did succeed. We were sadly mistaken, however, in our wishful thinking that white Atlanta would show any deep concern for Morehouse.

Miss Elizabeth P. Whitehead, a friend of the college, who wanted to help Morehouse, solicited funds among her wide range of acquaintances. One check came from Samuel Green, the head of the Atlanta Ku Klux Klan. The check was small, but Morehouse was desperately in need of funds, and for every dollar we raised we would get a dollar from the General Education Board. Nevertheless, I had to return Samuel Green's check to Miss Whitehead, urging her to send it back to him. All that I had read and heard, and all I knew about the Ku Klux Klan was bad—anti-Jewish, anti-Catholic, and, even more heavily, anti-Negro. The Klan was active when I came to Atlanta in 1921; I had witnessed its cruelty, its savagery, its malevolence. Booker T. Washington may have been right when he said that the only thing wrong with "tainted money" is that "it taint enough," but money from Mr. Green was too tainted for Morehouse to use. The amount didn't matter—it would have been refused had it been for a million dollars.

Mr. Kendall Weisiger of the Southern Bell Telephone Company was chairman of the Morehouse Board of Trustees when I came in 1940 and for many years thereafter. Virginia born, Mr. Weisiger was much further along in his interracial thinking and behavior than most white Americans—Northerners or Southerners. Intellectually and emotionally, Kendall Weisiger had risen above prejudice based on race. A kindly man, generous in spirit, he was devoted to Morehouse, having come to love the college through John Hope. Had Kendall Weisiger been a rich man I am sure he would have contributed largely to increase the resources of the college.

Despite all these virtues, however, Mr. Weisiger could not understand why I would rather see him in his home—though farther away for me—than visit him in his office; or why I would ask him to come to my office rather than go to his in the Hurt Building. My philosophy has always been that one endures only the segregation he is forced to accept, that which is inescapable, but one never voluntarily embraces it. Segregation on trains and buses and streetcars had to be accepted because travel was necessary. Segregation in theaters and churches did not. Mr. Weisiger was shocked when I walked up twelve flights to his office rather than ride on the segregated elevator in the Hurt Building. I am glad that segregated elevators no longer blight Atlanta, for it would be hard on me at my age to climb twelve flights, even though my health is very good. Mr. Weisiger was a splendid example of a white man who had thrown off the restraints of race, moved and mingled freely among Negroes, called them Mr. and Mrs. and Miss, and served Morehouse faithfully, but who still felt that it was nonsense for me to walk up twelve flights of stairs to his office rather than ride a segregated elevator. It is so hard—perhaps impossible—for one born white and free to understand the feelings and behavior of one born into the near-slavery of segregation, one who at the eventide of his years is not wholly free.

Mr. Weisiger, like most people, did not understand another thing: He did not believe and could not understand that salaries for Negro and white teachers would probably never be equalized on a voluntary basis. When A. T. Walden entered suit to force the Atlanta School Board to equalize the salaries of Negro teachers with those of white teachers, many white Atlantans thought it was a mistake. There were even Negroes in Atlanta who felt that Walden was pushing things too fast. Some felt that the suit should be stopped. Willis Sutton, Superintendent of the Atlanta Public Schools, and Mr. Weisiger were very close friends, and I am inclined to believe it was Mr. Sutton who asked Mr. Weisiger to speak to me about the suit, knowing that I had good rapport with Attorney Walden. Mr. Weisiger and I talked at length and our conference was cordial and friendly. But I had to refuse my chairman's request.

Mr. Weisiger's arguments were two: 1) The salaries were gradually approaching equality, and 2) the salaries of Negro teachers in Atlanta were higher than those of white teachers in the small towns of Georgia. Neither argument, I felt, was relevant. The salaries of Negro teachers in Atlanta were not equal to the salaries of white teachers in Atlanta, and this was the only issue to be resolved. I could not ask Attorney Walden to stop the suit. To have done so would have been an underhanded betrayal of everything in which I believed and for which I had fought for so long. I am glad that though Mr. Weisiger and I disagreed on this and a few other matters we remained friends up to the time of his death.

I was accused of being responsible for Horace Ward's filing an application to enter the law school of the University of Georgia in 1950. Though the accusation was not true, the suspicion was so strong that the lawyer for the Board of Regents asked Ward in court whether I had advised him to file the application. Ward had been graduated from Morehouse and had earned an A.M. degree from Atlanta University in Political Science. The late Dr. William H. Boyd, professor of Political Science at Atlanta University, was the head of the NAACP in the state of Georgia at the time, and he and I were good friends. The NAACP wanted a test case. Boyd felt that Horace Ward, who had both poise and the ability to do well in law, would be the best possible candidate. When Boyd talked to me about Ward, I agreed that he would be a good man. Ward did not ask my opinion, but had I been asked, I would have given my heartfelt approval.

It was very difficult in 1950 to get a Negro to be the test case to break down barriers erected to keep Negroes out of white, state-supported schools. Public school teachers were rightly afraid of being involved in sponsorship—several had allowed their names to be used for this purpose and had lost their jobs. Young Negro graduates looking forward to a teaching career felt they would never be employed as teachers in the South if they were involved in trying to enter Southern graduate or professional schools. Moreover, those who did allow their names to be used in test cases were often harassed and their lives threatened. The way white institutions of Georgia are recruiting black students in the late 1960's and in 1970 makes it hard to believe that it was physically and professionally dangerous for a Negro to apply to enter a white Georgia school in 1950.

Horace Ward was one of the few Negroes willing to put his career on the line and suffer the harassment sure to follow. For eighteen months the decision on Ward's application passed slowly through various levels of the university administration: from registrar to the committee in the Law School to the president to the chancellor and on to the Board of Regents. The case was pending from 1952 until the fall of 1956. It was during this period that a well-known, distinguished white man came to my office to request me to advise Ward to withdraw his suit and accept out-of-state aid. My caller assured me that Atlanta University could get money to build a law school for Negroes.

I promised the gentlemen who came to see me that although at the moment I saw no honorable way I could persuade Mr. Ward to withdraw his application and accept out-of-state aid, I would give further thought to his proposal and write him within a few days. In my letter, I reaffirmed my assertion that I could not be part of a scheme to get Ward to withdraw his application, and that it had long been my hope that the University of Georgia would open its doors to Negroes without federal mandate. Of course, my wish was not to be. The Ward case went to court in December, 1956, and the decision was rendered in early 1957. The District Court dismissed the case on the grounds that all administrative remedies had not been exhausted before the suit was filed.

Ward had an A.B. from Morehouse, with a very good record, and had earned a master's degree from Atlanta University. The University of Georgia lawyers argued in court that Ward was turned down because Morehouse and Atlanta University were not members of the Southern Association of Colleges and Secondary Schools. The fact is that for racial reasons, the Southern Association did not admit Negro institutions to membership until 1957. However, Morehouse and Atlanta University had been on the approved list of the Southern Association for approximately twenty-five years. When Ward applied for admission to the law school at the University of Georgia in 1950, the requirement was not that the applicant be from a school approved by the Southern Association, but that he must have completed a minimum of two years of college work. Morehouse and Atlanta University were on the approved list, and Ward had two degrees: A.B. and A.M. He was, in fact, better qualified than most of the white students being admitted.

I was shocked, stunned, and terribly disappointed when I heard top university officials swear in court that race had absolutely nothing to do with Ward's denial of admission to the University of Georgia Law School. I suppose these top officials had to lie, since admission that Ward was kept out because of his race would have forced the university to admit him. In September, 1956, Ward enrolled in Northwestern University and completed his work there in 1959. He returned to Atlanta the following year, entered the firm of Hollowell and Ward, and became an assistant to the attorneys of record in the Holmes-Hunter case that forced the University of Georgia to accept Hamilton Holmes and Charlayne Hunter as students in 1961. Ward is not only still in Atlanta, but is a senator in the Georgia legislature and a deputy lawyer for the City of Atlanta. Sometimes it happens that the man who stands up and fights for his rights fares far better than the man who "plays it safe." Thurgood Marshall's name was anathema in the South after 1954. He is now Associate Justice of the United States Supreme Court. Constance Motley, a sharp thorn in the side of Southern school boards, as she argued against segregated schools, is now a federal district judge. Nehru, who was jailed many times as he fought Britain for India's independence, became India's first prime minister. Such vindication occurs often enough to keep alive the spark of hope.

Hamilton Holmes had spent two semesters and three months at Morehouse before the federal court ruled that the University of Georgia had to admit him and Charlayne Hunter. Both had been graduated from Turner High School in Atlanta and had sought admission to the University of Georgia. Holmes had been eligible to enter Morehouse as an early admission student but preferred to finish high school, where he had an A average. He entered Morehouse in the fall of 1959, and withdrew in the first semester of 1960-61 when he entered the University of Georgia under federal court orders.

We were sorry to lose Hamilton to the University of Georgia because I was not then, nor am I now, in favor of all of the best Negro students being drained away from Negro colleges. Furthermore, I was convinced that Morehouse could prepare Mr. Holmes for medical school as well as could the University of Georgia. The records of Morehouse men in the various medical schools over the years are convincing proof of this belief. However, I wanted to see the racial barriers at the university broken down, and I wanted a Morehouse student to be the first Negro male to do it. We at Morehouse believed that Hamilton Holmes would make a good first representative. So I strongly advised him to enter the University of Georgia, which he and Miss Hunter did in January, 1961. Shortly after Charlayne and Hamilton entered, other students rioted in protest and they had to leave Athens, Georgia, hometown of the university, under cover of night because the administration feared for their lives. The federal court subsequently acted with dispatch and ordered their return. This time they stayed.

I kept in close touch with Hamilton Holmes during his three years at the University of Georgia. I knew from him directly how he was treated by the white students and by his teachers. I knew that socially it was rough, that the white students did not want him there, and that they would talk to him in class, then refuse to recognize him on campus. Having learned the high quality of his work during the first quarter, I challenged him to make Phi Beta Kappa. I told him that if he continued the same high quality of work until graduation, he would be elected to membership in Alpha of Georgia at the university, the oldest chapter of Phi Beta Kappa in the state. Mr. Holmes was skeptical, saying that even if he made it they wouldn't give it to him. I reminded him that by his own admission his teachers were fair and friendly, that the unfriendly students had no voice in electing him to membership in Phi Beta Kappa, and that when he and Charlayne had had to flee Athens three hundred members of the University of Georgia faculty petitioned for their return.

I thought it would be a great thing if one of the first two Negroes ever to enter the University of Georgia was elected to Phi Beta Kappa. Since I am not a betting man, I did not wager with Hamilton Holmes on his success in earning membership in Phi Beta Kappa, but I promised him fifty dollars to be applied toward his medical school expenses if he were elected. Holmes made it, and I was happy to write the check. If I am responsible, as Hamilton Holmes has credited me, for encouraging the first Negro ever to enter the University of Georgia to work hard enough to achieve Phi Beta Kappa, I am both proud and pleased.

For many decades, the South has tried to make the world believe that the Southern way of life (the segregated way) was acceptable to Negroes. They trumpeted loud and long that Negroes were happy and satisfied with apartheid, Southern style, and that whenever a Southern Negro complained it was not really he who was speaking but, instead, he was being "used" by white Yankees or by Communists. It was always "outside agitators" who were "stirring up trouble"; Southern blacks were content with things just as they were. Although this delusionary conviction was rarely, if ever, true, it was so strongly held that in 1942 when Dr. Gordon B. Hancock of Richmond, Virginia, called together a group of Negroes to formulate a memorandum for the enlightenment of the white South, he deliberately failed to invite any Negroes north of Washington, D.C., in the hope that the South would listen and respond to Southern Negroes.

But the South was committed to its fantasies. Every Southern Negro who spoke out against the status quo was automatically labeled a Communist or a fellow traveler. Those of us who were staunch supporters of the National Association for the Advancement of Colored People, the Federal Council of the Churches of Christ in America (later the National Council of the Churches of Christ), and the Southern Christian Leadership Conference were called radical. Those who contributed to organizations that were held in suspicion by the House Un-American Activities Committee were accused by the Committee of being fellow travelers. Anyone who attended a meeting where any Communists were present, no matter how few, was promptly accused of having "Communist leanings."

A friend of mine, chaplain in one of America's greatest universities, invited me to be one of the sponsors of the Mid-Century Conference on Peace, and I allowed my name to be used. Since I could not attend the Conference, I refused to allow my name to be used as an honorary officer; however, my name did appear that way. So-called Communists did dominate the meeting. Consequently, the Conference was labeled a "Communist front," and I was labeled as a member of a Communist-front organization. I had delivered thousands of speeches and written hundreds of articles which showed no trace of Communist leanings or sympathy; nevertheless, between 1930 and 1961 I was repeatedly referred to as being a Communist or a fellow traveler. How else could a self-righteous white South explain my opposition to segregation and the exploitation of the Negro? I have no regrets that I was accused of being a member of Communist-front organizations, for had I not been it would be prima facie evidence that in my entire career I had not been in the vanguard of those working for social justice. I find it interesting to remember that each of the three times I was considered too un-American to speak to an audience, that judgment was made by the American Legion, and each time it happened in the North—twice in Ohio and once in Indiana.

In the spring of 1950, to cite the first example, the executives of the Associated Churches and the YMCA of Fort Wayne, Indiana, invited me to speak to the citizens of that city. Three days before I was to go to Fort Wayne, I received a telegram from the YMCA executive secretary asking whether I would be willing to have an early lunch with a group of citizens who wished to talk with me about my political philosophy. I assured him that I had no objection to talking with anybody, but gave him the option of withdrawing his invitation. He urged me to keep the appointment, telling me that neither he nor the officials of the church group were apprehensive about me, but that the American Legion was trying to block my coming to Fort Wayne.

At the luncheon two men led the inquisition—one an officer of the American Legion of Fort Wayne, the other the son of a naturalized citizen born in Germany. Before answering their questions, I ascertained the source of their authority to question me. Since it was apparent that no government body, nor the city of Fort Wayne, nor the State of Indiana, nor the federal government in Washington had requested this investigation, I submitted to their questions—but not without making it absolutely clear that I was merely accommodating them.

The American Legion spokesman raved like a maniac for forty-five minutes, telling me what a wonderful country the U.S.A. is, and bleating that he was certain that I loved the country and was loyal to it. The German followed the same line. He sought to impress me with the story of his father, who had come from Germany poor and uneducated, but had found so many golden opportunities in America that he and his son had become quite wealthy. By this time, I had heard enough. Assuring them that I, too, was proud to be an American, I pointed out that there was one fundamental difference between their citizenship and mine: "You are white and I am black." Any black man can lecture for hours on this difference, but I was not as verbose as they, nor as noisy; but the thesis of what I said was unqualified: *Any white man's chance of getting ahead in America is many times greater than that of any black man.*

During the meeting it became evident that my questioners had done their home work: They had been in touch with Indiana's witch-hunting

Senator William E. Jenner, the Justice Department, and the House Un-American Activities Committee. Fortunately, other inquiries about me had also been made: Of the National Council of Churches, and the American wing of the World Council of Churches, of whose central committee I was a member. The executive secretary of the YMCA reported to the group that no evidence was found anywhere that would connect me with Communism.

Rarely does a Negro have to look far afield for a true experience to validate any statement he may make about racism. But even more rarely is the perfect example immediately at hand as it was for me in Fort Wayne. Hotels in Fort Wayne were evidently not open to Negroes in 1950, and so the YMCA executive had reserved a room for me at the YMCA. My train arrived in Fort Wayne at two-thirty Sunday morning. It was about three o'clock when I got to the YMCA, only to discover that the young desk clerk had, through error, assigned my room to another guest. There was no vacant room in the Y. The young man called several hotels on the Y's list but they either had no vacancy or did not accept Negroes. Finally the young man called the Jefferson Manor, a fifth-rate hotel within walking distance of the YMCA.

When I arrived at the Jefferson Manor, the desk man rang for the owner who, on seeing me, said, "Wait a minute." When he returned, he brought with him two policemen to have me arrested. The officers were decent when they learned that I was an invited guest to their city and there was no cause for my arrest. The owner went into a rage, yelling that he had told the Y executive not to send any "niggers" to his hotel. Though polite to me, the officers put no pressure on this man to make him rent me a room. Instead, they took me back to the YMCA to find out for themselves what had happened. At the YMCA they convinced themselves that the young man at the desk had made an honest mistake, but although I was the responsibility of the YMCA, they did nothing to get me housed in a Fort Wayne hotel. Since the Y clerk could not, and the police officers would not—or at least did not—help, I decided to fend for myself. I called the Reverend Phale Hale, a Morehouse alumnus who was a pastor in Fort Wayne, and asked him whether he could play the good Samaritan to his college president. He got up and dressed, and around five o'clock in the morning came to the YMCA and took me to his home.

This is the story I used to climax the conference called by my inquisitors to find out whether I was a member of the Communist party and whether

I was patriotic and loyal. I expressed the ardent hope that they would be as much concerned about rooting out racial prejudice in Fort Wayne as they were about ferreting out Communists. The meeting ended with their apologizing to me; and I was told that the leading inquisitor put a ten-dollar bill in the collection plate after my speech.

In the late 1950's, I was scheduled to give a Lenten sermon in one of the suburbs of Columbus, Ohio. The minister of the church where I was to speak called me at my hotel to tell me that I would be picketed by representatives from the American Legion protesting my right to speak in that town. The picketing turned out to be a puny affair and a good crowd came to hear me despite the picket line—perhaps because of it!

The women of Columbus had invited me to be the main speaker at their Seventy-fifth Anniversary World Day of Prayer on February 17, 1961. The meeting, sponsored by the United Church Women and the Columbus Area Council of Churches, was to be held in Veterans' Memorial Hall. Once more, that most "patriotic" organization, the American Legion, opposed my speaking in Columbus. They picketed the auditorium; but their effort to discredit me again met with no success, indeed was a fiasco. The press, commenting on the services, estimated that 2,200 people were in the auditorium that night.

I had represented this country in two world organizations—the World YMCA as a member of its Central Committee and the World Council of Churches as one of the ninety men on its Central Committee. For thirty-five years my life had been devoted to the church and to education in this country. But these facts meant nothing to the American Legion. It made no effort to learn the truth about me.

There are, of course, good and happy memories that should be told. One such concerns Margaret Mitchell. Countless thousands associate her name with *Gone with the Wind;* Morehouse men have a very special association with her. Not infrequently have Negro servants willed what little they have to white people for whom they worked. When Margaret Mitchell's devoted servant willed several thousands of dollars to her, Miss Mitchell gave it to Morehouse to be used for needy, worthy black students. The money was used to aid Morehouse graduates in their struggle through medical school. Since Margaret Mitchell was not inclined to proclaim her acts of generosity, I am glad to record this one here.

Chapter XV

Southern Negro Leaders Challenged the White South

For decades much of the white South argued that Southern Negroes were satisfied with their plight. They said this when lynching was widespread, segregation was "God," discrimination was rampant, and Negroes in large numbers were migrating North in order to escape the crippling circumscriptions which held them in bondage. It was said so often, so long, and so loud that I believe that much of the white South accepted this myth as law and gospel. All too many times I read in the press and heard from the platform—that if white Northern liberals and radical Northern Negroes would leave the South alone, the race problem would be happily solved. When the Negroes in the South expressed dissatisfaction with their conditions, it could always be blamed on the North. "Our Negroes are satisfied," the South said. Over many decades the famous phrase of the Southern whites was, "We know the Negro. We understand him and he understands us. If agitators like Northerners and communists would stay out of Southern affairs, all would go well."

Up to 1942 Southern Negro leaders in a body had never spoken their mind to the white South. Now the time had come. The aftermath of World War I was fresh in the memory of many of us. We had seen the birth of the Commission on Interracial Cooperation, which was brought into being primarily to ease racial tension that was mounting even before the First World War ended. We remembered the racial riots which followed that war. We had noted that the number of Negroes lynched increased in the years immediately following the war. In 1942 we were engaged in the Second World War. Interracially things looked gloomy, and Negroes did not want the tragedies of the aftermath of World War I repeated after World War II.

One of the Negroes most concerned about what could happen was Gordon Blaine Hancock of Virginia Union University, Richmond. In 1941, Doctor Hancock released an article to the *Associated Negro Press* entitled "Interracial Hypertension." This article was on the gloomy side and aroused the concern of Mrs. Jessie Daniel Ames of Texas and Atlanta who was an official of the Commission on Interracial Cooperation. Hancock observed that racial tensions were mounting all over the place and that the white South was determined to put down any hopes of larger freedom that the Negroes might entertain as a result of their participation in World War II. In his article Hancock compared American society, with its racial tensions, to a man suffering from high blood pressure which, if not soon treated, would result in disaster. The author took note of the sporadic racial riots that were appearing across the country, and of a speech he had heard a prominent Negro make which he thought could only serve to stir up racial strife. This article stirred Mrs. Ames so much that she got in touch with Doctor Hancock and made an appointment to visit him in Richmond to see what could be done about the situation. The article is so important in the history and organization of the Southern Regional Council that I have included it here.

Interracial Hypertension

Hypertension is a fancy name for high blood pressure, just as delinquency is a fancy name for old-fashioned devilment, or prevarication is a fancy name for old-fashioned lying. Medical authorities tell us that hypertension is not a disease but a symptom; even so, unless it is properly treated and relieved, it results disastrously by and by.

There can be no doubt that there is today in race relations a hypertension which, unless treated with the greatest care, will have disastrous consequences. In spite of the preachments of religion and the promises of education, the fact remains that we are definitely entering a dangerous phase of the interracial conflict. In proof whereof we offer the all-too-frequent riotous outbreaks here and there about the country. Those outbreaks must be construed as symptomatic of an undercurrent of interracial bitterness that demands the most serious thinking and careful planning, if unhappy results are to be averted.

In this situation the better-class whites and Negroes have one of the mightiest challenges of this generation, and the future of both races is indissolubly bound up with the way this challenge is met. If serious trouble is to be avoided, both white and Negroes must face the ugly fact that race relations are in a state of hypertension and rupture; that unless matters are speedily taken in hand and shaped according to some constructive plan, we shall probably lose many important gains in race relations that have been won through many years, through sweat and tears.

. . . . .

This article is inspired by a speech which a prominent Negro made within recent weeks before an audience of Negroes numbering nearly a thousand. This man stood for almost an hour and made one of the ablest speeches I have ever heard. But from beginning to end his speech was one continuous rehearsal of the wrongs and injustices which the Negro has suffered in this country. He built up one of the strongest cases against the white man I have ever heard. All the while he was casting himself in the role of hero merely by recounting the woes of his stricken race.

That large audience was deeply moved and the occasion was enveloped in a pall of resentment and bitterness that is bound to do damage sometime, somewhere. The speaker did not seem to know that when only one side of a question is presented to the exclusion of the other side, the speech becomes propaganda. That the Negroes of this country have suffered many things because of such one-sided presentation did not seem to concern him. Here was a Negro who was the victim of a cruel propaganda turning propagandist himself. He called himself "fighting fire with fire," patently forgetting that such fights and fightings never end in victory but call for more and more fighting.

This speaker said not a word about the improved and improving race relations mirrored in a hundred ways, if we compare what the Negro has and enjoys today with what he had and enjoyed two generations ago. He spoke not a word about the growing spirit of justice and fair play in the heart of the New South, evinced by the growing willingness to admit the Negro to full citizenship. Within recent weeks prominent white citizens of South Carolina petitioned the officials of that state to allow Negroes to vote in the Democratic primary. This easily constitutes one of the finest gestures in race relations that has been made since 1876.

When Mrs. Ames went to Richmond it was not an accident that she and Dr. Hancock met at the colored YWCA, although Mrs. Ames was a registered guest in a white hotel. In 1942, it was not possible for a Negro and a white woman to hold a conference in a white hotel in Richmond. Normally this conference would have been held at the hotel where Mrs. Ames was registered. Hancock points out in the January, 1964, issue of the *New South* that he and Mrs. Ames discussed the feasibility of Negroes themselves making a public statement that might become the foundation of a new basis of cooperation, and challenge the white South to a new basis of interracial programs. Mrs. Ames assured Dr. Hancock that if he could get a group of Southern Negroes to present a challenge statement to the white South she would assemble a group of Southern whites to speak to its challenge and consider its proposals. Dr. Hancock set about to find ways and means of assembling a group of southern Negroes to draw up proposals to be presented to the white South. After he consulted with P. B. Young, editor and publisher of the Norfolk *Journal and Guide*, a host committee was formed with Dr. Young as chairman. The Southern Negro leaders met at the North Carolina College for Negroes at Durham, October 20, 1942.

The question naturally arose as to who should be invited. Should Negroes from the North be invited as members or as consultants? Dr. Hancock and his advisers decided against inviting any representatives from the North. We were bitterly criticized for this by our Negro friends in the North, but even now I think Hancock and his committee made a wise decision. All of us at Durham, or most of us, were staunch defenders of such Northern organizations as the NAACP and the National Urban League and were working with Northern Negro leadership in general, but we knew that if Northern Negroes were invited the white South would have used that as an excuse to decline cooperation. The purpose was to disarm the white South completely, so that they would have no excuse whatsoever for not speaking to our proposals. Eighty Negroes were invited. Fifty-nine came, and twenty-one were represented by letters and telegrams.

The best Negro leadership in the South had met at Durham to speak to the white South: educators, ministers, businessmen, editors, physicians, social workers, labor leaders, and civil rights workers. The question was what to say that would not frighten the Southern leadership away. Just as we had to be careful not to doom the conference to failure before we assembled, likewise we had to be careful that we said nothing in our document that would give the white South an excuse to back away. After we had talked all day at Durham, the document we wished to present was not ready; certainly, fifty-nine persons could not in a single day shape a statement that would be acceptable. I was the first to suggest that a drafting committee should be appointed to complete the document to be presented to the white South.

This committee met in Atlanta, Georgia, and completed its work. The document spoke forthrightly against discrimination in politics and civil rights, industry and labor, service occupations, education, agriculture, military service, social welfare, and health. The full statement of the Durham Conference appears in the January, 1964, issue of the *New South.* Here is the preamble:

A BASIS FOR INTERRACIAL COOPERATION AND DEVELOPMENT IN THE SOUTH

A Statement by Southern Negroes

The war sharpened the issue of Negro-white relations in the United States, and particularly in the South. A result has been increased racial tensions, fears, and aggressions, and an opening up of the basic questions of racial segregation and discrimination, Negro minority rights, and democratic freedom, as they apply practically in Negro-white relations in the South. These issues are acute and threaten to become even more serious as they increasingly block, through the deeper fears aroused, common sense consideration for even elementary improvements in Negro status, and the welfare of the country as a whole. With these problems in mind, we, a group of southern Negroes, realizing that the situation calls for both candor and wisdom, and in the belief that we voice the sentiments of many of the Negroes of the Nation as well as the South, take this means of recording our considered views of the issues before us.

(1) Our Nation is engaged in a world-wide struggle, the success of which, both in arms and ideals, is paramount and demands our first loyalty.

(2) Our Loyalty does not, in our view, preclude consideration now of problems and situations that handicap the working out of internal improvements in race relations essential to our full contribution to the war effort, and of the inevitable problems of post-war reconstruction, especially in the South where we reside.

(3) The South, with its twenty-five million people, one-third of whom are Negroes, presents a unique situation, not only because of the size of the Negro population but because of the legal and customary patterns of race relations which are invariably and universally associated with racial discrimination. We recognize the strength and age of these patterns. We are fundamentally opposed to the principle and practice of compulsory segregation in our American society, whether of races or classes or creeds; however, we regard it as both sensible and timely to address ourselves now to the current problems of racial discrimination and neglect, and to ways in which we may cooperate in the advancement of programs aimed at the sound improvement of race relations within the democratic framework.

(4) We regard it as unfortunate that the simple efforts to correct obvious social and economic injustices continue, with such considerable popular support, to be interpreted as the predatory ambition of irresponsible Negroes to invade the privacy of family life.

(5) We have the courage and faith to believe, however, that it is possible to evolve in the South a way of life, consistent with the principles for which we as a Nation are fighting throughout the world, that will free us all, white and Negro alike, from want, and from throttling fears.

It is significant to note that nothing was said about ending segregation, and yet this was only twelve years before the 1954 decision when the U. S. Supreme Court declared segregation in the public schools unconstitutional. Paragraph (3) of the preamble printed above mentions segregation, but in such a way as to indicate that our immediate concern was not with abolishing it. I tried to insert a statement which went beyond our opposition to the principle and practice of compulsory segregation, saying in essence that we would work for the abolition of legal segregation in American society. I stood alone in this effort. My colleagues argued that if we came out honestly and said we would do what we could to abolish segregation, the South would never consider our proposal. Maybe they were right. We can never know, however, because we didn't say it. Although we were deeply engaged in a Second World War and Negroes were dying again for democracy, our group thought it would be unwise to do anything more than to say that we were against segregation in principle.

The Durham statement was well received by the South, and throughout the South the editorial comments on the whole were good and favorable. Almost six months later, on April 8, 1943, the leadership of the white South met in Atlanta, to respond to the Durham statement drawn up October 20, 1942. I do not know how many southern whites attended the Atlanta conference, but 292 signed the document which the Southerners released to the nation. This was a tremendous response to the challenge we had laid down in Durham, and representatives came from twelve southern states.

As in the Durham document, no case was made against segregation, which was the basic evil in the South in 1943 and which still lingers with us; and as the Negro leadership in Durham a few months before was afraid to argue for the abolition of segregation, so was the white leadership afraid to do so when they answered our challenge. It is also worthy of note that the emphasis was placed upon improving racial relations through evolutionary means: "The solution of these problems can be found only in men of both races who are known to be men of determined good will. The ultimate solution will be found in evolutionary methods and not in ill-founded revolutionary movements which promise immediate solution."

How strange! These words were written eleven years before the revolutionary decision of the United States Supreme Court in 1954, twelve years before the one-year-long bus boycott in Montgomery in 1955 and 1956, seventeen years before black college students violated Jim Crow laws and went to jail by the thousands in an effort to be free men and women in downtown establishments, and twenty years before 250,000 Negroes and whites marched on Washington, forcing Congress to pass a public accommodation law; twenty years before the Birmingham march and twenty-two years before the Selma march which contributed to other revolutionary congressional civil rights laws. And yet how cautious we were in laying down our manifesto to the white South, and how cautious the white South was in responding to our mild declarations! Negroes and whites were as careful in their declarations as men walking on thin ice, so explosive they thought the race problem.

Out of Durham and Atlanta came Richmond, where resolutions of the Collaboration Committee were adopted. "The Atlanta meeting of white southerners had authorized the appointment of a Collaboration Committee to meet with a similar committee of Negroes from the Durham meeting." Ralph McGill had chaired the Atlanta meeting, and he appointed the members of the Collaboration Committee. The two committees—Atlanta and Durham—met in Richmond on June 16, 1943. Out of their meeting came a statement of support for the Durham document and a bi-racial continuation committee to implement it.

Gordon Blaine Hancock might well be called the father of the Southern Regional Council. Beside him as founder stands Jessie Daniel Ames, who was disturbed by Hancock's article, "Interracial Hypertension." If Dr. Hancock had not written the article and if Mrs. Ames had not responded to it, it is conceivable that the Southern Regional Council would not have come into being. I quote from Josephine Wilkins' article printed in the January, 1964, issue of the *New South:*

> Thus when the Continuation Committee appointed at Richmond met at Atlanta University on August 4, Dr. Odum was elected chairman of the meeting, and a proposal was brought in to set up a southwide council with broad scope. Following a day-long discussion, the proposal was approved and a resolution establishing the organization now known as the Southern Regional Council was adopted. The Continuation Committee was made its nucleus.
>
> A charter was applied for by Dr. Rufus Clement, president of Atlanta University, Dr. Charles Johnson, Ralph McGill, Bishop Moore, and Dr. Odum. The charter was granted on January 6, 1944. A charter meeting was held at Atlanta University on February 16-17, and just prior to its opening the Commission on Interracial Cooperation met and merged the Commission with the newly formed Council. All those who had participated in the Durham-Atlanta-Richmond meetings, together with members of the old Commission, were made charter members. Bishop Moore was elected president and when he could not serve, Dr. Odum was elected. A board and an executive committee were chosen, and Dr. Guy B. Johnson and Dr. Ira DeA. Reid were made staff directors. The Southern Regional Council was launched!

The Council did not start out in 1944 fighting to abolish segregation. It was exceedingly cautious and timid, stepping lightly so as not to disturb the status quo of a segregated society. One of the reasons Dr. Howard Odum, chairman of the Richmond meeting, and others gave for not opposing segregation when the Council was organized was that the South would not support it financially if they spoke out against segregation. My retort was that if they pressed vigorously for justice within the segregated pattern, the South would not support the Council. My words were prophetic; the Council's support has come from the North. However, without a doubt, the Southern Regional Council became one of the most effective interracial agencies in the nation, working courageously to make the United States what it ought to be in the area of race. Without fanfare and without seeking publicity, it has supplemented and complemented the work of the National Association for the Advancement of Colored People, the Southern Christian Leadership Conference, and the Congress of Racial Equality. Negroes carried the ball in the movement. It was the Durham statement that laid the foundation for the work of the Southern Regional Council and not the pronouncements that came out of Atlanta. As Gordon Blaine Hancock and Jessie Daniel Ames advance in years, they can be proud of their work in paving the way for the establishment of the Southern Regional Council. I am glad that I too had a hand in its founding.

Chapter XVI
Politicians and President Kennedy

When Ellis Arnall defeated Eugene Talmadge in 1942, Negroes in Georgia were disfranchised. Therefore neither Arnall nor Talmadge had any reason to worry about the Negro vote. Nevertheless, the racial problem was injected into the campaign. Although Arnall was played up as having won with a more liberal stance on race than Talmadge, this was hardly the case. Talmadge declared in the July 19, 1942, issue of the Atlanta *Constitution* that "as long as I am Governor of Georgia Negroes and whites will never go to the same school." Since Talmadge was accusing certain professors at the University of Georgia of encouraging the coeducation of the races, Ellis Arnall evidently felt that he too had to use the racial issue in his campaign. The year before, Eugene Talmadge had forced the Board of Regents to oust Dean Walter Cocking and Dr. Marvin Pittman on the charge that they were advocating the coeducation of the races at the University of Georgia. I heard a radio address delivered by Governor Arnall in which he said, in essence, that if a Negro tried to enter a white school down his way (Newnan), the Negro would not live to see the sun set and there would be no need to call out the militia. This was tantamount to encouraging the mob to take any step necessary to prevent the coeducation of the races. The racial issue developed such heat in the campaign that the editor of the Augusta *Herald* wired Arnall and Talmadge, according to the Atlanta *Constitution* of August 13, to lay off the race question. The editor warned Arnall and Talmadge that future stress on race "may lead to serious disturbances and cannot possibly serve any useful purposes."

It was Talmadge's tirade against the university system of Georgia that defeated him in 1942. His false accusation against the university—that it was advocating the mixing of the races—turned the vast majority of the state papers against him and with them the students and professors of the university system. Rating boards, including the Southern Association of Colleges and Schools, were threatening to drop the university from its accredited list. It was the threat to the university system of Georgia and not the difference of the two men on race, as expressed in the campaign, that defeated Talmadge in 1942.

In all honesty, however, Arnall did not wave the red flag of race during his four years in office, and he made one of Georgia's best governors. During his administration, the poll tax was abolished. He humanized the penal system; he reduced the voting age to eighteen; when the white primary was abolished, he refused to call a special session of the legislature to circumvent the federal court's decisions; he fought the Ku Klux Klan; he revised the state constitution; and he wrote a good book, *The Shore Dimly Seen* (J. B. Lippincott Co., New York: 1946.) But there were two other things he did that I shall not soon forget. He made the speech just referred to, which did encourage lynching and the mob, and he wrote a letter to me with a revealing salutation. Unfortunately, I cannot find the letter but the incident is told in John Gunther's book, *Inside U.S.A.*

> I mentioned Dr. Mays above. Recently ex-Governor Arnall (one of the best progressives in the South!) had occasion to write him an official letter. Arnall was in a quandary. He could not, of course, address Dr. Mays as "Mister" or "Doctor," even in correspondence. The taboo on this has been ironclad for years. Finally he hit on the device of simply calling him "Benjamin."

It is still amazing to me that a man of Governor Arnall's position and standing in the nation did not know how to address me, for it has usually been easy for white people to give Negroes titles—anything except the verboten "Mister"! Of course, Mr. Gunther was in error in saying that calling a Negro "Doctor" was taboo in the South in 1946. "Reverend," "President," "Doctor"—any one of them would have been acceptable, but he began by addressing me as *Benjamin.* To the reader this may seem a small matter. But I have often wondered since if this reflected a disrespect which Mr. Arnall held for Negroes at that time. Of course it may be that his campaign utterances on race and the way he addressed me indicated what little respect a politician has for *anyone* who has no power to help him get in office. During the Arnall administration, the Negroes in Georgia were not voters.

One proof that Eugene Talmadge's anti-Negro stand did not defeat him in the fall of 1942 is the fact that he won the governorship again in the fall of 1946 but died before his inauguration. Mr. Talmadge's anti-Negro utterances were so vile and vicious that many of us were concerned about what might happen racially when the governor took office in January of 1947.

Negroes got the ballot in 1946, but they were not organized, and not enough Negroes were registered to vote to make any impression on Eugene Talmadge. And yet some of us wanted to do something. I got the idea that the General Missionary Baptist Convention of Georgia might be induced to adopt a resolution which I had drawn up, calling for January 9, 1947, Inauguration Day, to be a Day of Prayer for the governor-elect, Eugene Talmadge. Brief excerpts from the Resolution follow:

> RESOLVED, That the members of the General Missionary Baptist Convention in Georgia assembled in Annual Session in Savannah, Georgia, this 12th day of November in the year of our Lord 1946, set aside Thursday noon, January 9th, 1947, the day of Governor Talmadge's inauguration, as the day and hour of prayer for the Governor and his administration; and that we assemble in our respective churches and pray to the God of the universe for Eugene Talmadge, asking God to make of him a good, just, democratic and Christian Governor; . . . a Governor of all the peoples, Negroes and whites, Jews and Gentiles, Labor and Management, Protestants and Catholics, "with malice toward none", and with justice for all; and be it
>
> FURTHER RESOLVED, That we call upon all Negro Baptists in the State of Georgia and all other religious bodies throughout the State and Nation—Negro and white, Protestant, Catholic, Jewish—to participate in this hour of prayer, Thursday noon, January 9th, 1947, and if they cannot assemble in Church, we call upon them to stop for a few moments wherever they may chance to be: at work, at play, on their sick beds, in the air, on the sea, on the train, on the bus, in their homes, in the street and pray for Governor Eugene Talmadge and his administration. . . .

Before the governor-elect was inaugurated, death overcame him and put an end to our Day of Prayer. Whether our efforts would have in any way influenced the governor, we will never know. We had felt deeply disturbed and terribly frustrated, but we had tried to do something helpful.

President Harry Truman appointed me to membership on the National Committee of the Mid-Century White House Conference on Children and Youth. Oscar Ewing, the Federal Security Administrator, was the chairman of the White House Conference; Anne Hedgeman, his able assistant. It was the wish of President Truman, Mr. Ewing, and the fifty-seven persons who constituted the National Committee, that a conference on children and youth should include representatives of the different racial and ethnic groups as part of the various state delegations. It was left to the governor of each state to appoint the delegates from his state, or to authorize someone to choose the delegates, with the governor's approval. With one or two exceptions, the governors of the states did include members of minority groups in their state delegations.

As a member of the National Committee living in Atlanta, I was asked by Mr. Ewing to call on Governor Herman Talmadge (son of the deceased Eugene) and inform him on the point of minority representation, and to tell him that in due course he would get an official communication from President Truman. In my brief conference with the governor, he made no commitments but gave me the impression that the matter would be considered when he had received official communication from Washington.

Georgia was allotted thirty-six delegates, but we were unsuccessful in getting Governor Talmadge to approve Negroes as delegates to the White House Conference. At first he appointed Nelson Jackson, Southern field director of the National Urban League, and Mrs. Hortense Cochrane, of the Atlanta University School of Social Work, to serve on the Georgia Selection Committee under Mrs. Ralph Hobbs, chairman of the delegation. Mrs. Hobbs was president of the Georgia Congress of the Parent-Teacher Associations, and I am sure the governor had to approve each of the thirty-six Georgia delegates. Although Mrs. Cochrane and Mr. Jackson received letters from the governor stating that they were members of Mrs. Hobbs' Georgia Committee to select the delegates, they were never called to a meeting. When I questioned Mrs. Hobbs, I was told that the governor wanted an all-white committee. According to the Atlanta *Daily World* of June 13, 1950, when Mrs. Cochrane and Mr. Jackson wrote the governor complaining that they had not been invited to any meeting, their letters were referred to Jerome Connor, director of the Georgia Citizens' Council. Connor reportedly told them that the governor would not have Negroes on the state committee.

The governor's excuses for not appointing Negroes as delegates to the White House Conference on Children and Youth were fantastically flimsy. He argued that in Georgia Negroes did not represent the state in any official capacity: no Negroes in the legislature; none serving as judges; none on the Board of Education; and none on the Board of Regents or other governing bodies. Another alibi was that Georgia had laws of segregation and as long as he was governor he was going to enforce them. Obviously these non sequitur arguments had no bearing on appointing Negroes to the delegation. The real reason that the governor had no intention of naming Negroes to serve on the Georgia delegation was to him the best of all reasons—they were Negroes—blacks! There was no incentive for him to do so—he could go on to the Senate and stay there without a single Negro vote.

It should be noted that in 1950 the total population of Georgia was 3,443,330, of which number 1,062,762 were Negroes. The governor felt entirely free to ignore, really to insult gratuitously, slightly more than 30 percent of the people of Georgia. It took no great power of divination to conclude that the governor of Georgia was supremely indifferent to the welfare of the black people in his state. He may have had a few Negroes on his place whom he liked in a paternalistic way, and he may have been kind to them "in their place," but he had not the slightest conception of the Negro group as one to be treated with dignity and respect. Between March and September, 1950, the Atlanta papers carried full accounts of the controversy between the governor and me and the White House Conference officials relative to Negro representation in the Georgia delegation. No amount of publicity or protests prevailed: The governor would not be moved.

On September 19, 1950, the Atlanta *Daily World* carried an article with the caption "Talmadge Names Lily-White Body to White House," which stated that it was clear the governor wanted no Negro representatives in the Georgia delegation. I revealed the governor's attitude in a letter to Oscar Ewing, federal security administrator, who was in charge of the White House Conference. I said to Mr. Ewing, "We have done everything honorable on this end to get Governor Talmadge to include Negroes on the Georgia Committee. Every effort has failed."

In its September 19, 1950, issue, under the caption "Negroes Not Leaders," the Atlanta *Journal* quoted Governor Talmadge as saying:

> We do not have Negroes in the Legislature, on courts, on boards of education, the Board of Regents and other governing bodies.
>
> If Georgia citizens select the delegates, they will be white delegates. If Washington wants to choose the delegates and have Negroes attending the conference, they are at liberty to do so.
>
> We have segregation laws in Georgia. As long as I am governor of Georgia I will do my utmost to enforce them.

The Atlanta *Constitution* of September 19, 1950, quoted the governor as follows:

> . . . I have no objections if the chairman of the President's White House Conference on Youth desires to invite Negroes from Georgia. If he expects me to send a delegation from Georgia, we will send white people.

Considerable time was spent in the National Committee trying to find a way to have Georgia Negroes officially represented at the Mid-Century White House Conference. Should the Georgia delegation be reduced by approximately one-third? Should President Truman be requested to prevail upon the governor to send a biracial delegation to the Conference? Both of these suggestions were discarded by the National Committee. If the Georgia delegation were cut, Negroes would still be left out. We thought it unwise to bring the President of the United States into a controversy of this kind.

Either Mr. Ewing or his assistant, Mrs. Anne Hedgeman, suggested that I be empowered by the National Committee to assemble a group of Negro leaders from over the state of Georgia to select eighteen Negro delegates who would be officially recognized by Mr. Ewing and the National Committee. And this was the way in which the problem was solved. In addition to the eighteen Negro delegates whom the Negroes chose, there were a few chosen at large by the National Committee. Thus it turned out that Georgia had the largest Negro delegation of any state in the Union. If Governor Talmadge had elected to appoint one or two Negro delegates or had allowed Mrs. Hobbs' committee to do so, I am sure that in 1950 a token representation of Negroes would have made it difficult for the National Committee to complain. It was Governor Talmadge's adamant position which enabled Negroes to be so adequately and ably represented at the Mid-Century White House Conference on Children and Youth in December, 1950.

The National Committee, attempting to carry out the wishes of President Truman, worked exceedingly hard to make certain that segregation and discrimination based on race and color would be eliminated or reduced to the bare minimum. Most of the hotels in Washington agreed to take all delegates regardless of race or color; a few hotels were eliminated because of their unshakable refusal to take Negro delegates. Some hotels, if they were able to surmise from the reservations that the delegate was black, would assign him to a Negro hotel. I sent in my registration on Morehouse College stationery and accordingly was assigned to a Negro hotel. I had no objection to staying in a Negro hotel, but knowing that this assignment was an attempt to segregate me, I protested to the Central Housing Agency. I was re-assigned to the Willard Hotel.

All of this happened twenty years ago. The Negro is a political force now, and since the way of conversion for politicians is via the ballot, Senator Talmadge may be a different man. At any rate, his tactics must be different.

It is not by accident that Maynard Jackson, young Atlanta Negro attorney, polled more than two hundred thousand votes in his race for the Senate against Herman Talmadge in 1968, and that many white people voted for the courageous young Negro.

In 1961, President Kennedy was seriously considering me for membership on the Civil Rights Commission. Senators Russell and Talmadge vigorously opposed my appointment because I had never concealed my opposition to being segregated and discriminated against for no other reason than that God made me and my people black. I have often said that I came out of my mother's womb kicking against segregation and discrimination based on race, color, religion, ethnic or national origin. Throughout the years, I have found nothing in the Bible, nothing in the practice of the Christian Church prior to modern times, nothing in Christian theology, nothing in the findings of the best scientists, and nothing in the Constitution to justify segregation based on race and color. Certainly my views on this subject are well known by all who have heard me speak and all who have read what I have written, and I have never apologized to anyone for my position.

Senators Russell and Talmadge opposed my appointment on the grounds that my views on Civil Rights were well known and that I could not be objective in judging whether there were violations of the Civil Rights law. They argued that I would approach the subject with bias. Senator Talmadge attempted to bolster his opposition by what amounted to a smear campaign. He pointed out that my name was on the list of the House Committee on Un-American Activities as having had some connection with organizations labeled by the Committee or the Attorney General's office as being Communist-front agencies.

Throughout my career, I have seldom answered charges brought against me. With my friends, I needed no defense; with my enemies a defense would do no good. But now, in the evening of my life, I want to say something about these charges:

I plead guilty to the charge that I am a desegregationist. I use the term "desegregation" deliberately, because we can desegregate with court orders and congressional legislation. Integration, on the other hand, is a spiritual term implying oneness, wholeness, identity of aims and purpose. Integration has to be achieved in deeper ways. In this framework, however, I am both a desegregationist and an integrationist. Nevertheless, I do not agree with Senators Russell and Talmadge that I could not investigate impartially because of my opposition to segregation and discrimination based on race and color. I am a man of integrity; and what has been first and foremost in my life has been my honest endeavor to find the truth and proclaim it.

But even had I been biased and too subjective to deal fairly and impartially with facts, how could the senior and junior senators from the State of Georgia possibly point the accusing finger? Studying their records in the Congress, reading what the press has reported they have said about race, and listening to their utterances, I, a black man, conclude that so far as Negroes are concerned our senators have never been objective. The records all attest that Senators Russell and Talmadge have been staunch segregationists all of their lives; they have been opposed to every decision against segregation handed down by the federal courts; and they have voted against every civil rights law passed by the Congress. Both of these men signed the Southern manifesto denouncing the 1954 decision of the United States Supreme Court. A "little" black man like me cannot do nearly so much with his "bias" as can "big" white men like Senators Russell and Talmadge who occupy high places in the Congress and serve on and head powerful national committees. They had the power and the prejudice to implement their "bias" to prevent my appointment, and they did. Power in the hands of the bigot is what makes bias so dangerous and evil.

It really didn't matter particularly whether I served on the Civil Rights Commission or not; but the total situation which developed did matter a great deal. It takes an unusual politician to have respect for any man who is not in position to help him get in or stay in office. If Russell or Talmadge had needed the votes of Negroes, they would not have pounced on me as they did. Politicians for the most part are "tuned in" only to the voice of the vote. Votes have changed more politicians' minds and postures on the question of race than the Sermon on the Mount, the thirteenth chapter of I Corinthians, or the Emancipation Proclamation ever did. In the future, it may not be so easy for the politicians of Georgia (or any other Southern state) to ignore Negroes.

I do not recall ever having met Senator Russell formally. I have had occasion to write him about certain matters, and he has responded courteously and promptly. I have never talked with him personally a minute in my life. My association with Senator Talmadge has been only slightly closer. When Senator Talmadge was governor, I was invited to give the address when the Hughes Spalding Pavilion in Atlanta was dedicated. The governor and I shared the platform. When the program was over, Governor Talmadge did not use the steps but jumped off the platform. Negroes at the meeting interpreted that leap to mean that the governor did not wish to shake hands with me for fear a photographer would snap a picture showing him in the "disgraceful" act of shaking hands with a Negro. This might have been a false interpretation, but it was one that was widely circulated in the Negro community—and it is ofttimes truly amazing how accurately Negroes can explain the convolutions of the racist mind.

Twice I went to the governor's office to request small favors: President Tubman of Liberia was coming to Georgia to visit his mother's native state and to be given honorary degrees by Atlanta University and Morehouse College. We were told that protocol requires that the head of a state, coming to another state, should be invited by the Chief Executive of the host state or country. President Rufus E. Clement of Atlanta University and I made an appointment to see the governor and requested him to extend President Tubman an invitation to visit Georgia. He received us pleasantly, dictated the letter, had it typed, and signed it before we left. The other time I went to see Governor Talmadge, it was as a member of the National Committee of the Mid-Century White House Conference on Children and Youth.

All this is to say that Senators Russell and Talmadge certainly did not know me as an individual well enough to block my appointment to the Civil Rights Commission, but they did know of my attitude toward segregation based on race and, according to their convictions, I suppose this was enough to make them oppose me. When Mr. Talmadge was governor, he met a friend of mine, head of the Standard Oil Company of Ohio. My friend tells the story that when he inquired of the governor if he knew his friend, Benjamin Mays, in Atlanta, the governor said he did, and remarked further that I was "smart but dangerous"!

Senator Russell did not state or imply that I was a fellow traveler or a member of subversive organizations as Senator Talmadge did. According to Senator Talmadge, not only could I not serve objectively as a member of the Civil Rights Commission, but he thought it most significant that the House Un-American Activities Committee had listed my name as having had connections with subversive organizations. I should like to set the record straight.

I have written more articles and books and delivered more speeches than most Americans. I challenge anyone to find in my written or public statements one sentence that would indicate that I was a communist or a fellow traveler. I have been one of Communism's severist critics. When I was feuding with the University of Chicago about its segregated housing policy, I refused to allow the Communist students on the campus to assist me in any way. Nor was I ever tempted by the ease with which Communist girls socialized with black men. I doubt whether the senators have ever read anything I have written. Talmadge heard me speak only once.

It was exceedingly easy for one's name to be listed as a member of an organization accused by the Un-American Activitites Committee as being subversive. One could hardly know each time he lent his name to sponsor an organization that seemed worthwhile, or was a member of an initiating committee to get an organization going, or attended a meeting of an organization labeled by the Un-American Activities Committee as being associated with Communists, or made a contribution to an organization of which the Un-American Activities Committee did not approve, whether or not the organization was in fact subversive. Senator Talmadge was quoted in the press as saying that I had been identified or associated with at least four different Communist-front organizations. I am sure that my name was used by more than four organizations which the Committee called "Communist front." I recall one that used my name without my consent. I was a sponsor of the Mid-Century Conference for Peace which I never attended. I did not know who participated. This conference was listed as a Communist front. The Southern Conference on Human Welfare was listed; and persons like Eleanor Roosevelt and Mary McLeod Bethune were among the organizers. I have been definitely and proudly involved with the Federal and National Council of the Churches of Christ, and these organizations were also attacked as being Communist. I have never knowingly supported any organization that was Communist or subversive. Talmadge opposed my appointment to the Civil Rights Commission on two counts: 1) My name was associated with organizations listed as being Communist-identified, and 2) I was a desegregationist and therefore incapable of making impartial decision in cases involving Civil Rights. It was on only the latter charge that Russell opposed me.

If the House Un-American Activities Committee had wished to be fair, it would have released data only on persons definitely *proven* to be Communist or subversive. If Senator Talmadge had wished to be fair, he would not have used data about me from the House Un-American Activities Committee unless they had specifically said that I was subversive. His using these data without finding out the truth about my loyalty to my country was tantamount to using lies to smear me. It wasn't fair. This attempt to block my appointment to the Civil Rights Commission while at the same time trying to smear me by giving the public the impression that I might be a Communist, or had Communist leanings, was irresponsible for a man in high office.

The opposition of the two Georgia senators to my appointment was widely circulated in the press, which in almost every instance, came to my defense in editorials such as that in the Atlanta *Constitution* on March 2, 1961:

> The proposed appointment of Dr. Benjamin E. Mays to the Civil Rights Commission ought to be judged on its merits and not on smears of the man.
>
> The president of Morehouse College has been on public view in Atlanta for 30 years. His loyalty and his integrity are known by this community.
>
> What he believes in the field of civil rights is known beyond question, and if that is the basis of opposition to his appointment, then let it be. But let him be spared any further question about his loyalty. Atlanta knows there is no question about it.

and in the New York *Post* on March 8, 1961:

> The NAACP today urged President Kennedy to ignore protests by Georgia's two U.S. Senators and appoint Dr. Benjamin E. Mays, nationally known educator and religious leader, to the U.S. Civil Rights Commission.
>
> Roy Wilkins, NAACP Executive Secretary, assailed attacks on Mays by Senators Talmadge and Russell as "both ironic and outrageous." . . . "Both men have spent their public lifetimes," he said, "in support of a system which for more than 90 years has denied Negro Americans the enjoyment of their constitutional rights as citizens."

Despite heavy support for me, however, Russell and Talmadge won.

My first knowledge that I was being considered for an ambassadorship came from London. Someone phoned to confirm what he had heard in London "that you have been appointed Ambassador to Israel by President Kennedy." Shortly after the London call, *Newsweek* carried a brief statement, under the caption "More Appointments for Negroes": "Doctor Benjamin Mays, President of Atlanta's Morehouse College as an Ambassador —possibly to Israel." The press picked up the story, indicating that I was being considered because many persons were being interviewed about me by the FBI. My friend Ralph McGill of the Atlanta *Constitution* was so sure that the position would be offered that he called requesting me to let him know immediately after President Kennedy notified me of my appointment. One of the President's aides called a couple of times wanting to know whether I would be interested in a foreign appointment by President Kennedy. I gave him no particular encouragement, saying only that I was happy in my work, and that I would be more interested in other work after perhaps another two more years at Morehouse.

I heard nothing directly from President Kennedy about this. Some time later, when Mrs. Mays and I were guests for dinner at the White House, President Kennedy said to the Shah of Iran, as I went through the line, that he had wanted to make me an ambassador but I had preferred to remain in education.

Here again it did not matter that I was not appointed Ambassador to Israel. I loved being at Morehouse, despite the many difficulties inherent in the work. I never knew why the appointment was not made. I cannot charge it up to Senators Russell and Talmadge. Mr. Russell told the press that he would be willing to endorse me for Ambassador to Israel or any other ambassadorial post to which the President wished to assign me—but to membership on the Civil Rights Commission, never. If this was Senator Russell's attitude, I am sure it was the attitude of Senator Talmadge also. That Senator Russell was willing for me to represent this country abroad, but was opposed to my serving my country on the Civil Rights Commission here at home, would no doubt seem strange to anyone other than an American Negro—a black man in Georgia.

Some situations, no matter how protracted, how unremitting, never become acceptable. Negroes have lived in Georgia for many decades, feeling that the man in the governor's mansion was not their governor, and that in no way did he represent their interests. Indeed, most gubernatorial candidates in the State of Georgia have run their campaigns on anti-Negro platforms. When Governor Carl Sanders spoke at Morehouse in 1966, he was, according to our records, the first governor of Georgia to speak at Morehouse in this century. It was not that Morehouse did not want to have rapport with the governors of the state, but my predecessors and I did not know whether or not the Chief Executive might say something that would antagonize our students. It is hardly surprising that Negro students and Negro people have had little faith in governors who shouted from the house tops their loyal support of and identification with segregationists. Governor Sanders, on the other hand, made a good speech at Morehouse and was warmly received by students and faculty.

Most candidates for governor of Georgia have not wanted white people to know that they were soliciting Negro votes. I believe that "Bo" Calloway would have secured enough votes in the runoff to beat Maddox in 1967, despite his anti-civil rights record in Congress, had he not been afraid to seek the Negro vote. Negroes were not in love with Maddox. I was spokesman for a committee that went to see Mr. Calloway. He made some commitments relative to Negroes which we liked. Time was short. Our suggestion that he call together a group of Negro leaders from over the state and tell them what he had told us fell on deaf ears. I believe Calloway could have won that race. He thought he could win without the Negro vote and fear kept him from openly seeking their votes.

I was considered by President Kennedy for a position on the Civil Rights Commission and for an ambassadorial post. Neither appointment was made. Twice in three years Sadie and I were guests at the White House when the President and Mrs. Kennedy were entertaining foreign dignitaries. I was appointed by him to the Advisory Committee of the Peace Corps and represented the Peace Corps at an all-African Conference on Education in Ethiopia. The most signal honor he conferred on me was in appointing me as one of four Americans to represent our government at the state funeral of Pope John XXIII in Rome, Italy. The other three were: Lyndon Baines Johnson, then Vice President; James Farley, former Postmaster General and Chairman of the National Democratic Committee; and Doctor George N. Shuster, former president of Hunter College. Previously, I had met Lyndon Johnson only casually, but on this trip we talked quite a bit. For about ninety minutes on the plane, we discussed civil rights, and I was impressed by what appeared to be his genuine concern. What he did in the field of civil rights after he became President proved that he had been sincere in his words to me.

I was told by a Kennedy aide that the President had plans to involve me in government work. What would have happened had he lived, I do not know. Why he expressed an interest in me, I cannot say. Perhaps my friends in Washington recommended me. I had not campaigned actively for John Kennedy, but I had made it clear in many speeches that I was going to vote for him. I wrote articles in the Pittsburgh *Courier* defending his right as a Roman Catholic to be President of the United States. I could never see how anyone could reasonably oppose, solely on the basis of religion, a man who aspired to be President or to hold any other elective office. Few men in America have I admired as much as I did John Fitzgerald Kennedy.

Chapter XVII

Morehouse School of Religion and the Interdenomination Center

At Howard University, we had succeeded in developing the School of Religion into a first rate seminary which gained membership in the American Association of Theological Schools in December, 1939. Prior to the School of Religion's admission, Gammon was the only predominantly Negro seminary that had attained membership. For many years Gammon had been the most outstanding theological seminary among Negroes. Howard was now ready to join Gammon in a program to improve further the theological education among Negroes, although the doors at both Gammon and at Howard had never been closed to students of other racial groups.

Shortly after the accreditation of The Howard University School of Religion, I was called to the presidency of Morehouse College. Though founded primarily to train ministers and teachers, Morehouse had for decades placed more emphasis upon the liberal arts and sciences than upon the training of ministers. Before I came to Morehouse, the administration had decided to phase out the B. D. program in the School of Religion and concentrate on a major and minor in the field of religion, as in other undergraduate disciplines. This was in many ways a wise decision, for it was hardly possible to make both the college and the school of religion first rate institutions. And yet I felt that it would be most unfortunate if Morehouse abandoned its original intent to prepare men for pastoral leadership in the church. So we set out to develop a good program leading to the B. D. degree, which we had succeeded in doing before the end of the 1940's.

I knew all the while, however, that Morehouse would never be able to make its School of Religion what the times required while also striving to develop a first-rate college. I felt this when I went there in 1940. I saw only one hope for the Morehouse School of Religion, and that hope was to work out some kind of affiliated arrangement with Gammon Theological Seminary and the Turner Theological Seminary at Morris Brown. Consequently, I assumed the presidency with this in mind. I was certain, nevertheless, that it would take a long time to consummate the idea and that it would never be done without the wholehearted coöperation of Gammon, the only accredited seminary among the three and the only seminary that had a plant and an endowment of its own. Then there was the problem of getting the AME's, the Baptists, and the Methodists to work together in an affiliated program. It seemed that we needed someone to perform a miracle. Needless to say, a miracle didn't happen; but there existed certain stark realities which Gammon, Morehouse, and Morris Brown could not ignore. Morehouse and Morris Brown would hardly be able to secure ample funds to build separately two first-rate seminaries, even if two more seminaries were needed in Atlanta. As indicated above, Gammon had a plant of its own, a small endowment, and accreditation. Nevertheless, Gammon with its larger resources needed Morehouse and Morris Brown for its future existence just about as much as the Morehouse School of Religion and the Turner Theological Seminary needed Gammon. When the Candler School of Theological at Emory opened its doors to Negroes, would the Methodist Church support both Gammon and Candler? These factors lurked in the background as we worked to bring the three schools, later five, together.

The idea of cooperating in a theological program for Negro students in Atlanta had begun in the early 1930's between Gammon Theological Seminary and the CME Church and later between Gammon and the Morehouse School of Religion. When J. W. Nicholson and I were making our study of Negro churches in the United States, a program existed between Gammon and the CME Church. In the 1940's, Morehouse had a cooperative exchange program with Gammon.

Very soon after my arrival at Morehouse, a series of conversations was begun among President Willis J. King of Gammon, President William A. Fountain of Morris Brown (representing Turner Theological Seminary), and myself to explore some plan of future cooperation among the three schools of theology. As early as April 24, 1942, I presented the idea of affiliation to the Morehouse Board of Trustees and I presented it repeatedly thereafter. The conversations continued intermittently over a period of eighteen years. During this time, Dr. King was succeeded by Dr. John W. Haywood, and Dr. Haywood by Dr. Harry Richardson as president of Gammon. At Morris Brown, President Fountain was followed first by President John H. Lewis, then by President Frank Cunningham, and finally by by President John A. Middleton. My own unbroken tenure as president of Morehouse and my unflagging interest in a cooperation which would result in one strong seminary rather than three relatively weak ones helped to keep the idea of affiliation alive until the Interdenominational Theological Center actually came into being in 1959.

Shortly after President Richardson came to Gammon in 1948, a proposal was presented to the General Education Board for funds to coordinate or combine the seminary work of the three institutions. The officers of the GEB were ready to consider the proposal, but the Gammon leadership was hesitant and clearly not ready at the time to go forward with the merger. My correspondence with Dr. Henry Pitt Van Deusen, President of Union Theological Seminary and member of the General Education Board, which will be found in the Appendix, reflects the positions held by certain parties at that time.

It was not until 1956 that plans were laid in earnest for unification. It had been clear all along that Gammon held the key to a viable cooperative plan and that, in the nature of things, it would have to provide the leadership for closer cooperation. Gammon was a seminary in its own right, and foundations would hardly look away from it to two liberal arts colleges for leadership concerning theological education. In 1956, Dr. Harry Richardson assumed the role of leadership toward affiliation. It was very clear by that year that Morehouse and Morris Brown would not be able to build first-class seminaries, and it had also become clear that when Candler School of Theology at Emory opened its doors to Negroes, Candler—not Gammon—would be the fair-haired child with the Methodist Church. Even if Morehouse and Morris Brown had been able to continue their theological schools, the Southern Association of Colleges and Schools would hardly have permitted them to, since the theological schools would likely drain support from the colleges. These factors were the "miracles" that made the ITC possible.

In 1956, at the request of Dr. Richardson, the Rockefeller General Education Board gave Gammon Theological Seminary $15,000, which was to be used by a committee to study the Atlanta situation and decide whether to recommend the establishment of a new seminary to be affiliated with the Atlanta University Center Institutions: Atlanta University, Clark, Morehouse, Morris Brown, and Spelman colleges. Richardson of Gammon, Mays of Morehouse, and Lewis of Morris Brown met and named the members of the committee we wanted to undertake the study, all of them acceptable to the officers of the General Education Board. They were: E. C. Colwell, Chairman, then Vice President and Dean of Faculty of Emory University and later president of Southern California School of Theology; M. J. Holmes, president of Illinois Wesleyan University; Henry P. Van

Dusen, president of Union Theological Seminary; F. D. Patterson, president, Phelps-Stokes Fund; and Walter N. Roberts of the American Association of Theological Schools. This committee made an affirmative report, recommending that Atlanta be the place for the establishment of a new affiliated seminary. It was the efforts of this committee that made appropriations possible for the creation of the new seminary. The name, the Interdenominational Theological Center, is the brain child of Doctor E. C. Colwell.

The idea of a center for theological education on a non-denominational basis was so fascinating and challenging that the Phillips School of Theology of Lane College, Jackson, Tennessee, under the leadership of Bishop B. Julian Smith, became interested in the Atlanta plan. Soon the CME Seminary joined with the three Atlanta seminaries to make up what is known as the Interdenominational Center. Now the time had come for the four institutions, Gammon, Morehouse School of Religion, Turner Theological Seminary, and Phillips School of Theology to move jointly to get appropriations for the establishment of ITC.

The Sealantic Fund had been established by John D. Rockefeller, Jr., for the purpose of improving the quality of theological education on a non-denominational basis, and this new center was the kind of arrangement in which Mr. Rockefeller was interested. The General Education Board had been concerned with theological education in the Atlanta University Center for some time, as demonstrated by the $15,000 appropriated to Gammon for the purpose of the study. In response to a proposal presented to the Sealantic Fund and the General Education Board by the four participating institutions, the Fund appropriated $1,750,000 for the ITC—1958—$1,500,-000 for a new plant and $250,000 for endowment. The General Education Board appropriated $500,000 for endowment, but on a matching basis. It accepted the $250,000 from the Sealantic Fund as matching money, thus turning over to the new seminary its first $250,000, making an endowment of $500,000. The ITC was chartered March 14, 1958, and began operation on the Gammon campus in September, 1959. Construction of ITC on Beckwith Street began in December, 1959. With the completion of the buildings, the dedication of the new plant and the inauguration of Dr. Richardson was held in May, 1961. The new plant was occupied June 1, 1961, and the first school year for ITC in its new home began in September of the same year. Dr. Richardson had soon raised the $250,000 required to secure the second $250,000 matching money from the General Education Board. Almost at the start, the ITC had a million-dollar endowment.

The Study Committee laid down certain guidelines which the trustees of the four institutions adopted in order to guarantee the harmonious functioning of the four institutions. Each denomination has representation on the ITC Board of Trustees. The original number of ITC trustees was twenty-two, elected as follows: six by Gammon, three by Morehouse, three by Morris Brown, three by the Phillips Schools of Theology, and seven at large, irrespective of denominations. The number of trustees has since been increased to thirty, maintaining the same denominational ratio. Initially each denomination or participating institution contributed $20,000 to the ITC for every twenty-five students of its denomination, and $800 for each additional student over that number. Each denomination is responsible for instruction in its own history and polity. Each is also responsible for the housing of its unmarried students. Directors of the denominations on the campus and the president of the ITC sign the diplomas. Furthermore, each denomination provides counseling and financial aid for its students, with the ITC furnishing some aid for needy students. Excluding the denominational dormitories, their management, and the special denominational teaching, the ITC is under the management of the ITC Board of Trustees.

The campus at present is a $3 million establishment. Morris Brown is in the process of erecting a dormitory for AME students. The ITC endowment is $2,162,000, and a $3 million campaign is in process.

Bennett Hall, the Morehouse School of Religion dormitory, was made possible by contributions from churches of the National Progressive Baptist Convention, the General Missionary Baptist Convention of Georgia, the New Era Baptist Convention of Georgia, the Board of Education of the American Baptist Convention and Mr. and Mrs. John Nuveen of Chicago. Fully two-thirds of the money needed for the construction and furnishing of the Bennet Hall was given by the Nuveens. As the plaque at the entrance to the hall shows, the building was erected in memory of Mr. and Mrs. William Stiles Bennet by their daughter and son-in-law, Mr. and Mrs. John Nuveen. Mr. Bennet was a New York judge, lawyer, assemblyman, and congressman, and a member of the organizing group of the NAACP. The Nuveens dedicated the building in the spring of 1965.

Gammon was already accredited by the Southern Association of Theological Schools. Since the combination of the four institutions made the Center stronger than each institution standing alone, there was no difficulty in getting the Interdenominational Theological Center accredited by the American Association of Theological Schools. At the first meeting of the

Association after the ITC began its work, the Center was approved by the AATS. The Morehouse School of Religion, Turner Theological Seminary, and the Phillips School of Theology became accredited institutions by virtue of the strength of the whole. Thus, the Morehouse School of Religion is the only Negro Baptist Seminary that is accredited. If, however, one of these units should decide to go it alone and withdraw from the Center, that school would lose its accreditation.

There is another important factor about the ITC. Each of the four schools that constitute the ITC kept what it had. The four affiliated denominations made no financial contribution toward the establishment of ITC. Neither Baptist, Methodist, African Methodist Episcopal, nor Christian Methodist Episcopal contributed money for land, for ITC buildings or for endowment. The plant and endowment that Gammon had, Gammon kept. The other three institutions had less, but they kept that—so each institution entered the affiliation on the same basis, and this was good. The requirement that each denomination build its own residence hall was also sound. Each has a claim to something on the ITC campus that is uniquely its own.

The minds, hearts, and monies of many people went into the planning and the establishment of the ITC. But special mention must be made of the staff and trustees of the General Education Board and the Sealantic Fund, without whose initial gifts and subsequent contributions the ITC would not have been born. The committee of five who made the study and recommended that the Center be established deserve special commendation. Three members of this committee are still on the ITC Board and are rendering invaluable service: F. D. Patterson, E. C. Colwell, and Henry P. Van Dusen. The latter two have served as chairmen of the ITC Board. Van Dusen, who has helped greatly in fund raising for the Center, is the present chairman of the Board. The ITC is much stronger because the Phillips School of Theology joined the seminaries in Atlanta under the able and astute leadership of Bishop B. Julian Smith. Too much praise cannot be given to Dr. Harry V. Richardson, the Center's first president, without whose leadership the Center would not be what it is. Dr. Richardson retired, at his request, in the fall of 1968, leaving the ITC in the hands of his successor, Dr. Oswald Bronson. Since cooperation across denominational lines is the genius of the ITC, we must be grateful to Dr. Frank T. Wilson, chairman of Temporary Commission on Theological Education in the Southeast, under whose leadership the Theological Seminary of Johnson C. Smith Institution has become the fifth university to join the ITC complex, beginning in the academic year 1969-70. More recently the sixth school has joined the Center: The Charles Mason Theological Seminary. We hope the association will be permanent.

Fortunately, at the time of the merger of the four institutions, the Morehouse School of Religion as an integral part of ITC placed no financial burden upon Morehouse itself. The ITC took over the three of our School of Religion faculty members whose salaries did not exceed the $20,000 required of Morehouse for the first twenty-five Baptist students enrolled in ITC.

Having served as dean of the School of Religion at Howard University for six years, gaining accreditation for that school, I am very glad that I was privileged to play a small part in bringing the ITC into being and also to have been able to secure accreditation for the Morehouse School of Religion by the American Association of Theological Schools.

Chapter XVIII

The Church and Race

I believe that throughout my lifetime, the local white church has been society's most conservative and hypocritical institution in the area of White-Negro relations. Nor has the local black church a record of which to be proud. The states, schools, business enterprises, industries, theaters, recreation centers, hotels, restaurants, hospitals, trains, boats, waiting rooms, and filling stations have all played their ignominious roles in the tragedy of segregating the black man and discriminating against him; but at least none of these enterprises claims to have a divine mission on earth. The church boasts of its unique origin, maintaining that God, not man, is the source of its existence. The church alone calls itself the House of God, sharing this honor with no other American institution. The church is indeed sui generis.

The local white churches, the vast majority of them, have not lived up to their professed Christianity, because Christian fellowship across racial barriers is so inherent in the very nature of the church that to deny fellowship in God's House, on the basis of race or color, is a profanation of all that the church stands for. Secular organizations make no commitments, nor do they prate about brotherhood among men and a gospel of redemption and salvation. When the church maintains a segregated house, and simultaneously preaches the fatherhood of God and the brotherhood of man, then surely "hypocrisy" is the mildest term one can apply. "Whited sepulchre" comes to mind.

Although the local black church has never denied white people the privilege of entrance for worship in their churches, and has often inflated the white man's already bloated ego by giving him preferential seating, Negro church members would hardly welcome large numbers of white people to membership in their congregations. I believe this attitude is not based so much on race as it is on the desire of Negroes to maintain control of their churches. Then too, Negroes would hardly want to run the risk of being hurt or humiliated by whites who so often exhibit a superior air in their association with Negroes. The basic difference between the black and white churches is that the black church has never had a policy of racial exclusiveness. The white church has.

Leadership in the church is supposedly different from that in secular life. In earlier years, and even today, the minister was said to be specially "called of God" to do His work, to preach His truth. Early in my life I became aware of the dichotomy in the preaching and the practice of the church leadership. Now and then the Reverend James F. Marshall, my pastor, would invite white ministers to preach at Mount Zion, especially the Methodist minister, the Reverend Pierce Kinard. My father, though illiterate, was never impressed with the Reverend Kinard's message. He once remarked about the Reverend Kinard's emphasis on living right in order to be assured of God's blessings and of eternal salvation, while at the same time Negroes were being cheated, beaten, and lynched throughout South Carolina. As young as I was, I got the message. The few Negroes who attended the Reverend Kinard's tent meetings were thoroughly segregated. Members of my family never attended because they were Methodist meetings for whites, and, frankly, we were actually afraid to attend a white church.

The gospel in Negro and white churches alike was definitely otherworld-oriented and never even hinted at bringing whites and blacks of the county closer together for the improvement of social and economic conditions. After all, if the "righteous" were to be rewarded in heaven, where there would be no more night, no sickness, no death, where the angels had wings and the streets were paved with gold, it mattered little that black people were exploited and mistreated here on earth! The Negro's song, "Take All the World and Give Me Jesus," was never considered seriously by the white man, even though he may have believed in heaven. He had as much of Jesus as the Negro—and the world besides!

My early unhappy racial experiences explain my cynicism about the sincerity of many white ministers. I have never cared to listen to any minister who would deny fellowship on a racial basis. More than once I have turned off the radio or the television rather than listen to the preaching of a man known to advocate a segregated church. I tuned out Billy Graham as long as he held revivals under segregated conditions. When he came to Atlanta early in his career, the Council of Presidents of the Atlanta University Center was asked to provide a segregated meeting for the students and faculties of the Center. Needless to say, we refused, and we felt it was an insult to us to be asked to do this. I listen to Billy Graham now with appreciation of what he says and the hope that he is a sincere convert of his own teaching. Segregation in the House of God has been a great strain on my religion.

In the process of writing this book, I read widely the most reputable newspapers of the South published between 1880 and 1910. I was anxious to find out what they had to say about lynching, the most vicious evil of my early years, and what their attitude was toward the Negro. I do not recall ever having seen a single article by a minister, a group of ministers, or by anyone speaking in the name of the church and Christianity that condemned the horrible crime of lynching. During this time, the church was truly both in the world and of the world. Earlier in this book [also see Appendix A], I have related in detail examples of the horrifying lynchings which took place in Phoenix, South Carolina, in the county of my birth. The Phoenix Riot, with its accompanying lynchings, is one of the most hideous records in the history of this country. One would think that somewhere, in at least one of the South Carolina newspapers, the voice of the church would have been heard speaking out for justice and stamping its disapproval upon such savagery. I found no record of a church voice raised in protest. The church was so much a part of the system that lynching was accepted as part of the Southern way of life just as casually as was segregation. Ironically enough, when the Southern people did begin to cry out against lynching, it was not the voice of organized southern and northern ministers but of southern white women under the leadership of the Commission on Interracial Cooperation. The Southern Association of Women for the Prevention of Lynching was organized in Atlanta in 1930, under the leadership of Jessie Daniel Ames, and did much to denigrate lynching in the South. Time has not done much to change the silence of the local church in the midst of racial ills.

The local white church has always been conservative when it comes to taking a stand on social issues, especially so if the issue involves black people. Local black churches have been far more prophetic than the local white churches. So-called radical movements, such as the National Association for the Advancement of Colored People, have always had access to black churches. The Southern Christian Leadership Conference, under the leadership of Martin Luther King, Jr., and, since 1968, under Ralph David Abernathy, and the National Conference of Black Churchmen have involved the local Negro churches in programs designed to bring about social and economic justice for black people. But North and South, Negro and white churches remain highly segregated. A thoroughly desegregated church, embracing a representative number of blacks and whites, is a *rara avis* in the United States.

In the area of race, local churches have followed, not led. When segregation in the public schools was declared unconstitutional on May 17, 1954, one would have expected the local churches to urge compliance on moral and religious grounds. But for too long a time the local white ministers in Atlanta and in other Southern cities were silent, and when they did speak it was as a group. For the most part, the individual pastor was afraid to urge compliance, afraid to stand alone. He wanted protection from the group as well as the benefit of the impact that the group might make if he were to speak out.

The local Atlanta white ministers certainly did not lead in a program to abolish segregation in the public schools. Indeed, it can hardly be said that they even followed. It was three and a half years after the May 17, 1954, decision of the Supreme Court before some eighty white ministers in Atlanta broke their silence on the Court's decision. It is disgraceful that it took the Atlanta white ministers forty-two months to come out with a statement on segregation in the public schools, and it is even more shameful that when they did speak it was only as individuals, for they did not dare speak for their congregations. They felt that they had to say they were opposed to intermarriage and against the amalgamation of the races. They expressed belief in "preserving the integrity of both races through the free choice of both." It is utterly fantastic for white ministers to speak for white men against the amalgamation of the races. The white man's activities in this area of behavior are a matter of history the world around. The black race in America has been amalgamated for centuries. I suppose these men of the cloth felt compelled to say such things to please the white public.

Speaking three and a half years after the 1954 decision outlawing segregation in the public schools, the white ministers of Atlanta issued a statement both weak and inconclusive. They said, in part:

> As Americans and as Christians we have an obligation to obey the law. This does not mean that all loyal citizens need approve the 1954 decision of the Supreme Court with reference to segregation in the public schools. Those who feel that this decision was in error have every right to work for an alteration in the decree, either through a further change in the Supreme Court's interpretation of the law, or through an amendment to the Constitution of the United States. It does mean that we have no right to defy the

constituted authority in the government of our nation. Assuredly also it means that resorts to violence and to economic reprisals as a means to avoid the granting of legal rights to other citizens are never justified.

If I had been a segregationist, I could have freely signed this document.

A year later 312 Atlanta ministers spoke somewhat more pointedly to the issue at hand. This group was speaking in the interest of preserving the public schools. These ministers were also cautious. They were against massive integration and sincerely opposed to the amalgamation of the races. They pleaded for time where desegregation of schools was most difficult and expressed the hope that state and local authorities would be allowed to do the job when good faith in compliance had been shown. This group, too, urged law and order, and said that those who were dissatisfied with the decision should seek legal ways to change it. They insisted, however, that closing the public schools would be a tragedy.

All in all, their November, 1958, manifesto was a plea for gradualism. It called for intelligent discussion of the issues of integration, asked that creative thought be given to preserving the public schools, and advocated a citizens' committee to preserve harmony within the community. It was clearly not a manifesto for integration but rather one for law and Christian duty. And its sponsors did what "Christian" and "religious" people usually do when they lack the will to act: They called on God. They said, "Man cannot will himself to do this. The Christian, or Jew, can do this only with the help of God." They called for prayer and the strength to do it. It is indeed strange that when man does evil, he has the will, but when he faces a moral crisis and needs to do what is right, he calls on God to give him the strength to do it.

The one white minister who did speak on his own, Dr. Roy D. McClain, of Atlanta's First Baptist Church, preached a sermon that was absolutely safe, and this was two years after the May 17 decision. Any way one read his statement, it was clear that he was opposed to the decision of the Supreme Court outlawing segregation in the public schools. It was distinctly more pro-segregation than pro-integration.

Dr. McClain is an eloquent and convincing speaker. When in early summer, 1956, he spoke about the May 17 decision, his words were as usual carefully chosen and beautifully uttered. Both the Atlanta *Constitution* and the Atlanta *Journal*, in their issues of June 25, 1956, quoted heavily from Doctor McClain's pro-segregation sermon. The *Constitution* quoted Dr. McClain as follows: "... the last twenty-four months have engendered more strife and hatred than the last decade of normal progress." The Atlanta *Journal* quoted Dr. McClain thus: "Righteousness cannot be legislated any more than education can be; one cannot be forced into the acquisition of facts; instead he can be encouraged, shown and nurtured." He said that coexistence is possible without cohabitation, but that "this does not mean, however, that there is a first and second class citizenry. Such could never be justified in democracy, Christianity, or anything." Evidently Dr. McClaim had forgotten history. Negroes and whites had co-existed in this country for three and a half centuries, and a glance at any Negro audience testifies that there has been considerable cohabitation.

Organized church bodies, unlike the local churches, did support the Supreme Court's 1954 decision. Several denominations spoke out: for example, the Southern Baptist Convention, the Southern Presbyterians, the North Georgia Methodist Conference, and the Council of Church Women from fifteen Southern states.

However, even the pronouncements of these Southern church bodies made no real impact on the local churches. They continued their segregated ways. Dr. Martin Luther King, Sr., tells of his experience in a local Atlanta church:

> I had heard of Roy McClain's ability as a preacher, so, shortly after he came to First Baptist Church on Peacthree, I decided to go hear him preach. I asked Mrs. Crawford, one of the trustees of Ebenezer, since deceased, and Mrs. Hudson if they would like to ride out with me . . . for Sunday morning worship.
>
> We went early . . . and arrived before Sunday School was out. I parked and we went in the front door into the sanctuary. We were met at the door very cordially, and we went in and seated ourselves about two seats down on the righthand side, with me taking the aisle seat. We had been given bulletins of the order of worship at the door. A white woman came in, bowed to us, smiled, and seated herself alongside the two ladies who were with me.
>
> We sat for about twenty minutes, and then I noticed two or three people near the podium deep in a discussion. Finally, one of them came back and said to me, "You folks can worship down in our chapel." I told him we were quite all right where we were, and he went away muttering to himself. Another came, much rougher talking than the first, and said, "Now you folks know we have a place where you can worship down in our chapel. You will have to go down there and you will have to go *now.*"
>
> I said to my companions, well, I guess we'll just go back. The man kept saying to me, in a very ugly mood, "Well, are you going? Are you going?" Mrs. Crawford said, "We didn't come here to cause any trouble." The man

> said, "Well, you are going away somewhere!" and grabbed me by the arm. "You are just here to make trouble, that's all." I told him he was mistaken, and he shoved me, and we left.

The full story of the Atlanta experiences of the Reverend Ashton Jones is told in his book *After Prison What?* (Published privately by Reverend Jones in 1969: LaVista, California). In an editorial on June 9, 1965, the *Christian Century* commented:

> The Reverend Ashton Jones, sentenced to 18 months in jail for disturbing public worship at the First Baptist Church of Atlanta, Georgia, in 1963, has now been pardoned and released from prison by the Georgia State Department of Pardons and Paroles, after serving more than eight months of the sentence. The "crime" for which the nearly 70-year-old minister paid his heavy penalty was his effort to integrate public worship at the all-white First Baptist Church in June, 1963, by attempting to enter the sanctuary of the church in the company of a Negro student. Ashton Jones was guilty of something more than disturbing public worship; he disturbed in Atlanta a slumbering Christian conscience.

Even those responsible for his conviction were not able to get Ashton Jones out of prison until he had served eight hard months. Roy O. McClain, the pastor, appealed to the State Board of Pardons and Paroles for clemency for Jones. Jones had been convicted on a Georgia statute dating back to 1792 and revised in 1866. When kneel-in demonstrations started, the Board of Deacons of the First Baptist Church voted 58 to 2 not to allow Negroes to enter the sanctuary.

Paradoxical as it is, churches that believe in and practice segregation have been sending missionaries to Africa and Asia for years to convert the "heathens" to Christianity. In Chapter XI I have related my experiences with a few of these missionaries. I heard Africans talk about this dichotomy when I was in Liberia, Ghana, and Ethiopia. African students at Morehouse during my presidency remarked about the way missionaries from America segregated Negroes in the United States and sought to save the souls of black Africans in Africa. Many black people in this country believe that some white missionaries go to foreign lands to evangelize colored people in order to atone for the way in which black people are brutalized here in the United States.

Though persuaded to Christianity by Southern missionaries in Africa, the converted Africans would hardly be welcomed to fellowship and membership in the very local Southern churches that helped to foster the foreign missionary enterprises. The experiences of Sam Oni from Ghana, with the Tattnall Square Baptist Church in Macon, Georgia, are convincing proof of this assertion. Oni made his way to Mercer University, also in Macon, Georgia, upon the advice of a Southern Baptist missionary, an alumnus of Mercer University. Sam Oni succeeded in breaking down the color bar at Mercer, which at that time was 133 years old; but the officers of Tattnall Square Baptist Church advised their ministers to get the message to Oni that he would not be welcome at the church. He was accepted at the Vineville Baptist Church after the pastor of that church convinced the officers and the congregation that Oni was not a *Georgia* Negro—he was different from an *American* Negro! He was African and had been converted to Christ through their own Southern Baptist missionaries in far away Ghana. It has been true ever since Emancipation that any foreigner is better treated than are Negroes in the United States. Even German prisoners rode unsegregated in this country during two world wars, and Asians on the whole receive better treatment in this nation than black Americans. Now a black Ghanian was accepted into Mercer University and the Vineville Baptist Church—forbidden territory for a Negro American!

But Sam Oni could not break the color bar at Tattnall Square Baptist Church. In the summer of 1966, the Tattnall Church voted not to seat Negroes at its worship services. Two Negroes did worship there in June and were allowed to worship one time in peace, but the occurrence almost split the church asunder. In July the church voted 289 to 109 to close its doors to Negroes. Sam Oni was in California when he heard about this decision and the furor which precipitated it, and he felt compelled to try to become affiliated with Tattnall Square Baptist Church during his senior year. He wanted to tell the "Christians" at Tattnall how their policy of segregation was hampering their missionary work in Africa. Oni attempted to worship there that fall. This experience is best told by Dr. Thomas J. Holmes, pastor of Tattnall, author of the book *Ashes for Breakfast* (Judson Press, Valley Forge, Pa.: 1969):

> The young foreign student, neatly dressed, knowing impeccable English, fluent French, and three tribal languages, approached the red brick church on the corner of the Christian university. There he was stopped rudely by the ushers of the segregated congregation. They had been instructed to turn all Negroes away, and to these Georgia middle-class white men Sam Oni was just another "nigger." They blocked his way. He asked for the privilege of talking to the deacons or reasoning with them, but the

ushers wanted no part of Sam Oni. In their view he had been a troublemaker ever since he had integrated the university and brought integration pressures on the campus church.

When Oni politely insisted that he be admitted, he was seized by two deacons of the church. One applied a headlock on him, and the other dragged him down the steps. Oni kept his cool and did not fight back. He endeavored to reason with his adversaries from the sidewalk.

"Go to the church where you are a member, or some other church," a deacon ordered.

"No," said Oni.

Meanwhile the chairman of the deacons had called the police, who were conveniently nearby with a patrol car. Two policemen appeared in their summer gray uniforms, pistols on their belts, and led the African student to their car. They placed him inside and kept him there until he agreed to leave quietly—while the people inside the church sang the hymn by Frank Mason North:

Where cross the crowded ways of life,
Where sound the cries of race and clan,
Above the noise of selfish strife,
We hear Thy voice, O Son of Man!

Sam Oni tried once more in October, and once more he was denied. But this time he preached a sermon at the front of the church steps and his message was carried to the nation on television. Before he preached, he tried to enter. A plainclothes policeman, an off-duty deacon, and an inactive member of the church blocked him. On the very steps of the church, Oni told the three men, "Do you not see the inconsistency of what you are doing? You send missionaries to my land to tell me about the love of God, and then when I come to your land I do not find this same love in your hearts. Does God not love in the same way here? Do you not care if my people go to hell?"*

The pastor, the assistant pastor, and the minister of music of Tattnall Square Baptist Church wanted the church to be Christian and open its doors to Negroes. This was more than the majority of members at Tattnall could take, and in September the three ministers were ousted by a vote of 250 to 189. Later, in collaboration with Gainer E. Bryan, Jr., Pastor Holmes wrote his graphic and moving book from which I have quoted, above, *Ashes for Breakfast.*

On the local scene, prejudice looms largest in housing. As long as white

*(*Ashes for Breakfast*, p. 17.)

and black people cannot live in proximity, as long as one Negro moving into an area can chase out a thousand white families, and two Negroes can put ten thousand whites to flight, it is going to be very difficult to have desegregated schools and churches. It is my candid belief that the vast majority of white people do not wish to live next door to a black man, nor in the same block with him; nor do they want Negroes in large numbers in their churches. The professions of the Negroes and their standing in the community make no difference. If they are black, they are not welcome. And very little has been done to change this pattern of blind prejudice, as witness the following experiences of SWAP.

As Negroes began to move into southwest Atlanta, there was an honest effort on the part of SWAP (Southwest Association for Progress) to stabilize the community so that we could demonstrate that it is possible to have a successfully integrated neighborhood. We will hardly succeed. As black people moved in, the white people moved out. The West Manor Baptist Church, for example, had a fine plant and a fine minister. Before Negroes moved in, the membership of this beautiful, modern church was about 800. As blacks moved in, the white exodus was so rapid that within a few years the membership was reduced to approximately 200, thus placing such a heavy financial strain on the few who remained in the area or who remained loyal by commuting even after they moved, that the minister was forced to give up in defeat. The $750,000 plant was sold to the Free For All Baptist Church, a Negro congregation, for the unpaid balance, reported to be around $300,000, or a loss to the white congregation of about $450,000. Just two blocks away, the Southwest Christian Church sold its plant to a black church, the Trinity AME, in December, 1969, whose pastor, Reverend P. W. Williams, told me it was a good buy. Other churches in the area are sitting on the anxious seat. No price is too high for white Christians to pay to get away from black Christians!

According to an article in the Atlanta *Constitution* in October, 1969, the Southwest High School, in the SWAP area, formerly all white, had become about 96 percent Negro; and West Manor Elementary School, in the same area, also formerly all white, had only ten white students among its enrollment of 500. There are nineteen residences in my block. The first black man moved into the area in the fall of 1966. There are now sixteen Negro families and three white families in my block. One black family has just built there, making twenty families. The Negroes in my block break down in this way occupationally: public school teachers, college professors, ministers, a dental technician, a professional baseball player, a member of the family that owns the Atlanta *Daily World*, and a retired college president.

This job analysis, I believe, would be typical of the Negroes moving into the Southwest area. The whites who previously occupied the area, but have since run away, were of comparable, perhaps somewhat lower, economic identification. Nevertheless, this flight pattern is happening in Atlanta, perhaps the most enlightened city in the South—certainly among the most enlightened in the nation. The local church members are a part of the exodus, and the white ministers stand helpless, perplexed, not knowing what to do. It is more than probable that had the minister at West Manor Baptist Church and the one at the Christian Church gone out to recruit Negroes to replace their fleeing white members, the remaining white members would have fired them and then would have run even faster.

Although my career has been in education for thirty-four years and in research and social work for six years, I have been fortunate in having extensive contacts—local, national, and worldwide—with the church and the Young Men's Christian Association. National and world gatherings have been more Christian in character than have local ones, in that fellowship has never been denied. Even when national bodies have been all too cautious, in an effort to placate those coming from segregated sections of the country or the world, and those who are dyed-in-the-wool segregationists, fellowship across racial barriers in assembly and worship has always obtained. This has been true in the score or more national and world gatherings in which I have been a participant. However, it must be remembered that national and world gatherings are not empowered to pass resolutions which are binding on local bodies, and so are not subject to the same pressures. Nor do I mean to imply that race has not been a problem in national and world church bodies.

For the race problem is ubiquitous; and I have never been able to escape it. It came up in every national and world Christian conference I ever attended. It is ever present. One often hears that Negroes never forget the race problem, that they talk about it all the time. This is equally true of white people. In church and state alike, the black man has been continually in the white man's mind. One need only read anti-Negro newspapers reaching back a hundred years, and anti-Negro books written over the decades, or study the laws the various states and the federal government have enacted against the Negro to find that the black man has dominated the white man's thinking since the first Africans landed here in 1619. The Negro, I am convinced, is the white man's obsession.

The black-white relationship has been so crucial that black and white alike are inclined to attach great significance to any slight breakthrough a black man may make in this relationship. Thus it was national news when the Federal Council of Churches of Christ in America elected me its vice-president in Pittsburgh, Pennsylvania, in 1944. It was national news because it was the first time that the Federal Council, organized in 1912, had chosen a black man to serve in the second spot of the Council. The president of the Federal Council at that time was Bishop G. Bromley Oxnam of the Methodist Church. The Negro and the white press headlined my election, and *Time* magazine called me a "religious liberal," citing as proof that though I was a Baptist I had never tried to convert my Methodist wife to the Baptist faith!

I became widely known in church circles, and was invited to speak to white and black groups all over the nation, in state and city federations of churches—even in church councils in the South, especially in Virginia and North Carolina, and in the Baptist Convention of Florida. I was not invited to the local white churches, for few such churches in the South, in the mid-1940's, would have dared invite a black man to preach to them. I doubt that a single one would have had the temerity. Even to this day, excluding Glenn Memorial on Emory University's campus, only two white churches in Atlanta and vicinity have ever invited me to speak to their congregations —Trinity Presbyterian Church in Atlanta and Saint Paul United Methodist Church in Marietta. And Atlanta has been my home for thirty years.

Two experiences which happened during my two years as vice-president of the Federal Council are worth relating here.

First, the Council held a special meeting in Columbus, Ohio, March 5-7, 1946. President Truman was a guest speaker. Winston Churchill was traveling on the presidential train with Truman. Mr. Churchill chose to remain on the train while the President spoke to the delegates of the Federal Council. The officers of the Council thought it would be a good gesture if we went down to the train to greet Winston Churchill, and we did. He showed no particular enthusiasm for our visit, and I thought he received us rather coldly. Consequently, I felt no particular enthusiasm for nor was I impressed by this great man.

Though vice-president of the Council, I evidently posed a problem to some of the Council leadership. Where was I to sit—on the platform with the President of the United States or in a special seat up front in the audience? I have always wondered whether there would have been any debate if the vice-president of the Council had been white. As the second officer in the Council, I should have helped decide who would sit on the rostrum. The decision was made for me to sit in the front row in the audience. Several rows in front were being left for dignataries and secret service men. I was advised to take my seat in the front row before the presidential party came in and before other guests had taken the reserved seats.

Several persons came to request me to move, saying that the place where I was sitting was reserved for special people. I didn't move. Finally Earl F. Adams, secretary of the Protestant Council of New York, came to me and said, "Why are you sitting here? As vice-president of the Council, you belong on the rostrum with the President of the United States." He said, "Wait, I'll fix it." Another chair was placed on the rostrum and, when the President came in, I was escorted to the rostrum. Evidently I had presented a problem which Earl Adams solved. People in the audience had wondered why I didn't move as requested. When I went to the rostrum, the mystery seemed solved. They thought it was planned from the beginning that I would sit on the rostrum. Not so.

Secondly, at the same Conference, the Federal Council took a giant step. It issued an official document stating in forceful language that it was opposed to segregation in any form and that the Council from that moment on would work to eliminate it. This was, I believe, the first time the Federal Council had made such a declaration, and so was assuming national leadership among church bodies. It was significant, too, that Will W. Alexander, who had been head of the Commission on Interracial Cooperation until the new organization, the Southern Regional Council, was organized, was chairman of the seminar on race. The Commission on Interracial Cooperation never did declare itself against the segregated system. The seminar on race of the Federal Council, chaired by Alexander, raised its voice in opposition to segregation in every area of life. I think it important to quote one paragraph of a document from the seminar on church and race of which I was a member:

> The Federal Council of the Churches of Christ in America hereby renounces the pattern of segregation in race relations as unnecessary and undesirable and a violation of the gospel of love and human brotherhood. Having taken this action, the Federal Council requests its constituent communion to do likewise. As proof of their sincerity in this renunciation, they will work for a non-segregated church and a non-segregated society.

I was glad to see Will Alexander move to this position. He fought for this statement vigorously, and I am mighty glad that I was a member of the seminar that assisted in its formulation. The Federal Council, and now the National Council, never retreated from this position. The National Council has gone beyond mere pronouncements to participation in the arena where the action is. It has taken a leading role in such action projects as: The Delta Ministry; The Ghetto Investment Program; the Crisis in the Nation Program; and The Mississippi Summer Project on Voter Registration. It has also been active in the field of legislation, has participated in Project Equality, and given encouragement to the National Urban Coalition.

Two years after my term as vice-president of the Federal Council of Churches of Christ in America expired, I was a participant in the organization of the World Council of Churches in Amsterdam, Holland, in 1948. Unfortunately, the Second World War had made it necessary to delay the establishment of this great body. The seed of ecumenism, however, had been germinating for a long time. The historic moment came the second day of the Assembly, August 23, 1948, when delegates from 750 communions and 43 countries voted unanimously to organize the World Council of Churches. It was a great moment, and the delegates and visitors cheered long and lustily.

The United States was so heavily segregated in 1948 that I was always glad to get a breath of fresh air somewhere in Europe. Since the people in the Assembly came from the ends of the earth, there could not possibly be any segregation or discrimination. All hotels, restaurants, streetcars, churches, and government organizations were opened to everybody, a thing unheared of in most sections of the United States. One would have to be in an Assembly of the World Church really to know what Christian fellowship is. Segregated and discriminated against all my life, I believe that I can sense any form of discrimination instinctively. I found none in Amsterdam. At a communion service, I noted a Methodist sitting next to a Baptist, an Anglican sitting next to a Presbyterian, a Chinese communing beside a Japanese, an American white man seated with an American Negro, and an African communing with a Dutchman. As I sat there in the World Church, my mind reverted sadly to the United States, where local churches were the most segregated bodies in our country.

The same catholicity obtained in social affairs. The reception given by Her Majesty's government and the one given by the burgomaster and the aldermen of the City of Amsterdam were lovely, representing all shades and colors, ranging from the pure black to the lightest of the light. One of the persons to introduce the attendants to the burgomaster was an African delegate.

Despite the fact that this delegation of 450 people was mainly ecumenical, designed to bring about the unity of the non-Catholic churches, the race problem is so universal that it has to be considered wherever people meet. Thus in several sections, race prejudice and discrimination were condemned. Section I of the Assembly's "The Universal Church in God's Design" said: "Even where there are no differences of theology, language, or liturgy, there exist churches segregated by race and color, a scandal within the Body of Christ." From Section III, dealing with "Disorder of Society," came these words: "If the church can overcome the national and social barriers which now divide it, it can help society to overcome those barriers. This is especially clear in the case of racial barriers. It is here that the church has failed most lamentably—it knows that it must call society away from racial prejudice and from the practice of discrimination and segregation based on color and race as denials of justice and human dignity, but it cannot say a convincing word to society unless it takes steps to eliminate these from the Christian community because they contradict all that it believes about God's love for all his children."

When participating in a World Church gathering, black people often need to see to it that the church takes a strong position on race, and also that Negroes are not left out when offices and positions are being voted on. In world gatherings, as elsewhere, the Negro is likely to be the forgotten man. Several times in plenary sessions at Amsterdam, I or some other black man had to see to it that a section dealing with race was strengthened. On this point, the Pittsburgh *Courier* reported my own stand as follows:

> Dr. Benjamin E. Mays, president of Morehouse College and *Courier* columnist, electrified the World Council of Churches here last week when he vigorously proposed amending a resolution involving the Universal Church to include a specific attitude on the racial situation within the Church proper. His amendment was passed. Noting that the report on *The Universal Church in God's Design* covered the racial aspect throughout the world in just ten words, Dr. Mays took the floor of the assembly and proposed the following amendment:
>
> > In addition to differences in theology which divide the Universal Church, it is further divided into racial churches based entirely on race and color. It is to be regretted that this division is so deeply established that even where there is unity in theology, creed, ritual,

> liturgy and language, we find the body of Christ divided on grounds of race and color. This condition must be strongly condemned by the World Council of Churches and it should urge the churches to eliminate this condition within its fellowship.

There were six of us as delegates representing the National Baptist Convention, Incorporated. On discovering that a central committee of ninety persons was to be the official voice of the World Council between Assemblies (a five-year interval), we knew that the National Baptist Convention, Incorporated, despite its four million members, would not be represented unless we pushed for membership.

So I called our delegation together and we worked out a strategy. Fortunately, the chairman of the nominating group saw the reasonableness of our attitude and I and another American Negro were chosen. From 1948 to 1954, when the Second Assembly of the World Council of Churches met in Evanston at Northwestern University, I represented the Central Committee in Rolle, Switzerland; Chichester, England; Toronto, Canada; and Lucknow, India.

I have never been to South Africa, but everyone I know who has been there tells me that the race problem in South Africa is worse than anything in the most prejudiced sections of the southern United States—in fact, it is the worst in the world. Some people with whom I have talked believe that white South Africa would kill off the Bantus and "Coloured" people before they would abolish apartheid and grant equality.

I could never doubt what I heard about South Africa after working with representatives of the Dutch Reformed Church in world conferences. More than once it was necessary for me to take a position opposite to that espoused by Dr. Ben J. Marais of the Dutch Reformed Church in the Transvaal. Doctor Marais and I had stiff debates on race on the floor of the Third Meeting of the Central Committee of the World Council of Churches, which met at the University of Toronto, Canada, in July, 1950.

Dr. Ben J. Marais is a very enlightened man. He agonizes over the racial situation in South Africa. He does not try to justify segregation or apartheid on Biblical or Christian grounds, as he explains eloquently in his book *COLOUR: Unsolved Problem of the West* (Howard B. Timmons, Capetown, 1952). But Dr. Marais did believe in 1950, as well as in 1954 when we last met in Evanston, Illinois, that apartheid was a practical necessity in his country.

From this position, he defended apartheid in church and state in South Africa. Doctor Marais supported the idea that the Central Committee should send an all-white delegation to South Africa to help seek a solution to the racial problem there, arguing that an interracial study group would be unacceptable to the Dutch Reformed Church and to South Africa generally. He spoke ably for an all-white committee to visit the churches there. The situation in South Africa obviously was extremely bad if an honest man like Marais felt he had to take that position.

I respected Marais' position and that of others who supported him, but it was absolutely mandatory that I oppose him. I felt that I was in a better position to do so than any white delegate. I knew only too well what racial discrimination and segregation meant, and so I knew that the World Council of Churches could not afford to be a party to racism or apartheid in South Africa. Our debate attracted wide attention in the press in the United States and Canada. The Buffalo *Evening News* of July 15, 1950, carried part of the extemporaneous speech I delivered in a plenary session on the need to send a truly ecumenical, interracial delegation to South Africa.

> "I wish that I might do the impossible," said Dr. Mays. "I wish that I might speak for the 8,000,000 Bantus, who never have an opportunity to speak for themselves in Africa, who never have an opportunity to speak for themselves anywhere in the world.
>
> "Since 1937, in seven world conferences, I have heard the story of South Africa . . . It's the same old story. The only new element today is apartheid (segregation). They tell us: 'It's a difficult situation; outsiders cannot understand it. Stay out, leave us alone; anything you say except praise will make the situation worse.'
>
> "But the argument always comes from a representative of the Dutch Reformed Church or someone in sympathy with that point of view. I would like to see a Christian Bantu come here sometime and present his own point of view.
>
> "To say that apartheid is not segregation but separate development—to say that it is for the good of all—is almost blasphemy. To say that it is in the interest of the Bantu or the black man is a terrible thing to say. Why not let us be frank and say that apartheid is a system that has been worked out because two million Europeans feel that if they do not have apartheid they will be swallowed.
>
> "I was disturbed when Dr. Marais said that among all the political leaders, only the Communists oppose apartheid.
>
> "It is a sad situation. For if all the churches are on one side, the side of apartheid, and only the rank Communists are on the other side, then you are laying the foundations of Communism. You are setting group against group, race against race.

"You do not solve problems by drifting backwards; you solve them by tearing down barriers so that you can get at them.

"It disturbed me that the outstanding ecumenical body of Christendom should even raise this question. What kind of delegation could the World Council of Churches send except an ecumenical delegation?

"I think the Central Committee is a little too timid. I don't believe the situation in South Africa will grow worse if this committee speaks a word of protest in the name of God. I do not believe it can grow much worse unless an effort is made to do as Hitler did in Germany—to kill off the Bantus.

"It is for us to speak what we believe to be the voice of God and leave the consequences to God.

"I make no apologies for the racial situation in the United States; God knows it's bad enough. But we can honestly say that it is not getting worse, as it is in South Africa."

During the discussion, I had large support for a multiracial delegation. Only a minority of the members of the Central Committee would have voted to send an all-white committee to study the race problem in the churches of South Africa. A multiracial delegation was voted, with Dr. Marais casting his ballot in favor of the resolution. However, it turned out to be fruitless after all, because the interracial committee was to go only after consulting with the Christian Council of South Africa and its member churches. And that meant death to the idea of a black-white delegation being sent to visit the churches of South Africa.

Sadie, her sister Emma C. W. Gray, and I drove from Toronto to Cleveland, Ohio, to attend the Eighth Baptist World Congress which met in 1950. As we drove from Toronto to Cleveland, we did not expect to find any kind of discrimination. We were wholly unprepared for being refused accommodations at a motel in Niagara Falls, Canada. We had certainly not expected to encounter discrimination in Canada. Nothing we said moved the proprietor. We were black, and he didn't take our kind. We finally found a motel that housed us for the night.

This experience was grist for my mill. I was going to the Eighth Congress of the World Baptist Alliance, where representatives came from forty-eight nations and some fifty thousand people were in attendance. I had two important assignments in the Congress: I chaired the Commission on Social Justice; and was to give a major address on the subject "Christian Light on Human Relationships." The experience at the motel in Niagara apparently helped me in my seminar and in my address. My seminar got through a resolution calling upon all Baptists and affiliated organizations to use their influence to have discriminatory laws repealed and other laws enacted to safeguard the rights of oppressed racial groups. Our resolution further asked each Baptist to examine his own soul with a view toward freeing himself of racial and cultural prejudices and embodying in his own person the mind and spirit of Christ in all human relations.

My seminar subject, "Social Justice," was closely related to my speech. I have always tried to take an objective view of responses to my speeches, knowing perfectly and sadly well that such responses may be largely emotional outbursts and nothing more lasting. When I finished my address in Cleveland, the people in the huge auditorium sprang to their feet and applauded long and loud. As good as this made me feel, I knew that nothing would really change as a result of that address. I knew that local churches would remain segregated, that discriminatory laws would remain on the statute books, that, as I drove from Cleveland home to Morehouse, I would meet the discrimination I had always met in hotels and restaurants, and that national and world bodies would go on passing resolutions, and that things would go on as before. But, like the Hebrew prophets, one must make his witness even though we do not repent.

The Central Committee meetings in Rolle, Switzerland, in 1951, and in Lucknow, India, in 1952 and 1953, moved along about like other world gatherings. There was no segregation and no discrimination based on racial and ethnic origins. My great experience in Lucknow came when reporters from all over India questioned me for ninety minutes, not quite believing me when I gave evidence that Negro-white relations were better at that time in the United States than they had been when I was in India in 1937.

Back home again we had to answer the question: Where in the United States could we meet and be certain that Negroes and other dark people would not be humiliated and embarrassed in hotels, motels, and restaurants? We wanted to meet on some campus where facilities were adequate and space ample. Bishop G. Bromley Oxnam, one of the six vice-presidents of the World Council, and a leader of note in the movement, was anxious to have the assembly on a Methodist university campus. We examined the situation at Duke University in Durham, North Carolina. The university was satisfactory, but as no guarantee could be given that there would be no discrimination in Durham, Duke was out. Some Eastern campuses were ruled out for lack of space for all the activities of the Second Assembly. Bishop Oxnam was threatening to use his power to take the Assembly back to Europe. Some of us protested. Finally Northwestern University, in Evanston, Illinois, was chosen as the place for the Second Assembly of the World Council of Churches, August 14-31, 1954.

As in Toronto, the question of race received more publicity at Evanston than any other topic. The seminar on Intergroup Relations, of which I was a member, was in essence a seminar on race prejudice, segregation, and discrimination. W. E. B. DuBois was prophetic in 1903 when he wrote, in *The Souls of Black Folks,* "The problem of the twentieth century is the problem of the color line." Here, as in Toronto, Dr. Ben J. Marais, of the Dutch Reformed Church in the Transvaal of South Africa, and I were on opposite sides of the same question—race. My position and Marais' had not changed since our debate in Toronto four years earlier. My knowledge of the Bible, theology, and church history, plus my understanding of what leading modern scientists have to say about race, make it impossible ever to change my position that segregation in the church is immoral. Dr. Marais' position that segregation in South Africa is a practical necessity, though he personally opposed segregation, could not be changed either. Marais argued in his address, immediately before mine, that segregation in the church can be justified only on the ground that "the ultimate goal may be missed if we proceed over-hastily."

My address, "The Church Amidst Ethnic and Racial Tension," was, in my view, a moderate expression. However, many conservatives who heard sections of it quoted on radio, or who read excerpts from it in the press reports, thought it was a radical speech. As a result, I received more vilifying letters on account of that speech than of any I have delivered in my forty years of public life. In it I pointed out that, from Jerusalem in 1928, Oxford and Edinburgh in 1937, Madras in 1938, Amsterdam in 1948, London in 1950, and Lucknow in 1952-1953, every world conference had condemned segregation in the church, and yet it is still rampant in God's House. I made clear that there is nothing in the Old and New Testaments, nothing in Christian theology, nothing in church history of either the early church or of the Middle Ages that would justify segregation in the church. I quoted modern scientists to show that there is no basis to justify consigning a man to a segregated, inferior role in the church or anywhere else in society. I told the Assembly at Evanston that modern racial segregation is "tantamount to penalizing one for being what God made him and tantamount to saying to God, "You made a mistake, God, when you made people of different races and colors."

My address was an attempt to indicate that the only basis the church has for its segregated policy is the wickedness of church people themselves. During the speech the audience interrupted me ten times with applause, then stood and applauded me for several minutes at the end. And yet it was this speech (the full text appears in Appendix B) that provoked the ire of a goodly number of people. Here are two of the letters I received. The first was from Tennessee.

> Kingsport, Tennessee
>
> You dirty black *nigger* you will never change the minds of the white people. Each time you open your big black mouth more white people hate you and all the rest of the niggers. If you do not like it down here in the south go north or where you came from Africa.

Another letter from Cleveland, Ohio, began as follows:

> Dear Ben
>
> You sho do has a hard time bein' a Nigger don't you Boy! I dun read in the paper 'bout yo speech at the Assembly of the World Council of Churches, Evanston, Illinois.
>
> It makes me sad and sorry for you Boy. You, it seems to me, is just miserable all the time. Now, you is supposed to be a smart Niger, just answer me one question: Why can't a Nigger just go on bein' a Nigger like God dun made em, and be happy?

The Evanston conference was a great occasion. But, as after previous world gatherings, the character of the local churches was hardly changed by any of the activities of the conference.

It took a hundred years, but it happened—one hundred years after Lincoln's Emancipation Proclamation on January 1, 1863! On January 14, 1963, for the first time in the history of the nation, three religious bodies—Catholic, Jewish, Protestant—met together at the Edgewater Beach Hotel in Chicago to see what could be done to eradicate racism in churches, synagogues, and society. The Conference was sponsored by the National Council of the Churches of Christ in America, the Synagogue Council of America, and the National Catholic Welfare Conference. Sixty-seven additional religious and religiously identified groups took part in the meeting by sending participating delegates. The three sponsoring bodies honored me by choosing me to be the Conference chairman, with that good man, Archbishop Paul J. Hallinan of Atlanta (now deceased) as vice-chairman. It had been my good fortune to attend world conferences on three continents between 1937 and 1963, but none had dealt in depth with the question of racism as this one did. From my opening remarks as Conference chairman I would like to quote briefly:

> We come this week to think together, to work together, to pray together, and to dedicate ourselves to the task of completing the job which Lincoln began 100 years ago.
>
> We recognize the fact that we have had 100 years to make religion real in human relations and that we may not have another 100 years to make good on our theological commitment. We did not seek world leadership, but the second World War thrust it upon the United States. . . . But world leadership requires more than industrial and military might. It requires that we practice at home what we seek to sell to the world. So we are here because our consciences will not let us rest in peace until we implement more fully in deed what we expound in words. And as long as we say we believe in God, the brotherhood of man and in the Declaration of Independence, we have no choice but to strive with might and main to close the gap between theory and practice. Until we do this, we play a hypocritical role and wear an uneasy conscience.

But the real probing to get at the heart of this country's racism was done in the thirty-two seminars and in the eleven platform speeches, which included assertions such as the following:

In our "appeal to the conscience of the American people," we called for a reign of justice in voting rights; for equal protection of law; for equality in educational and cultural opportunities, in hiring and promotion, in medical and hospital care; and for open occupancy in housing. We called for a reign of love in which all barriers based on race would be eliminated, in which the stranger would not only be welcomed but sought after, and in which "any man will be received as brother—his rights, your rights; his pain, your pain; his prison, your prison."

In its closing appeal to the nation, the Conference foreshadowed our present racial tragedy:

> We call upon all the American people to work, to pray, and to act courageously in the cause of equality and human dignity while there is still time to eliminate racism permanently and decisively, to seize the historic opportunity the Lord has given us for healing an ancient rupture in the human family, to do this for the glory of God.

A very disturbing note was sounded by William Stringfellow, a New York attorney. He expressed a pessimism which almost turned out to be prophetic when he shocked the Conference by telling us that what we were doing in Chicago was "too little and too late." He told the delegates that the initiative on the race issue had passed from whites to Negroes and that the most "practical" thing the delegates could do would be to "go home and weep."

Our great hope soon faded away. The plan was to set up action projects on race in ten cities to demonstrate that racism could be conquered in a relatively short time. The cities chosen were Chicago, Detroit, St. Louis, Seattle, San Francisco, Oakland, San Antonio, New Orleans, Pittsburgh, and Atlanta. As National Chairman, I had several meetings with staff representatives of the three national sponsoring groups, but the Chicago experience could not be duplicated in the local communities. Several cities made a start but none proved very effective.

Back in Atlanta, Archbishop Hallinan and I found we were mistaken in our belief that since we were both Atlantans, and were vice-chairman and chairman of the Chicago Conference, it would be relatively easy to do there, on a local level, what we had done in Chicago on a national level. The Kerner Report (the United States Riot Commission Report, 1968) subsequently made it clear that racism is rampant in this country and sought to stir up the nation to do something about it. Yet the Chicago National Conference on Race was held five years before the Kerner Report, and only a short while later the race riots broke loose in many cities of the nation. We had tried to alert the religious world to the impending danger inherent in racism, but few people listened. Stringfellow seems to have been right —"too little and too late."

Again in Atlanta, Archbisohop Hallinan and I further sought the aid of Rabbi Rothschild, so that the three great religious faiths would be involved in any local effort to get a program going. We tried. We called together a group of Atlanta ministers of all faiths and explained the Chicago Conference and the racial implications for our city. We had several meetings, but we failed to persuade the ministers to set up a program to come to grips with the racial situation in Atlanta. They just wouldn't buy it. Perhaps we had the wrong committee—Catholic, Jew, Negro—or maybe Atlanta ministers were just not ready for an action program involving race.

It is not my purpose to indict and condemn all local churches for their racial policies. I am not unmindful of the heroic, ofttimes damaging, stand that many white ministers have taken to get all racial groups accepted into the fellowship of their churches. Nor am I unmindful of the scores of unknown ministers in the nation who have been put out of their churches, or have quietly left their churches because of their racial views, ministers who did not subsequently publicize their dismissals or withdrawals. I remember, too, the ministers and church members who participated in the March on Washington and the ministers who joined the freedom rides through the South. I recall that years ago, when it was very unpopular, the Reverend Charles Jones of Chapel Hill, North Carolina, accepted Negroes in his worship services, and finally, at great risk, received them in membership. When the Presbytery of North Carolina dismissed him for his racial views—supposedly on theological grounds—he organized a community church in Chapel Hill open to all races and remained its pastor until his retirement a short while ago. I hold, nevertheless, that my overall critique of the local church is accurate, and that it will be a sad commentary on our life and times if a historian writing in the year 2000 can still truthfully say that the most segregated institution in the United States is the "Church of the Living God."

Chapter XIX

Martin Luther King, Jr.

Before the Ford Foundation inaugurated its Early Admission Program, Morehouse had instituted one of its own. The Second World War was playing havoc with the College, for our students were being drafted in large numbers. In this crisis, we decided to take into the freshman class students who had finished only the eleventh grade. Among the eleventh grade students admitted to Morehouse in September, 1944, was Martin Luther King, Jr. At that time, he was just one freshman among many others. Only an omniscient God could have predicted his future.

One never knows what it is that triggers a response, but I am convinced that it was my contact with Martin Luther King, Jr., in chapel at Morehouse that brought us close together. There we began a real friendship which was strengthened by visits in his home and by fairly frequent informal chats on the campus and in my office. Many times, during his four years at Morehouse, he would linger after my Tuesday-morning address to discuss some point I had made—usually with approval, but sometimes questioning or disagreeing. I was not aware how deeply he was impressed by what I said and did until he wrote *Stride Toward Freedom*, in which he indicated that I had influenced his life to a marked degree. In public addresses, he often referred to me as his "spiritual mentor." Since his death, several persons, especially those seeking data for an article or book, have asked me whether I knew in what way I was influencing Martin's life. The answer is an unqualified "No." There is no way one can know the degree of influence one has upon another. I can only say that I am honored to have had a small part in helping to mold the life of one of the noblest spirits of all time.

It must be said in all candor that I feel that Martin Luther King, Jr. did as much for me, if not more, than I did for him. Perhaps if I had not known Martin through the Morehouse Chapel, and if his father had not been elected to the Board of Trustees of Morehouse College, our friendship would not have reached such meaningful depth. Our friendship continued to grow during his years of study at Crozer Theological Seminary and

Boston University, during his pastorate at Montgomery, during the years when he joined his father as co-pastor of Ebenezer Baptist Church in Atlanta, and throughout the civil rights struggles.

When Martin Luther had almost completed his doctorate at Boston University, I offered him a position on the faculty at Morehouse. After giving serious consideration to my invitation, he decided that he should accept the pastorate of the Dexter Avenue Baptist Church in Montgomery, Alabama. When he returned to Atlanta as co-pastor of Ebenezer Baptist Church, I again offered him work as a part-time professor, hoping that someday he would be with us at Morehouse full time and for many years. So great were the public demands on his time, however, that after one semester he had to give up his seminar on nonviolence. Had he accepted my offer to teach at Morehouse, he would no doubt be alive today; but his name would not be among the immortal few who have achieved real greatness.

Furthermore, had the city officials in Montgomery been enlightened—or even sensible—the life of Martin Luther King, Jr., would have been a different story. Then, too, had Mrs. Rosa Parks behaved as she was "supposed to," and as Negroes generally had behaved for decades—that is, if she had gotten up and given a white man her seat—there would have been no Montgomery Bus Boycott. Had the city officials met the simple demands of the Montgomery Improvement Association, perhaps the world would have never witnessed Dr. King's capacity for magnificent, selfless leadership in the interest of mankind. The demands of the Montgomery Improvement Association were all reasonable—too reasonable—and all within the segregated pattern. It also seems that any sane city officials would have agreed to permit Negroes to keep their seats if, when entering from the rear, they filled the bus, in which case whites would have to stand. The reverse would be true if whites filled the bus first. Sensible officials would have been willing to hire Negro bus drivers, certainly in predominantly Negro areas, and would have instructed white drivers to be civil in their treatment of black customers. All these demands were denied; hence the year-long Montgomery Bus Boycott.

It is highly probable that Martin Luther King, Jr., was the only man who could have led the Montgomery Bus Boycott for an entire year without violence, with the exception of the violence instigated by white people. Without Dr. King's charisma, his brilliant mind, and his unquenchable spirit Negroes would hardly have stuck it out. For Dr. King it was the beginning of an incredible pilgrimage which was to bring him world-wide honor and acclaim—and death. From that moment of the boycott on, until his assassination on April 4, 1968, he moved steadily from height to height, loved by his friends and hated by his enemies. I am sorry he did not come to Morehouse, but no college could have provided such an opportunity for leadership, a leadership so needed by all mankind and one for which he was so eminently qualified.

Of the countless incidents I could relate about Martin Luther King, Jr., I have chosen three because it seems to me that they illustrate so perfectly the quality of the man's soul—his vision, his courage, his magnificent capacity for self-denying love.

The first of these concerns Rosa Parks who was arrested December 1, 1955. Nobody knows just why, on this particular occasion, she didn't choose to obey the bus driver's order to get up so a white man might sit down. Perhaps she was tired after working all day; perhaps she was just tired of being pushed around all her life by white folks. At any rate, she sat—and the Boycott was on!

When the Montgomery officials discovered that violence could not stay the protest or stop the Boycott, they resorted to mass arrest, using an old state law against boycotts. Dr. King, who was in Nashville at the time, knew that if he returned to Montgomery he would be arrested too. En route to Montgomery, he stopped overnight in Atlanta. His father, frantic for his son's safety, assembled a group of friends to consult with them about the wisdom of Martin Luther, Jr.'s immediate return to Montgomery. It was on February 22, 1956 that we met at the residence of Martin Luther King, Sr., and according to Martin Luther's own book, *Stride Toward Freedom,* the following persons were present:

A. T. Walden, a distinguished attorney; C. R. Yates and T. M. Alexander, both prominent business men; C. A. Scott, editor of the Atlanta *Daily World;* Bishop Sherman L. Green of the AME Church; Rufus E. Clement, president of Atlanta University; and Benjamin E. Mays, president of Morehouse College. As I myself remember, Attorney Dan Duke was also present.

Reverend King, Sr., stated his reason for calling us together and expressed his conviction that his son should not return to Montgomery right away. In *Stride Toward Freedom,* Martin Luther King, Jr. writes that after his father's statement

> . . . there were murmurs of agreement in the room, and I listened as sympathetically and objectively as I could while two of the men gave their reasons for concurring. These were my elders, leaders among my people. Their words commanded respect. But soon I could not restrain myself any longer: "I must go back to Montgomery—my friends and associates are being arrested. It would be the height of cowardice for me to stay away. I would rather be in jail ten years than desert my people now. I have begun the struggle, and I can't turn back. I have reached the point of no return." In the moment of silence that followed, I heard my father break into tears. I looked at Doctor Mays, one of the great influences in my life. Perhaps he heard my unspoken plea. At any rate, he was soon defending my position strongly.

I had to defend Martin Luther's position. Here was a man of deep integrity and firm convictions. How could he have decided otherwise than to return to Montgomery? How could he hide while his comrades in nonviolent arms were being carried to jail? That, in essence, was what I said.

I am mighty glad that I had the wisdom to give him the moral support he needed at that time. I had admired him ever since he entered Morehouse as a freshman: now my respect for him mounted on wings. In the light of this definitive statement of Dr. King's, I shall always wonder why Louis E. Lomax, in his book *To Kill a Black Man,* stated that at this meeting I had been opposed to Dr. King's return to Montgomery.

As for the second event, the officials in Alabama, and particularly in Montgomery, took great delight in harassing Martin Luther King even after the Montgomery Bus Boycott ended. In 1957, when Ralph Abernathy was being tried on some trumped-up charge, the Montgomery courtroom was almost full. When Dr. King wanted to get in, the officers refused him permission, and upon his insistence, he was arrested. Twisting his arms, they pushed and kicked him into a cell. Before Mrs. King and others could plan a strategy for getting Dr. King out, he was suddenly released. At the trial, he was convicted of *loitering,* and given the choice: He could serve time or pay a fine. Here came the great decision. Convinced that he had been unlawfully arrested and unjustly convicted, and therefore could not in good conscience pay the fine, Dr. King announced that he would serve his time in jail. This pronouncement shocked and stunned the court. I understand that the judge almost begged Dr. King to pay the fine. Some person —at the time unknown—paid it. Later it was learned that Clyde Sellers, the chief of police, had paid it, remarking that it would be cheaper to pay the fine than to have Martin Luther King, Jr., in jail at the city's expense.

Dr. King's decision not to pay went almost unnoticed at the time, but to me it was one of the most momentous decisions of his whole civil rights career. It made a tremendous impression on me. He would obey an unjust verdict. But by serving time rather than paying a fine for something he should never have been convicted of, he registered for the whole world his protest against injustice. His great decision has motivated and will continue to motivate the actions of others as we pursue this long journey up the precipitous hill toward racial justice, democracy, and Christian living in this country.

A third incident will dramatize Martin Luther King's high regard for the law, even for unjust laws. Those who have condemned him for admonishing people to break unjust laws have not realized that when he himself violated them he was not being irresponsible nor was he advising others to be irresponsible. It was his way of seeking to achieve social change without instigating physical violence. If he had violated the law and then cried for amnesty, his action in a sense would have been irresponsible and would have indicated disrespect for law. But when Martin Luther violated the law he did so consciously and deliberately and was always willing to pay the penalty exacted by law, even though the law was blatantly unjust. He was willing to suffer for a righteous cause in the firm belief that this kind of suffering was redemptive.

I saw him demonstrate this belief on October 29, 1967. President Glenn H. Leggett had invited a group of distinguished Americans to Grinnell College to confer honorary degrees. Dr. King and I were among them—he to give the convocation address in the morning before the conferring of degrees in the afternoon, and I to introduce him. His schedule was so tight that he had warned Grinnell that he might not be able to get there, so an official of the college asked me to stand in if he couldn't make it. An emphatic "No" had to be my answer to this request—this huge crowd had come to hear Dr. King, not me. No substitute would have been adequate. To make his appearance, Dr. King had to come by a private plane provided by a friend. The crowd that had waited patiently for ninety minutes for his arrival gave him a standing ovation when he appeared, and applauded long and loud when he finished speaking.

This was the speech Martin Luther King, Jr., made just before he returned to Alabama once more to serve time for contempt of court. He had a heavy cold, and I was greatly concerned when he left me in Grinnell to go to Birmingham. He could have ducked another ordeal by staying out of Alabama, but true to his character he would not run and hide even though he knew he was being punished unjustly. Only one who has the highest respect for law is willing to serve time for violating laws whether just or unjust. This man never cried for mercy; he never asked for amnesty.

The Grinnell experience was five months and eight days before his assassination. My next public speech about Martin Luther was the eulogy I gave at his funeral on April 9, 1968.

Second only to my wife, my deepest loyalties were for Morehouse and for my desire to help bring full justice to black people in a country that had denied them justice since 1619. I loved Morehouse so much that I would have been ready at any time to give all that I had, even life, if such giving would have enabled Morehouse to become the school of my dreams. When Martin Luther King, Jr. led the Montgomery Bus Boycott, and afterward made civil rights his major activity, I was sorely tempted many times to become an activist in the struggle rather than just to give financial and moral support. Morehouse needed a full-time president, not one who would be often in jail or away speaking and marching. I knew that if I became deeply involved as an activist in the civil rights struggle it was only fair to Morehouse that I resign, and that I was too committed to the college program to do. (I did, however, participate in the March on Washington in 1963, and had planned to be in the Selma March in 1965, but I had to be with Sadie who was undergoing treatment at Mayo Clinic at the time.) I was striving with all my might to develop a sound and superior educational program at Morehouse, and I hoped to leave the college in a stable financial position. Although I did leave it stronger in every way, my accomplishments trailed far behind my expectations.

Martin Luther King, Jr., was a powerful man and I was, and still am, so inspired by his integrity, his courage, and his commitment that I have never been quite objective about him. I was wholeheartedly in accord with most things he did. Even when I had reservations about a certain course of action, I hesitated to criticize him, both because I thought his judgment might well be better than mine, and because I could never doubt the sincerity of his purpose. It angered me to hear him accused of being insincere, or of doing things for the plaudits of the crowd. Many, for example, condemned his stand on the Vietnam War. Even some civil rights leaders and other Negroes in high places were harsh in their criticisms. In conversations, on public platforms, and in my weekly articles in the Pittsburgh *Courier*, I found myself in the happy position of defending his stand on this and many other issues.

Why should Dr. King have confined his work to civil rights and left

Vietnam to the government experts and military professionals? I learned long ago that there are no infallible experts on war and that no leader has ever been able to confine his leadership to one area, a point I made in the Pittsburgh *Courier* on May 20, 1967;

> . . . I do not agree with the leaders who criticize Dr. King on the ground that he should stick to civil rights and not mix civil rights with foreign policy. If the critics differ with him because of his stand on the Vietnam War, let them say it. No leader leads in one particular area. I think most civil rights leaders speak on other issues as well. I see nothing wrong with a man speaking out on three or four different issues. He may be right in his stand on Vietnam and he may be wrong. History will finally record the verdict.
>
> It should be noted here that what Dr. King is doing now is consistent with his philosophy of nonviolence. He was a follower of Mahatma Gandhi before he led the Montgomery Bus Boycott. He has consistently expounded on the doctrine of nonviolence. The Nobel Peace Prize was awarded to him on this philosophy. He has expounded this philosophy on the home front and it is logical that he would expound it on the international front. I think we should at least make our criticisms of Dr. King on the major issue. . . .

After Martin Luther King, Jr. received the Nobel Peace Prize, I was eager to do two things: To see to it that Morehouse would be the first to honor Dr. King on his return from Oslo, and to do all that I could to get the city of Atlanta to honor this distinguished native son. The first I could do on my own. For the second I needed help. I wanted Atlanta to honor Dr. King because Atlanta had never been entirely happy over his leadership. Some considered him too radical, forever shaking the foundations of the status quo. Not only white Atlanta voiced this opposition—many Negro leaders were jealous of the man's tremendous power, his stature, his leadership; others sincerely believed that he was stirring up trouble.

The Morehouse Convocation recognizing the great honor that had come to one of her sons was held in Archer Hall in January, 1965. It was a huge success. Twenty-seven hundred persons, mostly black, came to honor him. After citations were given by the faculty and the student body, Martin Luther King, Jr., Morehouse alumnus, Nobel Peace Prize winner, delivered a brilliant address on the civil rights situation in this country.

But what about the city of Atlanta, black and white together? We formed a small committee—Ralph McGill, Rabbi Jacob Rothschild, Archbishop Paul J. Hallinan and I—to get things going. Then a larger group was called together: representatives of the Atlanta Christian Council, the Conference of Christians and Jews, the Southern Christian Leadership Conference, the National Association for the Advancement of Colored People, and various Negro ministerial groups. We wanted the celebration in the heart of Atlanta, downtown, not in the black community. The State of Georgia and the city of Atlanta had never produced a Nobel Peace Prize winner, so why shouldn't Atlanta rise to the occasion, welcome the opportunity to expand its image in the nation and the world?

Things got off to a slow start. The economic power structure was reluctant to support the project to recognize Dr. King. We needed the most prestigious names in Atlanta to sponsor the banquet: Atlanta needed to do this for its own self-respect; Dr. King needed to have the assurance that his native city honored him for what he had achieved, and respected his leadership, even if all its citizens did not agree with him, did not love him.

The Committee was discouraged at first, but finally things began to fall into line. *The New York Times* carried an article accusing Atlanta of dragging its feet on whether it would honor its Nobel Peace Prize winner. This article, along with the help of Mayor Ivan Allen, Jr., succeeded in getting the support we needed.

The dinner was an overwhelming success. Instead of the eight hundred persons we had hoped to seat on that notable night of January 27, 1965, we packed thirteen hundred people into the Dinkler Plaza Hotel to honor Atlanta's new First Citizen. These thirteen hundred citizens, black and white, came spontaneously to their feet after King's address and gave him a thunderous ovation. Only a man of superb courage and soul-deep conviction could have uttered that speech. In his hometown, where his philosophy and activities were not fully accepted, a lesser man would have given a speech designed to win over those who were critical of him. Not so with this man. He made it clear that while he himself was on the mountain top that night, the needs of the people in the valley were calling him, and he would forthwith return to the valley to help the man farthest down. In closing, Dr. King said, in part:

> . . . I must confess that I have enjoyed being on this mountain-top, and I am tempted to want to stay here and retreat to a more quiet and serene life. But something within reminds me that the valley calls me in spite of all its agonies, dangers and frustrating moments. I must return to the valley. Something tells me that the ultimate test of a man is not where he stands in moments of comfort and the moments of convenience, but where he stands in moments of challenge and moments of controversy. So I must

> return to the valley—a valley filled at the same time with little Negro boys and girls who grow up with ominous clouds of inferiority forming in their little mental skies; a valley filled with millions of people who, because of economic deprivation and social isolation, have lost hope, and see life as a long and desolate corridor with no exit sign. I must return to the valley —a valley filled with literally thousands of Negroes in Alabama and Mississippi who are brutalized, intimidated and sometimes killed when they seek to register and vote. I must return to the valley all over the South and in the big cities of the North—a valley filled with millions of our white and Negro brothers who are smothering in an air-tight cage of poverty in the midst of an affluent society.

It was a magnificent and moving experience. Black and white, rich and poor, Protestants and Catholics, Jews and Unitarians, politicians and statesmen were there, and we sang happily the civil rights song, "We Shall Overcome . . . Black and White Together." Atlanta was proud of itself and glad that it did it; and I was overjoyed that Dr. King's hometown had truly honored a most deserving man, even though he was black and was living a doctrine of militant nonviolence which was unacceptable to many of those who came to honor him.

Though the man's philosophy was nonviolence, it was militant nonviolence. Those who cherish the status quo will oppose that philosophy. It was a long time before we could elect Morehouse's most widely known alumnus to the Morehouse Board of Trustees. There were those of us who held that it would bring honor and prestige to the Board if Martin Luther King, Jr., were a member; others bitterly opposed his election. It was rumored that one trustee would not sit in the same room with Dr. King.

The prospect of Dr. King's joining the Board was slowed up, too, because Elbert Tuttle, chief judge of the Fifth United Circuit Court of Appeals and himself a Board member, had said that if Dr. King came before his court as a result of demonstrations, he would have to absent himself from the case if Dr. King were on the Board. This gave us concern, for we didn't want to lose Judge Tuttle from the Board, and we certainly didn't want him to be absent from any court involving King.

There was a time when, if we had insisted on Dr. King's membership on the Board, we would have split the Board. But those of us who wanted him could not rest in comfort if we gave up the fight to get him elected. When the time came that Judge Tuttle felt that he would not need to resign if King became a member of the Morehouse Board, we again pushed for his election; and we did elect him to membership on April 10, 1965.

Long before the world paid tribute to Martin Luther King, Jr., by awarding him the Nobel Peace Prize, Morehouse College had conferred upon him her highest honor. We wanted to be the first college or university to recognize his leadership in the Montgomery Bus Boycott. The Boycott had continued all through 1956, and our first commencement after that was in June, 1957. In April, I proposed that we honor Dr. King on June fourth by conferring upon him the honorary degree of Doctor of Humane Letters. The faculty and Board of Trustees accepted my recommendation unanimously. It gave me great joy to confer the degree when the day came.

The Eulogy which I gave at the funeral services for Martin Luther King, Jr., at Morehouse College, on April 9, 1968, was my last tribute to a great and good man. (Full text in Appendix C.)

Chapter XX

I Can Sing Atlanta: The Trail Blazers

I have never been able to sing "Dixie." I cannot sing "Dixie" because to me Dixie means all the segregation, discrimination, exploitation, brutality, and lynchings endured for centuries by black people. It means the riots I have seen, the personal insults I have suffered, and the mobs I have barely escaped. It means a system that disfranchised me until I was fifty-two, denied my worth as a person, attempted to clip the wings of my aspirations, and deliberately and relentlessly sought to crush my spirit so that I would be ashamed of being black.

If Dixie were Atlanta or Atlanta were Dixie, I could sing "Dixie." Not that Atlanta is what it ought to be or what it could and must be, but because Atlanta has come a long way, and I believe that Atlanta has the will to approach more nearly what a city ought to be. Atlanta did many wretched things to me, too. Yet having lived a black man in Atlanta for a total of thirty-eight years, I have experienced a new Atlanta, unknown to me when I first came there in the 1920's. I know from my wide travels that Atlanta is not the typical South. It is better.

I can sing and praise Atlanta as I sing the National Anthem and "America," as I recite the Declaration of Independence, read the Bill of Rights, and rejoice over the adoption of the 13th, 14th, and 15th Amendments. I know that the Declaration of Independence was not meant for me; that its chief architect, Thomas Jefferson, was a slave owner; that the 13th, 14th, and 15th Amendments have not been fully implemented; and that the "land of the free" and "sweet land of liberty" are not equally applicable to black and white. But these are the ideals to which the nation clings and the goals toward which it strives when it is at its best and thinks nobly. It is not always easy for a black man to swear allegiance to the flag, but the American dream is embodied in that allegiance, and until it is repudiated one can still hope for and work toward the day when it becomes a reality. As long as Atlanta struggles toward the dream, I can sing Atlanta.

I can sing the National Anthem and "My Country 'Tis of Thee" because after visiting many countries in Europe, Asia, and Africa, I have concluded that the United States, despite all its imperfections, is the best country for me and that my job is to continue the battle to make America in reality what it claims to be. Possibly Atlanta is overpraised, but having traveled in forty-seven of the fifty states, I can testify that black-white relations here are as good as in any city in the nation and better than in most.

Atlanta is a progressive city, and the people here want to keep it that way. In the 1920's, and even when I came back in 1940 to be president of Morehouse College, Atlanta was so depressing in its black-white relations that I saw little difference between it and Birmingham or Memphis. As I appraised bad human relations in the South, I rated Birmingham No. 1, Memphis No. 2, and Atlanta No. 3. The railroad stations in Atlanta were embarrassing enough, but Birmingham provided *separate stairways* for blacks and whites to go to and from the trains. They were not even permitted to go up and down the same steps. The Memphis waiting room gave the impression that Negroes were sealed off as if in some kind of prison. I mention these two cities only because at that time I dreaded so much having to alight from a train in Birmingham or Memphis.

The picture of Atlanta in the late 1960's and in 1970 must be contrasted with the one presented in Chapter V, and it should also be remembered that the great changes in black-white relations for the most part have come about since the middle of the century. Today, we take Negro policemen and firemen for granted. But it was terrifying to attend the public hearings in 1948 when Atlanta was trying to make up its mind about employing Negro policemen. The then Mayor, William B. Hartsfield, Chief of Police Herbert Jenkins, and the aldermen made the decision to employ Atlanta's first Negro policemen in 1948. Yet it is probably not generally known that not until 1961, thirteen years later, could a Negro policeman arrest a white man. Negro police officers were confined to Negro neighborhoods; separate precincts were provided for them; and civil service status was withheld until their worth had been proven.

During my earlier years in Atlanta, I always felt subdued, beaten down, restricted, circumscribed, and hemmed in when I went downtown. Perhaps many Negroes accepted the segregated conditions as inevitable—I never did and I never could. No doubt there are many who would still deny that Atlanta deserves a "new" name in black-white relations. I understand and sympathize with their opinion, but I feel that both sides of Atlanta must be shown. It is true that in the 1940's Atlanta was not in the same shameful category with the town of Monroe, Georgia, where, in 1946, two Negro couples were lynched in broad daylight—and thereafter nobody, including the GBI and the FBI, could find out who had lynched them. On the other hand, the Atlanta of the 1940's was not the Atlanta of today, which is far ahead of the rest of the state in the area of race relations.

Perhaps I can best describe the difference between the two Atlantas by a simple statement of my own feelings: I feel like a human being in Atlanta in 1970. I feel that I belong here and that Atlanta is mine. I feel at home, and I can move around relaxed and at peace. I know that in the Atlanta of today I can and do ask policemen questions and get courteous replies without being insulted, without being called "boy." My wife was treated decently when she went downtown to buy a dress or sat down to be fitted for shoes. She was given proper respect and title; and the clerk did not spend unnecessary time trying to elicit her first name so that she could be called by it. She could try on a hat or dress without agreeing in advance to buy it. I do not have to walk up several flights of stairs to avoid riding a segregated elevator. I am not required to drink "black water" from a fountain marked "colored." Rest rooms are provided for all on a non-segregated basis. I accept the ticket seller's word and believe he is telling the truth when he says "I have no Pullman space," or "all seats on the plane are taken." When I go to the best restaurants, I am served with courtesy and respect; no restaurant will be closed to avoid serving me; I am not arrested, and pistols and ax handles are not used to keep me out. I am not denied service or thrown out of the best downtown hotels if I wish to reserve rooms for my friends.

Although Negro conventions and racially mixed conventions are held in the hotels in Atlanta without discrimination, it cannot be concluded that there is complete freedom from racial discrimination. One of my research assistants had a long interview with a black entertainer of national reputation. The reservation which his manager had made for the entertainer at a well-known hotel was not honored upon his arrival. At another equally prominent hotel, although a known figure, he was required to deposit $85 when he registered. When he objected, the clerk was curt and rude. The next guest in line—a white man—was registered with no mention being made of a deposit.

In August of 1969, my niece, arriving by plane around three o'clock in the morning and not wishing to disturb us at that early hour, attempted to register at a hotel. Though not living in Atlanta, she gave my address, and was refused on the ground that the hotel does not accept reservations from Atlanta residents. This is hard to believe!

No longer are there special lines and segregated windows where blacks make returns and pay taxes. Black people ride on the buses of Atlanta unsegregated, and it is not an anathema when black and white sit together; the Negro will not be arrested. Taxis operating exclusively for whites and taxis for colored only are relics. White women visiting the Atlanta University Center today do not have to listen to drivers orate on the evils of visiting a black educational center. Pictures of Negroes appear on the front pages of the white Atlanta newspapers, and they are given the proper titles. The bad news stories about Negroes are not unduly played up in the Atlanta press. I have not, in recent years, heard a white clerk, observing my white hair, "claim kinship" by calling me "Uncle." Negroes and white people need no longer be furtive about interracial meetings; they meet now in churches and other places, unafraid. One finds at least token employment of Negroes in respectable jobs above the menial level in city and state governments, in banks and department stores, in hotels and motels, and in industry and the federal government. Whites and blacks meet on common and unsegregated ground at Atlanta Stadium, yelling their heads off for the Atlanta Braves and the Atlanta Falcons.

I really feel that the mayor of Atlanta and the chief of police are genuinely interested in all of the citizens of our city. I doubt whether any other Southern official had the foresight and the courage to go to Washington, against the advice of aides and friends, to testify in the interest of a public accommodations law which was passed by Congress in 1964. Mayor Ivan Allen so testified. Negroes and whites sit together when they visit the state legislature, and their presence does not create a panic in the legislative body. There are a token number of Negroes in the state legislature.

Negro lawyers are now treated with respect in the Atlanta courts, and a black man sits in the courtroom wherever there is a vacancy. Negroes have token representation on the Board of Education and on the aldermanic board. The public library is open to Negroes. A black man in quest of knowledge is not confined to the branch library in the Negro section. The black golfer can play golf on city courses; and the city parks supported by the taxes of all the people are available to black folks without difficulty. As I walk the streets of Atlanta and visit public places the racial atmosphere is not as tense as in previous years. Friendliness is in the air. A white girl in her teens or twenties, serving the public, seeing me for the first time and not knowing me, would hardly address me as "Benjamin." Even Grady Hospital is a more humane place where Negroes are involved. At least some of the segregation and discrimination there has vanished. The Atlanta public schools are slowly being desegregated, although not without travail, and the colleges in Atlanta are accepting an increasing number of black students.

I am not a nightclub man and never have been, but I did have two black couples visit a dozen nightclubs in Atlanta in the summer of 1969 to see what would happen. As nightclub operators are inclined to be very sensitive to black persons patronizing their places of entertainment, I wished to learn Atlanta's nighttime racial "climate." On the whole, the service was reported to be good—courteous and polite. There was one place where the host's greeting was: "What can I do for you people?" When asked about seats, he said that the main lounge was filled and suggested the bar. As my researchers went past the bar to the main lounge, they saw several empty tables, but since the waitress ignored them they finally went to the bar, served themselves, and left. But this experience was an exception. The following comments about the service and treatment are typical: "Service good"; "neither rude nor friendly"; "service very good"; "white guests congenial"; "atmosphere not hostile but much staring"; "businesslike service"; "hostile stares"; "hostess went out of her way to be nice."

At the time of the visits, the investigators found one black waiter in one club and two black waiters in another. One club had a black host. About 80 percent of the workers in the clubs were white. There were only several black customers in one group of 150 to 200; in another club there were eight blacks in a group estimated at between 250 and 300; another club had three black couples in addition to the two couples doing the survey; and there was still another place where sixteen other blacks were patronizing the club. In fact, they found one or more black couples in every nightclub except two. The research couples were not turned away anywhere. The entertainment was by black performers in one club. Our investigators did hear of one case where a couple who were dancing were asked to leave because the management thought the "white" woman, who happened to be the black man's wife, was Caucasian.

Ten years ago, not only nightclubs but all restaurants in downtown Atlanta were closed to black people. The spot check conducted by the researchers seems to indicate that, as of 1969, nightclubs in Atlanta are open to Negroes. This fact should not be too surprising since the worlds of entertainment and of sports have often taken the lead in racial relations, far ahead of many educational and religious institutions.

The racial atmosphere in the churches of Atlanta has changed a bit within the decade. Early in the 1960's, when the students of the Atlanta

University Center were staging sit-in demonstrations in downtown Atlanta establishments, they found many of the white churches hostile toward Negro students who attempted to worship in them. Many church members were as opposed to worshiping with Negroes as the restaurant managements were to serving Negroes in downtown Atlanta.

I do not agree with those who hold that the church is sacrosanct and should not be tested as to racial attitudes. If secular institutions are to be tested, why not the "House of God?" So, in the summer of 1969, students of the Atlanta University Center were commissioned to present themselves by couples for worship services in forty different Atlanta white churches. The students were advised to create no disturbances if refused admission—they were simply to leave the church without argument. Thirty-six, or 90 percent, of the forty churches visited accepted the Negro worshipers. What would have happened if the same students had gone Sunday after Sunday, I have no way of knowing. The experiment, though not done in depth, at least indicates a wholesome trend. Some of the students' comments are illuminating and heartening:

> I was greeted very warmly and invited to come again.
>
> We were accepted very cordially. After the service the minister asked for and wrote down our names and invited us back that evening for supper and evening worship.

The following letter from one of the ministers is indicative of his sincerity:

> Dear Mr. ——————:
> It was good to have you visit us last Sunday. I hope the service was enriching to your life and that we may again have the privilege of having you here at —————— Church.
> If you are looking for a church home, I hope you will consider our church.
> Whenever I can help you in any way, please let me know.

Two of the forty churches made no pretense of welcome. One student's report is illustrative:

> I was received by these people, but they still treated me as if I were a "nigger" boy. My friend and I were watched for several minutes by this

one little white girl. None of these people sat near us for we were escorted to an aisle where there was no one.

I concluded that we were admitted only to keep from having trouble with more blacks. They acted as if we were trash.

The remaining two churches turned the students away. One student writes that as he approached the church door a man, possibly an usher, confronted him, saying bluntly, "Hold it right there!" while he distributed programs to white worshipers. When the student ignored him and attempted to open the door, the man stepped in front of him saying again, "Hold it right there!" Then he asked, "Where do you think you're going?" The student replied, "Really, it is none of your business, but I plan to worship here this morning." One man told the student he didn't want to worship, he "just wanted to make a scene." An usher and five white "Christians" approached and one of the six spoke up: "Look, why don't you go to one of your own churches if you want to worship?" Another of the group mildly protested, "We can't just turn a man away from the House of God," but the majority contended that the student didn't want to worship, and the leader of the six-man committee concluded the whole matter: "We are the Board, and we have taken a vote, and we feel you should go to one of your own churches." Since the students had been instructed to create no disturbance, the black student quietly went away.

It is unfortunate that two churches turned the Negro students away, and that at two others the climate was unfriendly; but it is encouraging that thirty-six extended the welcoming hand of fellowship.

These are some of the reasons why I can sing Atlanta.

In the summer of 1969, the National Funeral Directors and Morticians held their convention at one of Atlanta's newest and one of the country's most luxurious hotels. A top official, who told me that this city was chosen because of Atlanta's good name in Negro-white relations, also said that the convention would bring the hotel $182,000 during the week they were there. Not bad business for good race relations. Nearly all of the radical changes in race relations in Atlanta have come about within the last twenty-five years, and most since 1960. Why?

No one factor can account for Atlanta's unique character in black-white relations. It is difficult, if not impossible, to answer adequately the question, "How and why did Atlanta, more than any other Southern city, achieve her present good image?" I asked a dozen knowledgeable citizens who have lived in Atlanta for thirty, forty, or fifty years to give me their explanations. The following paragraphs summarize their opinions:

They said that Atlanta has a natural advantage of location—it is at the end of the mountains, is on a river, has a good climate, is seldom devastated by hurricanes and gives free access to people from east, west, and south of Atlanta. These advantages have attracted people to move here from every part of the United States, and many of them have helped to improve our picture of race relations. Atlantans have influenced the racial attitude of Northerners, to be sure, but those from outside the South have also made their impact on black and white Atlantans.

Given these conditions, the economic growth of Atlanta has been phenomenal, making it one of the fastest growing cities in the nation and giving it a cosmopolitan atmosphere shared by no other comparable cities in the South and by surprisingly few cities in the North. When it comes to government agencies, Atlanta is a replica of Washington. Many of the nation's largest businesses operate here. People from all over the world come to Atlanta. The Atlanta airport is the third largest in traffic in the country—an international airport, making it necessary that Atlanta behave like an international city.

Rightly, the respondents to my query as to the reason for Atlanta's progress placed emphasis upon municipal leadership as represented by the three decades that William B. Hartsfield and Ivan Allen, Jr., served as mayors of Atlanta. The leadership of these two men, they felt, certainly made a colossal difference in bettering human relations in this city. Allen brought more than concern; he brought compassion. He went to France in the interest of friends and relatives of Atlantans who died in the tragic plane crash near Paris in June, 1962. Nor could any official have done more to console the bereaved than Ivan Allen, Jr. did for the King family after the unforgettable assassination of Martin Luther King, Jr. in April, 1968. Without exception, Ralph McGill was named by the respondents as having done more than any other writer to get Atlanta and the South to accept federal decrees and congressional legislation in the interest of justice and democracy in a sane and reasonable manner. One respondent said that there is no way to measure the influence that McGill had for good upon black-white relations in Atlanta and the South, especially from 1954 up to the time of his death in 1968. Eugene Patterson, another great editor of the Atlanta *Constitution,* was also mentioned as one who helped to improve Atlanta's good image.

Although those questioned made it clear that the Commission on Interracial Cooperation had never made an attack on segregation, they listed it as an organization that helped to improve black-white relations in Atlanta. Mentioned also was the Southern Regional Council, although it, too, in its early years sought to improve relations between Negroes and whites only within the pattern of segregation.

The institutions that the Atlanta University Center comprises—Atlanta University, Clark, Morehouse, Morris Brown, Spelman, and the Interdenominational Theological Center—were given high rank as forces that produced outstanding Negro leaders for a hundred years. These institutions, it was said, gave Atlanta leadership in law, education, medicine, religion, the press, business, and politics not equaled in any other southern city—a leadership that white Atlanta could not ignore and had to respect.

White educational institutions helped, too, but for the most part their efforts were feeble. On the other hand, the Negro colleges in Atlanta never slammed their doors in the faces of white teachers and white visitors. For many years before segregation was abolished, the Atlanta-Morehouse-Spelman Christmas Carol Concerts were given for what were perhaps the largest unsegregated audiences in the United States, in which whites and blacks sat together, stood together, and sang together three nights each year in Sisters Chapel on Spelman College campus. At a time when no white college and no white church would accept Negroes, the doors of the black colleges in Atlanta, and of the black churches, were wide open to whites to visit and worship.

The economic life of Negroes was judged to have been improved through the success of Negro business institutions such as the Atlanta Life Insurance Company, the Citizens Trust Company, and the Atlanta Mutual Federal. By providing competition, these institutions made white Atlanta businesses more liberal in making loans to Negro churches and home builders. And when Negroes were not a part of any other interracial policy-making board, there was the Atlanta Urban League, with a white and black Board, helping to determine policies designed to benefit the Negro community.

In addition to the contributions of black leadership and of black educational and economic institutions, as reflected in the responses of the twelve knowledgeable citizens who are long-time Atlantans, the total impact of the Negro upon Atlanta's good reputation must be treated separately and in depth.

The Negro has not been given due credit for his share in making Atlanta a better city. One could wish that the changes which have been wrought to give Atlanta a good name in black-white relations resulted wholly from a sense of justice and fair play on the part of the white citizenry and the white establishment. However, if this were true, it would be a reversal of history. Seldom if ever does a weak, powerless group receive its fair share of citizenship rights merely because it should. This fact obtains as surely in Christian and democratic countries as it does in totalitarian states. Atlanta is no exception.

Negroes got their first high school in Atlanta in 1924 only because Negroes defeated a $4 million bond issue in 1921 that excluded them from sharing in the benefits that would have accrued had it passed. Before the bond issue was voted on again, Negroes threatened to defeat it again unless they were promised in advance that they would be given a high school. Negroes voted for the bond issue the second time around and as a result the Booker T. Washington High School came into being!

Between 1908 and 1946, Georgia Negroes were disfranchised through various restrictions placed upon them by the state and local communities. The white primary was knocked out in Georgia in 1946 when Primus King, a Columbus, Georgia Negro sued for the exercise of his right to vote, a right guaranteed to him in the 15th Amendment to the United States Constitution. During a registration campaign, headed by Grace T. Hamilton and Robert A. Thompson of the Atlanta Urban League, 24,137 Negroes soon enrolled. Voter registration among Atlanta Negroes assumed a major emphasis after 1946, and John Wesley Dobbs, a civic leader prominent in fraternal circles, made this one of his chief concerns. As I have said, it was difficult enough to get Negro policemen in 1948, but I am sure it would have been utterly impossible had Negroes remained voteless.

Consequently, things began to get appreciably better in Atlanta when Negroes spent their money in federal court to earn the right to vote. The prophets of doom were vociferous in their predictions that there would be bloodshed in Atlanta if black people were allowed the franchise. Even the Atlanta papers were a bit apprehensive. When the time came, however, nothing was done to keep black people from the polls. In fact, not long after Primus King won his case in federal court, white politicians aspiring for office were writing and visiting me, soliciting my support in their campaigns.

Thus it happened that at the age of fifty-two I peaceably cast my first ballot. This is one of many illustrations of the fact that the things we fear most are often of things that never happen. In the long and rugged struggle to make more humane our black-white relations in this nation, rarely have changes been followed by the dire consequences that were fearfully predicted.

For a quarter of a century Atlanta has been fortunate in having good leadership in its city government. Both William Hartsfield and Ivan Allen gave Atlanta good and progressive leadership. Both gained national and international reputation as being among the best and most progressive mayors in the nation. Most Negroes believed that Hartsfield did a good job in keeping Atlanta sane and sober on racial matters. Though it is probably unfair to judge men out of their time, many blacks believe that Ivan Allen did an even better job than Hartsfield. I am confident that the Negro vote was largely responsible for keeping these men in office, giving them the opportunity to rise above much of the race prejudice that they inherited, and thus freeing them to give Atlanta superior leadership. More than once, in the past twenty-five years, the Negro vote was decisive in the elections of Hartsfield and Allen. And it is not without significance that in 1965, in the runoff for mayor between Lester Maddox and Ivan Allen, Maddox received slightly more white votes than Allen. One analyst who carefully studied the Allen-Maddox vote records states that Allen received 33,089 white votes in the runoff and Maddox 35,919. On the other hand, Negroes gave Allen 31,224 and Maddox 176. Clearly, without the Negro vote, Maddox would have been Atlanta's mayor from 1966 through 1969, and the Allen leadership would have been lost to Atlanta during these critical years. Had the Negro been voteless during the past twenty-five years, Atlanta would have been a lesser city than it is now.

In earlier years, the segregated streetcar was always a source of friction. The motorman, armed as he was in his effort to uphold an unjust law, was seldom if ever pleasant to deal with. Although most Negroes rode the streetcars silently, they nevertheless deeply resented and protested a system that forced them to ride in the back, often compelling them to stand when seats were available. The atmosphere was usually tense when a streetcar was filled with Negroes and whites. To get Jim Crow streetcars abolished, Negroes in Atlanta had to take the initiative. The Georgia state law of 1890, which sanctioned segregated streetcars, was challenged in 1957 when the Reverend William Holmes Borders of the Wheat Street Baptist Church led a group of black ministers to violate the law by boarding a bus and riding unsegregated. They were arrested but promptly released. They were never indicted. Later, the Reverend Samuel W. Williams, professor of philosophy at Morehouse College, and the Reverend John Thomas Porter, a student in the Morehouse School of Religion, sued the Atlanta Transit Company for segregating them on the streetcars and buses of Atlanta. On January 9, 1959, a federal court declared that segregation on the Atlanta buses was unconstitutional. Once more, by destroying a barrier that perpetuated friction between the races, Negroes furthered better human relations in Atlanta.

Not so many persons were involved or benefited, but Dr. H. M. Holmes and his sons went to federal court to win their right to play golf on city courses. As in most cases in the 1950's, Negro lawyers had to argue civil rights cases. It was Attorneys S. S. Robinson, E. E. Moore, and R. E. Thomas who won the Holmes case.

It is to Atlanta's credit that her colleges and universities are now wide open to black students. But it should be remembered that black people had to go to federal court to break the color bar in higher education. Donald Hollowell and Constance Motley, black lawyers, assisted by Horace Ward, also black, won the right for Hamilton Holmes and Charlayne Hunter to enter the University of Georgia. This victory opened the doors of white institutions in Atlanta to black students. Atlanta would not have so good a name if the public schools in Atlanta were still segregated. Negroes are mainly responsible for a school system that is now in the process of desegregating all its schools.

Black visitors from the North are amazed to find that Atlanta hotels, restaurants, and nightclubs are open to Negroes, and that black people are employed in downtown businesses. For many decades, Northern Negroes were afraid to come South even to visit relatives. After being away for several years, Negroes born and reared in the South were afraid to return. There was basis for this fear, especially if they came riding through the South in fine-looking automobiles. Certainly Washington is a Southern city, but I felt more secure in Washington in the 1930's, when I lived there, than I did in Atlanta when I came here in 1940. Yet today, in ten years since 1960, black folk all over the nation are singing Atlanta's praises. Students in the Atlanta University Center, supported by a large segment of the adult black community, played a dramatic role in effecting this miraculous change.

Chapter XXI

I Can Sing Atlanta: The Young Warriors

When the Morehouse students began to talk about doing something about the intolerable situation in downtown Atlanta, where merchants gladly took black people's money but would not allow them to buy a cup of coffee, I knew that demonstrations were not far off.

On February 1, 1960, four students from A & T College in Greensboro, North Carolina, went to a white store in that city, seated themselves at the lunch counter and requested to be served. They were refused service, and they refused to leave. They were arrested, and the sit-ins were on. As in the Rosa Parks case in Montgomery, no organization sponsored the Greensboro sit-ins. This statement must be true, for so far as I know no civil rights organization has dared claim credit for it, as surely many would have been proud to do after this simple act of courage on the part of four young Negro boys set off shock waves which are still reverberating around the world. The time inevitably comes when oppressed people no longer will put up with an unbearable situation. Perhaps these four students had reached the limit of their endurance when they bravely started the revolution against discrimination in eating establishments in the South.

On February 5, 1960, four days after the Greensboro incident, Lonnie King, Joe Pierce, and Julian Bond met to discuss the role Morehouse students and the students in the entire Center should play in the "new revolution" that was destined to cover the South "like the dew." I am indebted to Lonnie King, the chosen leader in the Atlanta University Center demonstrations, for much of the data about this significant and exciting period in the history of race relations in Atlanta.

According to Lonnie King, the Morehouse and Spelman students had set February 12, Lincoln's birthday, as the appropriate time for the Center students to invade certain restaurants in downtown Atlanta. That date was postponed, however, because they wished to involve as many Center students as possible. The students had been planning their strategy for twelve days before a committee of them came to see me, February 17, 1960, to discuss their plans to begin the sit-ins in downtown Atlanta on February 19.

Far from being surprised that our students were "getting into the act," I would have been dismayed had they not participated in this South-wide revolution. What advice could I give them? Actually, they didn't come to me for advice but rather to inform me of their determination to strike a blow for freedom in downtown Atlanta and to get my blessings. How could I tell them not to do in mass what I had tried to do alone in Pullman cars, in dining cars, and in restaurants? All my life I had fought a lone battle against some of the injustices for which the students were now ready to go to jail, serve time, even die to break the sacred law of segregation so dear and so precious to the white South. And yet I had mixed thoughts and mixed emotions about it all. The record of the Atlanta police in its dealing with Negroes had not been good. I knew the students would be arrested. Would they be brutally beaten or even killed? Should their parents know about their plans? I suggested that they wait a while, that they continue conversations before beginning their campaign. I was a bit fearful that demonstrations at Martin Luther King's college might affect adversely his trial in Alabama where he was being charged with willfully and deliberately lying about his income and expenses. They understood perfectly well, however, that I would support them, whatever course they decided to take.

The six presidents in the Center were in full sympathy with the students, and the Council of Presidents never tried to overpersuade, let alone dictate to them. We did ask that they keep us informed and assured them that our suggestions were theirs for the asking, to accept or reject. I made my position clear to the Morehouse students. Each student should make up his own mind about participating in the sit-ins, should be coerced by no one, and once he had made up his mind to demonstrate, he should be prepared to take the consequences for violating the law, however unjust it surely was. I admonished them further that time spent demonstrating and time spent in jail did not absolve them from meeting the academic requirements of the college.

On February 20, the student government presidents and two students from each of the six campuses met for the first time with the Council of Presidents of the six institutions and agreed to meet with the Council of Presidents twice a week thereafter. At a meeting of the Council early in March, one of the college presidents, Albert Manley, as I recall, suggested that the students draw up a statement making it clear why they were protesting. The students accepted this suggestion: before going out to demonstrate, they would draw up a manifesto to tell Atlanta and the world what they were demonstrating for. On the committee to formulate the manifesto, students placed Julian Bond, James Felder, Lonnie King, Willie Mays, Roslyn Pope, Mary Ann Smith, and Marian Wright. The manifesto was written by students, not by presidents, and not by faculty. When three members of the committee asked me to read the document, I made one or two minor suggestions which I thought would strengthen it. It was a dramatic work of art issued under the title: "An Appeal for Human Rights." The students' complaints covered injustices and inequalities in education, jobs, housing, voting, hospitals, movies, concerts, restaurants, and law enforcement. I quote the first three paragraphs of the Appeal:

> We, the students of the six affiliated institutions forming the Atlanta University Center—Clark, Morehouse, Morris Brown, and Spelman Colleges, Atlanta University, and the Interdenominational Theological Center—have joined our hearts, minds, and bodies in the cause of gaining those rights which are inherently ours as members of the human race and as citizens of these United States.
>
> We pledge our unqualified support to those students in this nation who have recently been engaged in the significant movement to secure certain long-awaited rights and privileges. This protest, like the bus boycott in Montgomery, has shocked many people throughout the world. Why? Because they had not quite realized the unanimity of spirit and purpose which motivates the thinking and action of the great majority of the Negro people. The students who instigate and participate in these sit-down protests are dissatisfied, not only with the existing conditions, but with the snail-like speed at which they are being ameliorated. Every normal human being wants to walk the earth with dignity and abhors any and all proscriptions placed upon him because of race or color. In essence, this is the meaning of the sit-down protests that are sweeping this nation today.
>
> We do not intend to wait placidly for those rights which are already legally and morally ours to be meted out to us one at a time. Today's youth will not sit by submissively, while being denied all of the rights, privileges, and joys of life. We want to state clearly and unequivocally that we cannot tolerate, in a nation professing democracy and among people professing Christianity, the discriminatory conditions under which the Negro is living today in Atlanta, Georgia—supposedly one of the most progressive cities in the South.

After stating their case in clear and forceful language, they concluded with these words:

> We, therefore, call upon all people in authority—State, County, and City officials; all leaders in civic life—ministers, teachers, and business men; and

> all people of good will to assert themselves and abolish these injustices. We must say in all candor that we plan to use every legal and non-violent means at our disposal to secure full citizenship rights as members of this great Democracy of ours.

The draft was completed March 8. To be sure that the Appeal, which was paid for, would be treated with proper respect, the students sent it to the press by Rufus Clement, president of Atlanta University and president of the Council of Presidents. The Appeal appeared March 9, 1960 in the Atlanta *Daily World,* the Atlanta *Constitution,* and the Atlanta *Journal.* It received national attention, and was published in *The New York Times.*

Reactions to the Appeal for Human Rights, though mostly favorable, varied. It would be virtually impossible to find anywhere a better statement on the subject of Human Rights than the one the students of the Atlanta University Center issued. No other student group had done this. It was so good that Governor Vandiver believed that black students could not possibly have written a document so outstanding. Indeed, he didn't believe that it was written in the United States. The length of his rebuttal (Atlanta *Journal,* March 9, 1960) must surely indicate how devastatingly good he found it. The governor said: "The statement was skillfully prepared. Obviously it was not written by students. Regrettably, it had the same overtones which are usually found in anti-American propaganda pieces. It did not sound like it was written in any Georgia school or college; nor, in fact, did it read like it was written even in this country."

Others did not agree with Governor Vandiver. Margaret Long, writing in the *Journal,* headed her column: "Appeal for Human Rights Was Intelligent And Most Moving." Mayor Hartsfield said that the Appeal expressed "the legitimate aspirations of young people throughout the nation and the entire world." He said further that the student manifesto was "of the greatest importance to Atlanta."

By the middle of March, the students were well organized, under their chairman, Lonnie King, and determined to desegregate Atlanta. On March 14, five days after the Appeal for Human Rights appeared in the press a group of students visited my residence around midnight to inform me that demonstrations were on. The next day students from the Center staged their first sit-ins at the Terminal Station, the State Capitol, the County Courthouse, bus stations, the Peachtree-Baker Building, the Peachtree-Seventh Building, Union Station, City Hall, and other places. In their first effort to desegregate eating places, 200 college students staged sit-down demonstrations in ten white restaurants in downtown Atlanta. The Atlanta *Constitution* headlined its front page with "77 Negroes Arrested In Student Sit-Downs At 10 Eating Places Here," pointing out the fact that the protests in each of the ten places were orderly, quiet, and peaceful.

As long as there had been no action in connection with the advertised Appeal for Human Rights, there was generally praise for what the students had done. But when demonstrations started, it was a different story. On the evening of the 16th, the Atlanta *Journal* carried an editorial praising the nonviolent character of the demonstrations, and the conduct of the police and public, but it concluded with these words: "The protestors having made their point, the hope is that they now will leave well enough alone. When zeal and common sense are in conflict, the former too often prevails. But now is the time for common sense. Old customs and traditions are not changed by battering rams and dramatics but by time and attrition and with the help of good will."

An editorial in the Atlanta *Constitution* on March 16, 1960, concluded: "We repeat, the processes of law have been started. These can be handled without any public interference by agitators bent on disorder. We are a nation which must continue to live by law and this is a good time to remember it. We all have too much at stake in the present and future of this city to besmirch it with violence or extreme action. Let none of us forget that important fact." But the writer of this editorial was not to have his way. The revolution was on, and segregated facilities in downtown Atlanta were destined to go through months of turmoil, demonstrations, and negotiations.

Early in the game we, the presidents of the six institutions, sought an audience with some of the leading white businessmen in town, suggesting to them and urging them to use their influence to get the eating places opened to Negroes without the need of further demonstrations; for we knew that the students were ready for a long engagement. Our proposal was ignored. One outstanding businessman told us: "You go back and tell your students that they will never eat in a white restaurant in Atlanta." One of us remarked, "Never is a mighty long time." How ironic: Not many months later, I received an invitation to a political dinner at the Top Of The Mart with this man's name as one of the signatures. *Never* was indeed a short time!

The editorial writers in the *Constitution* and *Journal* who wanted the sit-ins to end peacefully with the March 15 demonstrations were not to have their wishes fulfilled. It took eighteen long months—not a single day—

before "the walls came tumbling down." The spring of 1960 and the fall of 1960 were filled with student demonstrations. On March 15, 1960, seventy-seven had been arrested. On October 19, 1960, fifty-seven students chose jail rather than bail. On February 8 and 9, 1961, eighty-two students were arrested, choosing jail rather than bail.

The protests took many forms. The sit-ins soon spread to other private as well as public eating places, including prestigious ones like Rich's. Pickets were used first on April 22, 1960, against A&P after a series of telephone calls to A&P management had yielded no results. Colonial Stores authorities were approached April 16 and urged to hire and upgrade Negroes. Some stores, like Food Town, hired Negroes after a short period of negotiation. Students kept busy throughout the spring of 1960. On May 17, three thousand protesters marched through town to a mass meeting at Wheat Street Baptist Church. On the same day, students sat-in at *My Fair Lady* at the City Auditorium. On June 26, students sat-in at Rich's, and thereafter private stores were the targets, because other cities in the South had desegregated their department store eating facilities and Atlanta had not. On June 27, a conference with officials at Rich's brought no tangible results. The students chose Rich's because it is the most outstanding store in Atlanta and one of the finest in the nation. Students felt that if Rich's desegregated its lunch counters and dining rooms, others would follow. Stores were not only picketed but were boycotted. No one had believed that the Negro adult community would boycott prestigious stores like Davison's and Rich's, but they did. The Federal Bank reported July 28 that department-store sales were down 22 percent. On July 30, there was a sit-in at *South Pacific* at Chastain Park. Kneel-ins at churches began in August, 1960. Also in August, 1960, Negro doctors, followed by their wives, picketed A&P.

When the colleges opened in September, 1960, demonstrations took on added momentum. In the meanwhile, adult citizens and students were negotiating trying to get the power structure to abolish its segregated ways. On October 30, the students agreed to a thirty-day truce, during which time Mayor Hartsfield was to use the influence of his office to get things settled so that Negroes could be free to eat and work anywhere in downtown Atlanta. The mayor was to make weekly reports to the Adult-Student Committee. The students' aim was to gain the freedom in downtown Atlanta before Christmas. The truce in that sense was a failure. Other attempts to negotiate with merchants failed. One year after the sit-ins started in Greensboro, students of the Atlanta University Center celebrated by staging sit-ins on February 1, 1961. On February 7, 8, and 9, eighty-two persons were arrested. A group of ministers were arrested and jailed for a night on February 15. Several Negro doctors were arrested at the Biltmore for sitting-in.

Two strange things happened during the twelve months before an agreement was reached. One was that the Ku Klux Klan got into the act. On one side of the street they were picketing for continuing segregation, while on the other side the students and some adults were picketing for ending segregation. But the more important thing was that much of the adult Negro community supported the students in their demands: doctors, lawyers (through the courts), ministers, the Empire Real Estate Board (providing bail when the students would accept it), and many faculty people of the Atlanta University Center. The more conservative Negroes who opposed the boycott and demonstrations did not count. Even they participated in the boycott, for no Negro wanted it said that he or she was not in favor of abolishing segregation and was not with the students in their noble efforts to give Atlanta a good image and free themselves from the evil of living in a segregated society. When one or two trustees requested me to stop the Morehouse students from demonstrating, I politely refused.

The Atlanta merchants "died hard" on this issue. The stalemate between the merchants and the students was broken when an Adult-Student Committee agreed to end the demonstrations and the downtown establishments agreed to desegregate their facilities when the schools were desegregated under court order in September, 1961. Thus ended an eighteen-month struggle for freedom. But when a mass meeting was held to hear the negotiating committees' report, things almost fell apart. It was Martin Luther King, Jr., who, in an eloquent speech, expressed faith in the commitments made by the Committee and urged acceptance. A lesser person could not have saved this situation. The following persons were members of the negotiating committee that ended the boycott, picketing, and sit-ins, and at the same time ended segregation in downtown Atlanta for all eternity, I hope: Ivan Allen, president of the Atlanta Chamber of Commerce; the Reverend William Holmes Borders, pastor of the Wheat Street Baptist Church; Doctor Rufus E. Clement, president of Atlanta University; Harold L. Ebersole of Davison's; Jesse Hill, Atlanta Life Insurance Company; Leroy Johnson, now Georgia senator; the Reverend Martin Luther King, Sr., pastor of the Ebenezer Baptist Church; Lonnie King, of the Committee on Appeal For Human Rights; the Reverend Otis Moss; Frank Nealy of Rich's; Herschell Sullivan, co-chairman of the Committee On Appeal For Human Rights; Attorney A. T. Walden, Civil Rights lawyer in many court cases; Q. V. Williamson, now alderman; the regional director of Woolworth; Mrs. Johnnie Yancey, civic leader; and representatives of other chain stores. The student leaders, working under the able and astute Lonnie King and Herschell Sullivan, Chairman and co-chairman of the Committee On Appeal For Human Rights who were largely responsible for the success of the battle to desegregate Atlanta—called by *Look* Magazine the Second Battle of Atlanta—came from the six institutions that make up the Atlanta University Center. They were Marian Wright, Morris Dillard, Julian Bond, Albert Brinson, Lenora Tate, Lana Taylor, Frank Smith, Josephine Jackson, Roslyn Pope, James Felder, Carolyn Long, Wilma Long, Ben Brown (now in the Georgia Legislature), Danny Mitchell, Lydia Tucker, Leon Green, Mary Ann Smith, William Hickson, Johnny Parham, John Mack, Edmond Harper, Kenneth Crooks, John Gibson, A. D. King, Robert Felder, J. A. Wilborn, Doris Smith, and J. C. Harper.

Sherman fought the first battle of Atlanta with guns and fire and helped to defeat the Confederate Army. The black students of the Atlanta University Center, almost a century later, fought the second battle of Atlanta nonviolently and won freedom for black people and a larger freedom for white Atlantans.

Before closing this chapter, I must make three comments in connection with the demonstrations; two of them involve me directly. In the early days of the sit-ins, when our students were likely to take off for a demonstration at any time, I called on Chief Herbert Jenkins about some of our students who had been arrested. I thought I sensed sympathetic understanding of the problem in Chief Jenkins' attitude toward our students who were disrupting the normal flow of business in Atlanta. He said to me in essence: "Go back and tell your students that when they are going to demonstrate, sit-in, or picket, let me know in advance so that I will be able to dispatch the right officers to the scene. You know we have all kinds of men on the police force; some are members of the Klan. It makes a lot of difference who the officer in charge is." He said further, "I would like to talk to your students, so that they will understand my position as chief." I asked the chief how far in advance he should be notified that a demonstration was in the making. "At least twenty minutes," he said. As for meeting with our students, he said the students could come to his office or he would come to the campus. He came to the campus. There he told the students, as he had told me, that he would appreciate it if they would inform him in advance when they planned to march on downtown Atlanta. He made it clear that when they violated the law he was duty bound to arrest them but assured them that no brutality would be inflicted. I shall never forget him or his extraordinary behavior.

The second incident concerned a plan to march from the campus to a mass meeting scheduled at the Wheat Street Baptist Church on March 17. Lonnie King made a mistake, I thought, in announcing at a student mass meeting on the campus that in their march to Wheat Street the students were going to pay their respect to Governor Vandiver at the State Capitol. The governor responded with lightning speed, authorizing a hundred or more state troopers to protect the Capitol and the news media carried the word. Capitol grounds are not city property, so that once our students landed there, they would be beyond the jurisdiction of city officials. We also felt certain that our students would get no sympathetic treatment from Governor Vandiver and his state troopers. Early on the morning of the proposed march, I got a report that the troopers were there, bumper to bumper, and that the Capitol was completely surrounded. Both the mayor's office and the chief's office called me, saying that the situation looked explosive and suggesting that I urge the students not to go to the Capitol.

I felt duty bound to relay to the Morehouse students the opinions of Mayor Hartsfield and Chief Jenkins; so at our nine o'clock chapel, I apprised them of the situation at the Capitol and advised them to postpone their march until another time when they could take the governor by surprise. The student leaders made me no promises. They said that they had to confer with the committee that made the decisions, and that the students of the Center would have to vote on the committee's recommendation. Lonnie and his cabinet called for a mass meeting at 1 P.M. There the decision would be reached whether they would march to the Capitol that day or later. The meeting was a dramatic one with possibly 2,000 students waiting for the committee's report—to march or not to march.

When Lonnie read the decision that they would march to Wheat Street by way of the Capitol, there was no doubt in my mind that nothing was going to turn these students around. Meanwhile the waiting students had been singing songs, among them, WE SHALL OVERCOME They were poised and determined. After the decision to march was announced, someone offered a moving prayer. The most touching phase of the entire event was the speech of Lonnie King who urged that only the true and brave should go; only those committed to nonviolence should go; only those who could accept violent treatment from the police without striking back should go. Those not committed to this philosophy should drop out. Nobody did. They marched away singing, WE SHALL OVERCOME SOMEDAY and were joined by students from Morris Brown and others along the way. I knew then that regardless of what might happen to the students of the Center, they had reached maturity; they were free. I could not stop them, and I did not want to stop them. Sadie and I got into our car and met the assembly at Wheat Street Baptist Church. Rev. Otis Moss then gave a brilliant address, a funeral oration over the death of Jim Crow.

The students didn't get to the Capitol. As they marched down Hunter Street toward the Capitol, Chief Jenkins met them about two blocks away, pointing a firm finger through the heart of downtown Atlanta, and thus averting what might have been a tragic encounter with the state troopers. Lonnie stubbornly insisted on the march to the Capitol, but when the chief told Lonnie that he had no choice but to obey his orders, Lonnie did.

One may ask: how can I sing Atlanta when it took the white power structure more than twelve months to agree to desegregate the city and to allow eighteen months to pass before the students actually achieved their objectives? The answer is that both the city government and the business people of Atlanta were wise enough to know that the time had come when Atlanta could no longer cling to outmoded traditions and at the same time have peace and prosperity. They yielded slowly and grudgingly, but they made the concessions. And what I feared most never happened. I was afraid that our students would be harassed and unmercifully beaten by the police and the jailers. I was particularly uneasy about the girls in the Center who demonstrated and went to jail with the men. When I looked into this I did not hear one student say that he or she was brutally treated. The charges against the students were dropped. This was as it should have been, but nonetheless it speaks well for Mayor Hartsfield and Chief Jenkins. It is outrageous, of course, that we had to go through all this in order to get what others get by being born white.

Atlanta is a proud city that has much of which to be proud. Both Negroes and whites love their city and have a stake in its future. It is centrally located, with thirty million people closely tied to Atlanta by rail, air, and good roads. Without a doubt, Atlanta is destined to be and already is one of the four or five crucial foci in the further development of the American economy. Atlanta competes favorably with twenty-five of the largest cities in the nation in construction, banking, communications, sales, and transportation. Dr. Harmon Moore of the Atlanta Christian Council says that attitude alone is one of Atlanta's greatest assets and that it has played a significant role "in the promotion of the famous Atlanta spirit and in the building of the metropolitan area." It has been predicted that Atlanta and Denver will be the fastest-growing regions in the United States in the 1970's. No other city of its size in the nation can boast of so many good colleges and universities and business schools. Atlanta has a very high percentage of educated persons. As for black Atlanta, Professor James Conyers has said that Atlanta probably has the most highly educated Negro community in the United States.

Atlanta has all these assets, but a city, like an individual person, can die if its health—physical and spiritual—is not preserved and enhanced. I believe that Atlanta's good character is largely due to good leadership—Negro and white. If this leadership cannot be continued and improved in business, religion, education, politics, and social concern, Atlanta will become just another city. The slums and ghettoes of Atlanta are not part of the city's good name, and we cannot conceal from view such slum places as Plunkett Town and Lightning. There is enough wealth in Atlanta to make it a model city in housing for its poor, black and white. Never is there a question of what could be done; always it is a matter of priorities. The federal government does not have the vision to make the abolition of slums and ghettoes a priority in the next ten years, or at least it has made no such announcement. It would be wonderful if Atlanta, a southern city, would decide to make adequate housing for all its citizens a top priority in the 1970's. Future racial peace in Atlanta—and everywhere else in the nation—may well depend upon good housing and good paying jobs for all who are able to work.

I believe that Atlanta cannot move forward as it should in the area of race relations if white people feel they must flee to suburbia to get away from black people, leaving the inner city to them. I concede that Atlanta must expand, but I do not believe that our political racial problems will be solved merely by extending the boundaries of Atlanta to include the counties and nearby towns. It is also to be devoutly hoped in the area of housing that one Negro cannot always seem to chase a thousand white persons and two put ten thousand to flight.

The City of Atlanta can definitely improve its practice in the employment of Negroes. The study of the United States Commission on Civil Rights found that in the City of Atlanta, where one out of every three employees of the city is Negro, there is no Negro at the managerial level and only eighteen at the professional level, while there were but fourteen clerical workers. On the other hand, Negroes hold 87 percent of the laborer jobs. Although Negroes constitute 44 percent of the Atlanta population, a mere eleven of the more than 300 persons employed in general administration in the City of Atlanta were Negroes—ten of them clerical workers and one a service worker. There are 6,000 state jobs in the Atlanta area, and only 350 are held by Negroes. Negroes comprise fewer than 5 percent of the white-collar jobs—but 50 percent of the service workers jobs. In both state and city government, Negroes are drastically under represented. We hope the employment image of Atlanta will be greatly improved under Mayor Sam Massell.

Atlanta's image in public school education is not commensurate with its reputation in the nation. As in other cities, north and south, the depth of the chasm between black and white in Atlanta is most apparent when it comes to desegregating the schools and when it comes to black and white living together in the same neighborhood. The decision of the federal courts that the city's public schools had to be desegregated by February 1, 1970, on a ratio of 57 percent black and 43 percent white teachers, created consternation among many white Atlantans. Many white teachers contemplated the prospect of being sent to black schools with dismay, some part of which was because of the natural fear of the unknown and untried, but a great deal of which was race prejudice. Black teachers, although not happy over being uprooted and transferred to alien surroundings, accepted the situation as a part of the price of progress.

The degree of further desegregation of students is yet to be decided by the District Court as I write this section. While we wait, many people are emotionally upset for fear of mandatory bussing, although the Atlanta Board of Education has not proposed bussing and the Supreme Court has not ordered it. Mass meetings have been held in many sections of the city protesting the transfer of teachers as ordered by the Courts. Governor Lester Maddox has advised defiance of federal court orders. Some 20,000 persons supposedly signed a petition and carried it to Washington to urge the President, the Supreme Court, and the Congress to repudiate the decisions handed down by the Supreme Court on October 29, 1969, and by the lower courts since that date. Some white students stayed out of school to march and demonstrate. Several hundred teachers, mostly white, resigned for various reasons. Fortunately, however, at this writing the transfer of teachers has worked well and the number of resignations seems to be about normal.

All this happened in Atlanta, the pride of the South in race relations and the showplace of the nation for harmonious relations between black and white. And yet, excepting for Governor Maddox and a few other politicians of his brand, the leadership in Atlanta has acted fairly responsibly, and it is hoped that Atlanta will come through the school desegregation crisis with the cause of black-white relations advanced as has been the case in numerous racial upheavals in this city in the last quarter of a century. It is clear, however, that Atlanta is a long way from being what it ought to be in providing a model for the nation in school desegregation. There are too many schools that are all black and too many that are all white. Too much able leadership has been conspicuously silent during the school desegregation crisis of 1970.

These are some of the areas in black-white relations where Atlanta needs to move with speed if it is to keep pace with the growth predicted for the decades ahead. It would be a tragedy if Atlanta should move forward economically and politically, yet lag behind in building a community where black and white can live together in dignity and with mutual respect. It would be wonderful, the realization of my most cherished hope, if Atlanta proved conclusively my conviction that despite the way Negroes have been lynched, brutalized, segregated, and discriminated against in the South, it can and will be in the South that black people and white people learn to live together in such justice and peace as to be a beacon light to all the world. The southern white man is sometimes very determined and insistent when he is dead wrong. He often moves with equal determination when he is convinced that the cause is right and just. If only Atlanta would give top priority to making black-white relations in Atlanta the best in the nation—black and white together! How soon that goal would be reached, how quickly that dream would be actualized!

Just as we are all glad today that we took the giant step to eliminate segregation in public places in Atlanta in 1961—and no one, not even those who resisted the change, would go back to a segregated community—Atlanta citizens will be equally happy and proud if their city sets the pace for the entire nation in developing a metropolis where black and white live harmoniously together and where even the poorest citizens have adequate housing, good jobs, and quality education—a city where every man, woman, and child can stand straight and tall, a city where everyone is born free and can walk on the moon!

Chapter XXII

Retrospect and Prospect

For seventy years, I have been keenly aware of the continuing crisis in Negro-white relations. To see a mob of white men bent on lynching Negroes before one is five years old etches an impression on the mind and soul that only death can erase.

Since my boyhood days, I have longed for a solution to the Negro-white problem. At one time I was willing to consider the problem solved if only lynching and the brutalities inflicted upon Negroes by white people could be forever abolished. Unyielding resistance to these injustices was deeply woven into the very fabric of my soul.

During my time and earlier, no program has ever been proposed that has produced a solution to this problem, which has dominated the thinking of black people and white people for over three centuries. Perhaps when the slave traffic was at its height, little thought was given to solutions. The dominant motive in promoting and maintaining slavery was profit, and profit alone, no matter how hard evil men may have striven to salve their consciences by blaming God, proclaiming that the black man was ordained by Him to do manual labor for the white man. "What God has ordained, let no man attempt to overthrow," was the false defense of the wicked for their avarice and greed.

In my lifetime, four main solutions have been advanced to close the chasm of suspicion, distrust, hatred, prejudice, and racism inherent in black-white relations in this country: colonization, segregation by law, some form of "black separatism" here in the United States, and more recently, integration (desegregation, in my terminology). A few people have argued that miscegenation is the solution. Violent revolution has been seriously proposed by a small group who believe that the "system" is beyond reform and must be destroyed.

During slavery, many white people advocated colonization for the Negro, especially for the free Negro. Some masters felt that with free Negroes around it would be too hard to discipline their slaves. There were also

Negroes who did not "adjust" well to the "American way of life"; so the question arose, "What to do with them?" As the numbers of free Negroes increased, it was felt that they had to be sent out of the country "if property in slaves was to be secure."

Others insisted that free Negroes should be sent out of the country because the two races could never live together in peace and harmony. In his book *From Slavery to Freedom* (pp. 237-241), John Hope Franklin tells of a colonization movement which began as early as 1774, when a proposal was advanced to send the Negroes back to Africa. Not long after the end of the Revolutionary War, a program to send Negroes back to Africa was proposed. Thomas Jefferson also headed a committee which "set forth a plan of gradual emancipation and exportation." Franklin reminds us further that the Connecticut Emancipation Society had as one of their objectives "the colonization of the free Negroes."

Negroes also were interested in colonization. In 1815, Paul Cuffee took thirty-eight Negroes to Africa at his own expense. Two years later, the American Colonization Society was organized with men like Justice Bushrod Washington, Henry Clay, and John Randolph supporting it. Plans were made to set up a colony for Negroes in Africa, and federal and state aid was sought to support the project and to arouse favorable public opinion. Men were sent out to raise money to get free Negroes to emigrate to Liberia. Having secured money, ships were purchased by the Society and chartered to transport Negroes to Liberia. By 1832, a dozen legislatures, including those of such slave-holding states as Maryland, Virginia, and Kentucky, had given official sanction to the Society. North Carolina and Mississippi had local colonization societies. To begin with, only free Negroes were transported to Africa, but soon slaves were manumitted to be taken to Liberia, and by 1830 the American Colonization Society had settled 1,420 Negroes there. In the end, however, the Society did not have much success in persuading Negroes to go to Liberia, the final total being approximately a mere twelve thousand. In fact, all programs for sending Negroes to Africa and to other countries were mostly failures. They were not economically feasible. Too few supported the idea; and those who did could not agree on how the job should be accomplished.

The colonization movement gained what little support it did for various reasons:

1) Some wanted colonization to succeed so that slavery might end and all Negroes be sent to Africa.

2) Others supported the idea because of their belief that Negroes could not adjust to western civilization.

3) Some even supported the idea of colonization because it would give missionaries an opportunity to "carry Christianity and civilization to Africa".

4) Slaveholders were anxious to get rid of free Negroes, hoping thereby to strengthen the institution of slavery.

Negroes themselves did their part to kill the idea of colonization. A group met in Richmond shortly after the organization of the American Colonization Society and, though they approved its idea they preferred a location in the United States, not in Africa. Some Negroes in the slave-holding states, seeing no hope of emancipation, supported the idea of colonization. On the other hand, most Northern Negroes opposed it. The Humane and Benevolent Society of Philadelphia was urged by three thousand Negroes there to reject the proposal outright.

It is clear that Negroes were wanted in the United States only as slaves and never were they welcome as free men. Even Abraham Lincoln, who won immortality in history by saving the Union, and incidentally freeing the slaves, wanted to send Negroes back to Africa. It is safe to conclude that those Negroes who favored colonization, whether in the North or the South, did so only because they were convinced that the white man would never accord equal opportunity to the black man to rise in the economic, professional, and political life of the country; would never provide the black man compensatory education and economic aid to enable him to overcome the handicaps placed upon him for three and a half centuries. Those Negroes who argued for deportation believed that white racism was permanent and irrevocable and that no amount of education and no miraculous religious conversion would ever change the white man's attitude.

Booker T. Washington did not believe that colonization was the way out for the Negro. His concern was to keep Negroes in the South. He advised Negroes and whites, "Cast down your buckets where you are." His solution was a segregated society in which Negroes, certainly for the time being, would leave politics alone and entertain no idea of social integration. It was this undemanding philosophy that made whites proclaim Washington the greatest living Negro and the leader of the black people in the United States. Washington delighted the South because Southern whites had always insisted that the race problem could be dealt with only through segregation. But time has proved that legal segregation is not the solution; that in a segregated society, where the dominant group has all the power and administers it for its own gratification, justice and equality are impossible.

Against this background of white racism and the Negro's conviction that he can never achieve justice and equality in this country, the Marcus Garvey movement and modern programs designed to solve the black-white problem in the United States bear discussion:

All the strivings toward "black separatism" and "black nationalism" are the inevitable result of Negroes' hopes and expectations being dashed to bits in frustration and disillusionment. Marcus Garvey came on the scene in 1919, just after World War I, in which Negroes were led to believe that if they fought under Woodrow Wilson's banner "to make the world safe for democracy", things would be better for them in the United States. They were not. Lynchings increased, and race riots broke out all over. Thus the racial soil was fertile for Garvey. Negroes were desperate for a "savior" to lead them to the "promised land," or at least away from the land of their afflictions and humiliations. No matter how illusory his dreams, and regardless of what certain Negro critics thought of him, Garvey had the qualities of leadership to stir the "black masses." He had charisma, he was eloquent, he was black. No other black leader, in my time, had attracted the masses as did Garvey. He did for Negroes what no other leader before him had done and what no black leader would do again until the 1960's: He made them proud of their heritage, proud of being black. The young Negro who thinks that the current emphasis on black identity is new needs to read about Marcus Garvey.

Although much has been written elsewhere about Marcus Garvey, some information on the background of this fascinating figure in the history of the American Negro needs repeating here. Many of our readers may know little or nothing about Marcus Garvey. He was born August 17, 1887, in St. Ann's Bay, Jamaica, British West Indies, the youngest of eleven children. He did not have much formal training, although he received a good elementary education. His claim that he studied at the University of London was never established. Nevertheless, he was widely read and perhaps was quite as knowledgeable as many university-trained men. At fourteen he became a printing apprentice in Kingston, the capital of Jamaica; and at twenty-two he had mastered the trade and been appointed foreman of a large printing establishment. He was fired from his job because he joined workers who were striking and accepted their invitation to lead a walkout.

During the next year, while working in a government printing office, Garvey edited a journal known as the *Watchman,* and organized a political organization, the National Club. The failure of both motivated him to travel. He visited several other islands in his native Jamaica and journeyed to Central and South America. In Costa Rica, Garvey's uncle helped him secure a job as timekeeper at one of the banana plantations of the United Fruit Company. There he was appalled at the conditions under which black people worked; and afterward, wherever he traveled, he carefully observed the working conditions of blacks. What he saw affected him greatly. Two years later he set sail for London.

There Garvey met members of other dark races who had grievances against the white men. He heard phrases like "India for the Indians," and "Asia for the Asiatics." In this context he became interested in the conditions of the African Negro; and it soon became clear to him that the problem of the Negro was not confined to the West Indies and Central America, but that it was international in scope and required international solutions. Garvey noted that other dark races were demanding justice in lands which were theirs; and even though Africa was under the control of whites he argued that Negroes must seek a land historically their own—to do so, he insisted, would be far better than to continue their futile efforts to overcome white prejudice in the Western world.

In his musings, Garvey asked these questions: Where are the black man's government, his president, his country, his ambassadors, army, navy, and men of affairs? Garvey set out to fashion a country for the black man. He was dreaming of a world for black men—not slaves, serfs, coolies, peons, but a nation of blacks who would make their impact upon civilization. The slogan "Africa for the Africans" was coined, and when Garvey developed the idea of Pan-Africanism the phrase "Africa for the Africans at Home and Abroad" became very popular.

In 1914, Marcus Garvey returned to his native Jamaica where he worked to perfect an organization to unite the Negro people of the world into one government which would be their very own. He had become interested in conditions of Negroes in the United States from reading Booker T. Washington's *Up From Slavery;* consequently when the people of Jamaica were unreceptive to his plan for black world unity, he set sail for the United States in 1916.

The Negro masses in America, it seemed, were waiting for Garvey. He started by speaking to Negroes on the streets of Harlem, and in a year's time he was acclaimed as an orator and a leader. When he spoke at a black mass meeting in a Harlem church, James Weldon Johnson described him as "possessing a magnetic personality, torrential eloquence, and an intuitive knowledge of crowd psychology."

Negroes of today who insist on being called black should give credit to Marcus Garvey for promoting this usage over a half century ago. He urged that all men of African blood refer to themselves as *black* men—not Negro men, not colored men. The Negro, he insisted, must not belittle his past in Africa but rather be proud of it. He berated Negro leaders who advocated social equality, and accused them of being unwilling to work hard to carve out a civilization of their own. He said that the white world—the white American world—would never give Negroes an even chance—*so get out!* Negro leaders, like W. E. B. DuBois, Robert Russa Moton, A. Philip Randolph, and others had many unpleasant things to say about Garvey, and he vigorously returned their remarks in kind. He criticized the color-based caste system within the Negro race. Before Garvey appeared on the American scene, it had not been considered polite to attack this system. Garvey labeled DuBois "a mulatto whose white blood made him hate the black blood in his veins."

Finally, Garvey was able to launch here what he had not been able to start in Jamaica. He established the Universal Negro Improvement Association, in which, he claimed, there were two million members by June, 1919. His publication, the *Negro World*, was designed to build up the black man's pride in himself; and Garvey, who by now was the most talked about Negro in the world, set about to build a merchant marine to establish trade among black men all over the world.

On June 27, 1919, Marcus Garvey's Black Star Line was incorporated, and it is estimated that as many as two million persons purchased shares in the venture. By August, 1920, Garvey was claiming four million members of the Universal Negro Improvement Association. In the same year he called a convention of Negroes from all parts of the world, the purpose being to shape a program to uplift Negroes and redeem Africa. Black men came from Africa, from South and Central America, from Canada, and from the West Indies. The convention adopted a declaration of independence as a universal anthem. The anthem was entitled "Ethiopia." Garvey was named "His Excellency, the Provisional President of Africa." A mammoth mass meeting was held in Madison Square Garden with an estimated attendance of twenty thousand people. When Garvey spoke the applause was tumultuous. He said in part:

> We are striking homeward toward Africa to make her the big black republic. And in the making of Africa the big black republic, what is the barrier? The barrier is the white man, and we say to the white man who dominates Africa that it is to his interest to clear out now, because we are coming, not as in the time of Father Abraham, 200,000 strong, but we are coming 400,000,000 strong and we mean to retake every square inch of the 12,000,000 square miles of African territory belonging to us by Right Divine.

DuBois argued that the Garvey movement was built not on a solid foundation but on sinking sand, and he predicted its failure—a prediction that really required no great prophetic insight. Ships were purchased for the Black Star Line, and soon the Universal Negro Improvement Association ran into financial difficulties. On January 12, 1922, Garvey and three other UNIA officials were arrested and charged with using the mails to defraud in the promotion of the Black Star Line and the UNIA.

Garvey's arrest made a martyr of him, and black people from many places came to his rescue. Some Negro leaders, however, pressed for his imprisonment or his deportation. The United States did not prosecute its case immediately, and while Garvey was out on bail, and during his trial, when he acted as his own attorney, he became a greater hero than ever. Finally, however, Garvey was found guilty, fined $1,000, and sentenced to five years' imprisonment in the Atlanta Federal Penitentiary. In the latter part of 1923, Garvey estimated his followers to be six million strong. The UNIA, which boasted nine hundred branches throughout the world, was making plans to implement its program of colonization. The Black Star Line was reorganized under the name of the Black Cross Line. But Garvey's agreement with the Liberian government to bring American Negroes to that republic was broken, and the emigration of American blacks could not take place.

The Garvey movement to build a black nation failed because its financial structure was unsound and because Garvey had too many enemies, black and white, fighting against him. Nevertheless the movement made many Negroes proud of their blackness and caused them to cease being ashamed of the color of their skin and of Africa, and to this degree it was a success. However, even if Garvey had succeeded in getting sufficient money, and if his financial structure had been sound, it is hardly conceivable that ten million Negroes would have gone to Africa. Despite their suffering and hardships, Negroes have always loved this land and considered themselves an integral part of it. So the greatest scheme ever attempted to establish black nationalism on the continent of Africa ended in failure.*

Today other protest groups, such as the Black Muslims, share Garvey's convictions that the dice are loaded against the Negro in the United States, but their distrust and dislike of white men are more intense and searing. C. Eric Lincoln's book, *The Black Muslims in America* (Boston: Beacon Press, 1961), begins with a Negro prosecuting attorney delivering his indictment against a white man, symbol of the white race. The white man was charged with being "the greatest liar on earth; the greatest drunkard on earth; the greatest gambler; the greatest peace breaker; the greatest adulterer; the greatest robber; the greatest deceiver; and the greatest trouble-maker on earth." The verdict of the jury was "guilty"—the sentence was "death." The audience, happy with the verdict, applauded thunderously. This episode is a fairly graphic description of what the Black Muslims think of the white man. Under the leadership of Elijah Muhammed, they have become a force to be reckoned with. To them the white man is the incarnation of evil and the black man is the epitome of virtue. They point out that it took the white man to drop atomic bombs, run special trains to witness a lynching, and only a white man could have mercilessly killed six million Jews.

The Black Muslims advocate complete separatism as the only possible or desirable solution to the Negro-white problem; but whereas Garvey's program was Africa-oriented, the Black Muslims prefer to establish a black nation right here in the United States. They have no intention of abandoning this country to the white man. Justice, they claim, requires and demands that a black nation be set up for Negroes on "some of the land our fathers and mothers paid for in three hundred years of slavery." Although the Black Muslims are not aggressively violent, they are certainly not nonviolent pacifists. They are taught to defend themselves when attacked. When Malcolm X was alive and in good standing with the leadership of the Black Muslims, he said, in an address at the Boston University School of Theology (May 24, 1960):

> We are never aggressors. We will not attack anyone. We strive for a peaceful relationship with everyone. But we teach our people that if any-

*For data on Marcus Garvey, I have relied on Robert Brisbane's *The Black Vanguard* (Valley Forge, Pa.: Judson Press, 1969), Ch. IV.

> one attacks you, lay down your life. Every Muslim is taught never to [initiate a] fight. . . . . Never be an aggressor, never look for trouble. But if any man molest you, may Allah bless you.

The Black Muslims do not advocate violence as a way to establish a black nation in the United States; nor do they offer any other plan.

All programs thus far advanced by the Negro to free himself from domination and exploitation have been highly visionary and impractical. I simply do not see black nationalism, whether here or elsewhere, as a way out for the black man. Past failures of black nationalist movements do not necessarily mean that future efforts in this direction will also fail. I do believe, nevertheless, that any effort to establish a black nation for more than twenty million Negroes outside the United States, or through a combination of states within this country, is not going to succeed. I see no practical technique of achievement: of securing sufficient funds; of establishing the necessary unanimity among Negroes; of persuading state governments to turn over certain states to Negroes. To dream of black nationalism—whether Garvey's, the Black Muslims, or some other's—is little more than a mirage.

What the black man needs most are: a better education; technical skills to enable him to succeed in a highly competitive society; decent jobs that pay enough to enable him to live comfortably above the poverty line; adequate housing, with the consequent abolition of slums and ghettoes; political strength to influence voting to his benefit and to defeat racist politicians; a sense of pride, self-respect, and self-identity; and a sense of solidarity. I believe that neither black nationalism nor black separatism has any magic power to provide for the needs of black people. Separatism of itself will not wipe out slums and ghettoes, provide adequate jobs and wages, or create a superior educational system for black children. Separatism may mirror the despair which drives a black man to wish to escape entirely from association with whites. Or it may stem from the desire of blacks to control their own destiny for good or for ill. But it can never be a lasting solution.

The central questions confronting every black man are what he can do to enlarge his freedom, to create in himself a sense of his inherent worth and dignity, and to develop economic and political security. He must also consider what can be done to help build a society where each person has the opportunity to develop his mind, body, and spirit without the imposition of artificial barriers. Are these things more likely to be achieved in a separate or nationalistic society than in a so-called integrated society? There is no easy way; there are no certain answers.

The United States government and the vast majority of white Americans have never committed themselves to the idea of full-fledged citizenship for the Negro. Black people in America were emancipated 106 years ago, and a century has passed since the enactment of the 13th, 14th, and 15th Amendments to the Constitution. In all these years, the federal government has never been willing to enforce laws to give the black man the rights that are guaranteed to him by the Constitution. Not in needs, hopes, aspirations, fears, sorrows, or dreams do men differ: only in pigmentation! How different history might be had all men been the same color!

In 1954, the Supreme Court handed down a decree designed to desegregate the public schools; later, congressional laws were enacted to wipe out segregation and discrimination. Yet resistance to implementing the Court's decree and complying with the laws passed by the Congress has been so nation-wide that, much to the dismay of the white establishment, disillusioned and frustrated Negroes are forming and aligning themselves with radical groups which no longer are asking but demanding. Even as I complete the last chapter of this book, the October 29, 1969, decision of the Supreme Court ordering an immediate end to the dual system of education is meeting tremendous resistance. Moreover, the Nixon Administration has argued for a slower pace in desegregating schools!

Some maintain that the movement toward integration has failed completely, and that Martin Luther King's philosophy of nonviolence is out of date and no longer relevant to the needs of the black man. I am deeply disappointed at the slow pace of abolishing discrimination, saddened by the sympathy President Nixon has given the segregationists, nauseated by the way some so-called honest men deliberately use all their ingenuity to circumvent the functioning of federal law. However, I am not willing to throw in the towel after fifteen years of effort since the May, 1954, decision; nor am I willing to discard the program of militant nonviolence as an effective way of changing black-white relations. Segregation has been declared unconstitutional by the Supreme Court; court actions have been supported by congressional law; and certainly some Negroes have benefited greatly from actions of federal courts and the Congress. The changes that brought better job opportunities for Negroes came not through physical violence but through militant nonviolent action in the courts and by pressures exerted on the establishment from sit-ins and other effective demonstrations. No one can deny that the masses of Negroes are little if any better off than they were before 1954, but this bitter fact does not mean that the gains made in the civil rights struggle are meaningless, worthless. With many restrictions removed by the federal courts and Congress we should be in a better position to tackle and solve the economic problems that confront the poor.

Federal court decisions, following the 1954 Supreme Court decision, and the successful 1963 March on Washington, two hundred thousand strong, led Negroes to believe that a new era was about to emerge for the black man. The Civil Rights Acts of 1964 and 1965 further increased the hopes and expectations of black people. The plight of the poor blacks, however, was and remains so serious that the Johnson Administration's War on Poverty did little to improve their condition. Riots broke out in Los Angeles, Detroit, Cleveland, Newark, Washington, D.C., and other smaller cities, dramatizing the gravity of the urban problems. The assassination of Martin Luther King, Jr., the great apostle of nonviolence, in Memphis, on April 4, 1968, temporarily touched off more rioting. Militant black groups have emerged demanding radical changes not only in economic and political realms but in education as well. Within recent years, therefore, one hears much talk about *black power, black awareness, black consciousness, black capitalism, black studies,* and *black universities*—all aimed at improving the economic and political power of the Negro and creating in him the respect for and appreciation of blackness which thousands of Negroes had never possessed.

Since I retired from Morehouse College I have discovered a great deal in talking with many angry black students, on both white and black college campuses, hearing things I never heard or knew during my twenty-seven years in the president's chair. At Morehouse I had tried to develop an academic community that was supra culture, supra race, supra religion, and supra nation. I tried to build this kind of college because I believed then, as I do now, that unless we succeed in building this same kind of world mankind's existence on earth is indeed precarious. I knew I could make little impact on the larger society, but I did what I could in the small area over which I presided for more than a quarter of a century. There was a time when I felt that black students generally shared this philosophy, but I have found since 1967 that this is far from being a universally accepted view among young black students:

In 1968 I was dining with eight black students on the campus of a huge Midwestern university. Although the administration of the university apparently was doing a great deal to increase the enrollment of Negro students and was trying to make the black students an integral part of the life of the university, the students with whom I was dining felt alienated, in fact they were convinced that prejudice and discrimination against black students were rampant. One girl was bitterly critical of white people—*all* white people. When I questioned her universal indictment, speaking out of the experience of the many and varied friendships I have had with whites over the years, she was not convinced and challenged me to show her a single white person who could be trusted absolutely where the black man is involved. She maintained that on the surface white friends might seem sincere, might even feel themselves to be sincere, but that in the final analysis whites always thought in white terms and looked upon black men as being both different and inferior. These students saw no ground for hoping to solve black-white relations through a desegregated-integrated society. They believed that white racism was here to stay.

Since 1967, I have found black students on more than one campus who would dismiss all of the white faculty on the basis that white teachers cannot relate to black students. In humanities courses, they wanted to study only African art and culture—nothing Roman, Grecian, or later European. They wanted all-black faculties, insisting that only black teachers can understand the black experience. To me, on the other hand, it was clear that these students were far too inexperienced to understand that even if an all-black faculty were a realistic goal toward which to strive, there simply are not enough black scholars available to fill all the positions in the black colleges and universities. Moreover, the white colleges and universities are steadily enticing much of what is available away from the black institutions.

On one Negro campus in the South, ways of solving the race problem were being discussed at the time of my visit. I was genuinely shocked to find students at this school who were actually afraid that the white man was contemplating genocide as a way of getting rid of the Negro. To a few, genocide was no mere possibility, it was an imminent probability. When I expressed doubt that such a thing could happen in the United States, I was reminded that the American white man had killed off the Indians and that "enlightened" Germany had exterminated six million Jews. If what they feared did happen, they argued, the Negro had no choice but to fight to the last man. These students were bitter and afraid of what the future held for them.

Even at Morehouse, there was a small, definitely anti-white minority in 1969. This pro-black, anti-white sentiment was vividly impressed on me on

April 17 and 18, when I and others were harassed by students of the Atlanta University Center. On April 17, to begin with, a group of students crashed the Atlanta University Trustees' dinner and delivered the following ultimatum for the white trustees to sign:

> We, the undersigned, resign from the Board of Trustees of the schools within the Atlanta University Center. Our purpose in resigning is to enable the black community to control their own education and toward this end an entirely new process of control must be established. We recognize and support the necessity of Black Power in education, and so we step aside. This act will release us from all responsibility and leaves the schools in the hands of an interim committee of alumni, faculty and students to be elected from those respective groups.

The hostility implied in the ultimatum presented to the white trustees at the Atlanta University Trustees' dinner was intensified on April 18 and 19 when a group of students (three from Morehouse, one from Atlanta University, four from Spelman, one from Clark, and one from Morris Brown), and two professors from the Atlanta University Center (one from Spelman and one from Morehouse), locked up and chained in the Center's board room the Morehouse trustees as well as a few trustees from Atlanta University and Spelman who usually attend the Morehouse board meetings. Several officers of the Morehouse Student Government Association who were there to discuss certain matters with the board were incarcerated along with the trustees. Some fifty to seventy-five students guarded the hall to be sure that the trustees could not leave the building when they were permitted to go to the rest room. A Spelman visiting professor was the leader inside the board room, and a Morehouse visiting professor was in command in the hall. It all came about because on the day before, the chairman of the Atlanta University Board had agreed to meet a committee of students from the Center to hear certain demands they wished to present. This meeting took place at nine o'clock A.M. on April 18 and was adjourned at ten A.M. At that point the committee of "angry blacks" refused to leave the room, took charge of the meeting, dominated it, and held us prisoners for twenty-eight and a half hours.

I would not choose to be locked up and chained in again, but I am mighty glad I had this experience. Only in this way could I understand what kinds of demands a few students in the Center were making, and realize how insulting and vulgar some of our black students can be. Had I not experienced it firsthand, I could hardly have believed it. They put forth three demands and made it clear that we would be held indefinitely until all three were met. The conditions were:

1) That the Morehouse Board of Trustees accept as *fait accompli* that the name of the Atlanta University Center had been changed to the Martin Luther King, Jr. Center;

2) That there be black control of the colleges in the Atlanta University Center;

3) That the trustees of Morehouse support the idea of merging all six institutions in the Center into one single university and assume responsibility for persuading the other five institutions to accept the plan of merger.

The first two demands were not within the jurisdiction of the Morehouse board. Only the Council of Presidents of the six institutions could deal with the idea of changing the name of the Center, and only the Council could agree and recommend to their respective institutions that the Center become black controlled. By "black control" it was really meant that all white trustees on the boards of the six institutions resign to make way for boards of all black members. The militants were willing to compromise if the vast majority of trustees were black, but preferred that the white trustees step aside, raise the money needed, and turn over it and the control of the institutions to black trustees. They argued that black people must control their own destiny. Furthermore, self-perpetuating boards of trustees must go. Although there had been no recommendation to the administrators and boards of trustees of the six colleges that the name of the Center be changed to the Martin Luther King, Jr. Center, it was announced to the Morehouse board as an accomplished fact, that the change had been made by fiat.

A Morehouse freshman from Chicago was what I choose to call "the prosecuting attorney." He was young, loud, vulgar, and insulting. He had absolutely no respect for the trustees. The professor in charge in the board room was overbearing and insulting, too, but not vulgar. Both he and the students made obvious their supreme contempt for the trustees. During the twenty-eight and a half hours of our imprisonment, their antagonism was directed particularly against the white trustees. At first, there was a ridiculous but successful attempt to prevent white trustees from using the rest room. Some of us really had to "blow our tops" about this senseless manifestation of indecency and cruelty before our jailers agreed to permit white trustees the use of the rest room.

The students took over the telephone in President Gloster's office and at first attempted to deny me the use of the telephone to call my wife to inform her of my safety. During a long-distance call that had come through to me, I was rudely interrupted and told I had talked long enough. The white trustee who had given most to the college over the years was insulted more viciously than anyone else. The objective seemed to be to embarrass and humiliate the white trustees so much that they would resign forthwith. I was tongue-lashed, called "Uncle Tom," and accused of having no faith in black people because I had said, in an Honors' Day address at Spelman, that if we expected to get a $100 million from Negroes (the conservative estimate to build a university for ten thousand black students) we might as well forget it because Negroes did not have the economic resources to put up that much money—and if they had it, I doubted they would give it.

When our captors feared that the "pigs" (police) were being called, the students in the hall crowded into the board room and told us that the trustees would have inflicted upon them everything that the "pigs" might inflict upon the students. Actually, the police were not called. Instead, the imprisoned trustees asked an indignant crowd of students, faculty, alumni, and friends who had gathered outside and wanted to force our release not to aggravate the situation to what might bring tragic results. It wasn't until Martin Luther King, Sr., a Morehouse trustee, warned that the King family did not wish the Center be renamed for Martin Luther, Jr., in that manner and that they were exploiting his son's name; until the trustees accepted the idea of a merger, which was really nothing new; and until the trustees agreed to greatly increase the number of black members on the Morehouse Board, that we were released on Saturday afternoon, twenty-eight and one-half hours after we were locked in.

Where does the solution lie if not in black nationalism or in some form of separatism? Before speculating on the answer to this question, look at and appraise the current emphasis on blackness.

The term "black power" has never upset me. I believe in black power. Many white people are disturbed by the phrase, first used by Stokely Carmichael on a march in Mississippi. To some white people, the words mean violence. It is really rather strange that white people should get wrought up over the use of the words "black power." The white man has made his way through history on *white power.* The wonderful things he has done have resulted from his economic, political, and intellectual power. The evil things he has done, as well as the good things, have come from the white man's power and might. White power kept Negroes in slavery for 246 years and freed them without a dime in compensation for their labor. White power kept the black man segregated in the United States for one hundred years. White power robbed the Negro of the ballot, gave him inferior schools, lynched him, and saw to it that he was given only menial jobs and deliberately exploited and degraded. White power sees to it that desegregation in public schools moves at a snail's pace. Slums and ghettoes exist because the white man has the power to keep them in operation. In reality, white power determines in large measure the Negro's destiny.

I interpret black power as a good thing. It is a blessing if it convinces black people that their strength lies in solidarity, and that black men can never get political and economic power if they are divided and fighting among themselves. Carmichael and Hamilton are eminently right when they say: "Only when black people fully develop this sense of community of themselves can they begin to deal effectively with problems of racism in this country. This is what we mean by a new consciousness; this is the vital next step."*

But the phrase "black power," accompanied by the "clenched fist," is nothing more than a futile gesture unless it is filled with meaning and designed to develop a program to achieve for the black man that economic, political, and educational power which will enable him to bargain from a position of strength. I see nothing wrong with black power as used in Atlanta, in October, 1969, when Negroes gave Maynard Johnson, a black man, 90 percent of their votes which, combined with a sizable white vote, made him an easy winner in the race for vice-mayor. He received over 18,000 votes more than his formidable white rival. Black votes also elected several black men to serve on the aldermanic board. A unified black vote could have put a black mayor in office in the same election, or put Horace Tate, a black candidate, in the runoff, but in Tate's case the Negro community was split down the middle.

I see nothing amiss with what Negroes accomplished in the runoff election in Atlanta later that October when they increased the number of black aldermen from one to five and increased the number of Negroes on the Atlanta Board of Education from two to three. In this runoff between Sam Massell, a Jew, and Rodney Cook, the choice of the so-called white "Establishment," Negroes gave Massell approximately 43,000 votes, whereas the whites gave him approximately 18,500. Massell received a total of 62,632 votes, while his opponent got 51,289. The black votes made Massell mayor of Atlanta. Interpret those elections any way you wish, and they say

*Stokely Carmichael & Charles V. Hamilton, *Black Power* (New York: Vintage Press, 1967).

one thing: black political power was at work and it was nonviolent.

In addition to my being elected to membership on the Atlanta Board of Education in October, I was chosen president of the Board in January, 1970, the first Negro president in its history. Letters and telegrams of congratulation came from the Atlanta community and from across the nation and other parts of the world. There was only one really discordant note and it came from Tampa, Florida, signed by one "Willie Malone," but gave no return address. It said: "Dear nigger: How does it feel to get elected to a job strictly on your color?"

I do not see how we can exclude from a definition of black power or black capitalism the successful businesses built, owned, and controlled by Negroes, such as the North Carolina Mutual Life Insurance Company, the Atlanta Life Insurance Company, the Supreme Liberty Life Insurance Company, and many others; or the banks owned and controlled by Negroes such as the Mechanics and Farmers Bank, the Citizens Trust Company and the Black Press as forms of black power; and when I see Negro athletes performing superbly, Negro artists and entertainers at the top of the professions, Negro scholars holding significant chairs in black and white universities, Negroes holding high posts as judges in federal courts, black lawyers winning the May 17, 1954, decision of the United States Supreme Court, and student demonstrations being largely responsible for the passage of civil rights legislation in 1964, 1965, and 1968, I cannot exclude these from my concept of black power.

To me black power must mean hard work, trained minds, and perfected skills to perform in a competitive society. The injustices imposed upon the black man for centuries make it all the more obligatory that he develop himself. This challenge holds whether the black man lives in a desegregated society, an integrated society, or a black nationalist society. There must be no dichotomy between the development of one's mind and a deep sense of appreciation of one's heritage. An unjust penalty has been imposed upon the Negro because he is black. The dice are loaded against him. Knowing this, as the Jew knows about anti-Semitism, the black man must never forget the necessity that he perfect his talents and potentials to the ultimate.

I believe in black awareness and black consciousness. No man is free unless he accepts himself for what he is and can become. If black awareness means that black people are proud of themselves, proud of their heritage, apologizing to nobody, not even to God, for being what they are—black: wholly black, brown-black; yellow-black; or white-black, it is good. If it means that they will not be swept off their feet by the glamour of a partially desegregated society, it is indeed a fine thing for the black world. If "black awareness," "black consciousness," and "black is beautiful" mean that the Negro has rid himself of what Eldridge Cleaver, in his penetrating book *Soul on Ice* (New York: Dell Publishing Company, 1968) calls the "Negro's racial death-wish," the belief that "the race problem in America cannot be settled until all traces of the black race are eliminated," then the current emphasis on blackness is a benediction. If it means in the minds of Negroes that it is just as good to be a black American as it is to be a white American, I embrace the concept. On the other hand, if integration means or implies that one must forswear his identity as a Negro, I reject it.

Likewise, the current emphasis on black studies is a tribute to the black heroes of history who died fighting for freedom and equality during slavery and since emancipation, men who were never ashamed of being black. It is a tribute to such figures as W. E. B. DuBois, and especially to Carter G. Woodson, who spent his life studying and researching the Negro, past and present, and publishing books on the Negro at a time when white historians were degrading the black man and denying him his rightful place in history, and while many Negroes were denying their African heritage. I believe in black studies. American education is incomplete and partially false unless it gives due credit to the contributions that Afro-Americans have made to the development of this great country. Frankly, it doesn't matter to me how this is done—whether there are departments of black studies, majors in black studies, schools of black studies, or an honest-to-goodness integrated curriculum which gives black men their rightful place in the history of this country. This needs to be done not only to give the Negro a sense of worth and well-being, but also to set the historical records straight and to enlighten the mind of white America.

I believe in black colleges. For twenty-seven years I was president of one where the student body was almost one hundred percent black and where the faculty and board of trustees were racially mixed. But I do not believe in a black college or university if this means that all students, all faculty and staff members, the student body, and all financial support must be black. Even if the idea were a practical one, I could not embrace it, for setting people apart fosters segregation, which Negroes have fought against for a century. I do not believe that exclusively black colleges are necessary to engender race pride in black students, or that the salvation of black colleges lies in driving out white trustees, white faculty, and white students.

Nor do I believe that the black man's educational salvation lies in weakening black colleges by draining black scholars and students away from them to attend white colleges—colleges which for the most part are not free of racism. Colleges and universities that are deserving should be supported by state and philanthropic funds; racial identification should not determine the amount of support they receive. If race is a determining factor, this means there is racism in high places, and racism belongs nowhere in American education. White teachers should serve in black colleges, just as black scholars should be able to serve in white colleges. The emphasis on blackness must not mean that Negroes should not qualify to fill high positions in education and in all other areas of American life, whether integrated or desegregated.

Black capitalism as a partial solution to the black man's economic plight has been advocated. It is not clear to me, however, just what the term implies. President Nixon has endorsed the idea, but I am not sure that the meaning is clear in his mind either. Black capitalism may mean several things, depending upon which individual or group is espousing the concept. It may mean black ownership of business enterprises; it could mean the developing of black captains of industry and black capitalists "who own, control and accumulate resources and wealth and pass the same on to heirs in the interest of individual goals and aims." On the other hand, it could mean black business men exploiting blacks; or it may mean black business men seeking power and profit by whatever means possible.

If black capitalism means that more and better jobs will be provided for the working Negro poor and for the Negro unemployed, all to the good. Planners of any economic program should keep in mind the millions of Negroes who exist below the poverty line and who are unemployed. If the government or any private agency should provide funds to increase the number of black entrepreneurs, no one should quarrel with that, or if such an agency should assist black business men to provide the capital, this, too, would be gratifying.

The danger of black capitalism seems to be that it may depend upon a segregated Negro population to keep going. If this is so, it may fail because black people may not buy black if it is cheaper to buy white. I do not see how black capitalism can exist apart from American capitalistism as a whole. Another danger of the emphasis on black capitalism is that it may give the impression that black capitalism alone can solve the problems of poverty among Negroes and, of itself, can improve the quality of life of the masses of black people. This idea creates an illusion, for white capitalism has not been able to do this for whites or for blacks. Furthermore, I do not see how black capitalism can do the huge job that needs to be done to solve the problems that exist in the ghettoes and slums of our cities. I do not believe that black people can rely upon their own resources to eliminate poverty in ghettoes and poor Negro neighborhoods generally. Black capital and white capital can help, but it is obvious that huge sums must come from the federal government. However we look at it or define it, black capitalism is only one of the many factors necessary to help improve Negro-white relations in the United States and to improve the Negro's economic plight.

Despite my constant rebellion against a cruel and unjust system for almost seventy years, life has been kind to me in many ways. I have earned degrees from one of the best colleges and from one of the best universities in the nation. I have never had to ask for a job; offers—more than I could accept—have come unsolicited, and still do. I have traveled fairly extensively in North America, Europe, Asia, and Africa, on missions for my government, the church, the YMCA, and educational institutions. Twenty-eight distinguished colleges and universities have conferred honorary degrees upon me. Many people have helped me on my way, and Sadie and I in turn tried to help as many as we could. I have spoken and written what seemed to me to be the truth, even when there was the risk of being branded a Communist or a fellow traveler. I have always hated injustice and discrimination of every description, and I have fought them all of my life and shall continue to do so, but I am not bitter.

I have developed my friends across racial and religious lines, and I have never placed superior or inferior value on friendship on the basis of race or religion. I have never believed that the white man belongs to a race which is superior to other races of men. I believe that factors other than intellect and technical know-how must be taken into account when one is evaluating superiority. I believe that no race can claim superiority that has achieved its place by exploiting other peoples and conquering them through war. The criteria of superiority must include manifestations of justice, mercy, and social concern for the weak. If these are included in the criteria for superiority, the white man hardly qualifies as a superior race. He has exploited the weak, the ignorant, and the poor across the face of the earth.

I have not considered my social standing enhanced either by association with distinguished Negroes or by association with distinguished whites. I have enjoyed and appreciated my friends regardless of their stations in life. People are people. I have never sought "acceptance" as such, but I have wanted respect from all mankind. Love is wonderful; but if I could not have both, I would prefer respect. In the days when I was forbidden to ride Pullman, I insisted on doing so not because I wanted to be with white people but because I desired to ride comfortably and sleep well at night and because I had as much right to these accommodations as anyone else. It was fine when the passengers were friendly, but when they were not I was neither hurt nor embarrassed. When dining-car service and hotel accommodations were denied me, I kept hammering away at the problem because I wanted to be able to eat a decent meal and sleep comfortably—never just because I wanted to be with white people. When I ran into my black or white friends, and we visited together, I was delighted to be with them, but their color was incidental. Two and a half years ago, Sadie and I moved into a tokenly integrated neighborhood, now mostly black, in southwest Atlanta. We purchased our home in that vicinity because we wanted a pleasant location in which to spend our last years—that there were white people in the area neither attracted nor repulsed us. I have always felt that white people who defend segregation as if it were a very God must be shivering cold in their emotional insecurity.

I do not know whether there is a solution to the Negro-white problem. Whether racism in the United States can ever be abolished, I am not omniscient enough to say. To date, education and religion have not abolished racism, despite the fact that education is supposed to enable a man to find truth and follow it, while religion is designed to make men good. When I consider the Jew, I find no comfort in history for the Negro's plight. No other group in the annals of time has contributed so much, with so few in number, to the well-being of mankind. And yet anti-Semitism is centuries old and still shows its ugly face with alarming frequency throughout this and every other land.

It seems to me, however, that we have no choice but to continue our efforts to make this country a decent place for all Americans. As Henry van Dyke says, in *The Other Wise Man,* "It is better to follow even the shadow of the best than to remain content with the worst." I have the faith to believe that whites and blacks can improve their relationship to the extent that they can live together in peace, each respecting the other. Whether we like it or not, we can neither elude nor escape each other. I am convinced that any program designed to solve the black-white problem by providing a geographically segregated place for twenty million blacks is destined to failure. Moreover, believing as I do that offensive nonviolent actions of the Gandhi–Martin Luther King, Jr., type are the best way by which to improve Negro-white relations, I am convinced that any offensive, violent programs instigated by Negroes will profit little. Nor do I believe that the black man's salvation lies in the total destruction of the present social, economic, and political systems, and that on the ruins a new order of justice, freedom, and equality for all Americans will spring, full-blown. The same tainted and distorted humanity that built the present systems will build the new. Whatever the future holds for the American people, it must be accepted that the United States belongs to the black man as much as to the white man. Most of us were born in this country and we will live here and die here.

Finally, if the governments, private businesses, schools, churches, individuals, and the American people have the will, they can contribute to the solution of this problem. We can, within a ten-year span, provide decent housing for every family, make adequate jobs available for every able-bodied person, provide the kind of education that each child is able to absorb, make accessible medical care for all, abolish poverty and malnutrition, and permit each man to advance on his merit without his being penalized because he is black.

President John F. Kennedy could predict that in ten years we would place a man on the moon, and his prophecy came true. President Nixon asserted that we could fly to Mars in ten years or more. If we can set a timetable to get to the moon and to Mars—and meet it—God knows we can set a timetable to build a more just society. It's a matter of national will and commitment. It is also a matter of individual responsibility. If these things are not done, I predict that there will be terrifying days ahead in the "land of the free and the home of the brave."

Appendix A

The World in Which I Was Born and Reared

At the time of my birth in 1894, the Negro in South Carolina was rapidly losing the political ground he had gained. He had occupied the political spotlight since 1868, and for several years after federal troops had been withdrawn from the statehouse in South Carolina on April 10, 1877. South Carolina Negroes held high places in politics almost to the end of the century, certainly up to 1895, the year in which Negroes in South Carolina were stripped of the ballot, largely through the influence and leadership of Ben Tillman, who seized leadership of the Democratic party in 1890, four years before my birth. It was in the year 1890 that Mississippi disfranchised the Negroes of that state. Under the protection of the Republican regime during Reconstruction (1868-1877), and as a result of the new constitution of 1868 which placed no restriction upon universal suffrage, South Carolina sent eight Negroes to the United States House of Representatives in Washington: three served one term each, three, two terms each, and two, five terms each. Although Negroes never did control South Carolina, at one time during this period all the South Carolina representatives in Washington were Negroes.[1]

Negroes, Democrats and Republicans, were elected to the South Carolina Senate from 1878 through the election of 1886. Between 1878 and 1888, seven Negroes were elected State Senators. They were elected to the State House of Representatives from 1878 through the election of 1900. A total of forty-eight different Negroes served in the South Carolina General Assembly between 1878 and 1902. Before 1876, two Negroes became Lieutenant Governors; another became a Justice of the State Supreme Court; and one, Secretary of State. Negroes fared well not only in state offices but also in local politics, especially in places like Charleston, Beaufort, and Georgetown. Beaufort had a Negro sheriff and a Negro clerk of court; Negroes were county commissioners, coroners, probate judges, and school commissioners. On the local scene, however, the most productive source of public office for Negroes was federal patronage. Negroes were appointed postmasters in such cities as Marion, Branchville, Charleston, and Columbia. C. Vann Woodward reminds us, in his book *The Strange Career of Jim Crow*, that "dozens of Negroes were appointed postmasters in South Carolina during this period."[2] Despite the Negro's final fate in politics, the State Constitution of 1868, guaranteeing universal suffrage, contained elements that stood for thirty years, and some sections of it are in the present South Carolina constitution.[3]

What was happening in South Carolina was taking place in other Southern states. "Every session of the Virginia General Asssmbly, from 1869 to 1891, contained Negro members. Between 1876 and 1894, North Carolina elected fifty-two Negroes to the lower house of their state legislature. . . . In 1890, there were sixteen Negro members of the session of the Louisiana General Assembly which passed the jim crow railway bill that led to the case of *Plessy vs. Ferguson.* Southern states elected ten Negroes to the United States House of Representatives after Reconstruction, the same number elected during Reconstruction. Every Congress but one betweeen 1869 and 1901 had at least one Negro member from the South" (2: p.54).

Two things must be said about this era of Negroes in politics: Negroes never did control the cultural, economic, and political life of the South. The white man's dominance in every area was apparent. The vast majority of Negroes were at the mercy of the white man economically. Most of them were domestics, field hands, sharecroppers, and renters. Many of them were secretly held in peonage. Those Negroes who held public office were as honest, as just, and about as intelligent as their white colleagues. Constructive laws were enacted in the South Carolina General Assemblies in which Negroes participated. Prejudiced historians, however, have tried to distort the facts relative to the Negroes' part in politics in this era.

Robbing the Negro of the Ballot

Against the background which I have outlined, it should not be surprising that the political prominence of the Negro in my native state and in other Southern states was short-lived (1868-1902). The beginning of the end of Negroes' participation in South Carolina politics began legally in 1895, the year in which the Constitutional Convention of South Carolina stripped the Negro of the ballot. It was one year after I was born. The Negro's loss of the ballot in 1895 meant that I was completely disfranchised until 1946 when the white primary was declared unconstitutional in Georgia. Since I was equally voteless during my six years in Washington, D.C. (1934-1940), for thirty-one years after I was twenty-one years of age I could not vote in any local city and state elections—despite the fact that I was a college and university graduate and a college president. When I was one year old, another South Carolinian, Ben Tillman, born in 1847 in an adjacent county, Edgefield, was busy getting laws passed which kept Negroes in South Carolina voteless for half a century. Prior to the Constitutional Convention of 1895, Tillman had instigated and participated in brutal activities to intimidate Negroes and keep them from voting.

Disfranchisement of the Negro became law in all Southern states. Mississippi led the way in 1890. South Carolina followed in 1895. The Constitutional Convention designed to rob the Negro of suffrage in South Carolina was dominated by Ben Tillman and his followers. The delegation broke down as follows: 112 Tillmanites, 42 Conservatives, and six Republicans. The six Republicans were Negroes. The Negro delegates presented able arguments against the proposed scheme which would disfranchise Negroes in South Carolina (Note 3: Chapter v). According to the *Columbia State* (Oct. 26, 1895), James Wigg, one of the Negro members of the Convention, said this: "You charge that the Negro is too ignorant to be entrusted with the suffrage. I answer you that you have not, nor dare you, make a pure educational test of the right to vote. You say that he is a figurehead and an encumbrance to the state, that he pays little or no taxes. I answer you that you have not, and you dare not, make a purely property test of the right to vote." But despite such eloquence and logic, Tillman and his followers carried the day. The voices of Colonel John J. Dargan, a newspaper editor, and Wade Hampton, conservative, both of whom favored the Negro's political rights, were silenced. Hampton wrote the following from Washington:

> I have no fear of Negro domination—a cry used only to arouse race prejudice and to put the incoming Convention under control of the ring which now dominates our state. The Negroes have acted of late with rare moderation and liberality, and if we meet them in the same spirit they have shown, they will aid in selecting good representatives for the Convention. I, for one, am willing to trust them, and they ask only the rights guaranteed to them by the Constitution of the United States and that of our state (Note 3:p. 80).

Louisiana disfranchised the Negro in 1898; North Carolina in 1900; Alabama in 1901; Virginia in 1902; Georgia in 1908; and Oklahoma in 1910. Florida, Tennessee, Arkansas, and Texas robbed the Negro of the ballot by adopting the poll tax and by other means. No stone was left unturned in the South to disfranchise the Negro in my day. Hoke Smith of Georgia advocated using any method to keep the Negro from voting. The Atlanta *Journal* of December 5, 1905, reports from one of the campaign speeches of Smith as follows:

> This is a white man's country, and we are all agreed that not only in the State at large but in every county and in every community the white man must control by some means, or life could not be worth living.
>
> No matter how secure we may feel at present from Negro domination, if . . . there is danger to the State at large, or to any county or community in Geogia from this curse, it will be folly for us to neglect any means within our reach to remove the danger. . . .
>
> I plant my case upon the intellectual superiority of the white man; the capacity of every white boy who has a fair show to fit himself for duties the Negro can never discharge, no matter what his opportunites.

In opposing a proposed education requirement for voting in Georgia, Clark Howell, editor of the Atlanta *Constitution*, said, on September 15, 1895, that the educational clause would serve as a magnet to "draw the negroes of Georgia out of the cotton patch into negro colleges." The editor said further, "Whenever the nigger learns his (hic) haec, hoc, he right away forgets all about gee-whoa-buck!"

In his excellent book, *From Slavery to Freedom*, historian John Hope Franklin writes:

> On the floor of the Virginia convention Carter Glass had said that the delegates were elected to "discriminate to the very extremity of permissible action under the limitations of the Federal Constituion, with a view to the elimination of every Negro voter who can be gotten rid of, legally,

> without materially impairing the numerical strength of the white electorate."
>
> Southern whites said that the Negro had done nothing to warrant suffrage. But as he made progress in many walks of life, it became increasingly difficult to allege that he was naturally shiftless and incapable of advancement. The framers of the new suffrage laws, however, were committed to the complete and permanent disfranchisement of the Negro regardless of his progress. Their view was summed up by J. K. Vardaman of Mississippi, "I am just as opposed to Booker T. Washington as a voter, with all his Anglo-Saxon reenforcements, as I am to the coconut-headed, chocolate-colored, typical little coon, Andy Dotson, who blacks my shoes every morning. Neither is fit to perform the supreme function of citizenship."[4]

It should be noted in passing that it was rumored by Negroes living in the state at that time that Vardaman fathered a Negro family, despite his attitude toward Washington and his bootblack!

The statewide Democratic primaries became white primaries, often converted into white men's clubs, excluding Negroes. I was two years old when my state adopted the Democratic primary in 1896. Arkansas followed in 1897; Georgia in 1898; Florida and Tennessee in 1901; Louisiana in 1906; Oklahoma in 1907; Virginia in 1913; and North Carolina in 1915. A careful study of the state constitutions and codes of the Southern states reveals that various requirements were instigated to disfranchise the Negro, such as the ability of the voter to read any section of the Constitution; to write any section of it; to understand and interpret the section read; to pay poll tax; and to own a stated amount of property. Some states used the "grandfather clause," introduced by Louisiana in 1898 as a means of prohibiting the Negro vote, which provided that only those men whose fathers or grandfathers had voted prior to 1867 were eligible to vote. Since Negroes were not descendants of persons who voted prior to 1867, they were thus completely denied the ballot in states using the grandfather clause. If any one or all of the restrictions failed to bar the Negro from voting, there was intimidation, including beatings and sometimes murder.

For example, years before Ben Tillman became the leader of the Democratic party in South Carolina, he was working to advance the cause of white supremacy in the state and to eliminate the Negro from politics. He didn't hesitate to use any method to rid South Carolina of Negro participation in politics. Francis Butler Simkins says of Tillman:

> Regardless of law and of the opinion of the outside world, he believed that all means should be used in the fight for "civilization and progress in contest with barbarism and the forces which are undermining the very foundations of our commonwealth." "The Creator made the Caucasian of better clay than he made any of the colored people" was his simple creed and that of thousands less introspective. Acting on this belief, he joined the Sweetwater Saber Club. . . . Equipped with uniforms, sabers, and army

pistols, Tillman and his colleagues . . . prepared to use force if necessary to rid the state of control by its black majority.[5]

Tillman used force and threats when needed to put the Negro in his place. Anxious to assure the election of Wade Hampton in 1876, Tillman served as minority manager of election in a precinct in Edgefield County. In the early morning of election day, he and one of the Negro managers opened the polls, and Tillman threatened with death a Negro Republican who came to vote and who attempted to distribute Republican campaign material to a crowd of Negroes.

Even while Negroes were voting and holding high political jobs in South Carolina (1868-1902), Negro-white relations were far from ideal. By and large, white people in South Carolina were not happy to have Negro congressmen in Washington and Negroes in the South Carolina General Assembly. It did not please them to have Negro postmasters, sheriffs, clerks of court, school commissioners, and probate judges. After all, just a few decades ago these Negroes had been slaves, and it irked white people to have ex-slaves and sons of slaves ruling over them. With federal troops withdrawn, and Northerners sympathizing more and more with the Southerner in his attitude toward the Negro, and actually seeming to apologize for defeating the South in the Civil War, it was almost inevitable that the tide would turn viciously against the Negro. Economic adjustments alone caused considerable irritation between Negroes and whites; but for Negroes to seek the ballot and run for and hold office annoyed the whites still more.

Joel Williamson, author of *After Slavery*, enlightens us on this point. He tells us of a Charleston physician who said, after a Negro had been nominated for Secretary of State, that South Carolina was "a miserable land to live in." Williamson also writes of a white woman, disturbed about the Republican governor and Negro office holders, who described the legislature as "Crow Congress," "Monkey show," "the menagerie," and the constitution as the "Yankee-nigger government programme."[6] A Charleston woman complained, "Surely our humiliation has been great when a black postmaster is established here at headquarters and our gentlemen sons have to work under his biddings" (6:p. 255). It was humiliating to white lawyers when they had to plead before a Negro judge or Negro jurors. A white lawyer who had left South Carolina rubbed it in on one who stayed: "Well, Dick, you have a charming Supreme Court in South Carolina now—a contemptible scalawag occupying the seat once adorned by O'Neal and Dunkin, and two carpetbaggers (and one of them a Negro) in the seats once graced by Wardlaw and Withers. How do you feel before such a Bench? When you address such creatures as 'Your Honor,' don't the blood boil or grow chill in your veins? And how can you say 'Gentlemen of the Jury' to a panel of loathsome, leather-headed Negroes?"(6:p. 255).

It must be said, however, that there were voices of moderation and, for a time, there were white leaders who opposed efforts to rob the Negro of the ballot. Among these were Lamar of Mississippi, Stephens of Georgia, and Wade Hampton of South Carolina. These men, in public statements, proclaimed that disfranchisement of the Negro was both impossible and undesirable. Lamar was so optimistic in his position that he expressed the view that the South would not stand for it. Hampton was equally strong in his view that the ballot should not be taken from the Negro.[7] In the Constitutional Convention of Alabama in 1901, Governor Oates was disturbed over the way the Negro was being treated. "Why, sir," he exclaimed to a man of (J. Thomas) Heflin's generation, "The sentiment is altogether different now, when the Negro is doing no harm, why the people want to kill him and wipe him from the face of the earth!" (7: p. 353). Woodward also quotes another liberal man, Edgar Gardner Murphy, who said, "the extremist has proceeded from an indiscriminating attack upon the Negro's ballot to a like attack upon his schools, his labor, his life—from the contention that no Negro shall vote to the contention that . . . no Negro shall live" (7: p. 353). As time went on, however, the philosophy of these men, and of a few Southern papers that opposed robbing the Negro of his suffrage, was set aside, and white men united on the propositon that politics in the South was "for whites only." Tom Watson of Georgia, who first advocated the Populist movement in the interest of the common man—Negro and white alike—finally shifted his position and preached Aryan superiority. So bitterly intense was the feeling, I am convinced that by the close of the nineteenth century and the beginning of the twentieth, if Negroes had insisted upon their right to vote in my native South Carolina and other Southern states, genocide would have been the ultimate outcome. Negroes would have been shot down and killed like rabbits. What happened to the Indians in this country would have happened to Negroes, with whites having no more sense of guilt and no deeper pangs of conscience, except that Negroes would have been liquidated in a much shorter time than it took to suppress the Indians.

Mob Rule and Lynching

The sequel to the disfranchisement of the Negro in South Carolina was mob rule, lynchings, and riots. Woodward writes, in his second revised edition of *The Strange Career of Jim Crow* (2: p.87):

> Indeed, the more defenseless, disfranchised, and intimidated the Negro became, the more prone he was to the ruthless aggression of mobs. Three years after Tillman had completed his work of crushing Negro rights in South Carolina, colored people were victims of atrocities. While the state had accustomed itself peacefully to dozens of Negro postmasters before, the appointment of one in 1898 at Lake City touched off a mob that burned the postmaster up in his own house and shot down his family as they escaped. The same year mobs of "white cap riders" ranged over the countryside of Greenwood County, shooting and hanging an undetermined number of Negroes.

From this point on, things were not good for Negroes in the state of my birth.

When Tillman became Governor in 1890, and Senator in 1894, he set the pattern of Negro-white relations in South Carolina for decades to come. Mobs roamed at will and lynching occurred frequently in my county, Greenwood; in Tillman's,

Edgefield; and in counties adjacent to these. Tillman was a contradiction. In his first inaugural address, he praised the Negro as being "a staunch friend and a faithful servant during the war." He asked the white people, in that address, to hear "all reasonable complaints of the Negroes," to "grant all just, right, and safe privileges," and to give them "equal protection of the law and treat them fairly."[8] He even tried to get an anti-lynch law enacted. He claimed to be against lynching, except for one cause, that of rape.The Charleston *News and Courier*, on January 11, 1892, quotes Tillman as having said, "One crime which deserves lynching, and Governor as I am, I'd lead a mob to lynch a man who had ravished a white woman. . . . I justify lynching for rape, and before Almighty God, I'm not ashamed of it." In 1900, Tillman told the Senate, "We [the white South Carolinians] took the Government away. We stuffed ballot boxes. We shot them [the Negroes]. We are not ashamed of it."[9] When the first lynching of Tillman's second administration occurred, it was of John Peterson of Denmark, Barnwell County, who was accused of attempted rape of a fourteen-year-old white girl. Tillman had his secretary write to a Barnwell officer, "The villain deserves lynching and he [the Governor] has been hoping to hear that you have caught and lynched him" (9: p.224). Tillman was well received in the North, speaking at Chautauquas. He told Northerners that Negroes were "akin to the monkey . . . an ignorant and debased and debauched race"; and, "To hell with the Constitution when it stood in the way of mob justice to rapists" (9: pp.394-396). During Tillman's four years as Governor (1890-1894), twenty persons were lynched in South Carolina. In the ten-year span from 1890 to 1900, fifty-three persons were lynched in my native state.[10] A number of these lynchings took place in my county, a few miles from where I was born.

The Phoenix Riot in Greenwood County, about twelve miles from my home, began on November 8, 1898. Nothing so beastly as the Phoenix lynchings had occurred on such a massive scale in South Carolina since 1889, when eight Negroes were lynched at Barnwell. It was during these terrible days that I saw one of the mobs. It is the earliest thing I can remember. I was not yet five years old, but I can never forget that mob. It made an indelible impression on my mind.

For data on the riot, I have read articles in the Greenwood *Index;* the Charleston *News and Courier;* the Columbia *State;* the Columbia *Register;* and the Washington *Post.* I have also read the pamphlet, *The Phoenix Riot,* written some years later by James A. Hoyt, a cub reporter who saw much of the killing.[11] I have talked with my sister Susie and other Negroes older than I, in the county, who are still living.

The Phoenix Riot was precipitated by Republican leaders of Greenwood County trying to get evidence that Negroes were being denied the ballot, such evidence to be used in a contest for the congressional seat of the Third District. Negroes in South Carolina had been disfranchised in 1895, but no test case had been made challenging this disfranchisement. The Republicans chose Phoenix as the place to make a test case.

Around nine o'clock in the morning of November 8, 1898, Tom Tolbert, brother of R. R. Tolbert who was running for Congress as a Republican, appeared at the store of J. W. Watson where the state and federal elections were being held. He carried a ballot box which he placed on the small piazza in front of the store. He directed all Republicans who had no registration to drop a certificate, marked Blank

3, in this box. The certificate was really an affidavit swearing they had been denied the right to register and vote; that their votes had been rejected by the Democratic officials; and that if they had been allowed to vote they would have voted for R. R. Tolbert, the Republican candidate for Congress in the Third District. These affidavits were to be taken to Washington to contest the election of the Democratic candidate, and thus prove that the disfranchisement of the Negro by South Carolina was unconstitutional.

On page 1 of its November 9, 1898, edition, the Columbia *State* wrote of the Phoenix Riot:

> RIOT IN HOTBED OF REPUBLICANISM
>
> BLOOD SPILLED AT PHOENIX TEN MILES AWAY FROM GREENWOOD
>
> *The Negroes Start the Trouble by Shooting Down a White Man*
>
> About 9:00 A.M. Giles O. Etheridge, followed closely by R. C. Cheathem and several young men, approached Thomas P. Tolbert who was directing a protest vote in front of J. W. Watson's store. Tolbert was directing Negroes to deposit a blank paper in a ballot box stating that they had been denied their right to register, and if they had registered they would have voted for R. R. Tolbert, the Republican candidate for Congress in the District.
>
> As Etheridge protested Tolbert's actions, Tolbert struck him in the face. Someone else hit Etheridge in the head with an iron bar. Almost at the same instant, the hapless Etheridge received a pistol shot in the center of the forehead.

In this fracas, Thomas P. Tolbert was shot in the shoulder, but not fatally. "Twenty-two men had been refused the privilege of voting when the killing took place, two being white Democrats. Eighteen Negroes had deposited in Tolbert's box the certificate being copied" (11: p. 3).

The Charleston *News and Courier* and the Columbia *Register* of November 9, 1898, carried essentially the same story as the Columbia *State*, which wrote further:

> In the melee that followed, Tolbert and several Negroes were wounded but all escaped. The news spread quickly and in the afternoon about 100 armed men were in Phoenix. . . . There will probably be several lynchings at least. "Bose" Etheridge was a leading citizen.
>
> An afternoon inquest established that Joe Circuit, a Negro, fired the fatal shot. A memo book with his name was found on the spot. A relative of Tolbert, R. P. Henderson, who was about to be appointed postmaster at Edgefield, had promised to make Joe Circuit a clerk. Edgefield people notified him that this would mean death.
>
> Henderson, a young white man heretofore esteemed in this section, had been holding incendiary meetings with Negroes at weird places and unholy hours, saying Greenwood County (3 to 1 colored-white ratio) was theirs and they could carry the election.

When I was going over the newspaper reports of this incident with my sister Susie in the summer of 1967, she said the name of the Negro who allegedly fired the shot that killed Etheridge was not Joe "Circuit" but Joe Syrk; that the newspapers were in error. At any rate, Joe "Circuit" or "Syrk" was never apprehended, but several other Negroes were lynched for the death of "Bose" Etheridge. If the Negro who allegedly fired the first shot was indeed Joe Syrk, he was my first cousin. Negroes now living in Greenwood County believe that a white man killed Etheridge.

As a result of the killing of "Bose" Etheridge, an undetermined number of Negroes were killed—seven are known to have been lynched. Since the mobs sought to kill every Negro who went to Phoenix to vote, and since hundreds of Negroes left the county, historians admit that no one knows how many Negroes were lynched in the Phoenix Riot. Hoyt's pamphlet (11: pp.11-12) has this to say:

> There were eleven Negroes captured by the "mob" Wednesday, all suspected of participation in Tuesday's fight at Watson's store. With guns at their heads and ropes around their necks, they were all commanded to tell the truth and confess. Some of them did confess.
>
> Then they were lined up along a log, as I remember the story, and some of them were given the chance of escape, and they ran. Four were shot and killed. . . . Their bodies were left on the ground, and the "mob" went its way. I was told afterward that after the Negroes had fallen dead their bodies were riddled by volley after volley.
>
> The next day, Thursday, the Negro, Essex Harrison, believed to be another participant in the killing of Etheridge, was captured and taken to Rehoboth Church. The putrid corpses of the other four men were still there, some of them in a posture of sitting against trees. In this ghastly setting, Essex Harrison was executed. He was shot at from so many directions that the executioners endangered each other. He dropped dead across the corpse of one of those killed the day before and there he was left. That Harrison was an active participant in the Etheridge killing was apparently not established, but it was said to have been proved that he was at the Watson store that day "in response to Tolbert's orders." [Quotation marks as they appear in booklet.]
>
> Ben Collins, killed Thursday night on the Stalworth place, where he had hid, was said not only to have been present at the killing of Etheridge but to have fired into the store. . . .
>
> August Kohn, who arrived in Greenwood from Wilmington early Thursday morning, as soon as possible, of course, started for the scene of trouble.
>
> When he got to Greenwood he was told that there were two roads to Phoenix and was advised it would be safer to take the road by Casey's store. Reporter-like, he took the other road by Rehoboth Church and drove right into the story he was sent to get. These are his words: "Contrary to the injunction, we went by Rehoboth Church, and a stop was made to view the heap of dead bodies. Just then there came down the road a detail of

about 15 or 20 armed men with a solitary Negro marching in front. Addressing the reporters, one of the party cried, 'Get out if you want to do some work.' There was a frisky horse to manage; one of us went up to the shooting party unarmed. It was too unbusinesslike. The trembling Negro was standing on the roadside, a dozen rifles leveled at him. He looked at his slayers. He said nothing. He moved off. The rifles rang forth, and Essex Harrison fell headlong on the pile of already dead Negroes, his head pillowed on the bosom of a dead companion."

The Columbia *State* of November 13, 1898, told of five dead Negroes who were buried in a mass grave, and added that no relatives showed up at the burial. They were obviously afraid to be seen. Hoyt reports that "George Logan, colored, died Thursday, November 17, at the home of Joe Goode, colored, near Greenwood. Logan was one of the Negroes in the crowd at Rehoboth Church fired on by the whites"(11: p.10).

On November 9, 1898, the Columbia *Register* reported that "no less than 600 armed men are pursuing Tolberts and Negroes." The following day the *Register* reported: "SEVENTH NEGRO KILLED. Eight Negroes arrested, four released, four riddled with 150 round of buckshots and bullets. Murder of Etheridge and other crimes to some extent avenged. Estimated 75 men in lynching party. One Negro hanged at 8:00 A.M. today."

Contrary to press stories, there seems to be no evidence that Negroes were ever armed in large numbers to resist the mobs in Greenwood County during the Phoenix Riot. My sister and other Negroes whom I interviewed in the county in the summer of 1968, who were old enough to know something about the riot, had no knowledge of Negroes' being armed. There were rumors to this effect; but the press gives no evidence that Negroes were resisting whites. A white man had been killed, and several Negroes had to die for it, even though there was no absolute proof that a Negro killed "Bose" Etheridge. Then, too, Negroes had to be convinced, once and for all, that the ballot in Greenwood County was for whites only. On November 17, 1898, the Greenwood *Index*, my county paper, commenting on the Phoenix Riot, said this:

> The action of the white people of North Carolina, and the determination with which the men went into the Phoenix episode, demonstrated above all things else that the white people of this country will not entertain even a suggestion of Negro domination. It is a basic principle in our unwritten law that the white man must rule—a law firmly rooted in our natures and as unchangeable as that of the Medes and Persians. Everything that pertains to citizenship, to property, and the pursuit of happiness must conform to this law. A method, however unjust or unfair it may appear in theory, that does not take this fundamental principle into consideration, is inevitably wrong. It is a painful act, however, that in order to enforce this law harsh measures are sometimes necessary, but whether the measures are right or wrong, the higher law which brings about these measures is always right, and, in this instance, right is inconsistently consistent. No, our

> civilization won't allow us to entertain any thought of the Negro taking a part in a white man's realm, and any steps from him in this direction will result to the detriment of those who aid him and to his own destruction. It is better for white men to cease making him a tool for their betterment.

Most of the blame for the Phoenix Riot was laid on the Republican Tolberts, who were encouraging Negroes to register and vote. Oddly enough, however, no Tolbert was lynched—only Negroes. Though the mobs did go out to kill the Tolberts, they never did so. Negroes did not strike back. The truth is that Negroes were scared to death. They took to the woods, as my father did, and many fled the county and the state. According to the Columbia *State* (November 13, 1898), "there are several hundred Negro refugees in adjacent Georgia counties and more are fleeing, some have returned, some are going into town to trade and the situation . . . seems to be calm." Later, on December 21, 1898, the Columbia *State* applauded the Negro exodus from Greenwood County. Under the caption GREENWOOD'S NEGRO EXODUS, it said:

> 100 Negroes already gone, most to Mississippi, and an emigration agent has engaged several hundred families to go. This is good for everybody. It gets rid of excess Negro population in that fertile area. Since the war, they have rented land and, in collusion with white owners, have continued the evil system of one crop cotton with a deficiency in food crops. With whites taking over, they can diversify. Let nothing impede this exodus.

Although a Negro was charged with precipitating the Phoenix Riot, there are Negroes in Greenwood County who do not accept this accusation. Three Negroes with whom I talked in the summer of 1968 believe that "Bose" Etheridge was killed by a white man who was trying to kill Tom Tolbert, who had the Republican poll box in which Negroes were to deposit their affidavits. It was a stray bullet from the gun of a white man that killed Etheridge, they claim. A Negro friend of long standing, still living in Greenwood County, son of a man who lived on Tom Tolbert's farm for many years, who moved into his father's house and lived on Tom Tolbert's place for two decades after his father's death, has an interesting sidelight on the killing of "Bose" Etheridge. He swears Tom Tolbert told him that the bullet which killed Etheridge was fired by a white man and was meant for him, Tom Tolbert. Tom Tolbert thought the blame had been placed on Negroes to protect the white killer. I make no claim for the accuracy of this statement, but it is interesting to recall that no one was ever tried for the murder of Giles O. "Bose" Etheridge. It is also to be noted that R. R. Tolbert, the Republican candidate, was interviewed by a reporter from the Columbia *Register* at a train station in Greenville, South Carolina, on November 12, 1898, and is reported as saying he wanted to show that the Third District had a majority of Republican voters; that he voted for his opponent; that his brother had permission to put the box in front of the store; that he meant no trouble, for it was not a ballot box; that Etheridge knocked over the table and hit his brother; that Negroes had no arms and neither did his brother; and that Etheridge was "hit by green boys who didn't know how to shoot." This statement lends credence to the belief of Negroes that Etheridge was killed by a white man. If Joe Circuit (or Syrk) did not fire the fatal shot, it seems clear that the person who did was never apprehended.

Reactions to the Phoenix Riot were varied. The former Governor of South Carolina, now Senator Ben Tillman, seems to have expressed no regret. His position was that things would go well for the Negro if he accepted an inferior role. Tillman was interviewed by August Kohn of the Charleston *News and Courier* on November 14, 1898, and is reported to have said that the violence was caused by "race antagonism which will always exist and is uneradicable." "This prejudice," continued Tillman, "is stronger than law and religion." He said that the new constitution of 1895 was designed to "take the Negro out of politics legally. The Anglo-Saxon race has never been dominated by the colored race, anywhere in all its history."

There was a feeling of remorse in the community. Mass meetings were held placing the responsibility for the lynchings on the Tolberts (although still maintaining that a Negro fired the fatal shot) and assuring Negroes that they had no reason to fear if they "behaved." Some Negro leaders renounced the Tolberts, saying that they wanted to live in harmony with the whites. The Washington *Post* editorialized the hope that Phoenix had taught the Negroes a lesson—meaning, *stay out of politics.*

Other sections of the state and the South were having trouble, too. On November 8, day of the election in Phoenix, the Columbia *State* reported the killing of a Negro by a young white man in Blackville, South Carolina, because the Negro, Lloyd Lancaster, had jostled his killer, John McLendon, on the sidewalk the Saturday before. The Charleston *News and Courier* reported in its issue of November 12, 1898, that there was almost a riot in Charleston on that day. The Columbia *Register* of November 15, 1898, deplored the killing of an innocent Negro woman in the Phoenix area; and on November 13, 1898, in Smithville, Abbeville County, John Fell White killed a Negro accused of theft. Nor were the kinds of lynchings that took place in my home community in 1898 unusual. Jefferson Ellis, a Memphis Negro, accused of attacking a white girl and of killing a white woman two years before, was lynched in a horrible fashion. A mob of 350 men carried him before a bonfire and told him to pray. On his knees, Ellis began singing Negro hymns. Members of the mob cried out, "Burn him!" Others cried, "I want an ear!" "I want a finger!" and then they cut off his ears and fingers. They made him stand so the crowd could see him. They tortured him for thirty-five minutes; then his head was severed, and he was hanged by his feet. A sign was erected saying that the victim was to hang all day, and death to anyone who took him down before evening (The Columbia *Daily Register,* October 17, 1895).

Five years before my birth, the Charleston *News and Courier* told of eight defenseless Negroes lynched in Barnwell, South Carolina, Said the *Courier,* on December 29, 1898:

> It is impossible to describe how many shots each man received and where they were struck as their bodies and heads were literally torn to pieces. Michael Adams was tied to the post which marks the corporate limits of Barnwell. Just to his right was his accomplice, Ripley Johnson, fastened to a tree. The Martin murderers on the other side of the road were

> arranged in line. Some of the Negroes were old men, Morrell possibly sixty years old, and Peter Bell about the same age. As your correspondent viewed the corpses tonight, their frames were exposed, their clothes having been partially removed by physicians and the curious crowd. Some of the Negroes had their eyes shot out, others were wounded in the chest and face. Blood covered the ground upon which they laid (sic), and a more horrible sight could not be beheld by mortal man. The bodies of all the Negroes were brought to town tonight and carried to the guard house, where they will remain until tomorrow, when they will be buried. The lynched were accused of killing two white men. A mob of one hundred broke open the jail and took the Negroes out and lynched then.

In 1898, at the time of the Phoenix Riot, Charles B. Aycock of North Carolina ran his campaign on white supremacy and the disfranchisement of Negroes. According to reports in the Wilmington *Star*, on November 10 and 11, 1898, hundreds of armed men paraded in red shirts through the streets of Wilmington in order to frighten Negroes. Ben Tillman went up from South Carolina to assist his colleagues in their race-hating campaign. It is reported that 5,000 rounds of ammunition and a carload of firearms were sent to North Carolina a few days before the election. Not being satisfied with cowing the Negroes and winning the election, four hundred men, under the leadership of a former Congressman, destroyed the Negro newspaper, burned the building, shot up the Negro district, killed eleven Negroes, wounded others, and drove hundreds into the woods. The leader of the mob was adequately rewarded by being elected mayor.

In August of the year of the Phoenix Riot and the North Carolina mass murders, the Richmond *Times* reported a mass lynching in Arkansas. In an editorial on August 12, 1898, the *Times* wrote:

> The lynchers have been holding carnival in the state of Arkansas, and this time not only men but women have fallen victim of the fury of the mob. Nor were they executed for the "usual crime," but five persons, three men and two women, without any process of law, were taken by the mob and summarily deprived of their life, upon the charge of murder, either as principals, or accessories.

(Author's Note: The reports and descriptions of lynchings herein related have been taken from hundreds of microfilm copies of issues of the twelve major newspapers published in the South just before and after the turn of the century. All of the copies examined carried anti-Negro editorials, articles, or stories of atrocities committed against Negroes.)

In the year in which I was born, 192 persons were lynched in the United States. Between 1882 and 1946, a total of 4,716 persons were lynched in this country. Mississippi took the lead with 574 to her discredit; Georgia was second with 525; Texas third with 489; Louisiana fourth with 391; Alabama was in fifth place with 346; and South Carolina had 159. Forty-two states were involved in this savage and shameful crime during this period.[12] It is evident that what was happening in South Carolina was happening to the Negro in greater or lesser degree all over the South. His alleged crimes were splashed in huge headlines in Southern newspapers. Lynching Negroes had become a part of the Southern culture, engrained in the mores, condoned by the Church, and accepted as law by Southern states. John Sharp Williams, a respected Mississippian, once defended lynching on the floor of the Senate. Even the Congress of the United States winked at it, as evidenced by the fact that the National Association for the Advancement of Colored People could never get Congress to pass an anti-lynching bill. It is significant that as early as January 20, 1900, George H. White, a Negro, introduced in the House of Representatives a bill designed to make lynching a federal crime. The year before, 85 Negroes and 21 whites were lynched (12: p. 307). His bill didn't get through.

It is customary to put the blame for bad Negro-white relations on the behavior of "poor white trash" and "ignorant Negroes"; but such a claim cannot be validated. The "best" people in the South either favored lynching or condoned it. W. J. Cash, in *The Mind of the South*,[13] calls John Temple Graves "an artistocrat by birth," but Cash also points out that Graves advocated that, to protect Southern white womanhood, the South was justified in lynching any number of innocent Negroes to force the others to ferret out and reveal the identity of the man supposedly guilty of a purported crime. Facts or truth evidently meant nothing to John Temple Graves and his kind. He must have known that the vast majority of the Negroes lynched were not even accused of rape. Of the 4,716 persons lynched from 1882 through 1946, only 910, or 19.2 percent, were even accused of rape, and only 288, or 6.1 percent, of attempted rape (12: p. 308). In my county, a Negro was lynched for disputing a white man's word or failing to call him "Mister." The white people at the top, the white people in authority, the "best" white people were largely responsible for permitting and participating in the sadistic practice of lynching. I can add nothing to what Cash has written on this point:

> As for the ruling class in general, the evidence is equally conclusive, so far as these regions where lynching was still common were concerned. I mean the evidence that, far from attempting to prevent lynchings, the police in such areas almost invariably connived at them and very often actively participated in them, sometimes serving as master of ceremonies in the application of gasoline and torch or in adjusting the rope to the victim's neck; and (significant for the whole spirit of the South, for that matter) that customarily when a lynching took place, neither local nor state officials made any honest effort to apprehend and punish the criminals. The police either didn't investigate at all or reported, tongue in cheek, that they were unable to identify anybody, though who the guilty parties were was commonly neighborhood knowledge. Judges, attorney-generals and governors almost never made any attempt to spur them into the active performance of their duty. When, for a wonder, they did, they got no cooperation or support from the body of "best citizens" in the local community or state; on the contrary, the ranks closed now, as always, and all investigators got was grim warnings to mind their own business under penalty of tar and feathers (13: p. 302).

Innocent or guilty, it was almost universally accepted by white Southerners that if a Negro was accused of raping a white woman lynching him was all right. On the other hand, white men were not lynched for raping Negro women or for taking advantage of them. There were many people in the South who were opposed to mob rule and lynching, except when used under the pretext of protecting white womanhood, but their opposition was mild, because white people generally believed in white supremacy, and if mob rule was necessary to keep Negroes down, they condoned it.

Segregation in Depth

Stripping the Negro of the ballot and keeping him intimidated through the imminence of mob rule should have satisfied those who were determined to keep the Negro down. Not so. Segregation was instituted and enacted into law, in some cases even before Negroes were made ballotless. The Negro had to be segregated as one unfit to mingle freely with members of the white race. He had to be pushed aside so that he could be treated as an inferior. South Carolina's determination to segregate the Negro was bolstered when, in 1867, the right of a railroad to separate passengers according to race was upheld. There was a glimmer of hope for Negroes when Congress enacted the Civil Rights Act of 1875, which guaranteed nondiscrimination in public accommodations. In 1883, however, the Supreme Court unfortunately declared that Congress had gone beyond its constitutional power, and thus struck down the Civil Rights Act of 1875. This decision of the Supreme Court gave the South a free hand to segregate Negroes. From then on, jim crow laws grew rapidly, despite the fact that nothing in the United States Constitution gives the states the right to segregate their citizens.[14] The following list shows the dates on which twelve Southern states enacted laws requiring segregation on railroads, which included segregated waiting rooms, ticket windows, rest rooms and water fountains; and the dates on which these states enacted laws requiring segregation on streetcars and other forms of public transportation:[15]

State	Railroads	Other Transportation
Alabama	1891	1891
Arkansas	1891; 1893	1903
Georgia	1890; 1891	1890
Kentucky	1892; 1893	1892
Louisiana	1890	1902
Mississippi	1892; 1906	1904
North Carolina	1899	1907
Oklahoma	1907; 1908	1907
South Carolina	1898	1908
Tennessee	1890	1905
Texas	1907	1907
Virginia	1902; 1903; 1904	1901

The fetish and the practice of segregation developed to the point of absurdity. In some cities, a Negro could be arrested if he so much as *walked through* a white waiting room; he would certainly be if he refused to go back when the station policeman ordered him to do so. Parks and playgrounds, hospitals, prisons, schools for the deaf and blind, men serving life sentences—all these were segregated. Insane Negroes and insane whites were segregated—even an insane white man was held superior to an insane Negro! By 1908, Atlanta had segregated elevators, though not by law. In establishing segregation in transportation, the states gave motormen police power to implement the law. To satisfy federal law, the states called for "separate but equal" accommodations, but nobody saw to it that the separate Negro facilities were equal. Two important events gave wings to the segregation movement around the turn of the century: 1) Booker T. Washington's compromise speech in Atlanta in 1895; and 2) the decision of the United States Supreme Court in *Plessy vs. Ferguson* in 1896. I was born one year before Washington's Atlanta speech, one year before the death of Frederick Douglass, and one year before the Negro was disfranchised in South Carolina. I was two years old when the Supreme Court handed down its decision that segregation was constitutional if the two separates were equal. It was not only Washington's speech that made him acceptable to white America, but his acceptance of the philosophy of segregation in general.

His Atlanta speech made Booker T. Washington famous on two counts: By any standard of measurement, he was an able man; but, far more important, he said what white America wished to hear. W. E. B. Du Bois was just as able, but when he began to speak out at the turn of the century he was not whistling the right tune nor was he saying the "right" words. Consequently, he was never universally acclaimed by white America. The South, troubled, perplexed, and irritated by the presence of the Negro, saw in Booker T. Washington's speech a solution to the Negro-white problem. They liked, most of all, Washington's acceptance of segregation and his repudiation of social equality. They liked his admonition to Negroes and whites alike, "Cast down your buckets where you are." Two quotations from the Atlanta speech have been repeated and remembered more than any other: 1) "In all things that are purely social, we can be as separate as the fingers, yet one as the hand in all things essential to mutual progress"; and 2) "the wisest among my race understand that agitation of questions of social equality is the extremest folly, and that progress in the enjoyment of all the privileges that will come to us must be the result of severe and constant struggle rather than of artificial forcing."[16]

The advice to both Negroes and whites, "Cast down your buckets where you are," was a popular theme in the South. Overnight, Washington became not only the spokesman for the Negroes in this country but also, simultaneously, a world figure. Ironically enough, the man who said "in all things that are purely social we can be as separate as the fingers" enjoyed more social equality than any other Negro in the United States. He associated and dined with the "high and mighty." The man who discouraged Negroes from participation in politics suddenly became a fount of wisdom. Presidents of the United States sought his advice, not only with reference to Negroes but also concerning the appointment of Southern whites to political positions. Philanthropists sought his counsel when Negro colleges requested aid. Clark Howell, editor of the Atlanta *Constitution*, sent a wire to a New York newspaper saying that Washington's address laid down the platform "upon which blacks and whites can stand with full justice to each other" (16: p. 226). The Boston *Transcript* wrote in an editorial that "the speech of Booker T. Washington at the Atlanta Exposition this week seems to have dwarfed all the other proceedings and the Exposition itself. The sensation that it caused in the press has never been equalled" (16: p. 226). James Creelman of the New York *World Telegram* sent a telegram to his paper describing what happened after Washington's speech. "When Washington said, 'In all things that are purely social, we can be as separate as the fingers, yet one as the hand in all things essential to mutual progress,' the whole audience was on its feet in a delirium of applause" (16: p. 240).

It must be noted, however, that, great as Washington had become and in spite of having been given some social recognition, he was still a Negro, an "untouchable." The South was enraged when he accepted an invitation from President Theodore Roosevelt to dine with him at the White House. The President had gone too far! To eat with a Negro was tantamount to giving him social equality—a deadly insult to the South. Only when it was convinced that this was an isolated incident and that the President did not intend to make this a practice was the South placated. In an editorial in the Richmond *News Leader* on June 10, 1905, under the caption CHANGED CONDITIONS, the editor explained why he could welcome Roosevelt to Virginia:

> Unquestionably, the attitude of the entire South toward Mr. Roosevelt has changed within a year and the *News Leader* has participated in that change. This is because events and developments have proved that all of us were mistaken in supposing Mr. Roosevelt intended to practice and illustrate the doctrine of social equality. Evidently he realized that the Booker T. Washington incident was a mistake and has not repeated it.
>
> If he made colored people of any kind his associates and companions and had habitually or occasionally received them as his social equals, the feeling of the South toward him would continue to be one of bitter contempt.

The Jackson (Mississippi) *Clarion Ledger* said, in an editorial on June 24, 1905:

> The Booker T. Washington incident was a mere indiscretion. It was a blunder which a man of Mr. Roosevelt's sense should never have committed, but no sensible man in this section believes that the President is in favor of amalgamation. Our complaint against him was that in inviting a negro to his table he, as President of the United States, set the example of social equality between the races, and if he recognized and established that, amalgamation must follow as a logical sequence.
>
> Southerners have settled the matter that the races must be separated completely. President Roosevelt would be of the same mind if he lived in the South.

Booker T. Washington was acknowledged by the South as a great man, but not great enough to dine with a white man. It took an able, courageous man to challenge him. W. E. B. Du Bois was that man. He didn't like Washington's views on the disfranchisement of the Negro. He rejected Washington's endorsement of segregation. The "separate as the fingers" formula was inconsistent, in Du Bois' thinking. He felt that Washington had sold out to the South. (For a penetrating analysis of Du Bois's quarrel with Booker T. Washington, see John Hope Franklin's fine book *From Slavery to Freedom* [4: pp. 390-397].) Washington cannot be held responsible for the states' laws segregating and disfranchising the Negro after 1895, but it is probably true that Washington's speech enabled the South to do these things without any pangs of conscience. Washington's address made such a profound impression on white America that it is not only conceivable but highly probable that his philosophy influenced the 1896 decision of the Supreme Court which constitutionalized segregation.

How rapidly the Negro was bereft of the ballot, brutalized by mobs and individuals, and segregated in every area of life! It was inevitable that this same cruel discrimination would flourish in the field of education. Insofar as the *equal* part of the *separate but equal* doctrine of the Supreme Court decision, *Plessy vs. Ferguson*, was concerned, it meant nothing to the South. There was never any intention of the South to abide by that decision except as it favored whites. There is no evidence that the South even attempted to abide by it until forced to do so in 1935 when Murray sued to enter the law school of the University of Maryland. The most naïve optimist could hardly expect equality in education from people piously guilty of disfranchising, segregating, and lynching Negro fellow citizens.

Discrimination with a Vengeance

When I was a year old (1895), there was very little difference in the length of school terms for Negroes and whites in South Carolina—3.24 months for Negroes and 3.71 months for whites. In 1900, when I entered the first grade, the Negro school ran 15 weeks and the white school 24.4 weeks. In the five-year interval between 1905 and 1910, the white school term increased by 3.4 weeks and the Negro school term lost one week.[17] Writing of the educational situation in South Carolina, in his book *Separate and Unequal,* Louis R. Harlan says, "In the decade and a half from 1900 to 1915, South Carolina expenditures for education increased fourfold. The amount spent for Negro schools only doubled, while the amount for white schools quintupled; and the Negro schools made no gain for the five years after 1910. Insofar as education meant opportunity, the Negro child's chance, in relation to the white child, dropped from one-fifth to one-twelfth."[18] Harlan points out further that in 1900, the year I entered the one-room, four-month-term Negro school, South Carolina spent $588,414.53 for the white school system and $171,954.69 for the Negro system. In 1905 (when I was eleven years old), the amount spent for whites was $1,060,019.58 and for Negroes only $244,609.86 (18: p. 205). In the five-year span, the amount spent for whites had almost doubled, and the amount spent for Negroes had increased neglibly from $217,000 to $244,000. To state discrimination another way, South Carolina had increased its expenditures for the white schools from $588,414.53 in 1900 to $2,924,859.68 in 1915; whereas in the same fifteen-year period the increase for Negroes moved from $171,954.69 in 1900 to only $370,640,40 in 1915. In other words, dollar-wise, the increase for whites was $2,336,442 and the increase for Negroes only $192,682 between 1900 and 1915, approximately a 500 percent increase for whites and slightly over 100 percent for Negroes. Accepting the figures of the Federal Commissioner of Education for 1915, Harlan shows that there were 209,192 white students enrolled and 327,473 Negro children enrolled of ages from five to eighteen years. In that year, the state of South Carolina spent $13.98 per capita for each white child and $1.13 per capita for each Negro child (Harlan: pp. 204-205).

In 1900, expenditure per white pupil in attendance was $6.51; for the Negro pupil in attendance $1.55. In 1915, the per capita expenditure for the white students was $23.70, and for the Negro child $2.91 (Harlan: p. 208). The gulf of inequality continued to widen. In 1920, the per capita expenditure for the white child was $26.08, and for the Negro child $3.04. The same discrimination existed in salaries paid to Negro and white teachers. In Greenwood County, Negroes were 65.64 percent of the population in 1915, and received $11,653.74 of the school money; whereas the whites received $54,051.47, with 34.36 precent of the population (Harlan: p. 207).

The reports of other school systems of the South show similar discrimination: in 1899, the average monthly salary of white teachers in Mississippi was $30.64; the average of Negro teachers was $19.65.[19] The same average held for the year 1900 (salaries increased slowly for both white and Negro teachers). In 1915, the average monthly salaries for white teachers was $47.00; for Negro teachers the average was $25.00. In 1895, the per capita expenditure for the white child was $3.25; for the Negro child it was $1.45 (19: 1897-1898, p. 49). The Biennial Report for 1900-1901 lists $5.70 per capita for the white child and $1.87 for the Negro child. For 1920, the Biennial Report of the Mississippi State Superintendent of Schools shows that the per capita expenditure for the white child was $11.00, and $2.50 for the Negro child (19: 1920).

Though Virginia spent more for education than did Mississippi, the same pattern of discrimination was maintained. In 1895, the highest per capita expenditure among the counties was $11.49 for each white child and $3.31 for each Negro child. The lowest per capita expenditure in a county for the white child was $4.29; and for the Negro child $0.93. The highest per capita expenditure per student among the cities was $20.10 for each white child, and $7.70 for each Negro child. The lowest per capita expenditure for the white child in a city was $4.72, and $2.70 for the black child.[20] In 1900, the highest monthly salary paid white teachers in the county of Charles City, Virginia, was $98.05 for the white male, and $33.43 for the white female. The highest average salary for the Negro male, in the same county, was $32.50, and for the Negro female $25.00. In the same year, Richmond paid an average of $145.71 for the white male, and $50.09 for the white female. The Negro male's monthly average salary in Richmond in 1900 was $52.85; for the Negro female it was $48.36 (20: p.265).

The inequality of educational expenditures for Negroes and for whites began before the dawn of the twentieth century, and the gap of inequality increased steadily with the years. There was no real attempt to close this gap, the 1896 Supreme Court decision notwithstanding, until 1935 when the "separate but equal" doctrine was tested by Murray's suit to enter the University of Maryland. An example of how the inequality in education widened may be seen by an excerpt from an article the author wrote in *The Christian Century*, March 25, 1931:

Every silver lining has its cloud. I make bold to assert that the most discouraging trend in race relations is to be found in the area of public funds expenditures. The South is spending relatively less for the public school education of its Negro citizens. Thirteen Southern states in the school year 1918-19 spent $12.91 per capita for each white child of school age; $4.42 for each Negro child—a difference of $8.49. In the school year 1924-25, these thirteen states spent $27.95 per capita for each white child of school age; for the Negro child $9.52—a difference of $18.43. At the present time, these thirteen states are expending per capita for each white child of school age $40.92: for the Negro child, $15.78—a difference of $25.14. In other words, from 1919 up to the present time (1931), the per capita expenditure for the white child increased $28.01; for the Negro child $11.36.

As appropriations increase, the differences also increase. As the Negro child is advanced, the white child is advanced two, two and a half, three times faster. In the main, there is absolutely no approach toward equity, except possibly in Kentucky and Texas. Even North Carolina, with its vast program of improvement in education, is appropriating relatively less and less for public school education of Negroes—with the increased difference in per capita expenditure of $6.24 in 1919 to $30.18 at the present time.

Anti-Negro Publications

Around the close of the nineteenth century and at the dawn of the twentieth, the South had much going in its favor with respect to domination of the Negro; and things had been going the Southern way since 1877 when federal troops were withdrawn from the South. The Negro had practically vanished from Southern politics, thanks to state laws and intimidations. The federal government had extended a helping hand in 1883, when the United States Supreme Court set aside the Civil Rights Act of 1875 on the ground that it was unconstitutional. In 1895, Booker T. Washington had helped the white South by his debatable Atlanta speech endorsing segregation and the disfranchisement of the Negro and condemning social equality between Negroes and whites. The United States Supreme Court aided the Southern cause still further in its 1896 decision declaring segregation constitutional provided it was equal separation. The Northern press and authors looked kindly upon the South. Able Southerners were assiduous in their efforts to win the North to the Southern point of view and to assure the North that the Negro's destiny was safe in Southern hands. A Southern diplomat and novelist, Thomas Nelson Page, writing in *The North American Review* said:

The Negro has not progressed, not because he was a slave, but because he does not possess the faculties to raise himself above slavery. . . . Where the Negro has thriven it has invariably been under the influence and by the assistance of a stronger race. These wanting, he has inevitably and visibly reverted toward the original type. . . .

Slavery, whatever its demerits, was not in its time the unmitigated evil it is fancied to have been. Its time has passed. No power could compel the South to have it back. But to the Negro it was salvation. It found him a savage and in two hundred years gave seven million of his race a civilization, the only civilization it has had since the dawn of history.

We have educated him; we have aided him; we have sustained him in all right directions. We are ready to continue our aid, but we will not be dominated by him. When we shall be, it is our settled conviction that we shall deserve the degradation into which we shall have sunk.[21]

Another Southerner, Henry W. Grady, perhaps more than any other man, created sympathy for the South in the North, and gave body to the illusion that the South was dealing justly with the Negro. In his speech before the New England Society in December, 1886, declaring that the South had kept faith with the Negro, Grady said:

We remember with what fidelity for four years he guarded our defenceless women and children, whose husbands and fathers were fighting against his freedom. To his eternal credit be it said that whenever he struck a blow for his own liberty he fought in open battle, and when at last he raised his black humble hands that the shackles might be struck off, those hands were innocent of wrong against his helpless charges and worthy to be taken in loving grasp by every man who honors loyalty and devotion. Ruffians have maltreated him, rascals have misled him, philanthropists established a bank for him, but the South, with the North, protests against injustice to this simple and sincere people. To liberty and enfranchisement is as far as the law can carry the negro. The rest must be left to conscience and common sense. It should be left to those among whom his lot is cast, with whom he is indissolubly connected and whose prosperity depends upon their possessing his intelligent sympathy and confidence. Faith has been kept with him in spite of calumnious assertions to the contrary by those who assume to speak for us or by frank opponents. Faith will be kept with him in the future, if the South holds her reason and integrity.[22]

In the same speech, speaking of the Negro, Grady said, "He shares our school fund, has the fullest protection of our laws and the friendship of our people." It must be stated here that in the year that Grady delivered this speech before the New England Society, 138 persons were lynched in the United States and the majority of them were Negroes. Grady's attitude toward the Negro, expressed in this speech, must be compared with what he said the next year in a speech delivered at the Dallas (Texas) State Fair:

Those who would put the negro race in supremacy would work against infallible decree, for the white race can never submit to its domination, because the white race is the superior race. But the supremacy of the white race in the South must be maintained forever, and the domination of the negro race resisted at all points and all hazards, because the white race is the superior race. This is the declaration of no new truth. It has abided forever in the marrow of our bones, and shall run forever with the blood that feeds Anglo-Saxon hearts.

Mr. Grady reached his climax with this peroration:

> Standing in the presence of this multitude, sobered with the responsibility of the message I deliver to the young men of the South, I declare that the truth above all others to be worn unsullied and sacred in your hearts, to be surrendered to no force, sold for no price, compromised in no necessity, but cherished and defended as the covenant of your prosperity and the pledge of peace to your children, is that the white race must dominate forever in the South, because it is the white race and superior to that race by which its supremacy is threatened.
>
> It is a race issue. Let us come to this point, and stand here. Here the air is pure and the light is clear, and here honor and peace abide. Juggling and evasion deceive not a man. Compromise and subservience has carried not a point. There is not a white man, North and South, who does not feel its stir in the gray matter of his brain and throb of his heart. Not a negro who does not feel its power. It is not a sectional issue. It speaks in Ohio and in Georgia. It speaks wherever the Anglo-Saxon touches an alien race. It has just spoken in universally approved legislation in excluding the Chinaman from our gates, not for ignorance, vice or corruption, but because he sought to establish an inferior race in a republic fashioned in the wisdom and defended by the blood of a homogeneous people.[23]

Henry Grady of the Atlanta *Constitution* was one of the most outstanding men in the South. His view of the Negro inevitably made its impact on millions of whites and his speeches encouraged them to do things to Negroes which Grady himself would never do. It is interesting to note the orator's emphasis on "domination." Obviously, the Negro could share in government without dominating it; but Grady meant that the Negro must not even participate in affairs of state.

In an editorial on May 10, 1900, *The New York Times* commended the South:

> It has of late become the custom of the men of the South to speak with entire candor of the settled and deliberate policy of suppressing the negro vote. They have been forced to choose between a policy of manifest injustice toward blacks and the horrors of negro rule. They chose to disfranchise the negros. That was manifestly the lesser of two evils. In any community, North or South or foreign, this course would have been adopted. It was the only way to avert civil destruction. Northern men who have an adequate knowledge of conditions at the South no longer denounce the sup-

pression of the negro vote as it used to be denounced in the reconstruction days. The necessity of it under the supreme law of self-preservation is candidly recognized.

In his address on the Race Problem at Montgomery [Alabama] ex-Secretary [of the Navy:1893-1897] [Hilary Abner] Herbert spoke candidly of these hard conditions which confront the people of the Southern states: "Public opinion has made progress, and now sanctions, I think, these propositions: Negro suffrage has failed. It brought weakness instead of strength to the party that controlled it, piled up millions high the debt of every State where it was dominant, and did not better the condition of the black man anywhere. White men have obtained control and must keep it, if they mean to preserve the Anglo-Saxon civilization. But this is not all of it. Necessity has compelled us to resort to election methods which we desire to abandon" (*New York Times*, May 10, 1900).

On March 17, 1903, the Richmond *Times Dispatch* expressed satisfaction when a Northerner wrote an article in the *Outlook* favoring the South's treatment of the Negro. The *Dispatch* praised the writer for making it clear that blacks and whites, Africans and Anglo-Saxons, would never intermarry, that the Negro should not be led to vote against the white South, and that the North could help the Negro best by cooperating with the Negroes' white neighbors and under the leadership of his white Southern neighbors, in solving the race problem. The *Dispatch* closed its remarks by saying, "The solution of the race problem is not in sight, but it is a great point gained that the *North and South are coming nearer and nearer every day to the same viewpoint*." (Italics are the author's.)

Summing up the North's sympathy for the South, C. Vann Woodward, in *The Strange Career of Jim Crow* (2: p. 72) quotes Emma Lou Thornbrough as saying that before 1900 the North was only acquiescing in the way the South was treating the Negro but that "now there is a trend to imitate the South."

Uncomplimentary books written about the Negro, at the time of my birth and during my early years, were not new; they were centuries old. But writers around the dawn of the twentieth century gave support to those who were determined to deal injustice to the Negro. At the beginning of the twentieth century, several books were written designed to prove that the Negro was unworthy. In 1902, when I was eight years old, Thomas Dixon, a Baptist minister from North Carolina, wrote *The Leopard's Spots*, the theme of which was that the beastly nature of the Negro cannot be changed any more than the Ethiopian can change his skin or the leopard his spots. Dixon has one of his characters, the Preacher, say:

"The more you educate, the more impossible you make his position in a democracy. Education! Can you change the colour of his skin, the kink of his hair, the bulge of his lips, the spread of his nose, or the beat of his heart, with a spelling book? The Negro is the human donkey. You can train him, but you can't make of him a horse. Mate him with a horse, you lose the horse, and get a larger donkey, called a mule, incapable of preserving his

> species. What is called our race prejudice is simply God's first law of nature—the instinct of self-preservation."[24]

Dixon wrote *The Clansman* in 1905. Out of it came the motion picture *The Birth of a Nation*. He wrote *The Traitor* in 1900. Perhaps no writings in anybody's lifetime did as much to engender prejudice against the Negro as the writings and works of the minister, Dixon, did in mine. In 1907 came Robert Shurfeldt's book *The Negro a Menace to American Civilization*. In 1900, Charles Carroll wrote *The Negro a Beast.* The latter book was published by the American Book & Bible Society of St. Louis, Missouri. Carroll attempted to show, from hair, skull, cranial capacity, jaw, ear, chin, teeth, lip, nose, neck, spine, and pelvis that the Negro was inferior to the white man. He argued that the Negro was created along with the animals before God created man. The Negro was created a beast by God. Other racist literature, such as William P. Calhoun's *The Caucasian and the Negro* (1902); and William B. Smith's *The Color Line: Brief in Behalf of the Unborn* (1905), was appearing and making its impact against the Negro in the minds of white readers. Howard Odum, noted sociologist, strengthened the South in its attitude toward the Negro. In his *Social and Mental Traits of the Negro* Odum wrote:

> Back of the child, and affecting him both directly and indirectly, are the characteristics of the race. The Negro has little honor, conscience or love of home, no local attachment of the better sort. He does not know, in many cases for months or years, the whereabouts of his brother or even parents. Nor does he concern himself about their welfare. He has no pride of ancestry, and he is not influenced by the lives of great men. The Negro has few ideals and perhaps no lasting adherence to an aspiration toward real worth. He has little conception of the meaning of virtue, truth, honor, manhood, integrity. He is shiftless, untidy, and indolent. . . . The Negro shirks details and difficult tasks; he is incapable of turning his mind toward any other subject once morbid curiosity holds his attention.[25]

In all fairness to Odum, not long after he wrote this book, he repudiated these views and became an advocate of justice for the Negro—within the segregated pattern. He and other writers were simply following the line of nineteenth-century writers like the members of the Anthropological Society of New York, and like Josie Clark Nott, George Glidden, Louis Agassiz, and other men of science who were doing their considerable best to discredit the Negro.

Nothing could stop the relentless bulldozer of prejudice, segregation, brutality, and disfranchisement in its determination to destroy the Negro's faith in himself and so beat him down that the aspiration to rise would be completely suppressed. The eloquence and writings of Frederick Augustus Douglass, up to his death in 1895, could not stay it. The arguments of intelligent Negroes in the state assemblies of the South and in the halls of the Congress of the United States could not stop the grinding power of racism. Negroes were helpless. Neither the irrefutable logic of

William Monroe Trotter and W. E. Burghardt Du Bois, nor the eloquently commanding pleas of Booker T. Washington, the man the South had made, could hold back the rising tide of racism. Du Bois was prophetic when he said, in *The Souls of Black Folk* (1903), "The problem of the twentieth century is the problem of the color line: the relation of the darker to the lighter race of man in Asia and Africa, the Americas, and the islands of the seas."[26] Over a period of three hundred years, enough white authors used their talents to laud the superiority of the white race and to prove the inferiority of the other races of mankind so that every white child knew one thing quite early: "I'm better than a 'nigger'!"

All during this period, white church members were condoning what was going on in Negro-white relations, just as most of them had matter-of-factly accepted slavery for 246 years. People went to church; listened to sermons about God, Jesus, the Holy Ghost, the Virgin birth, sin and salvation; attended prayer meetings and revivals; but their religion had no relevance to the social issues of their time. Negro church members went to church, shouted, prayed, listened to their pastors who usually preached emotional and other-worldly sermons telling the people that God in his good time would set things right—if not here, certainly in heaven! But in the midst of their other-worldliness, Negro preachers during this period, as in slavery, emphasized the fact that God is Father of all mankind; that all men are brothers; and that in God's sight all men are equal. They affirmed the value of each individual; said that God is no respecter of person; said that He cares so much for us that the strands of hair on our heads are all numbered. There wasn't much else the Negro preachers could do.

Though the Negro was generally considered "nobody much," the churches of the North had faith in him. They believed that, given a chance, the newly emancipated people and their children could and would master the upper branches of knowledge. They went into the heart of the South and established schools, calling them colleges and universities. Methodists from the North went South and established schools like Wiley, Clark, Claflin, and Bennett. The Baptists went South and founded schools like Morehouse, Shaw, Bishop, Benedict, Spelman, and Virginia Union. Northern Congregationalists founded Fisk, Talledega, Tougaloo, and Atlanta University; and they had a hand in establishing Hampton and Howard. Northern Presbyterians gave Negroes schools like Knoxville, Johnson C. Smith, and Lincoln in Pennsylvania. Paine College in Augusta, Georgia, was established by the Christian Methodist Church and the Southern Methodist Church. From these schools came leaders, not only for Negroes but for all America. These churches gave the Negro hope. They lighted a candle in the dark.

Footnotes for Appendix A

1. Carter G. Woodson, *The Negro In Our History*, 7th ed. (Washington, D. C., 1941), p. 405.

2. C. Vann Woodward, *The Strange Career of Jim Crow*, 2nd ed., rev. (New York, 1966), p. 87.

3. George Brown Tindall, *South Carolina Negroes: 1877-1900* (Baton Rouge, La., 1966), pp. 80-84.

4. John Hope Franklin, *From Slavery to Freedom: A History of Negro Americans,* 3rd ed. (New York, 1967), p. 341.

5. Francis Butler Simkins, *The Tillman Movement in South Carolina* (Durham, N. C., 1926), pp. 39-40.

6. Joel Williamson, *After Slavery* (Chapel Hill, N. C., 1965), pp. 254-255.

7. C. Vann Woodward, *Origins of the New South: 1877-1913* (Baton Rouge, La., 1951), p. 321.

8. *South Carolina House Journal, 1890,* pp. 132-133.

9. Francis Butler Simkins, *Pitchford Ben Tillman* (Baton Rouge, La., 1944), p. 400.

10. National Association for the Advancement of Colored People, *Thirty Years of Lynching in the U.S.: 1899-1919* (New York, 1919).

11. James A. Hoyt, *The Phoenix Riot* (Greenwood, S.C., 1938), p. 3.

12. Jesse Parkhouse Guzman, ed., *Negro Yearbook,* 10th ed. (Tuskegee, Ala., 1947), p. 306.

13. W. J. Cash, *The Mind of the South* (New York, 1941), pp. 301-302.

14. James Wallace, *Segregation on Common Carriers* (Chapel Hill, N.C., 1947).

15. Pauli Murray, ed., *States' Laws on Race and Color* (Cincinnati, Ohio, 1951), App. 7, p. 698.

16. Booker T. Washington, *Up From Slavery* (Chicago, 1900), pp. 221-222.

17. *Reports and Resolutions of the General Assembly of the State of South Carolina 1896,* I.

18. Louis R. Harlan, *Separate and Unequal* (Chapel Hill, N. C., 1958), p. 204.

19. *Biennial Report of the State Superintendent of Schools of Mississippi, 1900-01,* p. 21.

20. *Report of the Superintendent of Public Education of Virginia, 1894-95,* p. 196.

21. Thomas Nelson Page, "The Southerner on the Negro Question," *North American Review,* CLIV, No. 425, 26.

22. *The Critic,* Jan. 1, 1887, p. 10.

23. Edwin Dubois Shurter, *Orations and Speeches of Henry Grady* (Austin, Texas, 1910), p. 34-35.

24. Thomas Dixon, *The Leopard's Spots* (New York, 1902), p. 460.

25. Howard Odum, *Social and Mental Traits of the Negro* (New York, 1910), p. 39.

26. W. E. B. DuBois, *The Souls of Black Folk* (Chicago, 1903), p. 4.

Appendix B

The Church Amidst Ethnic and Racial Tensions

(Speech Delivered at the Second Assembly of the World Council of Churches, Northwestern University, Evanston, Illinois, in session August 14-31, 1954)

Within the past quarter of a century, Christians have been forced to think about the bearing of their faith upon the problem of racial discrimination, and upon the meaning of the races in human history. Wars involving all mankind, the rise of atheistic communism, the development of the Nordic theory of racial superiority, the struggle of the colored peoples everywhere for freedom, and a new emphasis on the meaning of the gospel in our time have made us embarrassingly aware of the wide gulf that frequently exists between our gospel and our practice.

The Jerusalem Conference in 1928 prepared an extensive volume on the subject. Subsequent ecumenical conferences have devoted considerable time to the general topic "The Christian and Race": Oxford and Edinburgh in 1937, Madras in 1938. It suffices to say that in all these ecumenical bodies segregation in the church of Christ, based on race and color, has been strongly condemned.

Your present Commission has critically examined these documents and has benefited greatly by them. We have tried to build substantially on the works of previous scholars, and we believe we have dug new foundations. Since the church gets its authority from the Bible, we have searched the Scriptures anew—both the Old and the New Testaments—to see whether there is anything there to justify our modern policy of segregation based on race, color, or ethnic origin.

The members of your Commission, supported by the best biblical scholars, concluded that anyone who seeks shelter in the Bible for his defense of racial segregation in the church is living in a glass house which is neither rock- nor bulletproof. In the Old Testament the lines are definitely and sharply drawn, but they are drawn along religious and not along racial lines. For example, when Moses exhorted the Jews not to intermarry with the people in the land they were to possess, he did so on neither racial nor ethnic grounds. In Deuteronomy 7: 2-4 this is made plain:

". . . when the Lord your God gives them over to you, and you defeat them; then you must utterly destroy them; you shall make no covenant with them, and show no mercy to them. You shall not make marriages with them, giving your daughters to their sons or taking daughters for your sons. For they would turn away your sons from following me to serve other gods; then the anger of the Lord would be kindled against you, and he would destroy you quickly."

The objection to mixing is religious—not related to race, color, or ethnic group. Ancient Israel was held together by religion and not by race, just as the Jews today are held together by religion and culture. In fact, the nations that surrounded Israel belonged to the same racial stock as Israel. The Moabites shared Israel's language, the Edomites were tied to Israel by bonds of blood, and the Canaanites lived in the same country. But as long as they served their own gods, they were not accepted by Israel. On the other hand, the Gibeonites, who accepted Israel's God, ultimately became Israelites.

The drastic action of Ezra, on the return of the Jews to Jerusalem, in decreeing that the Jews had to put away their foreign wives, was not made on racial grounds. It resulted from an honest belief that they had trespassed against God by marrying wives of foreign religions. We search in vain, therefore, if we expect to find in the Old Testament support for our kind of racial and color segregation. The truth is that the Jews did not constitute a pure strain, and throughout its history Israel made proselytes from other nations and races.

When we turn to the New Testament, it is equally clear that separateness was based on religion and culture, not on the grounds of race or ethnic origin. Your Commission points out once more that from the beginning of his career Jesus proclaimed a religion that was supra-racial, supra-national, supra-cultural and supra-class. His doctrine of God as Father embraces the human race and makes us all children of the same God. God is our Father and we are his children. When we pray "Our Father which art in heaven," we acknowledge our kinship to him. And his concern for all his children is so great that the very hairs on their heads are numbered. Each is precious in his sight. To deny the universalism in the teachings of Christ is to deny the very genius of Christianity.

It is not surprising, therefore, that Hitler wanted nothing to do with Christ and nothing to do with the Christian religion, because they are antipathetic to everything that he stood for. His doctrine of Nordic superiority cannot stand up against the doctrine of the fatherhood of God and the brotherhood of man, nor against the brilliant account of Peter and Cornelius—a Jew and a Gentile standing face to face, confronted with the same Christ and with the same God—nor against the story of the Good Samaritan. It was a Samaritan, a member of another race, who responded helpfully and sympathetically to a Jew's needs, thus dramatizing forever the fact that anyone who is in need is a neighbor and that neighborliness cuts across race and class. Jesus challenged the proud Jews to do as well as the despised Samaritan in displaying love and dispensing mercy across racial and cultural lines.

Jesus declared that he found greater faith in a Roman centurion than he found in all Israel. On another occasion, he declared, ". . . many shall come from the east and the west, and shall recline with Abraham, and Isaac, and Jacob, in the kingdom of heaven: but the sons of the kingdom shall be cast forth into the outer darkness" (Matt. 8: 11-12). Speaking in the synagogue at Nazareth, Jesus made his audience angry when he reminded them that Elijah had been sent not to the widows of Israel in the time of famine, but only to the Gentile women of Sarepta, and that Elisha did not cure the Hebrew leper but only the Gentile Naaman. The position on this point is so clear that he who runs can read and understand.

Some Jewish Christians insisted that, in order to benefit by the gospels of Christ, one had to be born a Jew or become a Jew by accepting the rite of circumcision and being adopted into the Jewish people; but they were not arguing against Gentiles on the basis of race. Any foreigner who accepted circumcision and who was so adopted was readily accepted. Here we must draw a sharp distinction between Jewish segregation and ours. The kind of segregation or exclusiveness practiced by the Jews generally, and by the Jewish Christians, differed widely from modern segregation based on caste, color, and race. A non-Jew could become a member of the local Jewish group. He could qualify by meeting the conditions. But in our time, when segregation is based on race or color, there is nothing one can do to qualify. One cannot qualify even when he accepts the same creed, practices the same ritual, prays to the same God, and partakes of the same culture. Segregation based on color or race makes it impossible for the Christian of color to qualify, for one cannot change his color and he cannot change his race. And this restriction is tantamount to penalizing one for being what God made him and tantamount to saying to God, "You made a mistake, God, when you made people of different races and colors."

According to Acts, the Spirit descended on the people on the day of Pentecost, fifty days after the resurrection. The disciples and the people got a new sense of power, and they interpreted this to mean that the Holy Spirit was present. At Pentecost a new community was created. The church was born. Jews and proselytes gathered together, and representatives from some fifteen different nations were assembled. Acts 2: 1 makes this point clear, "When the day of Pentecost had come, they were all together in one place." There they were: Parthians, Medes, and Elamites; the dwellers in Mesopotamia, Judea, Cappadocia, Pontus, Asia, Phrygia, Pamphylia, Egypt, and the part of Libya about Cyrene; strangers from Rome; Jews and proselytes; Cretans and Arabians. In their own tongues, the proselytes heard of the mighty and glorious deeds of God.

Peter admitted in his encounter with Cornelius that it was unlawful for a Jew to associate with one of another nation. He told the group at Caesarea, "You yourselves know how unlawful it is for a Jew to associate with or to visit any one of another nation; but God has shown me that I should not call any man common or unclean." (Acts 10: 28). Continuing, Peter proclaimed the great universal truth: "Truly I perceive that God shows no partiality, but in every nation any one who fears him and does what is right is acceptable to him" (Acts 10: 34-35).

Paul carried this universal note further than Peter. Paul saw instantly that these differences could not establish the true church and could not further the missionary enterprise. He took the position that a Gentile did not have to become a Jew in order to be a Christian. The Jewish law had been fulfilled in Christ and had been superseded by him. In Galatians 3: 28, Paul declared, "There is neither Jew nor Greek, there is neither slave or free, there is neither male nor female; for you are all one in Christ Jesus." Again, in Romans 10: 12, we are told, "For there is no difference between the Jew and the Greek: for the same Lord over all is rich unto all that call upon him."

Paul set aside racial heritage, social status, and sex. In Christ all divisions are unified, and racial and ethnic groups become one. He declared on Mars Hill, "God that made the world and all things therein, seeing that he is Lord of heaven and earth . . . hath made of one blood all nations of men for to dwell on all the face of the earth."

(Acts 17: 24, 26). Thus, centuries before science discovered that all men are of one blood, that truth was apprehended by men of faith. My distinguished colleague, B. J. Marais, sought the thinking of the fourteen leading theologians of Europe on this subject, including Emil Brunner and Karl Barth. They all agree that we can find no justification in the Bible for a segregated church based on race or ethnic origin. This universalism in the gospel is climaxed and attested to by the fact that Christ died for all mankind. So if there are those among us who seek support in the Bible for segregated churches based on color, race, caste, or ethnic origin, they must turn elsewhere for support.

Your Commission has gone further. We have delved into church history: ancient, medieval, and modern. We have sought to find out what the churches have practiced through the centuries in their worship and fellowship. New Testament scholars and church historians all agree that since its inception the Christian church has had in its membership people of different nations, races, and even colors. Nowhere in the early church do we find distinctions drawn on the basis of country or race. James (2: 1-6) condemns the separation of cultural and social groups in the local church. The fact that the early church drew no distinctions based on race or color, and that Christians were often described as a "new people" or a "third race," drawn from many racial or ethnic groups, is attested by Tertullian, Origen, Ignatius, Hermas, Barnabas, Clement, and others. Their position is sustained by later scholars: Harnack and Ramsay, Cadoux and Moffatt, Griffith and Latourette. We seek in vain for signs of segregation based on race and color in the church of the first centuries of the Christian era.

What was true of the early church was true of the church of the Middle Ages. In both the ancient and the medieval church, the basis of membership was faith in Jesus Christ, our Lord. The basis of membership was faith, not race; Christ, not color; creedal acceptance, and not nationality. The creeds of Christendom have always been formulated and enforced in terms of certain beliefs about God, Jesus, man, sin, and salvation; never on theories about race or ethnic groups. In summarizing this fact, Marais says: "In the extensive literature of the history of the Church till after the Reformation, we look in vain for any sign of a racial basis for admission to the congregation." If color, race, or cultural background was a condition of membership in the local congregation of the early church or the local church of the Middle Ages, our survey does not reveal it.

It seems clear, then, that the color or racial bar in the church is a modern thing. It was not, in fact, until the seventeenth century that the outlines of the modern race problem began to emerge. It is the modern church that again crucifies the body of Christ on a racial cross. Race and color did not count in the early existence of the Protestant Church. It was when modern Western imperialism began to explore and exploit the colored peoples of Africa, Asia, and America, that the beginning of segregation and discrimination based on color and race was initiated. It was then that color was associated with "inferiority," and whiteness with "superiority." Our Commission writes: "The broad pattern of major racial group tensions which trouble the world today had its historical origins in the period of European overseas exploration and expansion into America, Asia, and Africa. The resulting exploitation of one group by another, involving groups differing in race, varied in the three countries. But the same general relation of asserted superiority and inferiority developed between the white world and the colored world. Color became first the symbol, and then the accepted characteristic of the intergroup tensions."

Your Commission concludes, therefore, that the modern church can find no support for this practice of segregation based on race, color, or ethnic origin in the Bible, no basis for it in the ancient and medieval churches, and none for it in the various theologists of the Catholic and Protestant churches.

Your Commission has probed beyond the church and the Bible. We have sought to find out what support modern science gives for segregation and discrimination. We could quote scientist after scientist on the question of whether there is or is not an inherent superiority which one race possesses over another. Forty or fifty years ago, scientists were divided on the subject. Also, men argued that some groups were biologically superior to others. Hundreds of volumes were written to justify a denial of equal opportunity to some peoples on the ground that they were inferior and that God had made them that way. But now there is no disagreement among the top scientists of the earth. As a recent UNESCO publication points out, "In matters of race, the only characteristics which anthropologists have so far been able to use effectively as a basis for classification are physical (anatomical and physiological). Available scientific knowledge provides no basis for believing that the groups of mankind differ in their innate capacity for intellectual and emotional development. Some biological differences between human beings within a single race may be as great or greater than the same biological differences between races." In another connection, the United Nations publication speaks for modern science on race: "All of us believe that the biological differences found amongst human racial groups can in no case justify the views of racial inequality which have been based on ignorance and prejudice, and that all of the differences which we know can well be disregarded for all ethical human purposes." At long last, science has caught up with religion, for it was Paul who declared, on Mars Hill nineteen centuries ago, that God made of one blood all nations of men.

If the church can find no support in science for ethnic and racial tension, none in the Bible for segregation based on race or color, none in the practices of the ancient and medieval churches, and none in Christian theologies, the questions naturally arise: How can segregation and discrimination in the church be justified? What can the churches do to put themselves in line with the gospel, the practices of the ancient and medieval churches, and in line with the findings of modern science? If the modern churches cannot practice full Christian fellowship in worship and membership, how can they preach the prophetic word to secular organizations that discriminate on grounds of race, color, and caste? To answer these questions is our task at Evanston. It is to these problems that the Commission on the Church Amidst Ethnic and Racial Tensions will address itself.

There is one aspect of this subject which we often overlook. Usually the question is, what does discrimination or segregation do to the person segregated, to the disadvantaged person? It is conceded that segregation and discrimination hurt the pride of the person discriminated against, that they retard his mental, moral, and physical development, and that they rob society of what the disadvantaged group might contribute to enrich humanity. We agree that imposed separateness breeds ill-will and hatred, and that it develops in the segregated a feeling of inferiority to the extent that he never knows what his capabilities are. His mind is never free to develop unrestricted. The ceiling and not the sky becomes the limit of his striving.

But we seldom realize what discrimination does to the person who practices it. It scars not only the soul of the segregated but the soul of the segregator as well. When we build fences to keep others out, erect barriers to keep others down, deny to them the freedom which we ourselves enjoy and cherish most, we keep ourselves in, hold ourselves down, and the barriers we erect against others become prison bars to our own souls. We cannot grow to the mental and moral stature of free men if we view life with prejudiced eyes, for thereby we shut our minds to truth and reality, which are essential to spiritual, mental, and moral growth. The time we should spend in creative activity we waste on small things which dwarf the mind and stultify the soul. It is both economically and psychologically wasteful. So it is not clear who is damaged more—the person who inflicts the discrimination or the person who suffers it, the man who is held down or the man who holds him down, the segregated or the segregator. Your Commission and the Assembly will wrestle with this problem.

The churches are called upon to recognize the urgency of the present situation. Even if we laid no claim to a belief in democracy, if the whole world were at peace internationally, if atheistic Communism had never developed, if Fascism had never been born and Nazism were wholly unknown, a nonsegregated church and social and economic justice for all men are urgent because we preach a universal gospel that demands that our deeds reflect our theory. To proclaim one thing and act another is sheer hypocrisy. It weakens the influence of the church, not only in its own fellowship but throughout the world. It hampers our efforts to evangelize Africa and Asia. It is not Communism, not Fascism, not the struggle between East and West, but the gospel itself which demands interracial justice and an unsegregated church. We should move interracially in the church, not from fear of Communism but from our "concern for our brother for whom Christ died." It has always been the responsibility of the church and the gospel to plow new ground, smash traditions, break the mores, and make new creatures. Such was the role of the Hebrew prophets, of Jesus and Paul, of the early church, of Savonarola and Martin Luther, of Livingston and Albert Schweitzer.

In the Commission we will wrestle with the ever present question, "To what extent is the church to be governed by expediency?" Is it wise to live up to the gospel we preach, or is it wiser to conform to the mandates of a secular society? Shall the church obey the laws of the state when they violate the laws of love, or the law of God which commands us to love one another? What should be the attitude of the churches toward laws that are obviously unjust and discriminatory? Obey them? Seek to change them? Violate them?

Finally, the task before the Commission and the Assembly is to show how the theme of the Assembly, *Christian Hope*, is related to racial and ethnic tensions, not only in the past days but in the present days. The major problem will not be to demonstrate from the Bible and from church history that it is only in modern times that race has become a basis for church membership. The task will be to show how the gospel of Christ can be presented and lived so as to make new creatures of men and women in the area of race, and bring hope and abundant life to all men—not only beyond history but in history. We refuse to believe that God is limited in history and that we must wait until the end of history before his mighty works can be performed.

We have known for centuries what the Bible says about race. We have known for a long time that the early church and the church of the Middle Ages did not segregate on the basis of race and ethnic origin. We know that there is no scientific basis for our treating one group as inferior to another. The gospel on race has been proclaimed for nineteen centuries. One world conference after another has condemned racial separation in the church. Yet segregation remains the great scandal in the church, especially in the United States and South Africa. The local churches permit secular bodies such as the state and federal courts, the United Nations, big league baseball, professional boxing, colleges and universities, the public schools, and theaters to initiate social change in the area of race. But even when secular bodies initiate the change, local churches, Negro and white, follow slowly or not at all. It will be a sad commentary on our life and time if future historians can write that the last bulwark of segregation based on race and color in the United States and South Africa was God's church.

We have plenty of light on the subject, but like Pilate of old we lack the will and moral courage to act on the light we have and the knowledge we possess. Clearly, knowledge is not enough. Paul knew this centuries ago when he said in essence, "I find myself doing that which I know I ought not to do and I find myself failing to do that which I know I ought to do." We quote Tennyson:

> Let knowledge grow from more to more,
> But more of reverence in us dwell;
> That mind and soul, according well,
> May make one music as before,
> But vaster . . .

Drinkwater likewise deserves to be used in this context when he profoundly wrote:

> Knowledge we ask not—knowledge Thou has lent,
> But, Lord, the will—there lies our bitter need,
> Give us to build above the deep intent
> The deed, the deed.

Here at Evanston the church will want to know how to deal with race within its own membership, the local congregation. The question will be: How can the local church so exemplify the spirit of Christ in Christian fellowship that the world will be compelled to follow its example?

At this Assembly, the people will want to know whether the church has any responsibility as an organized group for the alleviation of racial injustice in social, political, and economic life. What is the church's responsibility as an organized group? What is the responsibility of the individual Christian? What is the church's duty toward assisting the individual to fulfill his Christian task in his daily vocation? Above all, we should ask ourselves the question: Can there be a Pentecost in 1954?

If there can be a Pentecost in 1954, the individual Christian will be responsive to the gospel and he will act on his Christian convictions. There is no dichotomy between what we believe and what we do. We do what we believe. If an atheistic Communist can act on his belief, a Christian can act on his. If a Communist is willing to suffer for his convictions, go to jail and die for them, surely the followers of Christ's God can suffer for theirs. The true believer, like Peter, Paul, and Jesus, is not a slave to his environment. He can rise above it and transform it. He will testify to the unity in Christ by his daily deeds.

If there is to be a modern Pentecost, the church must do likewise in its worship and membership. It must also encourage its members to exemplify in their vocations this supra-racial unity in Christ. Being thus convinced, all Christians here in Evanston will take appropriate steps in their respective congregations to make it possible for the will of God to operate, to the end that all church doors will be opened in membership and worship to all who serve and love the Lord. For the church is God's creation, not man's, and it belongs to God. And in God's domain, all men are equal.

Appendix C

Eulogy at the Funeral Services of Martin Luther King, Jr., at Morehouse College, Atlanta, Georgia, April 9, 1968

To be honored by being requested to give the Eulogy at the funeral of Dr. Martin Luther King, Jr., is like being asked to eulogize a deceased son—so close and so precious was he to me. Our friendship goes back to his student days at Morehouse College. It is not an easy task; nevertheless, I accept it, with a sad heart, and with full knowledge of my inadequacy to do justice to this man. It was *my desire* that if I pre-deceased Dr. King he would pay tribute to me on my final day. It was *his wish* that if he pre-deceased me I would deliver the homily at his funeral. Fate has decreed that I eulogize him. I wish it might have been otherwise, for, after all, I am three score years and ten and Martin Luther is dead at thirty-nine.

Although there are some who rejoice in his death, there are millions across the length and breadth of this world who are smitten with grief that this friend of mankind—all mankind—has been cut down in the flower of his youth. So multitudes here and in foreign lands, queens, kings, heads of governments, the clergy of the world, and the common man everywhere are praying that God will be with the family, the American people, and the President of the United States in this tragic hour. We hope that this universal concern will bring comfort to the family—for grief is like a heavy load: when shared it is easier to bear. We come today to help the family carry the load.

We have assembled here from every section of this great nation and from other parts of the world to give thanks to God that he gave to America, at this moment in history, Martin Luther King, Jr. Truly God is no respecter of persons. How strange! God called the grandson of a slave on his father's side, and the grandson of a man born during the Civil War on his mother's side, and said to him: *Martin Luther, speak to America about war and peace; about social justice and racial discrimination; about its obligation to the poor; and about nonviolence as a way of perfecting social change in a world of brutality and war.*

Here was a man who believed with all of his might that the pursuit of violence at any time is ethically and morally wrong; that God and the moral weight of the universe are against it; that violence is self-defeating; and that only love and forgiveness can break the vicious circle of revenge. He believed that nonviolence would prove effective in the abolition of injustice in politics, in economics, in education, and in race relations. He was convinced also that people could not be moved to abolish voluntarily the inhumanity of man to man by mere persuasion and pleading, but that they could be moved to do so by dramatizing the evil through massive nonviolent resistance. He believed that nonviolent direct action was necessary to supplement the nonviolent victories won in the federal courts. He believed that the nonviolent approach to solving social problems would ultimately prove to be redemptive.

Out of this conviction, history records the marches in Montgomery, Birmingham, Selma, Chicago, and other cities. He gave people an ethical and moral way to engage in activities designed to perfect social change without bloodshed and violence; and when violence did erupt it was that which is potential in any protest which aims to uproot deeply entrenched wrongs. No reasonable person would deny that the activities and the personality of Martin Luther King, Jr., contributed largely to the success of the student sit-in movements in abolishing segregation in downtown establishments; and that his activities contributed mightily to the passage of the Civil Rights legislation of 1964 and 1965.

Martin Luther King, Jr., believed in a united America. He believed that the walls of separation brought on by legal and de facto segregation, and discrimination based on race and color, could be eradicated. As he said in his Washington Monument address: "*I have a dream!*"

He had faith in his country. He died striving to desegregate and integrate America to the end that this great nation of ours, born in revolution and blood, conceived in liberty and dedicated to the proposition that all men are created free and equal, will truly become the lighthouse of freedom where none will be denied because his skin is black and none favored because his eyes are blue; where our nation will be militarily strong but perpetually at peace; economically secure but just; learned but wise; where the poorest—the garbage collectors—will have bread enough and to spare; where no one will be poorly housed; each educated up to his capacity; and where the richest will understand the meaning of empathy. *This* was his dream, and the end toward which he strove. As he and his followers so often sang: "*We shall overcome someday; black and white together.*"

Let it be thoroughly understood that our deceased brother did not embrace nonviolence out of fear or cowardice. Moral courage was one of his noblest virtues. As Mahatma Gandhi challenged the British Empire without a sword and won, Martin Luther King, Jr., challenged the interracial wrongs of his country without a gun. And he had the faith to believe that he would win the battle for social justice. I make bold to assert that it took more courage for King to practice nonviolence than it took for his assassin to fire the fatal shot. The assassin is a coward: he committed his dastardly deed and fled. When Martin Luther disobeyed an unjust law, he accepted the consequences of his actions. He never ran away and he never begged for mercy. He returned to the Birmingham jail to serve his time.

Perhaps he was more courageous than soldiers who fight and die on the battlefield. There is an element of compulsion in their dying. But when Martin Luther faced death again and again, and finally embraced it, there was no pressure. He was acting on an inner compulsion that drove him on. More courageous than those who advocate violence as a way out, for they carry weapons of destruction for defense. But Martin Luther faced the dogs, the police, jail, heavy criticism, and finally death, and he never carried a gun, not even a knife, to defend himself. He had only his faith in a just God to rely on; and the belief that "thrice is he armed that hath his quarrel just." The faith that Browning writes about when he said: "One who never turned his back, but marched breast forward, / Never doubted clouds would break, / Never dreamed, though right were worsted, wrong would triumph, / Held we fall to rise, are baffled to fight better, / Sleep to wake."

Coupled with moral courage was Martin Luther King, Jr.'s capacity to love people. Though deeply committed to a program of freedom for Negroes, he had love and concern for all kinds of people. He drew no distinction between the high and the low; none between the rich and the poor. He believed especially that he was sent to champion the cause of the man farthest down. He would probably say that *if death had to come, I am sure there was no greater cause to die for than fighting to get a just wage for garbage collectors.* He was supra-class, and supra-culture. He belonged to the world and mankind. Now he belongs to posterity.

But there is a dichotomy in all this. This man was loved by some and hated by others. If any man knew the meaning of suffering, King knew. House bombed; living day by day for thirteen years under constant threats of death; maliciously accused of being a Communist; falsely accused of being insincere and seeking the limelight for his own glory; stabbed by a member of his own race; slugged in a hotel lobby; jailed thirty times; occasionally deeply hurt because friends betrayed him—and yet this man had no bitterness in his heart; no rancor in his soul; no revenge in his mind; and he went up and down the length and breadth of this world preaching nonviolence and the redemptive power of love. He believed with all of his heart, mind and soul that the way to peace and brotherhood is through nonviolence, love, and suffering. He was severely criticized for his opposition to the war in Vietnam. It must be said, however, that one could hardly expect a prophet of Dr. King's commitments to advocate nonviolence at home and violence in Vietnam. Nonviolence to King was total commitment not only in solving the problems of race in the United States but the problems of the world.

Surely this man was called of God to do this work. If Amos and Micah were prophets in the eighth century, B.C., Martin Luther King, Jr., was a prophet in the twentieth century. If Isaiah was called of God to prophesy in his day, Martin Luther was called of God to prophesy in his time. If Hosea was sent to preach love and forgiveness centuries ago, Martin Luther was sent to expound the doctrine of nonviolence and forgiveness in the third quarter of the twentieth century. If Jesus was called to preach the Gospel to the poor, Martin Luther King, Jr., fits that designation. If a prophet is one who does not seek popular causes to espouse, but rather the causes he thinks are right, Martin Luther qualified on that score.

No! He was not ahead of his time. No man is ahead of his time. Every man is within his star, each in his time. Each man must respond to the call of God in his lifetime and not in somebody else's time. Jesus had to respond to the call of God in the first century, A.D., and not in the twentieth century. He had but one life to live. He couldn't wait. How long do you think Jesus would have had to wait for the constituted authorities to accept him? Twenty-five years? A hundred years? A thousand? He died at thirty-three. He couldn't wait. Paul, Galileo, Copernicus, Martin Luther, the Protestant reformer, Gandhi, and Nehru couldn't wait for another time. They had to act in their lifetimes. No man is ahead of his time. Abraham, leaving the country in obedience to God's call; Moses leading a rebellious people to the Promised Land; Jesus dying on a cross; Galileo on his knees recanting; Lincoln dying of an assassin's bullet; Woodrow Wilson crusading for a League of

Nations; Martin Luther King, Jr., dying fighting for justice for garbage collectors —none of these men were ahead of their time. With them the time was always ripe to do that which was right and that which needed to be done.

Too bad, you say, that Martin Luther King, Jr., died so young. I feel that way, too. But, as I have said many times before, it isn't how long one lives, but how well. It's what one accomplishes for mankind that matters. Jesus died at thirty-three; Joan of Arc at nineteen; Byron and Burns at thirty-six; Keats at twenty-six; and Marlowe at twenty-nine; Shelley at thirty; Dunbar before thirty-five; John Fitzgerald Kennedy at forty-six; William Rainey Harper at forty-nine; and Martin Luther King, Jr. at thirty-nine.

We all pray that the assassin will be apprehended and brought to justice. But, make no mistake, the American people are in part responsible for Martin Luther King, Jr.'s death. The assassin heard enough condemnation of King and of Negroes to feel that he had public support. He knew that millions hated King.

The Memphis officials must bear some of the guilt for Martin Luther's assassination. The strike should have been settled several weeks ago. The lowest paid men in our society should not have to strike for a more just wage. A century after Emancipation, and after the enactment of the 13th, 14th, and 15th Amendments, it should not have been necessary for Martin Luther King, Jr., to stage marches in Montgomery, Birmingham, and Selma, and to go to jail thirty times trying to achieve for his people those rights which people of lighter hue get by virtue of their being born white. We, too, are guilty of murder. It is time for the American people to repent and make democracy equally applicable to all Americans. What can we do? We, not the assassin, represent America at its best. *We* have the power—not the prejudiced, not the assassin—to make things right.

If we love Martin Luther King, Jr., and respect him, as this crowd surely testifies, let us see to it that he did not die in vain; let us see to it that we do not dishonor his name by trying to solve our problems through rioting in the streets. Violence was foreign to his nature. He warned that continued riots could produce a Fascist state. But let us see to it also that the conditions that cause riots are promptly removed, as the President of the United States is trying to get us to do. Let black and white alike search their hearts; and if there be prejudice in our hearts against any racial or ethnic group, let us exterminate it and let us pray, as Martin Luther King, Jr., would pray if he could: *Father, forgive them for they know not what they do.* If we do this, Martin Luther King, Jr., will have died a redemptive death from which all mankind will benefit. . . .

I close by saying to you what Martin Luther King, Jr., believed: *If physical death was the price he had to pay to rid America of prejudice and injustice, nothing could be more redemptive.* And to paraphrase the words of the immortal John Fitzgerald Kennedy, Martin Luther King, Jr.'s unfinished work on earth must truly be our own.

Appendix D

Interracial Hypertension

(Paragraphs taken from an article by Dr. Gordon Blaine Hancock, of Virginia Union, released by the Associated Negro Press in 1941.)

Hypertension is a fancy name for high blood pressure, just as delinquency is a fancy name for old-fashioned devilment, or prevarication is a fancy name for old-fashioned lying. Medical authorities tell us that hypertension is not a disease but a symptom; even so, unless it is properly treated and relieved, it results disastrously by and by.

There can be no doubt that there is today in race relations a hypertension which, unless treated with the greatest care, will have disastrous consequences. In spite of the preachments of religion and the promises of education, the fact remains that we are definitely entering into a dangerous phase of the interracial conflict. In proof whereof we offer the all-too-frequent riotous outbreaks here and there about the country. These outbreaks must be construed as symptomatic of an undercurrent of interracial bitterness that demands the most serious thinking and careful planning, if unhappy results are to be averted.

In this situation the better class whites and Negroes have one of the mightiest challenges of this generation, and the future of both races is indissolubly bound up with the way this challenge is met. If serious trouble is to be avoided, both whites and Negroes must face the ugly fact that race relations are in a state of hypertension and rupture; that unless matters are speedily taken in hand and shaped according to some constructive plan, we shall probably lose many important gains in race relations that have been won through many years, through sweat and tears. . . .

This article is inspired by a speech which a prominent Negro made within recent weeks before an audience of Negroes numbering nearly a thousand. This man stood for almost an hour and made one of the ablest speeches I have ever heard. But from beginning to end his speech was one continuous rehearsal of the wrongs and injustices which the Negro has suffered in this country. He built up one of the strongest cases against the white man I have ever heard. All the while he was casting himself in the role of the hero merely by recounting the woes of his stricken race.

That large audience was deeply moved and the occasion was enveloped in a pall of resentment and bitterness that is bound to do damage sometime, somewhere. The speaker did not seem to know that when only one side of a question is presented to the exclusion of the other side, the speech becomes propaganda. That the Negroes of this country have suffered many things because of such one-sided presentation did not seem to concern him. Here was a Negro who was the victim of a cruel propaganda turning propagandist himself. He called himself "fighting fire with fire," patently forgetting that such fights and fightings never end in victory but call for more and more fighting.

This speaker said not a word about the improved and improving race relations mirrored in a hundred ways, if we compare what the Negro has and enjoys today with what he had and enjoyed two generations ago. He spoke not a word about the growing spirit of justice and fair play in the heart of the New South, evinced by the growing willingness to admit the Negro to full citizenship. Within recent weeks prominent white citizens of South Carolina petitioned the officials of that state to allow Negroes to vote in the Democratic primary. This easily constitutes one of the finest gestures in race relations that has been made since 1876.

Appendix E

Statement of Conference of White Southerners on Race Relations

(Conference of white Southerners on race relations, Atlanta, Georgia, April 8, 1943)

In October, 1942, a representative group of Southern Negro leaders met in Durham, N.C., and issued a statement in which they addressed themselves "to the current problems of racial discrimination and neglect, and to ways in which we may cooperate in the advancement of programs aimed at the sound improvement of race relations, within the democratic framework."

Their statement is so frank and courageous, or free from any suggestion of threat and ultimatum, and at the same time shows such good will, that we gladly agree to cooperate.

We do not attempt to make here anything like a complete reply to the questions raised nor to offer solutions for all the vexing problems. We hope, however, to point the pathway for future cooperative efforts and to give assurance of our sincere good will and desire to cooperate in any sound program aimed at the improvement of race relations.

These Negro leaders rightly placed emphasis in their statement on discrimination in the administration of our laws on purely racial grounds. We are sensitive to this charge and admit that it is essentially just. From the Potomac to the Rio Grande there are some ten million Negroes. While all citizens are governed by the same laws, it is recognized that Negroes have little voice in the making and enforcement of the laws under which they must live. They are largely dependent upon the will of the majority group for the safety of life and property, education and health, and their general economic condition. This is a violation of the spirit of democracy. No Southerner can logically dispute the fact that the Negro, as an American citizen, is entitled to his civil rights and economic opportunities.

The race problem in any Southern community is complicated by our economic limitations. The factors which have kept the South a tributary section have also kept it poor and lacking in sufficient industry to develop and to provide enough jobs and enough public funds for every public need. Yet the only justification offered for those laws which have for their purpose the separation of the races is that they are intended to minister to the welfare and integrity of both races. There has been widespread and inexcusable discrimination in the administration of these laws. The white Southerner has an obligation to interest himself in the legitimate aspirations of the Negro. This means correcting the discrimination between the races in the allocation of school funds in the number and quality of schools, and in the salaries of teachers. In public travel where the laws demand a separation of the races, primary justice and a simple sense of fair play demand the facilities for safety, comfort, and health should be equal. The distribution of public utilities and public benefits, such as sewers, water, housing, street and sidewalk paving, playgrounds, public health, and hospital facilities should come to the Negro upon the basis of population and need.

It is recognized that there is often practical discrimination by some peace officers and in some courts in the treatment of Negro prisoners and in the abrogation of their civil rights. There is no such discrimination incorporated in the laws of any of the Southern states. False arrests, brutal beatings, and other evils must be stopped.

In the economic field, unquestionably procedures should be undertaken to establish fully the right to receive equal pay for equal work. To do otherwise works a wrong to our entire economic life and to our self-respect. With so large a proportion of our wage-earning population belonging to the minority race, if we cannot plan for a well-trained, well-employed, and prosperous Negro population, the economic future of the South is hopeless.

Most of the Negroes in the South are on farms and in rural communities. Failure to provide for them all the facilities for improving agricultural practices through schools, county agents, and supervision, holds back all of the South. Fair wages, longer tenure of leases, and increased opportunities for farm ownership are also necessary.

All men who believe in justice, who love peace, and who believe in the meaning of this country are under the necessity of working together to draw off from the body of human society the poison of racial antagonism. This is one of the disruptive forces which unless checked will ultimately disturb and threaten the stability of the nation. Either to deny or to ignore the increased tension between the white and the colored races would be a gesture of insincerity.

That there are acute and intricate problems associated with two races living side by side in the South cannot be denied. But these problems can be solved and will ultimately disappear if they are brought out into an atmosphere of justice and good will. If we approach them with contempt in one group and with resentment in the other group, then we work on hopeless terms. The solution of these problems can be found only in men of both races who are known to be men of determined good will. The ultimate solution will be found in evolutionary methods and not in ill-founded revolutionary movements which promise immediate solutions.

We agree with the Durham Conference that it is "unfortunate that the simple efforts to correct obvious social and economic injustices continue, with such considerable popular support, to be interpreted as the predatory ambition of irresponsible Negroes to invade the privacy of family life." We agree also that "it is a wicked notion that the struggle by the Negro for citizenship is a struggle against the best interests of the nation. To urge such a doctrine, as many are doing, is to preach disunity, and to deny the most elementary principles of American life and government."

It is futile to imagine or to assert that the problem will solve itself. The need is for a positive program arrived at in an atmosphere of understanding, cooperation, and mutual respect.

Appendix F

The Richmond Statement

RESOLUTIONS OF THE COLLABORATION COMMITTEE

(Joint Committee of representatives of the Durham and Atlanta Conferences)

This is a day of great differences, strong feelings and epochal conflicts throughout the world. Yet the world's greatest need and hope is to find common ground for universal action and balanced harmony among all peoples. Manifestly, such a goal must be reached through cooperative approximation to the largest measure of agreement in line with the largest number of values and the largest number of people.

We face, therefore, the double crisis of standing firm for the conservation and preservation of human rights; yet to seek these ends by the way of peace and planning rather than by conflict and revolution. . . .

This is a rare challenge to the leadership of the South: to the white leadership to find new ways of cooperation and to justify increased confidence of the Negro leadership, to sense the difficulties involved and to meet increasing demands, without slowing down their essential efforts.

As evidence of the promise of this leadership, two recent Southern conferences on race relations, one at Durham, under the auspices of Negro leadership, and one in Atlanta, under the auspices of white leadership, have blazed new trails. As a follow-up of these and with the above problems and backgrounds in mind, we, a group of Southern whites and Negroes, representing both the Durham and Atlanta groups, meeting as a collaboration committee at Richmond, Virginia, June 16, 1943, and following the general trend of the Atlanta group, urge the general adoption of the Durham statement entitled "A Basis for Interracial Cooperation and Development in the South," which has had extraordinary nation-wide endorsement.

The framers of this covenant, realizing that the situation calls for both candor and wisdom, have included adequate and searching analysis of the principal issues involved, duly interpreted in their proper perspective. The problems so featured include political and civil rights, industry and labor, service occupation, education, agriculture, military service, social welfare and health.

In the area of political and civil rights: the essential problems featured were those of franchise and the ballot, jury service, personal security, service in public carriers, the elimination of violence within and without the law, the elimination of lynching, and the employment of an increasingly larger number of Negroes in the public service.

In the area of work opportunities: the increased training for all skilled, semi-skilled, and unskilled labor, and opportunity for employment; the readaptation of labor union policies both for the best interests of Negroes and labor unions; the problem of dual standards of pay; support of, but guarding against discrimination in, local, state and federal procedures; special problems of service workers and standards of living.

In the area of education: equalized opportunities in all aspects but especially including institutions of higher learning, professional training, and equal salaries.

In the area of agriculture: adequate opportunity for the Negro farmer, including a sound system of tenancy, adequate state and federal assistance, increased opportunity for farm ownership, fair farm wages, and the wider employment of Negro farm and home agents.

In the area of military service: along with the obligation to serve, the opportunity for full participation and advancement in the war activities and a continuing better adjustment of unsatisfactory situations.

In the area of social welfare and health: adequate provisions for safeguarding the public health, for training physicians and nurses, and for their employment. Also, the erection of low-cost housing and other facilities for improving community life.

We recognize now the importance of affirmative action, without which we shall fall far short of our hopes and possibilities. To this end, we direct that the continuing committee, as appointed by the two groups now consolidated in this larger collaboration committee, be charged with the responsibility for working out methods and practical means of approach. We urge especially that efforts be begun to prepare the postwar world for a wise and successful reception of our returning soldiers and to prepare both our soldiers and the people for attitudes and procedures adequate to carry the great load of postwar needs. In all these, we urge the public to a new sense of the meaning of these needs as they accord with our professed principles of Christianity and democracy.

Appendix G

Excerpts from Correspondence Regarding Merger of Seminary Work of Gammon, Morris Brown, and Morehouse

Benjamin E. Mays to Dr. Henry Pitt Van Deusen, May 4, 1950:

> . . . I am very glad you talked with Dr. Richardson of Gammon. . . . I can appreciate Dr. Richardson's point of view, but I fear he is more cautious than circumstances require. As far as I can gather, the Methodist Church officials are in favor of Gammon moving on this side.

Benjamin E. Mays to Dr. Van Deusen, June 14, 1950:

> . . . I am glad that you were able to sit in on the discussion about the possibility of Gammon's moving to the west side and the possibility of coordinating our theological work. I believe we are on our way. . . .
>
> I very much agree with your point of view . . . that we should think in terms of federating the work of the institutions. In this way we will be able to conserve actual values of the constituent groups and also the potential values. It is certainly a fact that Gammon has more to give when we consider faculty, library and physical plant. I say faculty because they have more people than we do. The quality of the staff is certainly no better than the Morehouse staff.
>
> Although we are not going to emphasize denominationalism in this system, I certainly think all values should be considered. Despite the fact that Morehouse has long since ceased to be a purely denominational school, there is considerable potential denominational support and good will for Morehouse among the Baptists of Georgia and the nation. There are many, many more Negro Baptists in Georgia and in the nation than all other Negro religious bodies combined. If there is a way to conserve the actual and potential interest here, it will be good not only for Morehouse but for the entire system. This also holds true for Morris Brown because the AME denomination is the second largest in the Negro group.
>
> I think we need to keep in mind too that Gammon will not be giving everything if their Board decides to move the institution. Physically, Gammon will give up more than Morehouse or Morris Brown, but in the long run it will be the salvation of Gammon to move on this side. It may be the case where the institution can save its life by losing it. Yet, there may be some of the Gammon people who feel that they have everything to lose

and nothing to gain if they move to the westside.

In addition to studying the federated faculties of Chicago, I think we should see what happened when Colgate and Rochester came together and what happened when Andover and Newton came together. . . .

Appendix H

Degrees

Earned:

1920: Bachelor of Arts, Bates College
1925: Master of Arts, University of Chicago
1935: Doctor of Philosophy, University of Chicago

Honorary:

1945: Doctor of Laws, Denison University, Granville, Ohio
1945: Doctor of Divinity, Howard University, Washington, D.C.
1945: Doctor of Laws, Virginia Union University, Richmond, Va.
1946: Doctor of Letters, South Carolina State College, Orangeburg, S.C.
1947: Doctor of Divinity, Bates Colleges, Lewiston, Maine.
1950: Doctor of Humanities, Boston University, Boston, Mass.
1954: Doctor of Divinity, Bucknell University, Lewisburg, Pa.
1955: Doctor of Divinity, Berea College, Berea, Ky.
1959: Doctor of Divinity, Kalamazoo College, Kalamazoo, Mich.
1960: Doctor of Laws, University of Liberia, Monrovia, Liberia
1962: Doctor of Humane Letters, Keuka College, Keuka Park, N.Y.
1963: Doctor of Laws, St. Augustine's College, Raleigh, N.C.
1964: Doctor of Education, St. Vincent College, Latrobe, Pa.
1965: Doctor of Laws, Lincoln University, Lincoln, Pa.
1966: Doctor of Divinity, Morris College, Sumter, S.C.
1966: Doctor of Divinity, Ricker College, Houlton, Maine
1966: Doctor of Humane Letters, Shaw University, Raleigh, N.C.
1967: Doctor of Humane Letters, Morehouse College, Atlanta, Ga.
1967: Doctor of Laws, Harvard University, Cambridge, Mass.
1967: Doctor of Laws, Morgan College, Baltimore, Md.
1967: Doctor of Letters, Grinnell College, Grinnell, Iowa
1968: Doctor of Laws, Michigan State University, East Lansing, Mich.
1968: Doctor of Humane Letters, New York University, New York
1969: Doctor of Civil Law, Middlebury College, Middlebury, Vt.
1970: Doctor of Laws, Centre College of Kentucky, Danville, Ky.
1970: Doctor of Humane Letters, Emory University, Atlanta, Ga.
1970: Doctor of Humanities, Benedict College, Columbia, South Carolina
1970: Doctor of Humane Letters, Brandeis University, Waltham, Massachusettes.

Index

(The Appendices are not included in this Index)

Made in the USA
Monee, IL
06 February 2021

59848242R00270